SHOCK
PEACE

CIECIE TUYET NGUYEN

SHOCK PEACE

THE SEARCH FOR FREEDOM

TATE PUBLISHING
AND ENTERPRISES, LLC

Published by Tate Publishing & Enterprises, LLC
127 E. Trade Center Terrace | Mustang, Oklahoma 73064 USA
1.888.361.9473 | www.tatepublishing.com

Tate Publishing is committed to excellence in the publishing industry. The company reflects the philosophy established by the founders, based on Psalm 68:11,
"The Lord gave the word and great was the company of those who published it."

Book design copyright © 2016 by Tate Publishing, LLC. All rights reserved.
Cover design by Joshua Rafols
Interior design by Shieldon Alcasid

Published in the United States of America

ISBN: 978-1-68237-944-8
Biography & Autobiography / Personal Memoirs
15.11.17

DEDICATED TO ALL heroes and casualties of the Vietnam War

TO THE THOUSANDS of dehumanised victims in the Vietnamese reeducation camps during 1975–1989

TO THE LOST souls in the journey in search of freedom

TO THE LIVING mortals who continue their voyage with faith and bravery

Heroes are often the most ordinary of men.

—Henry David Thoreau

Acknowledgments

My BOOK BASED upon many real characters from whom I sincerely thank them for providing me with their life stories and experience.

My mother, my sisters, and my brothers, whose presence were always somewhere in the book.

My sons, Kelvin, Abel, Mark, and Edward, for being invisible during my endeavour.

All of us, Vietnamese, Americans, Australians, and Allies of the South Vietnamese Republic who were parts of the story.

For help completing Shock Peace, I wish to thank Suzanne Collins, for her valiant editing efforts and advice; without her I would not have finished it; Huong, for her various inspirational anecdotes; Thanh, for hours of consultation; Chi, my pharmacy assistant, for her conscientious work in the pharmacy while I was absorbing in my writing; my neighbours from The Townhouse, Nguyen-Phuoc and her husband, with insightful significant details; my dearest childhood friend, Vi, with her resourceful energy and contacts; Trieu, Caitlyn, Maria, TD, and Drs. Q. Q. Bui, Q. Dao, N. Ho, H. Tran, and many others, who had supported me greatly throughout.

Last but not least, my dear Chris, who had provided me with valuable guidance, support, and advice, as well as given me enough confidence to jump start my book and complete it. Thank you for sharing with me the ups and downs of becoming an author.

Importantly, I must mention the spirits of deceased members of my family, soldiers, and boat people for their spiritual help during my darkest hours of doubts in writing my chapters.

Of course, my sincere gratitude also extends toward Tate Publishing, LLC and staff in turning my Shock Peace: The Search for Freedom into reality.

Contents

Prologue:
My Inspiration

THE THOUGHT OF writing a book occurred to me on the third day after I was diagnosed with macular degeneration (MD) by an optometrist. Ah, there I was with the usual goal: that of everyone with a story to tell, an attempt to write a book sometime in his or her lifetime. It was nothing new, nothing to get excited about, but it was a book! I was very brave to have thought of it: an inspiration before my eyesight had deteriorated beyond my ability to fulfil it.

I went for a long-overdue routine eye check-up and got a shock. It is extraordinary that we, as living mortals, usually care less about our eyes than what we are going to have for dinner tonight. It seems that our eyesight, the window to one's soul, is taken for granted by most of us.

An exclamation from the optometrist made me jump off my seat to come over for a closer look at what she was seeing on the screen. The pictures of my retina were clearly visible, showing various bright yellow spots at the centre.

She said, "Oh no, Trinh! Why have your eyes deteriorated this much since I last saw you? Three years ago, wasn't it? They were clear before, but now you have these dots, which shouldn't be there at all at your age! It's too early, Trinh! I am so sorry!"

My curiosity increased with what she had disclosed. Without any hint of anxiety, I asked, "What are those bright yellow dots, Clare?" She had been a friend since university days, a time that seems like ancient history now to me.

"You have macular degeneration, Trinh!" Clare said apologetically. "It's a condition that means you won't be able to see clearly later on when these dots get bigger. If the blood vessels in your eyes leak out and the proteins form scars preventing light from getting through, then you'd lose most of your central vision. Normally it happens to older people at sixty, sixty-five or so. I don't know why it has happened to you at this early age, Trinh. It must be all the stress of the last few years that is accelerating your condition." She looked at me and looked again at the screen. "I am sorry!" she said with finality.

All this technical information went into my ears and sat there without much insight, apart from the omen that I would not be able to see anymore. I started to worry by the urgent tone of her exclamation even though the shock of this entire discovery would not register its full impact until much later on when I got home.

"How long will it be til I can't see, Clare?" I asked casually.

"Ten, fifteen, twenty years…or something like that. You still have plenty of time, so don't worry too much about it. It just gives you more stress, and that's not going to help at all. In the meantime, you need to take Macu-Vision and omega-3 fatty acids. You should eat plenty of fish and green leafy vegetables. You should avoid meat and all things that raise your cholesterol." She said all these things in a casual manner. I was not sure now as the more time I dwelled on the condition, the more serious the matter became.

"You don't have high cholesterol, do you? High blood pressure, diabetes?" she added.

Feeling proud of being so healthy, I shook my head. How foolish of me! I left her surgery a bit overwhelmed with the term *macular degeneration*. It was only after I went home and sadness had actually overtaken me in every direction that I looked at it.

I opened the door, and when I saw my son, I blurted out dramatically, "Oh, Eddie, I've got macular degeneration! I'm going blind!"

"Are you sure, Mammy? How do you know?"

Luckily for me, like all ten-year-old kids, he did not fully comprehend the real nature of the condition and only asked that question absentmindedly. Then he went on with his Internet surfing after giving me a big hug and a kiss, which was quite rare coming from a teenager. And then he saw tears starting to fall down my cheeks.

Crying was the only thing I did that afternoon, apart from lying in bed and wondering why. Just like everyone else who was diagnosed with a terminal disease with no cure on the horizon, my reaction was just the same; I went from initial disbelief to shock to despair and finally to anger and frustration! How unjust! I was experiencing the "why me?" phenomenon that many of us do whenever disaster or unpleasant circumstances fall upon our heads.

In between crying, feeling sorry for myself, and still feeling sad, I started making phone calls. I declared my condition to my sisters, my brothers, and some of my closest friends as if the tsunami was of the least importance compared to my new discovery. I also realised how fragile happiness in life was! It could switch over in a fraction of a second, leaving the person numbed with sorrow by her misfortune. Again, anger started to build up as I remembered boasting to people not so long ago that I had never felt so content and so free in spirit as I had lately. After five years struggling with separation, divorce, and loneliness, this was the first time I had totally felt that I was happy with what I had and who I was.

Once, an acquaintance had said to me at a social function, "I don't know how a single, divorced woman feels, but as a single, divorced man, I feel so unbalanced living by myself. It's so unnatural!"

I smiled inwardly and thought, *Of course, everything in life usually comes in pairs—a pair of hands, a pair of eyes, or a pair of chopsticks.* With the absence of one, the other would have felt lonely and lost or would have even become partially useless! Ah, have you tried to use a single chopstick to eat rice or noodles? That is what I meant by partially useless. Moreover, just as man and woman are naturally meant to be a pair, being a single man or woman would bring about all sorts of feelings of solitude and asymmetry or unevenness, regardless of how much one tries to mask it. Hmm, these days, the definition of a pair has expanded beyond the boundary of a man and a woman now. However, a pair is a pair, regardless of gender. The dilemma in life is that mismatched pairs often come together and eventually end in terminations that make balancing a struggle to the odd ones out.

Even though the situation had not changed at that moment—I was still alone and divorced—all the bitterness in me had vanished like a miracle. The unsettled weariness and the lonesome anxiety of a woman who had been used to a quarter-century of marriage had fizzled out completely, leaving me as fresh as a cucumber recently. I was so proud to embrace the feeling of being an independent person who was not desperate or in need of any passion or comfort from another man. How sad that was for any woman whose years were ticked off the clock in chunks and was left vulnerable after a divorce! However, that independent feeling only resurfaced for a brief period. Now it was to be replaced by a feeling of grief. I was vulnerable again. How unfair life seemed to be! In all the tragedies I had had to go through, I had always managed to find a solution for each and was able to solve it regardless of how uneven my life had become.

But out of every other dilemma that I had to solve, it was the incurable state of macular degeneration that left me exposed, and there was no solution so far.

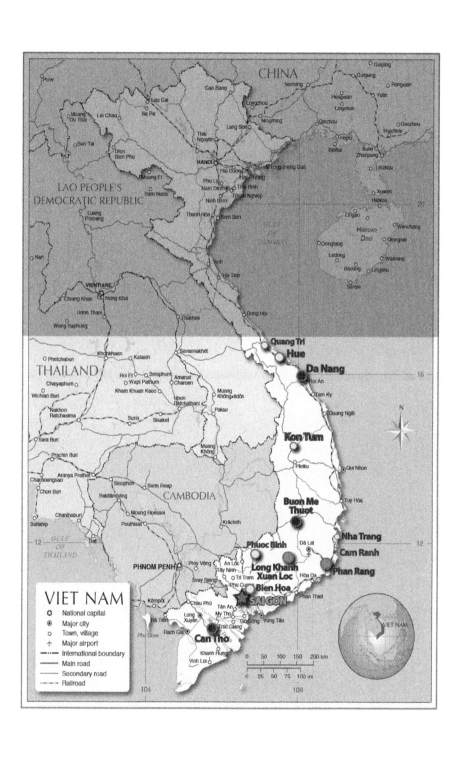

PART 1:

SHOCK PEACE

Chaos of Saigon

1975

THE MATH TUTORIAL class was quite empty today. It had been like this for the last few weeks. Everyone was on edge. Trinh sensed from the activities and expressions of the people around her that they were waiting for something to happen. This morning, the television had announced that the last day for all schools would be today, but Trinh still came to her private tutorial class because she loved her math. Numbers were always friendly and predictable; they were as simple as "two plus two equals four." They were never treacherous or deceptive to her. The puzzle was always solved, and the result was straightforward in the end; it was what Trinh liked about the subject. It was so much unlike literature and essays, which were mysterious and sometimes biased so that the boundary between truth and untruth, real and unreal was difficult to define. To go along with the thesis one had chosen to prove, one had to lean on one side or the other to stay logical (or conversely, illogical!) in the eyes of others, Trinh reflected. Today, she felt a hundred years old!

She was about to sit down, but then she had to stand up again as Ms. Mien had entered the classroom. It was a custom that students should stand up and be quiet when teachers entered and left the classroom.

"Please sit down. There're no more classes after today, students," Ms. Mien said without much hesitation. "Due to the state of turbulence in the country right now and the restrictions imposed on movements, all my tutorial classes will be cancelled. Come back now and then to check with me or the notice board for the date of resumption." She paused for a short while and then continued. "Good-bye, students, and I wish you and your family are all safe." Her voice trembled with emotion.

She looked about her classroom and took in the faces of those smart, keen kids. The bewildered looks of uncertainty and unease were displayed on those innocent young children as much as on the faces of many adults around her. The whole country was in mourning; the battles were closing in. They had lost Hue, Da Nang, and Buon Me Thuot to the Viet Cong (VC) last March. The sadness and perplexity of the near future was overwhelming for the Southerners. It was clear that the South was losing the war, and everyone was afraid that their life was threatened by the communists. There were talks of giving up the fight, and the war was ending; the South Vietnamese Armed Forces were withdrawing and losing bases. Many operations to evacuate thousands of US personnel and South Vietnamese refugees had begun a month before. The US was leaving, and that triggered panic and alarm among the conservative class. Ms. Mien was as afraid and helpless as many other teachers and scholars of similar social class.

She understood that scholars of the previous regime were not going to be appreciated and honoured in the communist system. The future was unfathomable, unclear, and horrifying. She had heard so many talks about how the Viet Cong treated intellectuals in the 1968 Tet Offensive in Hue. There were mass graves in Hue that covered hundreds of Catholics, South Vietnamese Armed Forces personnel, intellectuals, merchants, executives, and other suspected counter-revolutionaries after the city had been restored for a month under the occupation of the Viet Cong. With that knowledge, she was helpless; but she waited in apprehension like the rest of the population who had no means of escape or had chosen to stay.

The class was dismissed. The students had expected that to happen for some time, and they were not surprised. They felt melancholy filling the air; the pressure was almost suffocating. Trinh looked at her friends and the teacher; anxiety and tension was in everyone's eyes. They stood up and waited to leave after Ms. Mien's announcement, and talk broke out at once. Talk that seemed bottled up in their chests about the present situation started to brim over and spill out in every direction. Trinh gathered her books, stood up with the rest of them, and slowly walked out of the class. She saw a few students approach Ms. Mien and whisper something in a quiet tone. Ms. Mien nodded her head in agreement and waved good-bye.

Trinh bowed her head to the teacher on the way, another customary gesture of all Vietnamese students in her time, showing respect to the teachers and elders. It was deep respect, particular to Oriental culture. The teacher-novice relationship in her people was valued for as long as a person's lifetime.

To this day, almost forty years from the day she left Vietnam, Trinh knows many colleagues who keep in touch with their teachers and professors from high school to university. From a very young age in her culture, children are taught to appreciate whatever knowledge can be gained from whomever gives it to them.

Recently, Trinh received news from her high school friends that one of her Vietnamese literature teachers in year eight,

Ms. Thu, had passed away in her late seventies. That brought back some childhood memories of the beloved but stern teacher. The whole classroom would sit still, and no one dared to draw attention to themselves in case Ms. Thu would call them out to make an example of them to the class. Trinh was always one of the ill-fated students. She was singled out for criticism because Ms. Thu was very diligent in trying to keep Trinh's writing within the confines of the language. She was the best teacher Trinh ever had; Trinh still remembered some of her methods in teaching the rhetorical skill of the language. However, Trinh chose to express her thoughts differently, and she probably still did. Ms. Thu never liked Trinh's deviation, and perhaps the Vietnamese Literature League Club, if something like that exists, would not accept her writing. But then, in year nine, Trinh suddenly became the favourite of another literature teacher! She was chosen to represent the whole school for her year to give a speech at the end-of-year celebration. It came to her that with language, one either likes or dislikes the writer's expressions, and her change of fate might be just due to that. It came as always in math that Trinh knew when she was right or wrong, and she was confident with it most of the time.

Out of turn, she came up to Ms. Mien, gathered her courage, and asked, "Are you going anywhere, Ms. Mien?"

The teacher looked up at one of her beloved students and shook her head. "Where to, Trinh?"

"You know, going away from Saigon, from Vietnam...to America?" the little girl said hesitantly.

Ms. Mien smiled sadly in return. "Darling, you know that I'm a mere public high school math teacher. Where can I afford to go? I've got no connections or relatives or money to contemplate an idea like that, even though I've wished for it."

Trinh stammered. "But...but...Ms. Mien, everyone is talking of going or getting out of the city. I've heard that from every person I've met."

Ms. Mien patted Trinh's head gently. "Yes, it's a shame everyone's thinking of that. Even I am, but not everyone can, sweetie. I'm as poor as every other teacher in the country. Besides, what can I do once I'm out of here? I'm going to be just like a fish out of water, kiddie. I'm going to miss my students, and my life will be without a purpose."

She gazed into Trinh's eyes as if reassuring herself. "My students might still need me. Education and schools are bound to carry on, I'm sure. Math is a subject you cannot miss, isn't it?"

She laughed quietly with that statement and asked Trinh, "What about you and your family, Trinh? Are you leaving at all?"

Trinh shook her head. "No, Ms. Mien. We're staying as far as I know of. For now." Then she bowed her head once more in good-bye and walked toward the bike rack.

Waiting for her turn, Trinh pushed her bike out of the parking lot. Lien was next to her.

"Are you going?" she asked Trinh.

"Going where?" Trinh replied with a question, pretending ignorance.

"You know, going to America." The excitement of going overseas was apparent in the young girl's voice even though she was clearly uncertain and sad about leaving the country and her friends.

Trinh was amused. She had asked Ms. Mien the same question a moment ago. It was on the tip of everyone's tongue. "No, we're not going anywhere. Are you?"

"Yes, we are. My father has to. He's worked for the US company IBM. His boss insists he and the family must get out of the country. I was going to say good-bye to you and everyone even if Ms. Mien hadn't dismissed the class today."

Lien added quickly, "You know Trang and Trung, the twins, in year 7C? They left for France last week. They lived opposite my house. They came, said good-bye to me in the night, and left early the following morning. The house was a shambles the moment they left. The looters were so swift. It's unreal! That beautiful house and furniture!"

Trinh was not surprised at Lien's revelation; it was happening everywhere in the country in the last few months. The evacuations were the major focus of operations, and migration was the main motivation and discussion topic among the Southerners.

"My father doesn't want to go. His friends came and told him many times, but he refused, Lien. I overheard them talking. He has friends in the government, and many are leaving. One of them told him to come along as he had connections with the US embassy." Trinh added, feeling as proud and important as a strutting male peacock displaying his magnificent tail, "But my father is an ex-government official, so he has priority as well. Still, he doesn't want to leave Vietnam."

"You should go then," Lien announced with finality. She waved her hand and then looked at Trinh and swirled about her as if seeing the class and everything else for the last time. Lastly, she hopped on her bike and pushed it quickly away without looking back.

The rest of the day was quite humid and close. April in Saigon was always like this. The sky was cloudy, as if waiting for rain, and the sun was high and bright. The combination of the two made the air as steamy as a giant sauna. Trinh could feel beads of sweat dripping down her temples. The tutorial class was situated inside the local market, and today it was not crowded at all. *That was very unusual,* Trinh thought. She pushed her bike out of the labyrinth of walkways and market stalls. It took her half the normal time without having to shove and duck through the throng. There were not many people on the streets either. Many shops were closed, and in those still open for business, the owners were gladly reaping the rewards as there was little competition. The prices of goods went up dramatically overnight, especially rice, sugar, salt, fish sauce, dried noodles, and necessities. A kilogram of rice would cost five hundred dong the previous day but then would double that amount the next day. Everyone was stocking up on his or her supply as much as possible, if not going out of the country. Many vacant houses were looted, and everything inside was taken. Looters were running wild with people's property on the streets; they were making profits and acting gleefully happy with their ill-gotten gains all over the collapsing city. Regardless of the sombre atmosphere, they were pleased. In every ruin, there are always profiteers, it seems.

Rubbish was flying everywhere. There were bullet marks on some walls and a few holes here and there. The charred remains of a motorbike lay across the pedestrian path. An electric light pole was broken in half; the jagged edges looked sharp, and the wire was dangling loose on the pavement. It must have been very tall as the broken section was now occupying a large part of the pavement. The debris of a concrete wall from a vacated office overflowed messily, destroyed by the profiteers. They knocked it down mercilessly in their hurry to scoop up the furniture and booty. Inside the front yard, some piles of rubbish were still burning, and smoke was billowing high. Someone must have burnt their files before they left. *With this kind of weather, a real fire might start anytime,* Trinh thought.

Further down on her left, the guard station at the US-based civil service was deserted; the armed soldier with his M16 machine gun ready to fire at suspicious activity was no longer there. He must have been dismissed earlier and returned to his countryside homeland. *Lucky for him,* Trinh thought. He would be there for his family during the last few days of the war at least. The tall barbed-wire fence that served as a deterrent for intruders was intact, but the gate was wide open and the inner doors were unlocked. Nothing was left inside. Trinh was quite sure of that.

Trinh did not know how to feel; she was so confused and afraid. She pushed her bike faster home: at least home was still relatively safe. She passed a crashed helicopter lying sideways in the park near her home. Luckily, its body was on the grass and not obstructing the traffic. The pilot might have had a narrow escape as the chopper was broken and damaged, but there was no sign of burning or an explosion. Yesterday afternoon, when it was downed, its wretched body still had the impressive look of power of a sophisticated flying machine. It had been looted extensively overnight, and today, its pitiful remains were just an oversized metal dump that had been left behind because there was nothing more that could be stripped away by passers-by.

There was talk of going away to America, to France, to other foreign countries from everyone she met. Everyone wanted to leave, it seemed. The news and politics, mystifying and befuddling to a girl of thirteen at that time, added to her confusion. All she knew was that the fighting was very close, in the vicinity of the capital city, Saigon. It had escalated a few weeks ago; the war was approaching for real. At night, there was gunfire and distant bombings. Sometimes they were so close that Father had told everyone to sleep downstairs instead of the upper loft sleeping quarters.

"No one's allowed to sleep up there, all right, children? Gather around here at night, and the curfew is ten o'clock, so be home by then. Understand?" His voice was serious and heavy with anxiety.

Many households were building their bomb shelters right inside the living room. The makeshift shelter might have easily been destroyed by the smallest bomb. Trinh guessed the people had known that for a certainty. However, the effort to salvage a sense of stability and safety was a necessary step for all. *To keep their sanity intact*, Trinh thought.

At the same time, the bomb shelter might serve as a common burial ground for the complete family unit if a disaster like that really happened. They wished for that final escape to ease the pain for all if it ever did.

Some had declared casually, "If the bomb actually exploded in the living room, then we'd all go together. No suffering."

Trinh understood that was also her father's intent from his insistence in ordering all of them around the living room and kitchen at night. Their family shelters were made of double layers of sandbags piled on top of the sturdy solid wood dining table and the beautiful large divan in the kitchen. The divan was so low that only four of the children—Hoan, Kim, Trinh, and Luc—could manage to crawl in. Trinh recalled that it was strange that in a time of crisis, one could be very afraid but at the same time very indifferent to danger in their surroundings. These contradictory feelings were bewildering to them, citizens of Saigon, and to the population of the South. They could cry, and they could laugh. They cried when the imminent hazard was looming over their heads, and they laughed when it was quiet the day after. It was business as usual, they would just go on for another day.

However, when the gunfire and bombing was heard in frightening successive rounds, then Father would call everyone to emergency practice, the kids crawling under the divan and the adults under the dining table.

Oblivious of the gravity of the situation, the children behaved as if they were having a party, unaware of the anxiety displayed on their parents' faces.

"Here we go again," Hoan said.

"Have you brought the melon seeds, Trinh?" Kim asked.

"They're still here, I think." Crawling further inward, Trinh took out the bag of seeds hidden at the foot of the divan.

Then they started munching the seeds and giggling in the darkened space, enjoying the strange effect of dancing with danger. The adults could not make them be more conscious other than by ignoring their joyful innocence. Then, after a while, growing more immune to danger with so many practices, the adults joined in the party mood, behaving like children and starting to chat gaily in the crowded space; Father had to reprimand them and remind them to be quiet.

Flirting with death and peril was a common practice with people who were faced with crisis for an extended amount of time. Fear was replaced by indifference and unconcern. The Vietnamese were no exception after the prolonged periods of war since the Anti-French Resistance War in Vietnam during the Second World War till now, over thirty years of bloodshed and carnage. Consequently, the effect of the threat was no longer felt even though the threat itself was real and deadly. The possibility of exposure was diminished by individuals assuring themselves in times of calamity and danger that the worst might happen to someone else but that it would not happen to them, and so on. The longer they lived under the battle zones, the stronger their immunity to the effect of war. Trinh's brother, Dien, who was in the army, sometimes told her of walking in battle zones with gunfire crisscrossing his path and ignoring it completely. They simply convinced themselves they were invincible.

Similarly, the bomb shelters only served a few times in emergency practice, and then no one was willing to sleep or crawl under them anymore. Saigon was so hot and humid with the approach of May that it was torture in the crowded, suffocating space and a hundred times worse with fear. Gradually and strangely, the threat of being blown up was no longer accepted, as death seemed farfetched for many Saigon dwellers; the feeling of being invincible became widespread as they had lived under secured protection for so long. Even in the fiercest fighting periods of 1968 and 1972, Saigon dwellers were always safe with troops scattered on the outskirts of the city at all times.

Curfews had been in effect ever since Trinh could remember. They had always been imposed in the country over the hundred years of French colonisation; Trinh was sure of that. There were restrictions on movement in the city and around the country after midnight. It was even stricter now; no one was protected on the street after dark. Either they ran the risk of being accused as a Viet Cong, being shot at accidentally if their behaviour was considered suspicious by the South Vietnamese Armed Forces or the city army police, or, conversely, of being shot at by the infiltrated Viet Cong of the North if considered on the South side. That was the hardest dilemma for the people in a civil war; no one was safe to be considered friend or foe until proven so. Unfortunately, it could be too late to be perceived as an ally if the person was already a goner!

Father was at home when Trinh got in. He was at home more often than before since the intensity of the fighting had increased. He usually travelled to their ten-hectare block of land in Long Khanh, which was located a hundred kilometres from Saigon; he stayed there for a few weeks now and then. It was his retirement investment, his dream of a rambutan plantation. Rambutan was the prickly tropical fruit that Long Khanh was renowned for. Trinh approached him when he waved her closer. He caught her shirt, pulled her toward him, and quickly gave her an embrace and a kiss on the cheek. He had to be quick as he was expecting a rebuke from his daughter. Trinh was always annoyed and tried to break free; she was already too old for that! Her cheeks went red with embarrassment. For most Asians, hugging and kissing were not commonly practised. *It was only Father,* Trinh thought, *who had French influence and always showed his affection toward his children as freely as a Westerner.*

"Oh, Father! Let me go! Let me go!" She pulled herself vigorously away from his grasp.

"So no more school for you, darling?" Father let her go reluctantly, but he was amused at her reaction.

"Yes, Father. No more school! Yippee!" Trinh tried to inject some excitement into her voice.

Father laughed. "You wouldn't put up with doing nothing, my girl! I know you too well."

"Yeah? Why not? But I would! Because there is nothing I could do at the moment, Father!" Trinh declared stubbornly.

Nguyen shook his head at his defiant youngest daughter. "Cheeky devil! Now, run away, sweet pea. Go to the kitchen and help your mother. She's cooking lunch in there, and she's been by herself all morning. Be nice to her."

Everything had halted in Saigon and in the South for almost ten days since the change of presidency and after the talk of Americans leaving the country. Schools, offices, and some businesses were closed. The only activity that seemed lively was the discussion of how to get out of the country. Everything else was masked with despair and forlornness. People engaged in talk, debate, and speculation while waiting for destruction. At the same time, they were hoping for peace and stability to be regained. Their endurance was shredded thin. Regardless of the outcome and despite their dreadful fear of communism, they all wanted peace for their country, and Nguyen was one of them.

He was an ex-director in the finance department of the government and was well travelled. He had been to many places in South Vietnam as well as other Southeast Asian countries. Nguyen came from a wealthy family in Can Tho whose land was bountiful and which provided higher education and comfortable, affluent lifestyles for him and his siblings. His family wealth was severely affected after the imposition of the agricultural revolution in 1955 by President Ngo Dinh Diem, abolishing landlordism in the South. The majority of his family's land was divided into smaller sections for the peasants to purchase the land they were leasing.

Father refused flatly when his mates asked him to join them in leaving the homeland, saying, "Vietnam had fought with the French for a hundred years, and has been in civil war for a quarter of a century. Now it's going to have peace. It's not the peace I want to see with the rule of the Viet Cong, but it's peace after all. I was born when the First World War broke out, and

I have seen through the Second World War with the French, with the Japanese right here in this tiniest and remotest land. I have practically grown up with war all my life. Gunfire, bombing, destruction, and death have been familiar for most of my life, and now I want to live in my homeland and see how peace has actually arrived."

That was Father's opinion to whoever asked about his or her leaving or staying.

However, he told others who had worked for the Americans or had connections with them or had wanted to leave because of their phobia of communism, "Just go. It's sad in a situation like this, but if circumstances indicate choosing to leave the country, then you must do it. Don't risk making yourself and your family enemies of the Viet Cong (VC). I'm just a retiree, old and useless. I don't think I'm in any danger by staying back."

Trinh's half sister, Betty, her father's eldest who worked with a Taiwan agricultural company, also asked him, "Should my family and I leave too, Father? Mr. Kwo offers his help in getting all of us to Taiwan within the next week. The company's closing its business and vacating the office today. They offer the staff the choice of going with them. What do you think I should do?"

Father was reluctant to answer, but after a while, he said, "You're my daughter, a grown-up daughter with a family to take care of already, but you're still my daughter. I don't think I can bear the idea of your living in a foreign country that I'd have no connection with in the future. Being a past employee of the Taiwanese isn't as bad as being a past employee of the Americans. But if you think that's the best for you and your children, then of course, you must do what you think is right."

Betty was a divorcee with five children under eighteen at that time, but her salary provided her and the children a comfortable living. It was a difficult decision to make as she knew that life would be a hundred times harder with the change of the government. Betty's final decision was to stay, and she suffered the terror and cruelty after the Fall of Saigon with the rest of the population until her premature death. She could not leave her father at the time of the crisis, but she left him in the end after two years of living under the communists. She was a year short of turning forty.

The family was under strain, with relatives and friends coming to say farewell and crying as they left. Trinh had never seen the adults in so much distress. It was chaotic and frightening at the same time. Despite the speculation, the majority of the South was still in disbelief at the expected defeat. They were feeling dejected. The Americans were getting tired of the war, and the world was busy with other matters. Vietnam was only a small, pitiful, war-torn country that had had too much of their attention for long enough, and now that was it. There was no time to fuss over her anymore. It was time to turn to another page.

Rumours and Talks before the End

April 21, 1975

LAST NIGHT, THE bombing and gunfire got louder. Trinh could smell the fumes in her bed. The city was more alive at night than during the day with the artilleries and flares. Woken up by the thunderous noise of bombardment and the brightness of the unsettled sky, they gathered and talked outside the makeshift bomb shelters, longing to feel safe even though it was primitively constructed.

"It's getting closer. The fighting is here!" Father told them.

"There's still no news from Dien," Mother whispered. Her face was lined with anxiety.

Dien was an infantry soldier in the Eighteenth Division of the Army of the Republic of Vietnam, led by Major General Le Minh Dao. The last time they had had news from him was when the fierce fighting of Xuan Loc started. Today, two weeks later, Xuan Loc had been lost to the Viet Cong despite the courageous fighting of the Eighteenth Infantry Division since April 9. That marked the last defensive frontier of the capital city of the South: Saigon. Fearing the worst for her son, Mother was devastated at the news on television. She had cried, looking at the exodus of battered refugees running away from the lost city. Father was shattered at the realisation that the Army of the Republic of Vietnam was no longer able to stop the advancement of the North. Major General Le Minh Dao could not hold back the overwhelming force of the Viet Cong even with his emotional statement: "The communists could throw their entire army at Xuan Loc, and the Eighteenth would stand fast." His withdrawal made the adults even gloomier.

Right on the day Xuan Loc fell, they were not surprised to hear President Nguyen Van Thieu's resignation. Father had his friends coming to the house more often in the last week of April, and it was almost expected in their discussions.

"I knew it was going to happen! He's shedding crocodile tears! I bet he's almost glad that Xuan Loc was lost so he could resign quickly to get out of the country!" someone declared vehemently, shaking his head in disgust.

"He resigned so he could easily fly to safer ground!" another spat out with distaste.

"What's going to happen next?" someone else asked dejectedly.

"Is it true what he's telling people? That the Americans are leaving and are ceasing sponsorship? But that means the armed forces have no chance of holding on without their support."

"After his resignation, their morale has plummeted quickly, with so many generals and majors leaving their posts one by one! Don't you know that?"

"The Americans are withdrawing after the Paris Peace Accord signed in January 1973. It's the last soldiers that are leaving now. They're naïve in believing the integrity of the Viet Cong!"

"Nah, it's nothing to do with naivety. They simply did not want to have anything to do with the Vietnam War anymore!" Hai stated matter-of-factly.

"But the Eighteenth Infantry Division fought bravely at Xuan Loc for almost two weeks; the soldiers' spirits were high then. We still can hold the fort, can't we? What has happened?" Someone changed the topic.

"There was no direction, no reassurance, and no leadership! That's what's happened!" someone else sadly admitted. "The GIs could not fight without their captains, majors, or even generals! Their generals were so busy looking for ways to get out of the country. I believe they were leaving the responsibility of defending the frontiers to the mere lieutenants."

"Don't be too quick to condemn, Hai! There are courageous and patriotic majors and generals among those ready to flee. What about General Nguyen Khoa Nam and Le Van Hung in the air force? And the Brigadier General Tran Quang Khoi in the III Corps Armored Task Force?"

"What about them?"

"They're living up to their standards, of course! At least they're still around and fighting."

Mention of a few courageous and nationalistic generals was brief before they turned to more dismal discussions and pessimistic projections of the fate of the South.

Hai said sorrowfully, "Even television and radio were not encouraging in the least. News of retreat and defeat were quickly spread without a single mention of bravery or heroic fighting. The hoards of terrified refugees running wildly from one lost city to the next were appalling on television, and they gave little comfort to the remaining cities and citizens of the South. Those poor refugees did not know what to do, what to expect of them, and what to believe. The rumours were confusing and without any affirmation or correction from the authority. And thus, the general public was even more listless and unsettled."

"There is no direction given to the general public. They're running in a circle," someone agreed.

The Southerners were all wishing for something to happen, a miracle perhaps, to prevent the steadfast advance of Viet Cong. Something must happen soon. But what might that something be to rescue them from the pitiful fate of a losing battle? Someone had to do something urgently. But who was that someone to lead them out of this tiresome war? They did not know, and they simply waited in chaotic despair. A whole country was lost before the actual combat began for the lack of a real leader. No one took responsibility. No hero materialised in this saddest moment.

"Don't you all know that in the twenty-fifth hour, nobody wants to be a hero? Because nobody has the least idea what to do! Nobody trusts anybody with information regardless of the source. Even the rumours are discussed in secrecy. Believe it or not, the enemies are within us!"

"The US embassy is giving out the lists of names for evacuation, do you know that?" someone said.

"Yes, I know. That doesn't help, does it?"

"What doesn't help?"

"The negative effect on the morale of the armed forces from the evacuation operations, of course!"

"Don't you see that since March, pessimism is only made worse by the evacuation operations from the US embassy? It's an act that seems helpful and humane from their point of view, but in reality, it has destroyed the spirit of all the Southerners. They are lifting Vietnamese civilians among their citizens. Now, everyone wants to be safe, to get away from this war zone, to arrive at a peaceful destination. Now, no one wants to fight anymore. Why fight if you are the only one left standing? Why fight if they see a hope of leaving all this horror behind? Who can blame them?" Hai sighed heavily.

"Yeah, a pity!" another agreed. "Now many of them just want to return home to take care of their families and be rescued by the US embassy. Being safe and away from the danger zone suddenly becomes the priority rather than the urgency of defending the last frontiers of the South. Jealousy has started to show itself between the top-notch leaders and government officials in getting clearance to be in the evacuation lists. Do you know that as well? What a shame! I bet some are even waiting for the war to end quickly to be able to get out of the country without feeling guilty of deserting their units."

"I know some information was leaked out from among the US embassy employees even though they thought it was a secret!"

"What information, Hai?"

"The signal for total evacuation will be the moment they start broadcasting the song 'White Christmas' on the radio." Hai seemed to know many strong rumours, and he continued. "It's Operation Frequent Wind. Many know that hearing that song on the radio will be the warning of defeat. The war is practically over then. No help will ever arrive! Faint chance of anything like that! Run for your life if you hear that song. Believe me!"

"South Vietnam is doomed, my dear friends!" someone else agreed gloomily, tears brimming in his eyes.

The ease of capture of many cities of the South by the North Vietnamese Army was even a surprise to them. They had taken one city after another without much effort. Their advance was faster than they thought possible, and they seemed amazed at their victories. Many armed forces units just dropped their weapons and surrendered readily without putting up a fight.

Meanwhile, rumours about staying put or getting out of the country continued spreading from one general to the next.

"Vice President Nguyen Cao Ky is going to stay back till the last minute. I'm sure!"

"Who said so?" someone asked.

"There was an announcement from his office. He's going to lead the air force to strike against the Viet Cong."

"Bullshit! Faint chance that is going to happen! I'm sure he'll be the first to flee in his jet if he can!" Hai repeated his pessimistic statement.

"General Nguyen Van Toan is leading the battle to defend Saigon. He's not going to be beaten easily."

"I've heard that the Army of the Republic of Vietnam (ARVN) III Corps commander, General Toan, is organising five centres of resistance to defend the city. Is it true?"

"Yes, it seems so. These fronts are connected so as to form an arc enveloping the entire areas west, north, and east of the capital. He's using the Twenty-Fifth Division, the Fifth Division, the Eighteenth Division, the First Airborne Brigade, the Third Division, and the reformed Twenty-Second Division. He's going to protect Saigon at all cost!"

"More bullshit that the general public is naive enough to believe! Only rumours, mates!"

It seemed that the prolonged war had tired every soul. Some people wished the country had gained peace at any price so that they did not have to come back to fight the war anymore. Let it be anything but war and bloodshed! It was almost a relief that the war was ending. Even a bitter and sorrowful end, but it was the end at last. There had been so much death, misery, and combat that the spirit of fighting had worn thin and was now buried deep inside many combatants as well as frightening the civilians to the core.

The family normally sat around and listened, or they discussed the present situation in the living room, or in the kitchen around the divan despite their limited knowledge. The confusion of the state of the country was enhanced by the swift change in the cabinet of the South. After President Nguyen Van Thieu's resignation, Vice President Tran Van Huong took over the cabinet. Nevertheless, there were talks that President Tran Van Huong would not be able to keep up the fighting spirit of the soldiers. They wanted General Duong Van Minh to take over.

"President Tran Van Huong is too old and conservative. He won't be aggressive enough for a time like this," someone commented.

In fact, he did not hold office for long: barely a week later, he resigned.

April 28, 1975

"Newport Bridge! Cau Tan Cang has been taken!"

That was only a short five kilometres away from southwest of Saigon.

"Oh my god! They're coming!"

"Bien Hoa is lost. There is no chance for us now!"

Bien Hoa was thirty kilometres east of Saigon.

"What are we going to do?"

"We're not going to be spared!"

"There's nothing we can do but wait!"

"Wait for what? Doomsday?" someone mournfully declared.

During this confusion, President Tran Van Huong resigned, and General Duong Van Minh was appointed as the successor, leading a collapsing regime and a ravaged army.

"Poor old President Tran Van Huong. They should not drag him into this damn war in these last few days like this!"

"General Duong Van Minh is holding a disintegrating cabinet! It's not helping anything at all!"

"He's too lenient. He's not going to fight!"

"They only hope that he can negotiate with the Viet Cong through his friendly connections with them in the past."

"Fuck it if the Viet Cong is going to have anything to do with him!" someone said with finality.

"Yeah, don't be naive! Why should they negotiate? We're losing anyhow!"

"But he might persuade them to form a neutral government, mightn't he?"

"Bullshit!" someone said with distrust.

"General Toan has fled to Saigon already. He told everyone that most of the troops have lost their leaders as many have accepted defeat."

"See, I guessed that already!" someone said triumphantly, as if losing the battle was quite a happy conclusion for him!

During these last few days of April, a humanitarian mission called Operation Babylift was conducted, bringing thousands of abandoned orphans to many places around the world. As many as three hundred tiny babies in shoeboxes arrived in Australia. This was also an unforgettable image that the Vietnam War had left to the world.

"We're losing ground to the Viet Cong," Father sadly concluded. "The South has shrunk, and the president has lost interest in holding the country against the invasion. General Duong Van Minh will not fight, I'm sure."

"It's not going to be long."

Father had said less and less the last few days. The family could not sleep or eat much with all the disturbance and rumours, but they were sure that they were going to stay put. Father was indifferent to the commotion around them. There were large crowds in front of the US embassy for almost twenty-four hours every day. Helicopters whirled around the air relentlessly. In the end, the prevailing image that Saigon had left to the whole world was just that: helicopters and masses of refugees hanging on to the flying machines on rooftops; they were just so desperate to get out of the country. The twenty-one years of war was just abandonment and chaos in the conclusion.

"It's madness! The whole country is leaving!" Father shook his head in disbelief.

— ✪ —

April 29, 1975

Boom! Boom! Boom!

The whole house was awake again. A total twenty-four-hour curfew had already been imposed two days ago. Rockets and heavy artillery continued to hit Saigon.

"Tan Son Nhat Airport has been bombed," Father declared sadly. His eyes were dull.

The chaos continued to escalate even with the reinforced curfew. American radios had been playing Irving Berlin's "White Christmas" since eleven o'clock this morning. The US embassy was overwhelmed with crowds. Some desperate women even tossed their babies over the fence in the hope that they would be taken to the promised land, however remote that chance could be.

Everyone was staying in the house, sad and fearful of the hours ahead.

The Fall of Saigon

April 30, 1975

THE FAMILY WAS all gathered around the living room. The television was on. President General Duong Van Minh had announced a total unconditional surrender at around ten o'clock in the morning. He had asked for all armed forces of the Republic of South Vietnam "to calmly cease hostilities and stay where they are." The morning had been dragging on, heavy with suspense after the announcement. The adults looked preoccupied and sorrowful.

Trinh drifted to the front of her house by herself. The house was on the main boulevard, a kilometre from the Palace of Independence. The little girl stood at the gate looking out for hours, absorbed and baffled at the scenes of disarray. There were people running in panic along the streets in every direction; some were on foot, and others were on motorbikes. Their eyes were wild, their faces dull and expressionless. *All seemed in a hurry to get to their destinations regardless of the fact that the destinations might now be meaningless,* Trinh thought. Somehow everything had lost its purpose at this instant.

There were South Vietnamese Army soldiers passing the house. All looked tired and bewildered. There must have been a first, who put down his M16 on the pavement in front of Trinh's house, and then every soldier who went past that point automatically laid down his gun on top of the previous one. By lunchtime, the pile was getting higher. The trickle of soldiers walking past seemed to increase in volume, and more and more hurried by, some even stripping off their uniforms and putting them in a heap next to the discarded guns.

Trinh turned her head. She was awestruck as an armoured tank materialised suddenly from nowhere. It was slowly rolling down the boulevard from the direction of the Palace of Independence; the menace of its appearance lessened by its slow pace as if it hesitated in its purpose. She heard her heart thumping clearly from her chest but stood still. The little girl was not sure what the tank was going to do even though she could see from the familiar shape that it belonged to the South Vietnamese Army. Its heavy body rolled sluggishly past her house, went on over to the kerb, then stopped next to the carcass of the downed helicopter on the grass near the park. Followed quickly by his mate, the tank commander climbed out of it hastily. Both looked up and down the deserted street a few times and briefly made eye contact with the few onlookers standing in front of their houses. They were silently apologising for their intrusion. Then, as if on cue, both swiftly took off their uniforms, military hard hats, and threw them onto the pavement, away from the pile of the others. Afterwards, each ran in opposite directions without further exchange of words, clad only in white cotton vests and boxer shorts, abandoning their tank on the kerb of the public park. Their heavy army boots looked solid and powerful on their skinny legs; the last residue of the war to accompany them to a new, unknowable existence.

Trinh went inside when both running figures had disappeared from her sight. There was not much happening after that. The street was deserted again. In the dining room, the radio was giving out the irritating noise of static. Nothing was on television, just some neutral soundtrack with the flag of the Republic of South Vietnam flying high in the background. Its yellow base signifying its people's skin colour, and three red horizontal stripes representing the three main regions of Vietnam; North, Central, and South, vigorously displayed its grandeur as if unaware that its end was near.

It was past lunchtime, but no one was interested in meals. Lately, the family often had cold meals and bread. Distress and terror normally steered human minds away from mundane daily routine as the brain needed to concentrate on the anxiety and anguish it had to allay. Even the stomach was unimportant. Trinh was hungry, but she did not want to disturb her mother or sisters as she could see how tense the adults were. They did not talk or move about the house but sat around the divan, waiting in silence.

Minutes later, the radio came alive with some unintelligible sound at first, then a strange voice came on to the microphone with a thick, heavy Northern accent: "This is the announcement of the National Liberation Front. Victory now is ours to rejoice in! Our tank has crashed through the gates and advanced into the Palace of Independence. We have successfully seized power. You will hear the voice of your President Duong Van Minh to confirm."

President Duong Van Minh followed with his forlorn declaration. "The government of the South Vietnamese Republic is completely dissolved on all levels."

After that statement, deadly silence fell upon the whole city instantly, snuffing out all sounds at once. The strange atmosphere was as unnatural as it may have seemed hours ago, but the eerie silence had increased in intensity after the radio announcement. As if all the sounds of footsteps running away, of uniforms being stripped off the bodies, of machine guns being strewn across the pavement, of the armoured tank rolling down the streets, or of a helicopter being caught by power lines and catapulted down into the park were absorbed into it instantaneously and intensified a thousand times in its deadly void. All talk and rumours were gagged. Reality kicked in with such forceful brutality that the shock was clearly visible on everyone's face.

The air was still, willing everything to stay frozen in its place. Even the dead leaves from the tall *Dipterocarpus zeylanicus* trees in front of Trinh's house did not dare to part the branches lest their descent disturbed the sepulchral feeling in the atmosphere. Their two-winged fruits hung on to the last threads of connection lest the force of gravity pull them away and make an impact on the stillness. Trinh did not dare to breathe. She was afraid that her breathing would make too much noise and disturb the silence. She was afraid that her grumbling stomach would betray her of its own accord and emit an echo from the emptiness within.

Without a word being spoken, everyone moved slowly out to the front door. On both sides of the boulevard, there were people standing still. The whole city was standing still. Then, a sound erupted in the air, soft and hoarse. A chorus of fearful "Ohs!" broke involuntarily from the throats of the people, as something materialised suddenly that they were afraid to see. Their terrified gazes were directed toward a very strange-looking armoured tank rolling down the street. The shape, the colour, and the aura were so wrong. It was tracing the same path as another armoured tank not so long ago. In contrast, though, the speed was determined, and its menacing power was clearly visible. It carried the ominous-looking flags, half-red and half-blue with a yellow star and full red with the yellow star of the National Liberation Front and the Vietnamese Communist Party. *Perhaps that same T-54/55 tank was the one that crashed through the gates of the Palace of Independence a few moments ago,* Trinh thought.

The adults exchanged brief glances; everyone was trying to hide their shock and remain blank. No one dared to say anything, not even a whisper, as if a word escaping their lips at this moment would betray their vague grip on reality and push them further into the quicksand below the surface of sanity. The stunned and depressed looks of Saigon citizens were somehow unexpected by the Communists, who thought they had given the Southerners a victory to rejoice in. That shocked silence was not allowed for long, however; the South Vietnamese citizens were forced to show jubilation and ecstasy in welcoming the Northerners as enthusiastic traitors and conquering soldiers. They were forced to restore sound to the sepulchral atmosphere.

The tank continued parading down the boulevard with the entourage of Northern Army Soldiers; some were on foot, and others were on heavy Chinese buses and trucks. Trinh could see a few people, unmistakably wearing familiar civilian outfits and obviously traitors of the South, who appeared as if the victory was part of their reward. They were markedly different to the anomalous and peculiar-looking Northern soldiers, who carried distinctive AK-47s on their shoulders and wore black rubber sandals. Most soldiers seemed awkward and surprised at their victory, their features somehow as stunned as the Southerners.

On the other hand, the traitors and camp followers were wild with excitement. Their eyes were ablaze with fire. Two of them were holding the large victory flags and running on both sides of the tank. Later on, the South named those traitors "the 30th Aprils," or opportunists, who jumped hastily into the circles of celebration and reaped the rewards by quickly identifying as followers.

Those followers, who readily turned against everything of the South, were once a cleaner, a busboy in a restaurant, a clerk in an office, or a fishmonger from the local market. They were now fast becoming authoritative, granted positions as "people's chosen representatives" by the new communist conquerors. They were being used effectively to become informants who terrorised everyone from the old regime for fear of being named traitors or rebels, a crime that they had no chance of defending themselves against.

Amidst the commotion, Trinh heard a voice with a Northern accent, from a commander perhaps. He was yelling between gritted teeth, "Damn it! Those ungrateful brutes! Showing no sign of gratitude! Stupid idiots! Tell them to cheer, to salute with shouts of triumph, to make happy noises, to look jubilant! Don't just stand there and stare as if in shock!"

Another voice answered, with a Southern accent from which Trinh recognised as the cleaner of the school principal of her high school.

"Yes, comrade! I will make them greet the victorious soldiers in gladness and with joyful salutation."

Then he turned and started harshly shouting orders to other "30th April Communists." "Did you hear that? Come on, give them the flags and tell them to cheer, to be grateful for the victory gained by our comrades! They must, understand? Make sure they know that's what's required of them. Tell them to shout 'Victory to Great Uncle Ho and the National Liberation Front! Long live the Vietnamese Communist Party!' You've got that?"

He was obviously a long-time member of the Communist Party in its secretive operation in the South, who now had the authority of a senior comrade.

"Victory to the National Liberation Front!"

"Long live Uncle Ho and the Communist Party!" From the orders given by the cleaner, the group started shouting, urging the Southerners to join in.

In their hands were bundles of miniature National Liberation Front blue-red and Vietnamese Communist Party red flags, which had somehow clearly been organised well before in secret and now appeared liberally in the open air. They started to distribute these to bystanders, pressing them to "Wave the flags and cheer on. Don't just stand there! It's peace. Joy and happiness! Not bloody shock! Come on!" Their commands were curt and compelling. Hours later, the flags were to be left on the front doors of Saigon residents as a strong reminder to the South of which side had now taken charge of their city.

Moments later, the fierce heat of the April afternoon sun was marked by the sea of red communist flags. The brightness of the colours combined with the strong glare stung the eyes and subtly intensified the pressure in the air. Some bystanders resignedly obeyed the orders to cheer on, but their eyes were still dulled by shock and their hands waved the blue-red flags awkwardly. They repeated the phrases with restrained expressions as if in a language totally unheard of before.

"Victory to the National Liberation Front!"

"Long live Uncle Ho and the Communist Party!"

"Louder!" a voice tersely urged.

Then the crowd put more effort into the cheers, but their enthusiasm still lacked conviction. The tone was as flat as if coming from wired-up automatons, lifeless and inert.

The same cleaner went past Trinh's house on foot. Trinh looked at him, waiting for some recognition, but he refused to acknowledge her. His face was grim, and his gestures were completely different from the person he had seemed before. The eyes were filled now with hatred and vengeance. The voice was rough and coarse, not at all the timid, pleasing voice of the manservant doing simple chores for the principal. His manner was arrogant and triumphantly self-important, not like the submissively compliant school staff member of a few days ago. He must have thought the change was justified by his betrayal of the people and the land of the South.

He turned abruptly towards a boy her age, Trinh's next-door neighbour, and shouted, "Go inside and change! How dare you wear the colour of our victorious flags! Imprudent fool!" he sharply ordered.

The boy sheepishly turned bright red. He happened to be wearing red boxer shorts the same colour as the red flag of the Communists, only lacking the yellow star.

"I'm very sorry. Please ignore him. It's an honest mistake. He didn't think about it. I won't let him wear it again," his mother apologised effusively.

"Go on, apologise to the officer, son," she hastily urged the boy.

"I sincerely apologise, officer. I didn't know." The boy was still shy and confused about what had been so wrong, but he quietly obeyed his mother.

She hurriedly ushered him inside, her hands shaking with fear. The family was originally from the North, immigrants of the exodus in 1954, after the division of the country in half by the 17th parallel. She probably had experienced some of the cruelty, injustice, and harshness that the Communists had exerted over their citizens in the past.

The cleaner was satisfied that he had found some victims to show off his newly acquired power. His eyes squinted; the brows knitted together. Standing with his legs wide apart and his hands on his hips, he shook his head in disapproval. How could he! That was the most thoughtless act a citizen could have done to the country, wearing the same colour boxer shorts as the flag. What a stupid fool! He waved authoritatively to one of the followers on the street then hopped on the backseat of the motorbike. The miniature flags were raised high in the air in one hand, and his shout was loud, a spray of saliva escaping from his mouth with the cheers "Victory to Great Uncle Ho and the National Liberation Front! Long live the Vietnamese Communist Party!"

The parade went past. The commotion was short, but it left awkwardness in the rest of the bystanders that lingered on the street for hours later. The Southerners were still reluctant to look at each other; their gazes averted quickly whenever their eyes met. Some turned their back and went inside in slow motion and subdued quiescence. A few stayed still, searching for something familiar, something from the nostalgic past, even though the past was just hours ago. But it was futile now in the environment made suddenly strange by the yellow stars in the sea of blue-red flags hanging on the doors. One person on the opposite side of the street was silently scraping the painted-on Republic of South Vietnam flag on his wall. As if on cue, the others followed suit. Then the rest of the street was busy scraping off their walls the symbol of the last government. The past was now truthfully vanishing. Father looked on and sighed.

He turned and urged everyone to come inside the house, "Come on. The show is over. Nothing we can do now." His voice was gentle. Then he said after a moment of hesitation, "Time for lunch. We still have to eat."

Mother's eyes were watery. She looked at the direction where the tank had appeared before. "Dien is still not here! I'm so worried for him!"

"He should be okay, Chi. He's a clerk for Colonel Huynh's command unit. He's under his protective wings and not a combat soldier. He will be safe. He'll be home soon." Father did his best to allay her anxiety with faint reassurance.

"But how's he going to get home?" Mother asked. Her voice was weak, almost a whisper. She would be crying openly if not held firmly by Giang, her oldest daughter.

"Mother, our family has been lucky so far. My half brother, Sam, sacrificed his life for this war three years ago, and that should be enough. No one else is going to be hurt. I believe that Dien is safe and finding his way home. We have to be patient and believe it," Giang said with conviction.

Mother reluctantly agreed to come inside. She looked back twice in the same direction before walking in with her daughter.

Luc stared at the flags on the front door. He was quieter than usual. He could sense a big change was taking place and was as sorrowful as the others. Nevertheless, in his young mind, Luc could not imagine anything worse than the conditions and the suspense they had been living under during the last few weeks. At last, the chaos and confusion from the rampage of the looters in daylight and the bombardment and gunfire at night had stopped.

Hoan was looking into his underwear drawers for any red ones.

"Hey, I haven't got any red boxer shorts. Lucky me!" he declared. His relief from having nothing red in the wardrobe seemed odd in the distressing present situation, but seeing the terrorised expressions of the neighbours forced everyone to wonder about the magnitude of the matter.

Vy, Trinh's second oldest sister, was preparing a belated lunch in the kitchen.

Quietly, without prompting, Kim brought out a small knife and started to scrape off the old flag imprinted on the wall as the rest of the neighbours on the street had done. Trinh followed her sister and stayed by Kim's side, devoid of the small talk that was her habit. They both went in when the meal was served.

From that day, Saigon no longer existed in Vietnam. It was abolished on the world map and replaced by the name of "Ho Chi Minh City." However, regardless of the Communists' attempt to remind the whole population of their leader, Ho Chi Minh, the Southerners refused to call their once beloved Saigon by the whole name but referred to it just as "the city."

Still, persistently, for so many years, Saigon lives on in the heart of the Vietnamese around the world. It is named at various places in Australia, New Zealand, Canada, England, and France as well as in many other countries and in the United States as a symbol of freedom for expatriates in the free countries.

The Aftermath: Whispering

THE FAMILY GATHERED on the divan again, the males sitting with legs crossed in the yoga posture; the females all on one side, leaning inwards. All were quiet and restrained. A large square plain cloth was spread in the middle of the divan for serving meals. Chopsticks and bowls were grouped together in a corner, as Mother was not sure of how many were going to eat. It was late afternoon already, and the air was stuffy with a heavy stillness. There was no breeze to help clear the atmosphere. The markets were not open, and so the meal was very plain as there was no fresh meat, fish, or vegetables. A saucepan of thick rice congee was in the midst with six half-opened salted duck eggs and a dish of radish pickled in sweet fish sauce. Surrounded by creamy white, the egg yolks were dark orange in the centre, the only bright colour in the whole gloomy picture of the meal. It was almost the same as the food served up in the last few weeks.

At first, Trinh thought that the depressing atmosphere had dissipated her hunger pangs successfully, but sitting down with the bowl of rice congee in her hands, she realised that she could eat after all. Regardless of the simplicity of the meal, she was indeed ravenous. No one had had any breakfast since dawn, but only the children had any appetite; Hoan, Kim, Trinh, and Luc ate in silence. Their boisterous nature was subdued by the sad faces of the adults. They did not dare to make any unnecessary noise apart from the clinking of chopsticks and bowls.

Mother's eyes were watery, and her nose was red. Quietly, she picked up the corner of her blouse and used the inner side to wipe away droplets of tears from her eyes. Trinh noticed her sniffing in long deep breaths intermittently as if to control the flow of emotion. She saw Mother raise her bowl and put it down many times throughout the meal, but it was still very full when Trinh had almost finished hers. Mother hardly ate at all.

No one dared to speak up. Everyone was whispering as if the walls suddenly had ears, as if eavesdropping was a new practice acquired recently by every citizen in the new communist world. From the moment Saigon had fallen, the whole population of the South started whispering. They were unaware of the loss of their freedom to their own fear. As with the rest of the world at that time, the phobia of Communists and Communism was extraordinary. It was hidden in an invisible code. The defeat of the Republic of South Vietnam triggered that phobia, and the citizens of Saigon began to cower in terror. The meaning of human rights and freedom was swiftly taken away. In the lives of the Southerners, those became extravagant words in their vocabularies and replaced slowly by suspicion, horror, panic, and despair.

They did not dare to congregate in public. A crowd of more than three or four was considered dangerous and might be accused of conspiring to rebel. And chances were that they would be put in detention without further explanation. They talked in low, quiet tones inside their closed doors with only trusted members of their family or friends. They looked at each other and searched for signs of betrayal. Their careful use of words when talking to strangers was distressing; any misunderstanding and misinterpretation might be followed by disastrous results.

"I hope President Duong Van Minh is okay. He's so unlucky to be dragged into the mess in the last minutes like this," Father started the conversation, keeping his voice low.

"He's so naive to think that he could negotiate with the Communists. But why surrender so quickly, Father?" Mac continued. Mac was Giang's husband. Of the seven children in the family, only Giang, had been married a year before the war ended. They were staying in a separate part of the house with a rear entrance, which had recently been renovated into a fully self-contained modern apartment.

"Of course, they wanted him to believe so. He was the last means they had of trying to stall the advancement. However, the speed of the Viet Cong approach was so fast that it did not help. He was forced to surrender unconditionally."

"Why surrender without any effort to fight at all?" Mac was still dissatisfied with the answers and kept insisting.

"No one was willing to hold the fort anymore, Mac. Didn't you see that the top-notch leaders were leaving weeks before?"

"Yes, I know. The whole population was prepared to leave if there was a chance!" Mac shook his head sorrowfully.

"What are we going to do now?" Giang followed her husband's line of questioning.

"What can we do?" Father sighed. "We'll have to wait to see what's going to happen, and then we'll try to conform, dear. They're going to take action soon. In the meantime, we need to get back to our daily routine. Try to regain our normality, make the most of our time, and be calm. At least we're alive now." Father shook his head, trying to escape from his reverie.

Mother looked at Father; there was a meaningful exchange between them. Only at dawn the day before, he had discussed with her briefly how he might have to make a decisive move if the situation came to an unfavourable end. He had called a meeting with Betty, his oldest daughter from a previous marriage,

Giang and Mac, and his wife in the lounge when the fighting was closing in. The children were still asleep.

It was still very dark when Nguyen got up that morning. While waiting for the rest to arrive, he went to the large, heavy combination safe occupying a permanent corner in the room and took out a small pistol. He put it on the coffee table then beckoned them to sit down on the floor. The women were huddled together, squatting in a group and eyeing the pistol timidly. Mac sat next to his wife, his face showing lines of anxiety. He was curious about his father-in-law's request for a meeting at this early hour.

"I know I told everyone to stay calm and remain in the country for the last few weeks," Nguyen began. "I believed that the war was coming to an end and Vietnam was gaining peace after all, and I'd like to live and die here in my homeland. My oldest son had fought and died for this war, and at long last, peace is approaching. It's my sincere wish to stay. However, there are moments now that I'm doubtful of the Communists, and I'm afraid of their vengeance toward ex-government officials, intellectuals, soldiers and their families, or whoever they think of as their enemies. I could not sleep last night because the doubts became more and more profound. I thought of the killings in the 1968 Tet Offensive in Hue and in the darkest corner of my feeble mind, I was afraid. That's why I asked you to come and listen to me this morning." He looked at them squarely in the eyes.

They all started to talk at once after his last sentence, but he motioned for them to be quiet and then picked up the pistol and showed it to them.

"This only has a few bullets in it, but there are more in the safe. I'd thought of this solution only if the VC bastards were going to show cruelty or do anything to harm anyone, or anything that I foresee as a threat to any of you. Then I'll use it to shoot each one of us before letting us suffer in their barbaric hands." He spoke in long sentences without a pause, as if stopping would prevent him from finishing what he had to say.

Nguyen breathed deeply to regain his composure. Mother was shocked to hear his statement. Everyone else was stunned and speechless.

"But...but...No! No! It's...it's so...so frightful!" she stammered.

"Yes, dear Chi." Nguyen nodded his head and looked at his wife of twenty-five years. "I know it's outrageous to think of that last solution, but I cannot let myself witness the brutality the Viet Cong might treat us with. Even though I truly hope that the bastards will not do anything, considering I'm just an old retiree and useless. But as the days and hours are drawing closer, the fear begins to surface, and I'm afraid I might have made a bad decision in letting us all stay back!"

"No...no...It's...it's...impossible! Oh dear...dear! Buddha, help us, please...please!" Chi continued her stammering and then started to cry openly, drowning in her sorrow and panic.

"Yes, I'm praying for the help of the Almighty as well," Nguyen whispered.

"Father, please. Don't be too pessimistic. They're our own people. They're Vietnamese, and they speak the same language as we do. I don't think they can be as barbaric as we thought they were." Betty was in shock at Father's dreadful plan, and she tried to convince him with her own optimism.

"Yes, Father," Giang added. "We must remain calm. We will go along with the rest of the country. They could not possibly kill all the Southerners. It's absurd that they could be that bloodthirsty."

"Don't be too alarmed, Father. We're citizens of the South," Mac continued. "This is still our homeland. We're staying back, so we're already accepting our defeat and appearing to be willing to cooperate with them, Father. They could not do more harm to us, could they?"

"I hope not, Mac." Father sighed.

"Besides, I'm afraid you might not have the courage to pull the trigger too many times, Father! There are...there are...too many of us!" Betty reasoned. The last phrase was broken up, as Betty was overwhelmed with emotion.

"Betty is right, Father," Giang pleaded, "You could not finish us all and..." She stopped in mid-sentence. She was appalled at the horrific image and started crying with the rest.

"Don't worry too much, Father. You've made the right decision to tell us to stay back and we're going to enjoy peace in our country with you and the rest of the population of the South. There's nothing to be afraid of." Mac remained calm and spoke slowly, enunciating each word. He was trying to convince the group and himself, apparently.

Nguyen looked up. The morning sun was beginning to show its first ray of light through the front door. Floating freely within its realm were tiny dust particles dancing animatedly in total silence. He turned and gazed into the weary faces of his beloved wife, daughters, and his son-in-law for a long moment then walked to the corner of the room where the safe was. Then he reassured them. "No, I won't do anything. I'm sorry that I've brought this up. We'll be okay. Let's forget this dreadful discussion." He put the pistol back and closed the heavy door.

Later that night, Nguyen walked out as far as he dared from the house and disposed of the gun and the rest of the bullets in the sewage waste, the night before the Fall of Saigon.

In hindsight, through many sleepless nights, Nguyen realised that the weakness of the South Vietnamese people was their own naivety. The majority of the Southern population could not imagine the Northern Vietnamese Communists could be so barbaric and cruel. He thought most of the stories relating to that barbarism and cruelty from other Northerners who escaped in the 1954 Exodus or in the Tet Offensive in 1968 were mere disinformation. The horrific treatment inflicted on one human being by another of the same blood and ancestors could not be that horrifying. He could not possibly believe the hatred and revenge their own people, with the same mother tongue, could have imposed upon the people of the South. The blind animosity and fierce malevolence of the Vietnamese Communists toward capitalists, landlords, and foreigners had developed slowly and effectively. It was the extensive and continuous brainwashing propaganda of Ho Chi Minh and his followers for over twenty years during the civil war. Bitterly, that malevolence was also the driving force behind the single-minded advancement of the Communists toward the South. The Communists had won this war through gaining the trust and devotion of their people to fight for the land that they thought needed to be liberated.

Little had he known that that concept, based on hatred, led to much mistreatment and cruelty of the defeated citizens of the South and that it had gone on for more than another decade after the war ended.

The Reunion

THE EVENING WAS slow. Time passed even more slowly than in the morning. Television was still inactive, and most of the time it broadcasted the new national anthem of the National Liberation Front, reminding the South of the dramatic change of government in their land. Mother was sitting on a small stool in front of the house after the meal, waiting for Dien to come home. She longed to see the familiar outline of one of the three boys in her brood of seven children. Pitifully small and fragile in the dusk, she was the picture of an anxious mother waiting for her beloved son's return. Her arms were folded tightly against her chest, body leaning forward, hands crossed on opposite arms, chin almost touching her knees, and eyes gleaming with choked back tears—hoping for a young man to materialise.

The street in front was not as busy as it was at lunchtime, as if the curfew was still in place. Everyone was inside their house, whispering.

Mother stayed on her small stool until the street went dark. Even though there was a continuous flow of soldiers passing by the house, Dien was still nowhere to be seen. Mother recognised the South Vietnamese soldiers by the look on their faces and part of their outfits or appearance, as most were in civilian clothes. Some were wounded with bandages on their arms, feet, or heads. They wore the same look of tiredness and despondence as the soldiers who appeared in the morning before the Fall of Saigon. Some walked past and looked back at her, knowing that she was waiting for her son; their walk was taking them home to their loved ones.

Feeling sad and disappointed, Mother went inside. Her shoulders stooped, and her steps were slow. She was sick with worry.

That night there was less noise than on previous nights. There was no more bombardment but there was still occasional gunfire to be heard. The sky was darker than usual. It was pitch-black; not a star was in sight. After many frightening nights bright with flares and bombing, it seemed darkness was not friendlier after all. A feeling of foreboding had fallen on the city since lunchtime. No one wanted to go to sleep. Everyone was staying downstairs near the useless bomb shelters, but not inside. No one wanted to be separated from the family unit. Perhaps out of fear, togetherness seemed to be important to all of them at that time. Somehow, the terror of facing the Northern Vietnamese Communists increased in intensity with the passing hours. Even the children could sense the naked fear from the adults' outward appearance. Trinh was curious about its palpable horror even though it was so obscure, and strangely, the words were just "Communist" and "Communism." In her young mind, she could not understand the adults' fear, regardless that she too had felt it for no apparent reason. The mysterious panic and trepidation were real. To this day, Trinh was still able to recall the terror of the Fall of Saigon. From the memory of a young girl of thirteen, the effect of that appalling threat from the Communists and Communism was still vivid.

They were whispering to each other in the dark. Adults to adults and children to children, retelling the events of the day as if they still could not believe what had happened.

"It's spooky!" Luc said.

"Yeah, everything's spooky! Even their tank, it looked scary," Kim also commented.

"Poor Liem. He's scared stiff." Hoan laughed softly. "Served him right! Wearing red boxer shorts on a day like this!"

"You're cruel! No one noticed that. But everyone was scared too," Trinh said softly. "I know I was."

"Me too!" Kim agreed.

"Yeah, weird silence and a strange feeling in the air! Like a horror movie!" Hoan admitted, even after his lighthearted laugh.

Then they went quiet trying to get some sleep. Trinh lay next to her mother and listened to her long sighs during the night. *Poor Mother. She was worried sick,* Trinh thought. No one was able to sleep much, as whenever she was awake Trinh heard tossing and turning or rustling of pillows in the dark inside the mosquito net.

The next morning, full of anxiety, Mother could not do anything but wait at the front door again. She set up a station with the limited supply of food available to her. Kim and Trinh helped her to fill up her bucket of water whenever it was empty. The trickle of soldiers passing by the house continued. Like Mother, even in civilian clothes, Trinh could tell they belonged to the now defunct Army of the Republic of Vietnam (ARVN) from the look, the gait, the walk. All that made them different. Mother tried to stop as many as she could by giving them boiled rice, salted fish, dried bananas, and water from a bamboo basket next to her station. Some waved their hands in a negative gesture and walked hurriedly past, obviously uninterested in any conversation, their faces haggard and their expressions blank. Some stopped and were very grateful for what Mother was offering.

Tears streamed down Mother's face when they said, "Thank you for your kindness. I'm so hungry," and hugged her good bye after gulping down what she gave them.

Most knew where they were heading to, but some were lost and asked for directions. Their unit had disintegrated somewhere as far away as Long Khanh where Dien was last heard of and where Father's plantation was situated.

"How did you get here from so far away, son?" Mother asked one of them.

"I walked and hitchhiked my way, Missus."

"How did you manage with food and water?" She was surprised.

"Most of us were given food and water from kind people like you, Missus. Lucky for us, most of the Southerners were still from our side and not Viet Cong infiltrators!" He spilled out the heated sentence and continued the report quickly.

"There are dead bodies on National Route 1, scattered along the whole stretch, but I did not have the time and energy to bury them. I just kept walking, Missus." He was sorrowful and full of regret for what he had failed to do for his unfortunate fellow soldiers.

"They gave us some clothes to wear too as we did not want to walk with our uniforms on, and we put down our guns, military hard hats, and grenades on the way."

"What about shelter?"

"We slept in the kitchen of their houses or under their verandas. Yeah, there are people still caring for us soldiers!" he concluded sourly.

"I'm glad to hear that, son. I am as worried as all the mothers in the country are now. Go home to your mother, son. She'll be glad to see you."

Mother continued to ask for more information from the soldiers who stopped.

"Which battalion were you from, dear? The Eighteenth?" She hoped for some recognition.

"Yes, Missus." The soldier hesitated a little while before answering, as if afraid of giving away too much information about himself.

"Are there many of you walking home like this?"

"Yes, from what I've last seen, many of us are walking or hitchhiking. The army buses took as many as they could to some destinations, but the rest were on foot."

"When were you dismissed from the army unit, son?"

The soldier thought for a while as if unsure of the time frame. "It must have been three or four days ago, Missus. I'm not sure. Everything seemed so confusing!"

He stopped then said again, "I'm sorry! I…eh…" He apologised and did not finish his sentence.

Chi was not sure of what he was sorry about, whether it was his losing the war or his confusing of the time; but she let it pass. She was so relieved to hear that the soldiers from the Eighteenth Battalion were finding their way home by themselves and that Dien might be coming home late after all.

She pushed her luck. "Do you know a GI Nguyen Van Dien?"

The soldier shook his head again. He chewed on the piece of dried banana and swallowed it down hastily with a gulp of water before he answered.

"No, I'm sorry, Missus. I don't know of anyone of that name."

"He's a clerk for Colonel Huynh. You must know Colonel Huynh! He's in the Eighteenth Battalion!"

"Yes, I know Colonel Huynh." The soldier apologised once more. "But I don't know GI Nguyen Van Dien. I'm very sorry, Missus!"

Mother sighed heavily. She released the soldier's arm and let him go reluctantly, as if he was the last thread of connection with her son.

The day was almost gone, and the sun went down slowly, leaving a reddish trail in the sky and some faint light on the horizon. Mother was more anxious with the coming of darkness, and no one knew how to allay her distress.

"It's one more night that your brother is not safe!" she whispered.

It had been a day as futile as the previous one in her longing for her son's return. They packed up whatever was left of their supply and were about to give up. With one last effort, Trinh looked further to the right and saw a silhouette one hundred metres away walking hurriedly in their direction. She hastily pointed it out to Mother and Kim, and then the little girl ran toward him without speaking another word.

"Dien, Dien! There he is!" Kim was running with her, and now both were shouting with joy. It was unmistakably their brother, walking home for one hundred kilometres in his civilian clothes and army boots.

Mother stood still, her tears streaming down in rivulets, her hands shaking and her legs giving way so that she had to sit down on her stool, waiting for her son to come home at last.

The Disappointment

May 1975

THEY WERE SO glad that Dien was safely home. Like most other soldiers, he had walked and hitchhiked along the way.

The twenty-year-old soldier was barely an adult. The civil war was even older than he was. On the way home, he had seen many corpses from both sides lying exposed on the stretch of National Route No 1, and the mutilated and decomposed corpses were sadly ignored. The patriotic heroes of the South Vietnamese Armed Forces in the twenty-fifth hour were disturbingly being erased from history, and their death was agonisingly unjustified.

He had cried and exchanged his uniform for civilian clothes like the rest of his mates to avoid being gunned down when the news of total surrender was heard. Piles of guns, grenades, army boots, and uniforms were scattered here and there, and no one dared to touch them. They had suddenly become an encumbrance and a liability for the owners. Nevertheless, broken-down army buses were stripped empty by civilian scavengers. The pitiful sights of the last hours of the war were sad and depressing.

Walking along the highway home, he could not believe that the South had lost so quickly and bizarrely. It was so swift and surreal: a bad dream in which Dien could not understand the sequences. Was it the end, or was it the beginning? The dream was so odd, and it ended abruptly, just like the twenty-one-year civil war. Nothing made sense. If it had been a movie, he could not comprehend the director's objectives. The courageous fighting and the heroic sacrifice of his buddies, where did those fit in? The fierce and fearless combats of the South Vietnamese Armed Forces were still vivid in his mind, so why had they surrendered? Perhaps the soldiers were mere playing cards; the dice had been cast and the deal done well in advance, Dien concluded.

And what about the fate of the refugees of the South from the lost cities during the last few months? They had left the battle zones en masse, running wildly in horror and shock, abandoning their homes to escape the invasion of the Communists. They had formed tattered entourages and followed the retreating battalions in cross fire and bombardments. The images of those pathetic civilians broadcasted nationally on TV were still troubling his mind. What had they gained by believing in the protection they rightly deserved, only to realise that the fate they had been so terrified of was heaped on them in the end by the leaders of the country, who had left them high and dry? The betrayal was sharp and brutal. No one had expected it.

Ah! Here he was, at last! Dien was relieved. He could see the lines of *Dipterocarpus zeylanicus* trees along his street leading him home. Quickening his steps, he was breathing faster with the adrenaline coursing through him. The journey had taken him five days since his farewell to the command unit near Long Khanh, his last battle zone. Home was only a few steps away; there would be no more fear and anxiety. He was coming home, and he would finally be safe. He did not have to solve the puzzle any more. Let that become someone else's liability. He did not have to fight any longer. That was what eventually came out of this war.

Kim and Trinh caught up with him. In the fading light, his expression was indistinguishable, but Trinh could feel that her brother was very pleased. His smile broadened, and his eyes twinkled. Their radiance was deepened through his skin, darkened from hours of sun. The two little girls, fifteen and thirteen years old, were walking side by side in fast strides. Each was holding tightly to his hands, crying and laughing at the same time.

"We were so worried about you!" Kim said. "All of us!"

"Oh, I'm so glad. You're home. You're home now!" Trinh giggled, wiping her tears away with the back of her hand, the other hand not letting go of her brother's.

"Yeah, home and hungry!" Dien remarked lightheartedly, trying to suppress his emotion.

They laughed and broke into a run in the last ten metres when they saw Mother sitting on her small stool.

"Oh, son!" Mother could only mutter those words between hiccups.

Dien smiled sheepishly with tears running silently down his cheeks when Mother held out her hands. They held hands briefly, and then she gently patted his shoulders. Relief was clearly visible in her stance. She stood taller. The crouching figure of the last few weeks transformed as if a thousand tonnes of anxiety had been lifted off her soul. Then they all went in together. There was good reason at last for the family to rejoice.

Dien did not talk much about his experience in the final episode of the war, and strangely, no one dared to probe, seeing that he tried to avoid the topic, as if it was a torture for him to be reminded of the painful memory.

Slowly, family members were reunited, husbands to wives, sons to mothers, lovers to lovers; the lost fighters of a prolonged war were returning home at last. Like Dien, many did not want to recount their story; it seemed they wanted to bury it deep. Happiness was balanced by heartache. Mingled with the blissfulness of welcoming their loved ones home was the sadness of having to clean up the wreckage of war and the bitterness of the defeat. The Southerners started to look for missing relatives and loved ones in their own way.

"Go to his last combat zone and try to search for him, dear. He might be wandering about dazed and confused, unable to come home." Mother would advise some of her friends whose sons were still missing.

"Did you ask any of his friends? They might be able to help," she suggested.

"They did not know anything much. Everything was a blur to them," some would answer between sobbing.

"I went to Bien Hoa. There are many exposed mutilated corpses in the charred ruins. It's depressing and so sad. I had to help the villagers and peasants gather the corpses and bury them on their land with the kindness remaining to the compatriots."

There was no system to rely on in the search, and the new Communist government refused to have anything to do with it. The mass graves of the unknown soldiers marked the final chapter of the war. The mourning for the deceased in the less fortunate families was carried out quietly as if it was a crime to show anguish at the time of the victory. They were robbed of their honour to lay down their beloved men, fathers, sons, and brothers who had fought and died heroically for this civil war; instead, they were silently grieving their men as if in shame. Their hearts filled with anguish as the citizens of the South were forced to celebrate with the victors.

The Theory

Nguyen, Mac, and Dien had many small talks in the following months, and their discussion always revolved around the frustration of how the South had failed.

"I guess it's because we were so naive!" Mac said quietly.

"Yeah, to fall for their wicked manipulation, the Southerners were naive. But don't you see, Mac? To many Southerners, the frustration of defending their border was enough to tire them of the war. At heart, we are a peaceful and fun-loving people, gentle and simple. Do you agree?"

"We are gullible and straightforward, especially farmers and peasants," Nguyen continued without waiting for Mac to reply. "And remember, the majority of the Southern population are farmers and peasants! Their fertile land and extensive, intricate system of rivers and dams easily provided plenty of rice and, freshwater fish, and prawns for the whole country in the past, and even in wartime. Don't you forget that Vietnam was a leading exporter of rice to other Southeast Asian countries in the sixties and seventies. The complication of politics and power struggles was not in their interest, and most of the time they left it to the people of the north or central regions. They are content with their lifestyle, Mac.

"Okay, now tell me. Why were many guerrillas among the peasants led by a handful of thoroughly trained Communists?"

"Because the Communists insinuated hostility and resentment into the peasants' unsophisticated minds, along with the concept of antilandlordism, anticapitalism and anti-Americanism. They led them into believing the fight was for equal rights and freedom from foreign oppression!" Dien quickly replied, eager to voice his opinion.

"I can't put it any other way, son!"

"I thought the same, Father. The majority of the Southern peasants had limited education. And unfortunately"—Mac chuckled at his choice of words—"some literate ones were given freedom of choice, albeit partially. Nevertheless, they still had some freedom of speech and exerted their influence on others. However, they didn't understand the sophisticated information given to them, or it was not explained. So it was easily confused by the misinterpretation of Communist infiltrators. They thought they would have equal rights and share wealth if they were living in the communist system. Pity, how wrong they were!" Mac reached up to fill the cup with more hot tea for his father-in-law, shaking his head sorrowfully. "How naive!"

Nguyen replied, "And with skilful propaganda, the Communists formed resistant guerrilla units scattered throughout the length of Vietnam that brought havoc and vexation to the Americans and South Vietnamese Army in terrorist combat. The horror and dread of not knowing who were friends or foes in the guerrilla war were enough to demoralise many of the US GIs."

He picked up the dainty cup of tea, slowly inhaling its vapour. He then carefully sipped a few small gulps, enjoying its faint jasmine fragrance before putting the china gently back onto its saucer. Nguyen was savouring the few last pleasures in this transitional period of life. He was not sure if sipping tea in his ceremonial tradition would be considered outlandishly arrogant in the world of the Communists. He might be forced to abandon his enjoyment sooner. *It was too grand for their liking!* Nguyen thought.

"The Americans got involved out of the kindness of their hearts, but they put their people into our war needlessly. Don't you think so, Father?" Mac questioned his father-in-law again, jolting Nguyen out of his reverie.

"I'm not quite sure, Mac. Nevertheless, I'm inclined to agree with you that they should have only provided help and advice without actually sending their troops onto our land. Their presence gave the Vietnamese Communists a strong motivation for their war, the noble thrust of patriotism in people's hearts to throw the Americans off their land and regain independence. They won because of that too, I think," Nguyen said sadly.

Mac followed quietly. "I know they meant well, and they helped us tremendously. We cannot thank them enough. But American involvement had an adverse effect on our morale as well. Don't you think so? The entire population of the North was fed a noble and unique goal: 'liberate South Vietnam from the oppression of the Americans and reunify the country.' On one side, the South's sole purpose was to defend the homeland, and on the other side was to attack, to take over. The Northerners were fed limited, distorted news or biased truth and were totally ignorant of the outside world for the entire duration of the civil war. Ho Chi Minh and his Communist Party were successful in misleading their people and exerting a powerful determination to 'liberate South Vietnam and reunify the country.'"

Mac went on without waiting for anyone's response. "That was stressed resolutely by the name chosen for their army: the National Liberation Front, which included many patriots from the South who had volunteered to follow Ho Chi Minh to the North after the anti-French revolution and the Geneva Agreement in 1954."

"We were poorly led! Our leaders didn't use politics as skilfully as they did. We should have had some goal. Don't you think if the South had initiated the advance toward the North and put forward the great cause of liberating the people from Communism, then perhaps we would have had a greater chance of winning?" Dien was agitated. He thought of his fellow soldiers who fought bravely for nothing.

"I often wondered the same. It was a pity the South did not use that possibility. They were content and prosperous in their own land. Perhaps their selfishness prevented them from thinking that, as they might have had to share their wealth with the North once it had become their responsibility?" Nguyen smiled.

"And now the South has been stripped bare from their invasion any how! So much for thinking of having to take care of them! Now they're taking everything away from us." Mac was more agitated.

Father agreed, "Yes, I know. Our fertile land and high standard of living might have failed us in this war. We didn't see the need to fight. However, it was the opposite for the North. Their standard of living was always poorer. They never had a staple diet from their own food supply but relied heavily on the South in the undivided country of the past. Ho Chi Minh and his party members relentlessly pushed forward solely for the profitable gain they were going to reap once they got hold of the South. I'm sure of it now. On the pretext of a noble mission, the Vietnamese Communist Party led the whole nation into ghastly, prolonged bloodshed and the transformation of the North into a poor, undeveloped, and backward country. Everything seemed to stop growing or flourishing since his leadership began in 1954."

Mac added, "Then because of the guerrilla fighting and the demoralisation of the GIs, the antiwar activists used this extensively and artfully in their campaigns. Obviously, they had won over the confidence of a small proportion of the South population, the US citizens, and congressmen as well as the rest of the world over the prolonged period of fighting,"

"Thus the cry for peace was louder than the real threat of communism, and so they had to give up! The troops had to leave us without help and support!" Dien concluded.

"So the more pity for us, no help from them anymore!" Nguyen repeated regretfully.

Their discussions went on and on, but that did not change the fact that the South had failed through their general indifference.

"You see, even our own people were divided and fighting proudly for the opposite side as guerrillas. The peasants-during-daytime-turned-guerrillas-at-night were a nightmare for everyone, especially the armed forces and citizens. Besides, the peace-loving attitude of the Republican Southerners prevented them from seeing the war as a goal they had to win, but only trying to defend themselves whenever they had to." Nguyen admitted sorrowfully.

"Even with strong, courageous armed forces and personnel, without a noble cause and a goal, then the fighting spirit would fade with time. Unfortunately, that time factor was very much the challenge at the core. Eventually, it eroded the willingness of the defending side to retaliate. People got tired of the war after so many years of bloodshed and misery. Between the attackers and the defenders, the seesaw was always inclining to one side, and the latter was always at the weaker end."

Mac agreed. "Even the Americans were beaten by the time factor. They could not finish off the war as quickly as they planned to. Their aggressive tactic in warfare was to conclude the conflict between the two sides in the shortest time possible. It didn't happen, did it?"

"Yeah, it's a pity! It went on longer than necessary. In the end, they were tired of it too. That led to the abandonment of their assistance after more than a decade of costly military aid. The high number of US casualties in Vietnam War was also a sad fact in their futile attempt. Would you believe there were fifty-eight thousand casualties in total? No wonder the protest for peace was much louder than for war. I can't blame them!" Nguyen concluded.

"Our number of ARVN casualties was shocking too, Father: 260 thousand in all." Dien shook his head. "Sadly, war is always a big loss!"

Their discussions did not change the fact that for years after the Fall of Saigon, South Vietnam and its citizens suffered incredibly barbaric treatment. The hatred and animosity from the Communists were only understood belatedly by the Southerners. After a short initial recuperation period, the Vietnamese Communist Party began their revenge and punishment of the Republic of South Vietnam.

"We're their second-class citizens!" The Southerners were aghast at how the new state government considered their status even in peace.

"They only wanted to inflict revenge and punishment on us, as if the Southerners had to pay for the damage and suffering of the relentless twenty-one-year civil war waged by themselves, those northern communists!"

"Yes, those bastards! There's no government to revive and reunify the nation but a band of profiteers and robbers who come to take away what they think they are freely entitled to seize, the reward of the conquerors!"

"A bunch of liars and hypocrites!"

"Filthy communists!"

"Bloody savages!"

"How could they be so cruel to their own blood?"

"They still think of us, Southerners, as their enemies! We're not their own blood, mate!"

"Yeah, you're right. They can't get over the animosity feeling toward us, and they're treating us with the vengeance of the conquerors, not brothers reunited with brothers, I'm afraid!"

"What good to come with peace and unity but shattered dreams!"

"Part of it was our own fault! We should have been more diligent in fighting them!"

Those were the frustrated whispers among the Southerners following much mistreatment dealt out to them in the subsequent days. It was an appalling experience for the people of South Vietnam after the war ended that they had felt the shock peace hitting right at them, and that eventually led to the ghastly exodus of approximately more than one million people by sea in search of freedom.

The Disbelief:
The National Reserve Bank Closure

FRIDAY CAME. IT was almost the end of the week. Two days had gone by since the fall of the Republic of South Vietnam. The shock was still visible on everyone's face, but life had to continue. The Southerners were trying to patch up the fragments and were waiting in suspense for what was going to happen to their future, if there was a future.

Giang had been awake since dawn. The street was still quiet. Her self-contained apartment faced the avenue at the rear entrance of her parents' house. She missed the usual morning hubbub of the last few months. Even in the heat of the war, even in the chaos of a collapsing regime, there were relatively normal activities and the sense of belonging. Somehow, she did not feel like she belonged any more. Everything had changed in a short few days. She felt like an alien in a very strange country; even the language on radio and television was bizarre. The vocabulary of the Northern Vietnamese Communists was foreign to her ears. The songs they played on television were all very odd, with their strong Northern accents and high-pitched voices. The lyrics were all very much on the same theme, repeated again and again, praising the Vietnamese Communist Party, Ho Chi Minh, and the National Liberation Front. The propaganda had already started. She turned off the television, uninterested in the programs. Besides, she did not want to wake her husband. Both of them had stayed awake almost the whole night, whispering in bed. They were discussing the unknowable prospect of the South, both telling each other to stay calm.

Giang quietly put on a pair of dark beige flared pants and an eggshell-coloured T-shirt, a fashionable outfit in the Saigon of 1975. The printed picture of a cute purple kitten was prominent on the front of her shirt. The charm of the little animal was clearly portrayed by the artist. Long lashes adorned the sparkling eyes, and whiskers radiated from the adorable muzzle. Its right paw was touching a ball of wool tentatively, as if testing a safe toy to play with. The loveable creature was evidently unaware of any real danger out there; the harsh wide world did not exist in its pure, innocent attitude. The words "predator" and "prey" were unheard of.

"You're up early. Did you sleep at all, darling?" Mac asked, waking suddenly. His voice was croaky.

"No, I could not sleep at all. Perhaps on and off for a short while, and then the sun was up so I got up." Giang came closer when her husband patted the bed, inviting her to sit down.

"You are very worried, aren't you?"

"Why shouldn't I be, Mac?" Giang smiled weakly.

She held out her hand to him. They were wedded as recently as last year and were still very much in love. Mac had started his career as deputy tax commissioner in District Eight just before their marriage, a year before the war ended. After eight years of university and graduating with an honours degree, he could only serve the South Vietnam Republic for a short term: eight months in all. Now, everything was a shambles. His career was as shaky as the future of the whole of the South.

"I don't know, Giang. Part of me says it's peace and that we should enjoy it. The other part screams about the uncertainty of the communist system and whether the South is able to go along with them or be destroyed by them. I really don't know!"

Mac reached up and stroked Giang's hair. Her big, beautiful eyes locked with his, the tenderness in his touch warming both their hearts. Giang gradually became less agitated and more relieved. She had her husband by her side all the while at a time of crisis, and that was a blessing. She must remember that. Many of her friends were still watching and waiting for theirs to come home. They were probably in great distress and without anyone to turn to.

"We'll be okay, darling. We have each other, and we're alive today. Together, we'll manage. There are others in worse conditions than ours. Cheer up, sweetie!"

"Thanks, Mac. I know I'm very lucky. The family is lucky. No one got hurt. Even Dien came home in one piece!"

"Yeah, that's better. You've got me, honey. Don't forget!" He winked at her and pulled her down to the bed.

"Oh no, no! I've got to go, Mac. See, I'm dressed up already," Giang protested lightly.

"Really? Where to, honey?"

"Eh, I've got to buy some groceries, Mac. Just go out to see if any of the stores are open." Giang hesitated a little before answering. She was thinking of telling Mac her real reason for going out but decided to keep it to herself for now. She did not want him to worry about anything else in the meantime.

"Oh, all right. But just a cuddle, darling. I want to hold you in my arms for a little while. I want to feel your warmth, please," Mac pleaded.

"Okay, only for a little while." Giang smiled at her husband.

They lay in bed spooning and listening to each other's breathing. Their intimacy was needed to bring hope and calm to both of them. Giang stood up when she heard Mac's gentle snore.

Poor Mac. He was even more worried than her, but he made an effort to assuage her anxiety for her sake. Giang knew that.

She had a mission today. She was going to the South Vietnam National Reserve Bank to deposit some money. The last few weeks of the war had been so chaotic that Giang had withdrawn a large chunk of their savings and kept it at home, just in case they might need it. Now, it was over. The country was at peace, but the commotion was even more disturbing. Giang was uneasy with so much cash at home. There were talks of violence and robbery of people's property, cash, and jewellery in the greed that followed the 30th-April-Communist invasion. The worst and most feared spies knew who was who and took advantage of the period of disorder to strike. She did not want Mac to worry any more than necessary for her safety or the safety of the whole family. It was her decision to get to the bank today and return their money without telling him.

In her thinking, it was clear there was going to be a change of government, but Giang still believed in a system. The communist system was unfamiliar to her, but it must have a system, regardless. They were going to govern the country with a different ideology, and that was sad; but there must be a government in the reunited country, Giang reassured herself. Their language might be strange and peculiar. Their manner might be weird and alien or even crude, but they were still her fellow citizens from the North. There were no doubts about that, Giang supposed. The Southerners were vanquished citizens, but they were going to be treated as citizens in a country once more at peace, Giang trusted. They were not enemies any more. The civil war had ended already, Giang reminded herself.

Giang did not know that the naivety of a twenty-four-year-old Southern woman was as clearly visible in her as the kitten on her T-shirt. She had been too well protected in a traditional and influential middle-class family all her life. With never a harsh day out of her comfortable cocoon, Giang was as naive and gullible as ever. She had been raised as a young lady in a posh neighbourhood. She then went to the best-known high school in Saigon, Gia Long, and then on to a few years of university, but she dropped out eventually to get married. She never had to deal with the nastiness and malice of the real world out there when under her parents' care. She became a wife. Mac had taken her into his care, and Giang continued to bask in protection again. The malevolence and wickedness of the communist ideology was unknown to her.

Giang did not judge the communists by their reputation, and she could not convince herself of their cruelty because that was so outlandishly merciless. The harmonious, gentle character of a Buddhist Southerner did not allow for such ruthlessness in her thinking. How could they force businessmen, capitalists, landlords, scholars, religious priests, Americans, and all involved with the ex-government or armed forces personnel to their death? How could they force those people to dig their own graves and bury them alive? She heard stories so disturbing that Giang thought only barbaric animals or sick minds could act like that. She did not believe it. It was absurd, unthinkable.

Giang went to the pantry cupboard and rummaged into the stocks of noodle and rice where she had hidden the two million Republic of South Vietnam dong. The dong is the usual currency of Vietnam, like the dollar in Australia. They were wrapped carefully in four crisp bundles of five hundred notes. Giang gathered them into a large brown cloth bag. She grabbed a few packets of noodles to put on top and placed the bag inside the storage compartment of her motorbike. She pushed her motorbike silently out of the back door, mounted it, and rode it to the bank. There was light traffic on the streets. People were involved in their own business. *So was she*, Giang thought.

There were crowds shouting jubilantly, "Peace! Peace! Vietnam has peace after all!"

"Hurray! Hurray! We are at peace!"

"Let's enjoy it! Oh, beautiful, holy peace!"

"No more fighting! No more bombing!"

"No more death, no more misery!"

"No more running away from battle zones! No more war! It's peace now!"

"Vietnam is one whole country!"

"No more division, no more 17th parallel borderline! Hurray!"

"Our country is unified!"

"Hurray! Peace! Peace!"

The crowd continued in their ecstasy about peace and the unification of Vietnam.

There were red-blue and red flags with yellow stars everywhere. Giang avoided streets with crowds, and she turned into a different route.

Although it was just eight o'clock in the morning, people were already jam-packed in front of the door of the National Reserve Bank. However, only a small number of patrons were allowed in and out at intervals by the security doorman. The crowd was hectic and noisy. Many were trying to shove in, pushing forward, despite the closed door. Giang was very nervous; she was holding on to her brown cloth bag tightly. There were times Giang wanted to go home, but she was in the midst of the crowd now and unable to turn back.

"Geez, I did not know that everyone was desperate to be here!" Someone commented.

"Back out a bit, would you?" An agitated voice growled.

"I can't. They're pushing from behind. It wasn't me!"

A woman was walking out of the bank hurriedly, and the crowd was more alive, eager for information. Someone pulled her in.

"Could you get anything out?" she asked.

"Yes, but not entirely though. I wanted to withdraw more, but they only allowed one hundred thousand each. They said they were afraid they might not have enough cash for everyone."

"That's very lucky of you."

"I've been here since six o'clock! There were people here before me. Yes, lucky that they've still got some cash left to hand out."

"I wonder if there will be something left for me with this crowd!"

"Oh dear, oh dear! Yesterday they allowed two hundred thousand dong each."

"At this rate, they might run out of cash very soon."

"I only want to get fifty. We have no money to buy food. They should have that, I hope," another woman wished. She looked at the door and sighed, a concerned expression on her face.

Giang was perplexed. She thought of returning home without depositing her money as it seemed everyone else was withdrawing but her. Then the door was opened, and Giang was pushed through with the throng. She went to the cashier and mechanically pulled out her four bundles from the cloth bag then she placed them on the counter in a heap. She gave the entire two million dong to be deposited back in her account without further thought. The hell with it! Giang gave up. She did not know what to think anymore.

The cashier was surprised at the large amount of cash that suddenly materialised in front of her booth. She was hesitated and looked up at Giang, unsure of what to do.

"I want to make a deposit, please," Giang said.

The cashier looked at Giang penetratingly again, about to say something. Then she decided against it and accepted the four thick stacks of five hundred dong notes without another word. Whether or not she was glad that the bank was bailed out for another hour at least with this amount of cash, she did not show it. There were going to be another twenty people relatively happy at home with a hundred thousand dong each. Thanks to the young woman who was the only depositor in thousands of withdrawers on days like this.

Giang took the receipt from the cashier, looked at her balance, and walked out of the bank as if in a daze. She was not sure if she had done the right thing, but she did it anyway. The flow of thoughts was somehow very fragmented. Giang tried to make sense of things, but it seemed there was not a logical thought in her mind now. She was confused, not knowing what was right or wrong, as if in a trance. *Ah, the money was safe for now*, Giang reassured herself again.

Giang did not know that was the last time she would see her balance on her account as the bank closed permanently a few days later. After the National Liberation Front had transferred all authority to the Provisional Revolutionary Government of the Republic of South Vietnam, things changed dramatically. The closure of the bank was one of the first measures. As the days passed, people were devastated by shocks of growing intensity.

"Have you had any news from the bank?" Some would whisper in their discussion.

Without a word, without any official notification or letter of announcement, the Provisional Government took what remained in the National Reserve Bank as belonging to them.

"What's happened to our money?"

"Strangely, it's not ours anymore!"

"Every account has been raided. They've taken everything!"

"It's not ours anymore!" They repeated the phrase solemnly.

"They seized it all. All is now the treasure of the Communist Party without any regard to us and the rest of the population of the South. You must get used to that idea even it seems impossible, but our money belongs to the state now."

The account holders had had no notice whatsoever to get access to their accounts in which all the money, jewellery, gold, etc. were now no longer theirs, and there were no explanations offered.

"What are we going to do?"

"What can we do?"

"We've no right to protest. We're on the losing side. No one would be brave enough, foolish enough to ask. Would you?"

"No, no, of course not! They'll label us as capitalists. I'd rather be without my money than being called that!" Some would shake their heads at the projected fear.

Then, no one had dared to ask. They were stunned to be deprived and robbed of their life savings, but they were also scared to death of being classified as capitalists in the communist world! The new government defined capitalist very narrowly: "If you have money in the bank, then you are a capitalist!" That was a crime punishable by the Party and the People; the function of the capitalist was unforgivable. In the classification of Communism, only labourers and party members mattered. "Capitalist" was one class amongst those to be abolished, and the new government had already started its horrendous process of abolition. The terror had started.

A Violation of Freedom

ON THE WAY back, Giang saw groups of people with bands of red-and-yellow stars around their arms. They were forming barricades on the streets and stopping men passing by on motorbikes. They were the 30th April Communists and infiltrators, and their appearance was one of pure arrogance and superiority. They were "the People," and the band on their arm gave them a sense of power and authority. It had transformed them into someone else very different. The law was in their hands now, or more precisely, there was no law at all.

Together with the new conquerors, the Northern Communists, the 30th-Aprils, and the underground spies from the South were taking roles that were beyond their status—roles that controlled other people's life and death, happiness or misery. Their ultimate power seemed to give them great satisfaction, and human rights had no meaning in their view. There was no other justice system in the communist world but "the justice of the People," which decreed the final sentence without trial.

"The opportunistic 30th-Aprils were the ones who jumped on the bandwagon to escape from their low social economic status and become authorities overnight," Mac had tried to explain to Giang in their previous talks.

"Most of the underground communist party members were labourers or peasants, whose rough, hard life had prompted them to join the party in order to defy the upper class in the previous republican regime. They believed they would be able to change their life and status in a communist society with equal opportunities. Wealth had urged them to become traitors because what else could they do to achieve that so quickly? And now they were reaping the rewards by becoming terrorists literally."

Mac sighed, shaking his head. "Other underground Communists were university undergraduates and high school students who were gullible in believing in ideal doctrines of collectivism and communism like most youths of their era. Our world is divided into two main ideologies, and it's always the lesser one that attracts the young minds. I wouldn't blame them because who would support capitalism if they only see themselves as Robin Hood in an oppressive world?

"Collectivism or communism will never work in reality!" Mac raised his voice. "Human nature is naturally selfish." He smiled. "We work hard for our own needs first before thinking of others, and the Communists ask their people to think otherwise, which is the reverse side of human nature. It's unrealistic, and that's that!" Mac concluded flatly.

They were sitting in silence, their hands entwined and their minds mulling over their thoughts.

Mac stood up and, more or less trying to find explanations for the sad facts of treachery, said, "On the other hand, it's easy to see that the two classes in the new era of post-war Vietnam, the 30th Aprils and infiltrators, are the willing subordinates of their new leader! Those two classes were gaining in confidence and influence from the National Liberation Front and the Party by performing many outrageous acts in those early days of uncertainty."

Together with the illiterates from the North, they were slowly reversing the twenty-year social advancement in the South to the same level as 1954, which was very crude and basic in every way, from traditional national attire to cultural development and etiquette. Together with the Vietnamese Communist Party, they terrorised the Southerners. They initiated many despicable schemes in their hateful vengeance toward the defeated citizens. They instilled suspicion and scepticism within families and friends. The list was long.

One of her friends, a high school teacher, had warned Giang in confidence. "Guess what? The national attire isn't the traditional ao dai anymore. That's become something of an aristocratic symbol belonging to the capitalist world. Some teachers and students are now afraid to wear them to school. The Party members will sneer at you and reprimand your choice of attire as backward and nonconforming in front of the group political meetings. They'll say you're a capitalist if you're not careful. You can wear the basic *ao ba ba*, a simple white peasant's blouse and a pair of black pants and be called advanced by them. Be careful, Giang. They're judging our appearance, and they'll make us pay dearly. You can't afford to reveal your level of education or your standards. Remember their motto, 'the People demand a one-class society'? I truly don't mind that if there's something as a 'one-class society," but why lower your standards and not vice versa? Advancing the society and the people for betterment, but why go down to the crudest form possible in everything, even in language!"

She continued. "Don't you know that they especially enjoy victimising Saigon citizens as they thought we were given special treatments by the previous regime throughout the war? And they spread panic and dread as much as distrust and apprehension amongst us. So much so that I'm now afraid to confess my beliefs or opinions to any of my colleagues now. One of them was sacked last week because he said something like 'He can't expect us to respect him as a principal if he's only a high school graduate!' He said that to his friend just in passing. An 'advanced' student overheard his statement and reported it to the so-called principal in the school assembly. Poor guy! He and his family are going to suffer dearly."

Jolted out of her reverie, Giang was taken aback by an order from among the groups with the armbands, and she stopped in her tracks.

"Stop! Stop right there!" One of the red-banded officials shouted and waved to two young men riding together on a motorbike.

The look of alarm was visible on the faces of the victims. The young men were merely boys around twenty, who were perhaps university undergraduates. They slowed to a full stop in front of the man in charge.

"Get off the bike, arseholes!" the same one ordered curtly.

Both hesitated, unsure of what was wrong. Their fear was more pronounced with the offensive language and the violent gesticulations of the whole band.

"Stupid idiots! Don't you understand? Get off the fucking bike!" Another red-banded one yelled. His face was the same colour as that of the band on his arm.

The young men did not have enough time to get off the motorbike before being jerked by their collars and thrown roughly to the ground. They fell to the pavement together with their motorbike.

"Get up! Yes, both of you! Get up, long-haired swine! Slaves of the Americans and a treacherous regime!" the first one spat on the ground and swore angrily.

The victims were trying to stand up quickly, but they were clumsy in their efforts as their bodies were weak with apprehension. Their faces turned white. Looking down at their feet, they avoided eye contact with the terrorisers, still did not understand what was going on.

Another two were pointing their AK-47 at the men as if they were criminals. Two other red-banded terrorisers came closer with two pairs of shears in their hands. Without another word spoken, each jerked the victims' hair brutally from the base of their neck and started shearing away the hair up the back of their skulls. The young men were timid and weak with fear as lambs in the shearing shed, their hair falling on the ground in a heap.

"Bloody fucking bastards! You think you're better than us! Come on, we'll show you who's better than who!" one shouted vehemently, as if the act of humiliation was long-wished for in his mind, as if the words were his hidden inferiority complex waiting to lash out if given a chance. The coolie from An-Dong Market was enjoying his newly acquired power. For in his lack of intellectual knowledge, the insensitive and callous acts of insulting or humiliating the defeated citizens or destroying the cultural heritage of the South, of which he did not have a chance to enjoy before, was giving him so much pleasure.

"It served them right, cocky bastards!" he said gleefully to his scumbags after the young men were released.

Giang was in shock at witnessing the vicious attack of the red-banded people on the two young men her age. She was also trembling with fright and panic. What was it that was happening so quickly on the streets of her beloved city? The vicious harassment lasted only a few minutes, but it raised terror in passersby.

For some time later, that act of terrorism continued to strike many young men with hair longer than the communists thought appropriate. The men were humiliated harshly in public and stripped of their freedom of choice in a matter that was very personal.

The length of hair was to the communists a symbol of a relaxed and easy "hippy" lifestyle and a carefree attitude. For the Northerners, it was not permitted because they had seen so much hardship and suffering throughout the entire length of civil war. Ho Chi Minh and his Communist Party had made sure the population of the North tightened their belly for the Southward advancement. The Northerners had lived in poverty and been deprived of luxuries for a quarter of a century to satisfy their fanatical leader and his obsession. It seemed to them now that it must be punished because it was not allowed.

"Those Southerners must be punished for their wayward lifestyles!" their party leaders had ordered.

It had bound them as a strict law from the practice of Ho Chi Minh throughout his whole life. "Our leader, Uncle Ho, always appeared humble, lived a celibate life, and had little luxury in his daily living until his death," they boasted.

However, there were stories now from his own party members revealing his hypocrisy, with hidden whims and strings of women, whose death followed quickly after his secret sexual involvement with them to protect his facade.

Curiously, the Communist Party had not had definite regulations or precise policies in their management system to govern the unified country, apart from exerting pressure and forcing demands on the citizens of the South to submit completely in every control they initiated at that particular point. They invented many myths and schemes to suit their Party's policies without understanding the real consequences or impact on their people. Their capabilities were rudimentary, with only a limited number of academics or professionals to govern the country, and they had only a vague idea of how to take over the administration of a new territory. South Vietnam was completely different to their expectation in every way. It was the case of hit-and-miss, and the result was that the local authority had the power to preside over the matter at hand as it came along.

From the moment Saigon fell, news from Vietnam was completely blocked, and there was no connection to the outside world. Total ignorance of their current situation apart from propaganda or misleading information from the state government pushed the Southerners further down into their abyss.

Unlike the twenty-first century where information is at everyone's fingertips, Vietnam in 1975 was isolated and forgotten. The citizens were in a dark tunnel without any light on the horizon, and they experienced fear that seemed to spread as rapidly as an infectious disease. Once commenced, it was unstoppable, as during that delicate time, the Southerners had had no immunity. They were defenceless and unprotected, like abandoned orphans thrown out on the streets naked, unloved, and uncared for. The orphans were left on their own, vulnerable and helpless in the hands of their newly adoptive parents who had no concern and cared even less about their welfare. The Southerners were totally under the mercy of their Communist victors who took pleasure in instigating tortuous treatment on lesser beings without any concerns for human rights.

The orphans were deprived of care and attention for twelve years, as if the world had passed its limit for extreme compassion at that time and found it easier to ignore. They were nameless, pitiful, nonexistent citizens of a vanquished country from a war that nobody wanted to remember. From 1975 until 1987, the suffering and horrific experiences of the citizens of the South was poorly documented, especially the torment and affliction of the "enemies" of the Vietnamese communists, of their own countrymen from the civil war. Of this class of "enemies" of the Communists, the majority were remnants from the bitter, prolonged war, who were jailed in so-called reeducation camps. They were ex-government officials, judges, lawyers, armed forces personnel, religious leaders, ex-US employees, and whoever the Communists thought of as their enemies.

It was only from normalisation of relationships with the United States of America in 1987 and the rest of the free world that the citizens of South Vietnam had recovered their identity, and more than one million men were rescued from their hellish "reeducation" camps.

Dark Days

May 1975

THE BANK CLOSURE had stripped Father of everything he had accumulated over the years.

"Will we still be able to withdraw money from our savings account, Chi?" Father asked Mother, as if she was the treasurer of Vietnam at the time. He looked at her wishfully for an answer, as if she would have a solution for everything.

Perhaps Mother was always the figure of authority in Father's mind, Giang thought.

"The bank has closed indefinitely, Father," Giang said resignedly.

"Yes, I know." Nguyen nodded his head. He had already got that information from his friends who had put their money in the Republic of South Vietnam National Reserve Bank. "But what happened to my savings and pension? And my government bonds? Am I going to be compensated for those? Who's going to benefit from them? Are they all gone?" He found that too upsetting to even think about.

"And how are we going to live?" Nguyen continued his line of questioning.

"How are we going to survive? We've got nothing left," Nguyen repeated, "Nothing." He was awed by the circumstances his family found themselves in with the permanent closure of the bank.

For an influential and knowledgeable man, sometimes her father was so simpleminded, Giang thought. On the other hand, this righteous man was probably in shock and his mind had probably refused to accept the brutal reality. Giang sympathised with her father as she and Mac had shared the same fate. There was nothing left for them either. No one was able to answer his queries now. Even Mother was quiet for a while.

Chi looked at her husband and tried to find a plausible answer to ease his anguish.

"We'll manage, dear. We'll be okay," Chi reassured Nguyen, her voice soft but firm, with a resonance that was deeper and more powerful than it sounded. She had somehow become a tower of strength for him in matters like this. She just knew that she had to, Chi thought. He seemed lost, poor man. His vigour had evaporated, and he had aged a decade in just a few weeks after the Fall. His joie de vivre had disappeared; there was no more drive in him. Chi understood her husband's shock. His optimism had always been infectious in many dire straits before, but Chi knew that this final blow was gradually destroying him. He came from a family whose past wealth had bestowed many privileges and an affluent lifestyle. It had made him a trusting, carefree, and generous man throughout his life. Even though his journey had been eventful in the war-torn country, Nguyen never had to worry about his financial situation. He had taken his luck for granted.

Nguyen felt helpless. Now everything was crumbling. He had never thought that all his life savings, government bonds, and pension would vanish into thin air. His family did not have any other source of income but had relied solely on Nguyen's for many years. Except for Giang, who had married recently, the rest of the six children were dependants, and Chi had been a housewife all her life. Nguyen had been a high-ranking government official in various departments throughout his employment in the Republic of South Vietnam before his retirement in 1970. He had hoped to live in a unified Vietnam in peace, in a plantation of his own, and enjoy a country lifestyle away from the hubbub of a bustling city like Saigon, a dream that he had had for sixty years. In the present situation, it seemed that his dream would never materialise after all. He did not know how he was going to sustain his family through the difficult times ahead without money! Life had suddenly become a burden.

He tried to stand up but had to sit down again as his legs refused to hold him up. The patriarch of the family had lost control of his composure for once. After a minute of heavy silence, seeing that his wife and children were waiting for a statement from him, he had to say something to reassure them somehow; he knew that much. He wished that he could delegate the power now to someone else.

"Yes, I know. The family is going to be fine. We're going to be fine. We just have to..." Nguyen repeated his phrases and continued. "I know we're going to live on despite everything else," he declared gravely. He stood up again and walked slowly into his room to lie down.

He needed a rest. He was too tired to think. He still had his wife, and she would take care of the family for him, Nguyen reminded himself. He believed in her as much as he had loved her since she was a young bride of eighteen. Twenty-five years of marriage had not changed her much; she was still a beautiful, petite woman in her early forties, a delicate beauty. No one else was worth looking at in his eyes. She had fallen for him from the first day they met as much as he had fallen for her. They were courting when he was the young, handsome district commissioner of a small district at the far southeastern region of Bac Lieu. It was in the fifties, when the country was in the turmoil of internal conflict between various patriotic parties, fighting for independence to overrule French oppression. They had been together throughout the most dreadful period of the Vietnam War and had managed to stay alive. Now, when peace had finally arrived, when they did not have to worry about death and misery, somehow their stability had vanished along with financial support.

He felt old and useless.

Violation of Cultural Heritage: Books and Music Burnings

ANOTHER FEW WEEKS passed with more turbulence and unsettled news spreading throughout the city.

"Hey, Dien. Have you been out to the Central Plaza yet?" Khai swirled his bike over the kerb and shouted agitatedly toward the house. He and Dien had been best friends since childhood.

"Hell, no. What's up?" Dien walked out to meet his friend, a puzzled expression on his face.

"Saigon is ablaze. There are piles and piles of books burning on the streets."

"What books?"

"Every kind of fucking book!" Khai said with frustration.

"No! Oh shit! It can't be right! Who's burning them?" Dien exclaimed in disbelief.

"Of course, nothing is right! It's fucking wrong if you ask me! Who else, Dien? They're burning everything, all the books, and cassette tapes, music sheets, collections of albums, all the music of the South! People are adding theirs to the piles. It's utterly crazy."

"Why?" Dien could only utter monosyllables. He still could not fathom the meaning of all this madness.

"The 30th-Aprils and 'they' are promoting anti-intellectualism. That's bloody why!"

"They're insane. Do they want us all to be illiterate? Why burn books? It can't be all of them?" Dien persisted.

He could not understand the meaning of this vandalism of the intellectual heritage of the South. He felt a genuine sense of pain. He loved books. They had walls and walls of books at home. His father's collections were real treasures for him and the rest. They used to be able to take a book off the shelf and enjoy reading at home at their leisure. It was a real privilege as many of his friends had to go to the central library to borrow them.

The family had a private library that was quite precious—from cartoons such as *Lucky Luke* and Herge's *Tintin* to literature such as Tu Luc Van Doan, Confucius, ancient Chinese warfare, and even *Gone with the Wind* and *Les Misérables* in translations. Some were bound beautifully with hard covers and gold emblems. They were all very proud of them.

"Man, they're using AK-47s to come to houses and force people to bring out books that they classify as unsophisticated, distasteful, anticivilisation, and anti-Communist. Ah, especially *Playboy*!" Khai ended with a wink, lightening up a bit. He still had some sense of humour left, despite the seriousness of his voice.

Mimicking the Northerner's accent and pointing his fingers to Dien, Khai said, "You. Yes, all of you who had been nourished by the ham, cheese, and milk from the Americans and Thieu's insurgent puppet regime now have corrupt and filthy minds. Thanks to magazine pictures like these!" Shaking his head, Khai continued his playacting. "You've got to be ashamed by your behaviour! These disgusting magazines need to be confiscated and examined carefully to determine your level of reeducation by our party leaders!" Then Khai laughed sarcastically, pretending to shove a *Playboy* magazine into his pocket reluctantly.

"All kinds of books, man!" Returning to Dien, Khai continued, shaking his head and repeating himself. "All literature—historical, fiction, nonfiction, autobiographies, ideologies, and whatever—differs from their communist beliefs. Whoever is not their ally, then they've just got to destroy them all. Unbelievable!"

"I understand that they don't tolerate books out of their doctrine, but why destroy other literature that is historical or neutral?" Dien was talking to himself as if trying to find a plausible explanation.

"Come with me. You'll see how crazy it is!"

" Okay. I'll come, Khai." Dien hopped on to the back of his friend's motorbike, and they rode away at an alarming speed.

The crowd had formed a circle around the blazing fire in front of the Central Plaza. Dense black smoke rose high, adding to the already humid atmosphere of the monsoon season. The 30th-Aprils and their gang were bringing more books on motorbikes; they threw hundreds of beautiful, thick paperbacks into the fire without remorse. There were colourful magazines. *Perhaps not the Playboy or Penthouse as those must have been confiscated quickly by the comrades*, Dien thought. Even children's books and historical volumes were being brutally destroyed. Cassettes of music with beautiful love lyrics—the love of man and woman, of children and parents, of the magnificent scenery of a country, of patriots and their nation, of peace and humanity—were harshly thrown in. Music with phrases of fine poems in sophisticated language and with harmonious tunes as well as books full of valuable insights were destroyed indifferently, to be replaced with crude and monotonous praise of the Communist Party, Ho Chi Minh, their propaganda, their myth-making successes, and their make-believe victorious achievements in the war.

Khai and Dien were standing well back. They did not want to come too close for comfort, afraid of mixing with the crowd.

Similarly, some onlookers looked sorrowfully at the ashes rising slowly in the air as if lingering to watch them die. The light grey ashes were momentarily suspended midway in the thick tropical atmosphere before descending into the ferocious flames and being destroyed without a trace. In darkness, their silhouettes were reflected vaguely by the fire as mystifying as wandering ghosts, before breaking free and escaping into a different world, away from this madness.

Dien could feel the heat emanating from the fire even at that distance, and his heart fluttered as if part of his body was burning with the books. The cultural heritage of South Vietnam in its twenty-one years of freedom was turning to ruin at the hands of ignorance. He could feel his anguish blending with the heat.

"I think I've seen enough, Khai," Dien whispered, unable to raise his voice, unable to cry.

"Yeah, it's so ugly and painful."

"Let's go home."

They returned home in silence.

Mixed with bewilderment was the restlessness that had already fallen upon Saigon citizens; they were terrified by the violations, one by one, of their rights. Using armed force or just by intimidating already vulnerable minds with vague threats, the communists had begun their stabilisation process by eliminating unfavourable factors and tightening their control over every aspect of daily life. From psychological manipulation to the more obvious physical restriction of movements, the new Communist government was making certain that the Southerners had no control over their well-being. The local authority was one of the vehicles they used to monitor even the smallest act of the citizens.

New Era

THREE MONTHS PASSED. Schools had not resumed as the Fall of Saigon coincided with the commencement of the national summer break. Because of the chaos, the break began earlier than usual, and now it made going back to school an anxious prospect. *What would the curriculum be?* Trinh wondered. She was nervous about the new situation, unsure of what was going to happen. However, she was also curious to know who of her schoolmates had left and who had stayed. During this summer time, she was kept inside or near the vicinity of the house by her parents. It seemed a whole lifetime since she had ventured out with her friends, a real torture to the little girl.

The week before, the new government had announced that all high school students and university undergraduates had to make a contribution of labour toward their induction as citizens of a Communist country. They had to report to schools, not to start the new term but to be tallied up in the total number remaining for the new term.

Woken up early that morning, Trinh changed into white shorts and a flowery top that tied with a large bow at the back. She put on her thongs and stood waiting in front of her door for Lan. She could see her friend approaching in the distance, wearing black gabardine shorts, a pink T-shirt, and open-toe sandals. Lan had been one of her best friends since kindergarten. Being only five hundred metres from the school, Trinh's house normally served as a rendezvous for her friends so they could go to school together.

This would be their first meeting since the curfew declared a few months ago. All communications in the country were cut off after the Fall. The media and bulletins from the new government were not trusted as they were mostly fabricated or exaggerated reports. Like going back in time, the Southerners relied on themselves and word of mouth for information.

Trinh ran out to greet her friend. They smiled at each other and joined hands. They were so happy to be children again.

"Hi, Trinh! It's great to see you. It's been a long summer, and it's so scary, isn't it?" Lan blurted out.

"Hi, Lan! Yeah! Is your family okay? No one hurt?" Trinh asked. "I'm dying to go out, but I'm not allowed! It's not only scary but awful!"

"Yeah, I was trapped inside too," Lan said. "Mine is all right. And yours?"

"Yeah, everyone is safe. Even my brother is home. He's sad because of our surrender and tired because of his long walk home, but he has no scratches, believe it or not! A miracle! My mother was so glad. She vowed to be a vegetarian for three months if he was all right."

"Wow! Lucky him! You wouldn't believe it, but I saw so many dead soldiers on the highway that day coming home with my family from Thu Duc. I was so frightened. It's so ugly!" Lan beamed with this ghastly information as if she were proud of witnessing something so graphic and brutal.

"Yeah, it's nasty for sure. Did you see the tank?" Trinh added, putting on an important air. She did not want to be second best.

The girls were boasting about what they had witnessed on the historical day, excited with their gossip.

"The tank that paraded the streets on 30th April?"

"What else, silly girl!"

"No, my house is not on the Main Street, and like you, my parents did not allow any of us out of the house. But I heard that it was truly awesome and eerie."

"It was utterly weird! Scary and unreal!"

"I wish I could have seen it! But my streets went wild with all the 30th Aprils, and they celebrated like mad! A million of red flags filled up the entire area. Yeah, it's unreal!" Lan smiled and continued. "And I saw lots of helicopters flying around the US embassy with a lot of people crowding about at the landing ground, waiting to be picked up. They were desperate to get out. Funny! Wonder why!" Lan shook her head disbelievingly.

"The boy next door, the younger brother of the two with the thick glasses"—Trinh pointed to her right, animated with her story—"he had to go in and change his red shorts. They scolded him severely, poor thing, and he was scared stiff. His face was as white as a corpse. His mother had to hurry him inside." Trinh giggled.

She was amused now at the incident despite being so apprehensive at the time and secretly pleased that the boy was embarrassed. It served him right, as he sometimes stared at her through the common gaps between the two houses when Trinh was studying, and he did not even avert his glance when Trinh looked back. Naughty boy!

"Red is their colour, you know," Trinh whispered, going back to her gossip and changing the subject.

"True, red is their colour!" Lan admitted, whispering also. "Eww! You like it?"

"Of course not! It's ugly!" Trinh put out her tongue in a gesture of disapproval.

Only a few months had passed, but the city had swiftly changed its facade into a sea of red and yellow. All the signs and decorations before the Fall had been taken down and the bicolour theme of the victors' flag became the main colours of the nation. It was monotonous and daunting at the same time. Everywhere and everything was covered in red and yellow; the solid red canvas with yellow words were on all banners, billboards, office signs, notice boards, signposts, and flags. The dominating scarlet background on the walls, in the sky, on the trees, in the school, in the offices, on the desks, and everywhere she turned to look made Trinh quite dizzy. Every corner was decked to show that the Reds dominated the country now. The victors were erasing the last traces of the previous era, even down to the smallest details.

"Are you going?" Lan asked, back to their main purpose.

"Yeah, of course! I want to see if everyone is there. Don't you?" Trinh answered, ready to go. They did not have to wear the school uniform of the traditional white ao dai, as it was not a school day.

"Yeah, of course! Are you nervous, Trinh?"

"Are you?" Trinh repeated the question, instead of her answer.

"Yeah, what are they asking of us?"

"Cleaning the toilets, what else?!? *Labour is the essence of glory*, haven't you learnt?" Trinh shrugged her shoulders matter-of-factly; the little girl put on a grown-up air. "But let's go and see."

"Of course, I've learnt. The esteemed comrades stress that even though it means doing the cleaner's or gardener's job, collecting rubbish or digging the earth, it's an honourable duty each citizen has to carry out, an obligation we have to fulfil before being able to gain a place in our education." Lan quickly repeated her "learnt phrase," feigning a serious expression.

Labour contribution was a compulsory aspect of their qualification regardless of their academic results or achievements. It had to be accounted for by each individual in his or her resume. It was a brand new endeavour for the students of the South, and they were quite amused by it at first. They did not realise the ridiculous implications that would influence their future academic qualifications. Political studies were also an important part of their learning program.

The pair walked quickly to the school and were joined by many others who smiled sheepishly at each other, not sure of what to say.

It was not much past eight o'clock in the morning, but there was smoke rising in various corners already. There were open woodstove cooking fires in the playgrounds. Blending in with the wood smoke, the aroma of cooked rice filled the air along with the fresh smell of steamed sweet potatoes and cassava. These two root vegetables eventually became the staple diet of the Southerners, replacing rice, as it grew more and more expensive and scarce.

There were clotheslines crisscrossing from one tree to the next, and on the balconies in front of the classrooms, heavy with the light green army uniforms of the North. Somewhere in between, there were also black pyjamas and checked cotton scarves, the two trademark garments of the guerrilla's outfit that formed a frightening image in the minds of US soldiers and the rest of the Southerners in the war. Trinh was suddenly taken aback looking at them. Her heart skipped a beat. At first glance, for a transient moment, she thought of those as the outfits of the enemies invading her school.

"Ah, they belong to the current 'comrades'!" Coming back to her present state of mind, Trinh sighed with relief, and her fear was lifted off her chest. However, Trinh knew that the enemies were now within, nevertheless. She looked about and was surprised at the changes in her school.

There had been a small flower garden in the middle of the school, where the tall flagpole was; but now it was transformed into a garden of bok choy, the most popular vegetable of the people of the North. On one side, rows of corn plants were shooting up, the green leaves bright and energetic and full of life. Some young cobs protruded between the stems, golden silk flowing lightly with the summer breeze.

A sow and her brood of half a dozen piglets were enjoying the giant pile of rubbish near the tall crimson jacaranda tree. She looked happy and content; she had found a feast for her family. They were busy diving their snout into it. The old tree was in full blossom, the herald of summer vacation in the south. The fallen flowers were streaming around the base of the thick trunk like a red carpet, its extensive branches shading a wide area of the school grounds on hot summer days. Some blackened fruits had dropped onto the ground, joining the messy litter.

A few hens were picking away happily alongside the pig family in relative harmony. The fat sow did not mind the feathered creatures much, but the piglets were not pleased. They were annoyed at the industrious chooks with their continuous up-and-down pecking motions. They turned their heads and snouts toward the hens, shoving them away with irritable "oink oinks." The chooks scattered quickly but soon resumed their rhythmic pecking, ignoring the angry piglets. Belated cock-a-doodle-doos vibrated through the sunny morning from a noisy culprit who was still invisible to the listeners. He must be perched somewhere up on a branch, feeling very important and full of himself, Trinh was sure.

She was quite amused. "Geez, what's happened?" she asked Lan.

"We've got a farm in the school grounds! Wonderful! We don't have to travel to the countryside to study farming any more. Yippee!" Lan shouted excitedly.

"What's missing is a duck pond, Lan!" Trinh added, wishfully.

It was disappointing to see that the soldiers had turned their beautiful school into something very different, but the girls could not help feeling amused even in this weird and anxious environment.

From that day on, every school or university ground had been changed into a nationwide political forum.

The Northern Communist Soldier

DAYS AND MONTHS went by, and Trinh forgot what had happened as everything had taken place all at once. She lost track of the time. There were still talks, discussions, and rumours among the Southerners behind closed doors, as most had no other means to gather information. Only a few had radios to listen to, which secretly connected them to the outside world.

Relating to his thoughts while walking home on the last few days of the war, Dien said to his friend, "It's like seeing a bad movie in which the actors and actresses are acting from bizarre scripts. They don't know what to expect of their roles, and the director cares nothing for his final production. He's just happy creating a mad scene. In effect, after leaving the cinema, the viewers remember only seeing something horrendous, and everything else is a blur. They do not even want to recall the experience. It is plain ugly, an event to be forgotten."

"Yeah. Isn't that strange? And that's exactly how it's affecting us," Khai agreed. "Everything seems unreal! Many of us are amateurs, untrained actors and actresses being shoved out there onto the set, not knowing what is going on. Looking stupid and lost! Ah, but some are viewers, and some can act remarkably. And I don't know which ones are luckier!"

It became clearer that most of them had tried deliberately to forget those dark days and buried deep in the back of their mind the tortuous images from that period of their life, the period of playacting. Go and ask the Vietnamese Southerners, the boat people, in latter days, if they could remember much of what had happened in detail. A fraction here and there was all they had kept. No one seemed to remember all the details. The few memories that remained were those that were not so painful but still significant.

However, there were days Trinh remembered very well in this disturbing period.

Trinh's house and almost every other household in Saigon got into an arrangement to accommodate one or two Northern soldiers as a matter of course. It happened a few weeks after the invasion and might have been the way the new government exerted control over the Southerners during that critical early period. A soldier's station placed randomly here and there within the civilian residence would keep the defeated in check, snuffing out any rebellious conspiracy before it hatched. Especially, a house that had a retired government official and soldier of the former regime was under scrutiny, and that was Trinh's house.

His name was Sinh. The soldier walked up to Trinh's house one day, introduced himself, placed his AK-47 down in a corner, together with his rucksack, and since then had taken up residence in the kitchen as comfortably as in his own home. No one dared saying anything, and so he stayed. He was only nineteen, young and shy.

At first, the family was very reluctant to have any conversation with him, intimidated by his presence and afraid of revealing too much information that might harm them, especially Dien.

"Hey, I saw him looking at our grandfather clock like he has never seen one like that before!" Luc excitedly reported to Dien.

"Shhh, don't talk too loudly!" Dien reprimanded his brother. He was wary of the Northern soldier. Being in the same house with him was like an itch that he had to refrain from scratching.

However, Mother was polite to him. She was generous in sharing with him the family meal, but she kept her distance like the rest. He was quiet and used his time polishing his AK-47 to a bright shine. He usually sat on the small stool that Mother had once sat on while waiting for Dien's homecoming at the front door, and he looked about with a half-eager and half-mystified expression on his face. He was curious about everything going by but had no one to talk to; he was a lonely soldier. He knew that they were wary of him, but they did not know that he secretly had a similar feeling about them. He felt inferior for his lack of knowledge about everything here.

Everything was so strange. The South and the Southerners were completely different to what he had imagined. From what he had been told by his Communist Party and Great Uncle Ho, and through his entire life, Sinh had believed that the South and the Southerners lived in poverty and oppression and were a backward civilisation. In fact, what he had witnessed in his stay here, right now, had proven the opposite.

"Liberate the South and reunite the country!" He was told that the citizens of the North had to fight in the war for those ultimate goals.

"Putting all your devotions toward the Vietnamese Communist Party is showing love for your country!" He had seen billboards all over his hometown reminding the peasants of the loyalty they had committed to the Party.

"Following the Vietnamese Communist Party and loving your Uncle Ho is the duty of a patriot."

He was taught those slogans from a very early age. Family was considered an insignificant vehicle in the state government system. The Party was the universal essence, and its vitality was utmost importance. Sinh was always reminded by his party leaders.

Time moved on, and as the weeks passed, the children started to be curious and became friendlier to him as children normally are.

Sinh was very pale, almost greenish, as if lacking in vitamins. He was about Hoan's size, skinny and diminutive; and Hoan was only sixteen, two or three years his junior. The four kids used to form a circle on the floor in the kitchen, sitting cross-legged and talking to him on almost every subject. They were as curious about him as he was about them. They tentatively asked him about things in general in the North at first, but as time went by, they got bolder.

"Do you have any motorcars at all in the North, comrade?" Luc started, stressing the word "comrade" importantly. He clearly took pleasure in the new terminology of the Communists.

"No, we are very poor," he answered timidly and quietly.

Sinh was honest and truthful with them, unlike many others who would have boasted, "Oh, plenty! We have so many of them that the streets are jam-packed all the time!" as if proving their imaginary richness to the Southerners. Indeed, later on, the South knew that they were all just wishing for a bicycle, their only precious belonging, if they could have had it. Many of them made up lies with outrageous stories that turned into hilarious jokes for the whole South to laugh at when they discussed the North.

"Do you have motorbikes?" It was Trinh's turn to ask.

"No, we only have bicycles mostly."

"Oh dear, so do you have a bicycle at all, Comrade Sinh?" Luc was enjoying his questions and his "comrade" word.

"Erm..." Sinh hesitated then continued. "No, I wish I could have one." He was fidgeting on his feet, his eyes were hazy. *He was surely dreaming of a bicycle of his own*, Trinh thought.

"Really, so what do you have in the North?" Kim was surprised at his answers.

"Eh, we have nothing very much. We had to put everything toward the war as Uncle Ho taught us." Sinh was clearly uncomfortable revealing this information; he started to look down at the floor, visibly embarrassed.

"Hey, I like the sound of 'comrade'!" Hoan remarked boisterously, subtly changing the subject. The kids were all aware of his awkwardness, and they did not want to embarrass him further.

"Yes, it has a nice ring about it, hasn't it?" Trinh agreed. "Right, Comrade Luc?"

"Hmmm, I'm not sure if you're right, Comrade Trinh," Luc said in a more serious tone, his eyes twinkling.

"Why, Comrade Luc?" Kim joined the game, equally straight-faced.

"Because you're a girl, Comrade Trinh," Hoan teased, keeping his tone level.

"Nonsense, Comrade Luc and Comrade Hoan!" Trinh declared evenly, reprimanding them. "May I remind Comrade Luc and Comrade Hoan that sexism is not allowed by Uncle Ho's teachings. Right, Comrade Sinh?"

"Yeah, 'equal opportunities and equal rights for all,' comrade boys and comrade girls!" Kim announced. She was quick to copy one of the slogans that had been hanging all over the country.

Sinh smiled at their exchange; the Southern accent was peculiar to him, and he liked those kids. They were friendly to him at least, even though he knew they were teasing him. But they meant no harm. He remembered the first few weeks staying in their house when everything was unfamiliar to him from the kitchen utensils to the stove, the sink, the water faucets, and even the toilet. The house was so beautiful with running water from the tap with the turn of a handle, unlike his house in the village where he had to get water from the well. The cutlery was elegant with fine bone china dishes and bowls, and the furniture was attractive. He did not dare to sit on the lounge. It looked so grand. There was no way he could have afforded those things in his life. The Southerners' lifestyle was indeed far more advanced, and they seemed to be extravagant, with many conveniences. He was not sure why he had to liberate them; they seemed to be comfortable as they were.

There was one time he stood in front of the washing machine, scrutinising its minute dials and buttons, quite fascinated.

"That's for making ice cream." Trinh walked past and told him offhandedly, mischievously enjoying showing her superior knowledge to the "people of the other side."

"Ah, but what's ice cream?" Sinh asked.

"Oh my, really! Get real! You don't know what ice cream is? Are you sure?" Trinh was aghast at his question. She had only wanted to tease him at first to see if he knew about the washing machine.

Truthfully, Sinh had never tasted ice cream. He had grown up in the remotest rural area up North and had difficulty getting simple necessities, let alone an extravagant item like ice cream. It was obviously unheard of!

"Er, I don't know what ice cream looks like," he answered hesitantly, his face reddening.

"Okay, if you give me some money, then I can run out and get two ice cream sticks for us. One for you and one for me, and then you'll know what ice cream's like. Is that cool?" Trinh was pushing her luck, becoming more mischievous. She liked to test the boundaries. She would love to have an ice cream on this humid afternoon, and there would never be a better chance to ask.

Then there was the first time Sinh went to the bathroom and was surprised at a strange object in the corner about knee-high above the floor.

"Comrade Luc, what is it?" he asked Luc, pointing to the white oval basin, a puzzled expression on his face. Sinh had used the term "comrade" to address them initially, and that was the reason why Luc liked to tease him later on.

"It's a fish tank," Luc replied out of mischief.

The little boy enjoyed his game. He could not help but play practical jokes on these simple, unsophisticated, primitive Northerners.

"But what is this fish tank doing here without any fish in it?"

"Oh, we don't have any fish because they all died without food during the chaos." Luc continued with his joke. He winked at Trinh, motioning her to keep quiet.

Poor Sinh, he had never seen a toilet suite in his life, and he believed Luc wholeheartedly. He had been squatting down to relieve himself for his whole life. Minutes later, he went out to see some of his mates at the nearby school they had turned into their camping base, and when asked the same question about the toilet suite, he declared confidently to his commanding officer, "It's a fish tank, comrade major."

The major, who had the right to occupy the principal's office with a private and proper toilet, did not know its function and did not want to ask any Southerner, afraid to show his ignorance. He had to go to the common restroom with the soldiers and squat as he used to do. The major was delighted at Sinh's intelligence.

"Ah, is that so!" He patted Sinh's shoulder joyfully. "Go and buy some gold fish for me then, Comrade Sinh. I've never had a fish tank in my life. It is such a beautiful tank."

When the four colourful fish finally arrived, he carefully put them in the bowl and was happy to look at them swimming about every morning. He was very proud of his fish tank and pointed it out to everyone who came to visit him in the office. Until one morning, he went rushing out of the office, astounded, his face bright red. "Bloody hell! My gold fish have gone!"

He had accidentally pressed the button and flushed the toilet by mistake! There went the four fish down the sewer.

Cooking with Books

TRINH HEARD KIM entering the kitchen with her groceries, but she remained very quiet in her corner. The family was having fish today. Trinh could smell the ocean the moment Kim opened her grass-woven hamper. Her sense of smell was always very keen. The market was still trading freely during those early times.

"Hey, Trinh, come down and help prepare lunch with me, lazy bum," Kim yelled up from the base of the stairs.

Mother was out trying to sell a piece of her jewellery today, and so they had to prepare and cook a meal for the whole family. It was not easy at all for the two little girls at that time. City girls all their lives, they did not know how to start a stove with wood. That first step of turning on a portable gas or kerosene cooker, as they had before the Fall, was long behind them. Every kind of fuel was hard to get and expensive. They could not afford that anymore. The family had practically no income from Father, and none of the rest of them had a paid job. Their living conditions were the worst Trinh could remember. Some furniture had had to be sold already for daily expenses, food, and rice. Each month, a piece of furniture, valuable belongings, or jewellery went to feed all of them, six children, and her parents. Their refrigerator had gone.

Trinh reluctantly put her book back on the shelf after marking the page and walked slowly downstairs, counting every step.

"Damn!" she muttered aloud when she reached the twentieth step down on the ground floor.

"Why can't you do it by yourself, Kim?" she protested right away to her sister.

"Why? Why do I have to do it all by myself?" Kim asked, challenging her sister.

"Because I hate it. That's why!" Trinh declared.

"Hey, you can speak for both of us, cheeky monkey. Do you think I like it, you little runt?"

"You can start the stove today. It's your turn," Trinh retaliated.

"No, wait a minute! It's your turn. I did it yesterday."

"But I did it in the afternoon too."

"So?"

"So?" Trinh defiantly refused to give up.

"Okay, we'll do it together." Kim gave up. She knew that her sister had begun to show her stubbornness and that it was best to avoid a full-scale war. Kim had no more energy after bargaining and tackling all the choosing and buying at the market. She was not used to it; the timid, soft-spoken girl was still shy doing the tedious task.

Trinh started to collect some kindling from the pile of chunky wood in the corner and to bring it over. This was the hardest part. Sometimes it would take her more than a quarter of an hour to get it going.

"Here, use this." Kim gave her a book from one of Father's collection.

Trinh tore a few pages from the inside to light up her kindling. The hard covers were impossible to light at first. Not until the flame was high enough could they throw that in. There were moments when Trinh forgot what she had to do, squatting down near the wood stove and becoming deeply absorbed in the pages that she was about to burn. The teenage girl was as absentminded as most teens and sometimes unaware of the circumstances around her.

"Look, Kim, this is the book of warfare tactics in ancient Chinese times that Mother used to ask us to read aloud for her every afternoon when we were in primary school. Remember?" Trinh ran over to show Kim the beautiful book, its brown hard covers embossed in gold. The books were Father's pride. He had spent a lot of money building his private library from every kind of book, but now they had to pull them down and burn them in fear that they would be branded intellectuals.

"Lucky that Father was not here to see his books turned into ashes," Kim said in between tearing the pages and throwing them into the stove. Their father had often gone out and had stayed very quiet, uninterested in family business, ever since he realised his dream of retirement had been shattered.

There was a time when, instead of buying wood to use as fuel for cooking, the two girls used papers from the books on the shelves. Unbelievable as it was, it had been a month now before they came to the last few volumes, sitting at the bottom of the rows.

"Can't we keep those last books?" Trinh asked her sister.

She loved books; in fact, they all loved books. Their parents sometimes had to restrict their reading time as the children tended to get deeply absorbed in books and forget about homework or household chores. Trinh knew now that they could not keep them because many books were not in line with Communist doctrines. Now many Southerners were selling their beautiful books to peddlers by weight for use as wrappers, scraps, or uses other than reading. Their family was burning them because Mother did not want to let strangers know that they had those books in their library.

"It's safer to burn them, children. Do not let anyone suspect anything about us. We don't want to draw anyone's attention.

Make sure you all understand that!" Mother was adamant in her instructions.

Trinh was sorry to do what Mother asked of them because she realised that her ability to write and dream was the result of her reading advantage in early childhood. Books from a wide range on a variety of topics were readily available to her in the comfort of her home. They had provided her with knowledge and a vocabulary beyond her years.

"Yeah, if you must." Kim nodded her head. She remembered that book as well as the afternoons reading aloud for her mother. It seemed so far away, she reflected, a lifetime away! "I used to hate doing that, reading aloud words in those chapters that I didn't understand at all!"

"Yeah, all funny ancient Han-Viet vocabulary, and those are useless to us now! The Communists only use direct or crude words in their language." Han-Viet is the ancient Chinese-Vietnamese language normally used for literature or compound words. It is not easily understood by the average uneducated person.

"Yeah, they changed the name of Tu Du Obstetrics Hospital to 'Baby Factory' for a short while. Those crazy 30th Aprils or their illiterate commanders were trying to show their keenness by getting down to basics and refusing to use Han-Viet. How crude and downgrading the name was!"

"I heard that too, but I think they changed it back to its original name after acknowledging their own ridiculous mistake. Baby Factory! How could they!" They laughed together at the gossip.

Kim returned to their task and urged, "But hurry up! Stop daydreaming! You haven't started the stove yet! We still have to cook the rice, remember?"

"Oh, you sounded just like Mother, Kim!" Trinh teased.

"Yeah, yeah." Perhaps she had taken her mother's role when she was not here, Kim pondered, what with all the scheming and planning for a family meal!

She returned to scaling the freshwater fish. First, she rubbed some salt onto it as it was not very fresh! She had bought it because of that too. It was cheaper than the ones swimming in the fishmonger's basin. Mother always told her to use salt if the fish was stale. Last time she put too much salt and it was so salty that no one was able to eat a bite. But that was also the idea! Her family had little money to spend on food now, and a meal sometimes consisted only of a salty slow-cooked fish and some boiled vegetables dipped in fish sauce. This time she was careful to use only a teaspoon. They were going to have fried fish today as she had managed to get some lard from the butcher for a very good price. That was a treat! She was glad that she could manage something different from just slow-cooked salty fish for the family. After a while, that had become impossible to eat! For the growing teenagers, the amount of nutrition going into their body was scarcely enough to keep them alive, let alone make them grow. They were constantly hungry, and their bodies were constantly demanding sugar for the energy needed to feed the growing cells. She longed for her previous life. It was only a short while ago; only a month had passed, but it seemed like history now. Kim resignedly steered her mind away from that longing thought.

Cooking rice with an open-flame stove was very trying too. It was an art, turning the raw rice grains into cooked rice without burning half the contents. They could not afford to waste any of that either and still had no other choice but to eat it if it was burnt! They had had an electric automatic rice cooker before, but electricity was another extravagance that Mother was trying to avoid. It was frustrating for the teenagers to master the art when an electric rice cooker would do all the tricks. It was only after a time of trial and error that they began to have decent meals on the table and relieved everyone of having to eat uncooked rice. First, the heat must be high for the rice to boil in the open-lid saucepan, and then it had to simmer down with the lid closed at a lower heat until it was cooked. If the heat was still too high when the water drained completely then the rice at the bottom of the saucepan would be burnt and the upper part of the rice would be half-cooked without enough steam. At the beginning, they left the saucepan lid on; and when the rice boiled, it spilled all over the sides, leaving the rice with insufficient water.

Mixing with the rice was stones and husks from a poor-quality rice milling machine, which failed to sieve them out from the grains.

"Blast those stones and husks! There're more of them than there are rice grains! This could be a deliberate act to increase the weight of the final product!" Kim was furious, looking down at her tray. The girls had to sit for hours separating the impurities before getting on with the next stage of cooking the rice. Kim sighed heavily before starting her "Cinderella task," leaving her sister to light the fire by herself.

The girls immersed in their own chore in silence for a while.

"You've got to air it, Trinh!" Kim shouted, wiping tears away from her eyes as smoke began to billow out after Trinh threw a chunk of wet wood into the stove.

Their kitchen was not designed for wood fire cooking either, and the smoke from the wood was choking them and bringing tears to their eyes.

"How am I able to air it and get the fire going at the same time?" Trinh was coughing too. "I have to feed more kindling into it, you see?" she protested. The kitchen was mysteriously hazy with smoke.

"Hey, what are you two doing in here? Wow! It's like stepping onto a cloud! It's like being on a movie set of an ancient fantasy!" Luc exclaimed, excited despite the situation.

"Bloody hell! Fire! Fire!" Running downstairs, Hoan shouted over the noise and dense smoke.

"Come and fan the stove for me, Luc! Don't just stand there," Trinh demanded of her younger brother urgently.

"Where are you?" Luc pretended not to see her, stretching his arms in front and waving them around like a blind person.

"Silly boy! I am over here!" Trinh stamped her foot, waving her hands in the air.

Whoosh! A bucket of water was thrown over the stove, extinguishing the tiny flame and making the smoke ten times worse by Hoan's quick action.

"Damn! What are you doing?!" Trinh jumped up, ducking away from the splashing water. Ashes were flying up from the stove, mingling with the smoke and scattering everywhere.

The two sisters and two brothers burst out laughing, holding their stomachs and doubling up their body in hysterical laughter. They looked at each other and laughed harder, seeing their situation made funnier still by soot-smeared faces and watery eyes.

There was no chimney, so the corner of the wall was covered with black soot. It stained at the slightest touch. The girls also happened to go to school sometimes with their underarms smeared with black soot or even with spots on their cheeks or nose from the soot on their fingers, giving them the appearance of sad clowns.

Ration Book and Food Coupons

Months had gone by. The Southerners were getting used to the worsening conditions of living and the Communist ways.

"It's meat day today, folks. Come and get it with your ration book." The public announcement was loud; the speaker was very proud that it was the turn of her suburb to get meat rations today. Indeed, the person in charge put in extra effort by going around the neighbourhood and knocking on everyone's door, announcing the news separately.

"Don't forget to bring your family ration book, Kim," Hoa reminded. The Politburo party member for the Group 2, District 1 Division of Ho Chi Minh City was in her midforties. She was friendly toward Kim for some unknown reason, and the family was always the first to know the news. It saved a hell of a lot of time queuing, Kim often thought, if she rushed to the public government store and was the first in line. However, they had to bring their ration book to the Group 2 office to be stamped and to collect their coupon before being permitted to queue for whatever they were to buy.

"It's the fortnightly ration of half a kilo of meat for a family unit. Aren't we lucky?! Thanks to Uncle Ho and the Communist party. Fellow citizens, don't fail to acknowledge that!" Hoa trailed on, unable to resist adding the unnecessary phrase. It became a routine emphasis now for her and the rest of the administrative force.

"They've got to remember who has given them food, comrades. Only the Communist Party and Uncle Ho have provided them with the basic necessities. Tell them and remind them of that all the time, comrades!" Hoa had been given that order by her leaders, the high-ranking Politburo Party Members from the North, and she followed it diligently.

What an irony it was! Kim remembered that before the war ended, even during the fighting, they were living in comfort with an abundance of rice and food for everyone. The market was a free trade, and everyone could go and buy whatever they wanted. Now, thanks to the Party, their half a kilogram of meat rations per fortnight for the whole family of seven or eight people on average was a privilege. It was pitifully small and hardly enough to sustain anybody.

"Thank you, sis." Kim did not dare show her scepticism but breathed her gratitude before letting out a heavy groan when Hoa had disappeared. *Here we go again*, Kim thought.

Kim turned to face Trinh. "Whose turn is to queue this time?" she asked.

"I went to buy rice last time, Kim, and it was very heavy, don't you forget!" Trinh said.

"It's only eight kilos! Not that heavy, you little runt!"

"Hey, it might not be for you," Trinh protested, "but it was awfully heavy for me. It was a quarter of my weight, mind you! I got to carry it home, remember? And all by myself! It's hard work, you know!"

She continued. "I had to sometimes drag the bag and sometimes carry it in the bloody hot, fierce summer sun. It's a kilometre, and it wasn't fun at all!" Trinh complained. The girl was obviously tired of the task that her tiny body had to undertake.

"It doesn't help to swear like that, Trinh!" Kim reprimanded. "I will have to tell Mother if you don't stop!"

"I'll stop swearing if I don't have to queue for food," Trinh said defiantly.

Their family ration of rice was four kilograms per month per person because their parents were not in the work force and that was their allocated portion. For a permanent worker, it was thirteen kilos; and for a nonpermanent one, it was nine kilos a head. It meant that for being a citizen in the glorious Vietnamese Communist society, a person only had half a cup of rice a day and a tiny morsel of meat barely filling the cracks of his or her teeth. The national staple diet was rice; it was never an issue with Southerners. Before, they always had more than an adequate supply through their farmers. These days, with nothing else to complement half a cup of rice a day, the amount was too little, scarcely enough to sustain anyone, let alone the growing bodies of teens. The children suffered a great deal in those times, and their stomachs were constantly growling for food. Trinh remembered being hungry all the time.

A few months or so after the Fall, everyone, from infant to adult, had to have their name officially recorded in a Registry of Residency, and then the registration card had to be presented to the Politburo Officer at any time of day or night if requested. The registration was a legal procedure allowing the resident to stay in his or her own home and to have access to the available ration later on. The census listed names and details of every member in the family or household. That was the first control imposed on the South by the new regime. The registration card was also used to control all movements from a distance as short as five kilometres in the radius of their registered residence or from one district to the next. A trip longer than that had to have proof of purpose and had to be assessed by the group or district leader before being granted.

The citizens had to obtain a permit for every trip they planned overnight. A search was conducted randomly by the Politburo at any time or any day, and if a culprit was caught without a permit to stay overnight where he was at that time, then he would be led away and held for questioning. It was even worse if he had no proof of residency anywhere else; his or her fate would be sealed. In those times, it was almost a death sentence when a person was summoned to the Politburo Office for questioning.

Her house was searched one night. Just the knock on the door at night scared the wits out of everyone. An entourage of two soldiers and a commander was at their door with the announcement "It's a search. Open up!" Reinforced with an AK-47 machine gun, the authority had full power to apply justice in any way they wanted.

Father presented them with the family registration card then a roll call was conducted. The young commander looked Father up and down and asked, "What's your name?"

"Nguyen," Father answered, trying not to show his displeasure at the commander's insolent manner to a senior citizen. *It was poor etiquette*, Nguyen thought.

"Age?"

"Sixty-two."

"Profession?"

"I'm a retiree, officer."

"Okay, step aside now. Next!"

"Speak up! I can't hear you!" He tersely addressed Chi.

One by one, every member of the family was called out. When it was Dien's turn, everyone was tense, expecting some hassle.

Following the same line of questions as before, the commander then added, "Which battalion were you in?"

"The Eighteenth." Dien tried to remain calm. He knew that Mother was nervous, afraid that they would cause trouble since Dien was an ex-South Vietnamese soldier.

"Ah, that one! Lucky for you, I didn't fight in Long Khanh!"

Dien remained quiet. He did not know what the Communist was trying to say. If he had fought in Long Khanh with the Eighteenth Battalion then Dien would not be spared now?

"Report to the office tomorrow morning at 7:00 a.m. and every day after that until further notice, understand? If you fail any day, then your family will be held responsible for your action!" he ordered coldly, and then he went through all the list of names before leaving their house at one o'clock in the morning.

They felt powerless in the land of the People's Republic of Vietnam, an ironic name for a country where people were stripped of their human rights openly and disturbingly.

"Remember Thuy? My high school friend, the one with a large dimple on her right cheek?" Giang told the family, gathering around the divan as usual. "She got married just a month before the Fall, and her husband was not registered in time when the census took place as he wasn't with her but staying at his parents' house. He was taken into custody and was not allowed to stay in the house even with the marriage certificate on hand when the house was searched. They had to go through many steps over a period of months through the convoluted layers of the Communist system, with bribes offered for every step, before husband and wife were allowed to live under the same roof."

Until this day, the bribery regulatory system is still strongly entrenched in the administration of the Vietnamese Communist government. Bribery is necessary at every step. It is very much like a code of practice, a set of standard protocols applicable to all levels. *The Vietnamese government ought to have made it into a national act of law*, Giang thought. It is a highly regarded rule. It opens doors to everything. Nothing moves or goes beyond the desk without that first protocol: bribes and bribery.

After the short initial period of free market before regaining their composure, the state government enforced the collectivism policy, which prohibited all privatisation in every trade and transaction. The restrictions started with the stomach. It came as a shock to the Southerners as they had never had to worry about food in their life before, even when the country was at war. They were content with the available rich fertile land and abundant natural resources with rivers and dams crisscrossing the regions, irrigating their meadows and giving them more than enough rice, grains, and fresh water fauna. The Pacific Ocean alongside the S-shaped country of Vietnam provided a plentiful supply of seafood. Not, however, when peace arrived, when the Southerners started to have periods of hunger, and that were a puzzle to all.

"A ration book is required for each family. You must keep that ration book safe and bring it with you to record every purchase the family is allowed," they were instructed by a Politburo Party member. Then the whole nation revolved around that book from that time on.

Trinh flipped the pages and looked into the entries of her family's book. There were eight people in their unit, as Giang and her husband belonged to a separate unit.

1. 10/12/75 – 100 g of sugar, 100 g of cooking salt, 100 ml of fish sauce

2. 12/12/75 – Eight kilos of rice, two cakes of soap, 100 g of laundry powder, 100 ml of cooking oil

3. 16/12/75 – Ten kilos of cassava, ten kilos of sweet potatoes

4. 17/12/75 – Two kilos of fish, a kilo of bok choy, 100 ml of soy sauce

5. 18/12/75 – Ten kilos of wood, 100 g of dried prawns, five kilos of sweet potatoes

6. 20/12/75 – Two kilos of mixed vegetables, a small packet of monosodium glutamate

7. 25/12/75 – Half a kilo of pork, 100 g of salt

8. 26/12/75 – Twelve kilos of rice

9. 29/12/75 – One kilo of fish

10. 03/01/76 – Six duck eggs, some mixed vegetables, a can of condensed milk

11. 07/01/76 – Half a kilo of mince meat, a small pack of pepper, some garlic, some ginger

12. 10/01/76 – Eight kilos of rice, two kilos of wheat flour

The list was endless; there was an entry for every little thing in life! Trinh thought they would probably even count the grains of sugar if there were enough staff. Everything was accounted for in minute detail.

"It's a pain in the arse!" Luc sometimes yelled out in frustration.

"Mother, Luc is swearing!" someone reported.

They had to queue in line every time the coupons were handed out. Kim, Hoan, Luc, and Trinh were assigned the tedious task, and they all hated it. Hoan was always the one to duck out cleverly, leaving the other three to carry on the abominable duty.

Trinh did not know how other kids her age were supposed to study at school. She often wondered about it. Her entire free time before or after school was being used to get hold of all those goods to keep her family from starving. Sometimes she had to bring her schoolbooks with her; she would be standing in line and studying at the same time. The anxiety was the worst! Every time the family was given some coupon, there was the exchange of frustration between the sisters, Kim and Trinh, as Luc was still too young to handle most of the transactions. They were assigned to the unavoidable task!

There was no other way the average citizen could afford to live because black market prices were outrageous. Without any real source of income, they had no means of purchase. Stale fish or meat; poor quality soaps or shampoos; sticky, wet brown cane sugar; or unprocessed, discoloured salt, and the like—all were welcome to them. As time went by, it became worse. Even though the quality of those things was far lower than from the black market, many others who had money to afford better things still did not dare to refuse the coupons for fear of raising suspicion. In those days, they lived very much in fear. Fear of being betrayed by others for crimes that they might not be aware of. Fear of being exposed of committing crimes as simple as having more money to spend than the average person, having more food to eat, having expensive soaps to use, and having tender meats, fresh fish, and new-cropped rice to consume! It was a capitalist crime, forbidden and severely punished in the state government of Communist Vietnam.

"Do not let anyone see you having a whole chicken for dinner tonight. Make sure you close all the doors and dim all the lights!" A distant relative of the family and a Communist party member from the North gave Mother a fresh chicken, bought from the black market as a gift in exchange for her medication to treat his boil. He had to tell her to eat it in secrecy!

Many times when Trinh stood in queue, she saw in front and behind her the same expressions of fatigue on the faces of various ages, from teens to youth, to mature men or women, to old grandmothers or grandfathers. Many faces had become familiar after a while as the same people had to queue for each family, appearing at the same time of the day. Teachers, students, secretaries, clerks, factory workers, professors, doctors, or people from other professions of society—they all had to stand in line, holding on tightly to the food coupons and their ration book in the hope of getting the most basic necessities to live on. Every day, every hour, seven days a week, twenty-four hours a day, the whole population of the South had just a single goal in their life: enough food to fill their stomach and enough essentials to keep clean and be free of contagious skin conditions.

"Have you bought rice yet?"

"When is the next time for sugar?"

"Have you got your coupon for vegetables yet?"

"How come we haven't got it yet but you have?"

"Hurry up, the meat stall is going to run out soon!"

"The fish is fresh today, at least! Not like last time, I had to soak them in salt, but they were still smelly and awful to the taste!"

"It's rotten fish, and we still have to purchase it with coupons!"

"Hey, that's a privilege in the Communist country! Don't you forget that!"

"Yeah, yeah. *Communism means queuing in lines all day long.*" Then they laughed hysterically, weary and all!

"Last time, the wood was wet and in such large chunks that my brother had to chop it up with an axe. I had to run around borrowing the axe. It suddenly becomes a precious tool! And we had to air-dry it for several days before we could use it."

"Talking about chopping wood with axe, I had a terrible accident! Lucky no one was hurt. The handle flew off suddenly, hitting the glass cabinet and shattering it into pieces! It's the family's heirloom! What a shame!"

"It's crazy, isn't it? That family's heirloom might cost a thousand times more than the value of that stupid chunk of wood."

"Yeah, I should have sold it off and bought better commercial fuel."

"But they'll accuse you of spending extravagantly as a capitalist."

"Haha, back to square one. Chopping wood and toiling away with hard labour is safest now."

Then someone changed the subject. "Last month's rice was hard and dry. It must be an old crop from a few years ago!"

"Nevertheless, less stones and husks! It becomes a tedious task, picking out those impurities."

"Next week is meat time again!" Someone else was eager at the promising schedule.

Trinh pleaded, "Can you queue in line for me this time please, Kim. I'll do it next time. I have an essay to finish."

Those were the exchanges between them now. It was as if nothing else mattered. It was how the new government kept South Vietnamese citizens in check. It was impossible for them to think of anything else but that single goal: staying alive.

Animated, secretive talks of rebellion or revolution to overthrow the communists in these early periods after the war ended was just wild talk and hollow dreams or hopelessly futile battles ignited by a handful of frustrated and ill-treated ex-soldiers. Of course, those flickers of rebellious flames were easily extinguished as the rest of the country was so busy queuing for food or necessities that they had no energy or enough clarity of mind to join in. These hopeless battles then served as examples for the new regime to boast about their mighty power in defeating the Southerners again!

First Currency Change

September 1975

ANOTHER PUBLIC ANNOUNCEMENT was being made; Trinh was sure. She was woken up by it. It seemed that in the controlled world of the new Vietnam, citizens' activities were forever being dictated by the PA system.

"Time to get up!"

"Time for morning exercise, comrades!"

"Time to go to the weekly meeting at unit level! Each household has to have one representative there. Don't be late!"

"Time to go to group meeting for self report."

"Time to go to do labour contribution at group level."

"Time to do labour contribution at school level."

"Time to do labour contribution at party member level."

"Time to go to group meeting for political study."

"Time to go and buy rice. Time to buy food."

Trinh sighed. So many times in her daily life, she had to behave like an automaton.

This time, it announced, "Comrades and people of the Republic of Vietnam, this is to inform you of a total curfew tomorrow morning. Starting at 12:00 a.m. and effective immediately, no one is allowed to stay outside their residence. Severe punishment will be applied for anyone who disobeys."

This was announced at ten o'clock the night before September 22, 1975. Everyone was perplexed about what was going to happen. Early in the morning, at six o'clock, the PA was on again.

"We have an important announcement today."

The head district party member almost said "a really significant and important announcement," as it seemed to him they had so many "important announcements" every day. This was far more important than the average importance; he was sure of that. However, his Northern accent prevented him from saying the letter *l* correctly. "Really" would have become "reany" in his pronunciation, and so he regretfully omitted the word "reany." Damn! Damn! Sometimes he "reany" wanted to make them notice that one was more significant than the next because even he, an esteemed member of the Communist Party, could not see the difference.

This was real, however. He could sense the weight of his words. They were like tonnes of bricks, and he liked that. It made him feel "reany" important! He was the one to deliver the blow. How about that? The magnitude of the economic change was going to knock the shit out of a lot of cocky Southern capitalists for sure. It served them right! He had no sympathy for them, bloodsuckers of the real people like him. They were in for a nasty surprise! Everyone was—except the party members, of course, who had already got hold of the news and had managed to find some way to dodge the effects of what was to come.

"The currency of the previous regime is now obsolete. The transition time is for today only. Starting from tomorrow morning, all transactions involving currency are to be mainly in new dong. Each household is allowed to change a maximum amount of two hundred new dong, regardless of how much they have in old dong. I repeat, regardless of how much in old dong you have in your possession, you are only allowed to receive a total of two hundred new dong maximum per household. Each new dong equals five hundred in old money. Bring your family ration book and all your cash to the group office of your residence so you can change. Each household is allowed one transaction. I repeat, each household is allowed one and only one. The last hour for currency change is six o'clock this evening. That is final. No later than that."

There! He had finished his sentence with glee. He looked down at the piece of paper that even with utmost care and through his elementary year five educations, his handwriting was still childishly untidy. Bloody hell! This was so confusing, all this talk about new dong and old dong. He had had to memorise and practice reading the lines a few times last night, and he was still bewildered by what he had just said. Who could understand it all? He wondered.

While holding the official letter in his hands the previous night, he already knew this was coming. Scraping up all the available cash at home, he barely got ten thousand in old dong. Damn, it was so little! All he had was equal to twenty in new currency. That was all the reward he had for being a member of the Communist Party for twenty years! It was so wrong! Bloody immoral! He could not let this happen. He had to rise above this somehow. His contribution toward the victory of the unification of the country was worth more than that. When would it be his turn to reap the richness of the land, if not now?

Walking up and down the office with the key directive from the central office, he racked his brains for a solution. He had to think of something urgently. This was his chance to balance the injustice. Ah! A brilliant idea emerged miraculously out of his fuddled thinking. He knew what to do now. He just needed to recruit some of his subservient underlings to carry out his plan. He jumped on his bicycle and rushed to meet them. He was sure they would gladly join in with his clever plan. They would form a pact, and with clever bookkeeping, they could manage to pocket a substantial amount by having changed more cash for people who had more than the maximum amount allowed. He would tell them that they would get 50 percent of the amount as commission. Indeed, he would demand 70 percent and that extra

20 percent was solely for him. For each new dong the capitalists received, his gang would have the same amount in their pocket and even more for himself. How clever that was! They would swear an oath to keep it a secret, and no one would find out.

He was so proud of himself. He must tell his mother sometime later of this. The nutritious food and the affluent lifestyle he had allowed himself as the district officer since the Fall of Saigon had paid off at last. His brain was working much better than before. For over twenty years, while fighting in the civil war under the esteemed leadership of Uncle Ho and his Communist Party, he was quite dumb. He had to admit it. He had followed the doctrines of "equal opportunity and equal rights" and "work to the maximum level of your contribution but receive the sustainable level of your requirement" diligently, and what did he have? A mere twenty new dong for his life savings! It was absurd and ridiculously wrong!

Later, to his amazement, it seemed every other party member had thought of a similar scheme and were reaping the cash that had come their way in unexpectedly huge amounts. So he was not the only one to turn out smarter than he used to be, after all! They had turned into clever people in the short time of living in the South.

"Here is the plan." He gathered his underlings around in the district office in the night and explained.

"We will have two books, one on the day, and one for us. The first book is to record the real thing. The second book is to make it up. If Mrs. A had only one hundred in new dong, then there was one hundred extra for us in her allowance. If Mr. B gave us his cash, which was much more than his allowance, then we put his surplus into Mrs. A's column and so on. There are two ways: we can ask for a commission of 50 percent or we can always collect extra cash from the idiots who brought it all to us. Remember, each household is only allowed two hundred in new dong, regardless of how much they are holding in their hands. Their old currency will become useless plain paper just to wipe their arse the following day. They will agree with what you offer them, I am sure."

He stopped to look around at the faces of his group, seeking agreement and understanding.

"Do you all understand? Any questions?"

They looked up at him admiringly.

"Wow! That's the smartest plan I've ever known, comrade district commander."

"You're the best, comrade commander!"

"It's so smart! It's unbelievably clever!"

"So if I have forty thousand in old dong, then I will only get eighty in new dong. Yeah?" one raised his voice and asked. He then continued. "And we'll collect 160,000 in old dong from the 'pool,' then tally it to make it equal two hundred in new dong? Correct?"

"Yeah. But don't make it too obvious that all amounts equal two hundred, okay! Make it vary between 170 to 200, right, guys? Don't let them suspect our scheme," he stressed again, feeling very brilliant about it all.

The hectic day went past with a population of approximately twenty-five million Southerners, at that period of time, in shock at having their cash reduced even further. Some had thought they could manage to withdraw their savings from the National Bank in time before its permanent closure and keep the cash for the future. They had thought they were safe for a while at least. Obviously, nothing was safe! The change of currency had pushed hundreds of thousands of businessmen, well-off individuals, and wealthy families into the ground. Within twenty-four hours, their wealth and lifetime savings had gone down to a mere two hundred in new dong. It was very clever, indeed. The battle to abolish capitalism from the government was so swift and brutal that no one was able to avoid it. The ideal of equal opportunity from the madness of Communist doctrine was carried out at the expense of the lifetime savings and family wealth of the citizens of the South. Ironically, the battle gave birth to another class of capitalist: the Communist capitalists who emerged out of their corruption to rule the wayward country of Vietnam. In the incongruity of it all, the Communists were already contradicting themselves.

In the process of abolishing capitalism, the Vietnamese-Chinese businessmen were among the most targeted group. Many of them had been stripped of their properties not long before. Anyone who had more than one house was automatically branded as a capitalist, and his or her properties were inevitably seized. Many houses, factories, and businesses were confiscated from the hands of their owners by the sheer force of the "law of the People." Many were evicted from their mansions in the middle of the night by a mere piece of paper from the central office of the Vietnamese Communist Party. With the currency change, many suicides occurred among overwrought and depressed middle-aged and elderly men and women whose minds snapped at seeing the fruits of a lifetime taken away from them. The shock of facing the future destitute was too much for them to bear. Many had simply retreated into insanity.

"You know the Siu Siu restaurant owner, Mac?"

A friend of Mac's came by and told them of the entrepreneur's fate.

"Siu Siu was the name of a successful chain of restaurants in Cho Lon, a Chinese Town in Saigon. He started his business before 1975 from a small takeaway specialising in chicken and rice. After twenty years of labour and accumulating his wealth, he bought three adjacent houses on the same busy street of the commercial district in Cho Lon. The houses were turned into one large restaurant that was famous for his special dishes. Within a few months of the invasion, he was down to almost nothing. They took all his three houses into their possession. The takeaway ownership was transferred to one of his relatives to avoid any more trouble from the authority. He became just another one of the workers in the restaurant."

It also came to their knowledge that three years later, in 1978, all his family, brothers, sisters, cousins, distant relatives, a hundred lives in all, were escaping on a boat that sank not far from where it started. He was the only one who survived that fateful journey by floating on debris to the nearby shore of Ben Tre. All were gone without a trace, but he remained alive. He went mad shortly after being rescued and revived. As he was without any identification papers and was insane, the locals did not know who he was. They eventually found out that he was the Siu Siu restaurant owner, and so he was repatriated back to An Dong, Cho Lon. He became a vagabond, living on the streets near his once beautiful and famous restaurant. He died a few years later very poor, desolate, and lonely—the miserable end of the life of an industrious man.

Perhaps he was lucky to erase all his past tragedies and to immerse himself in a world apart, out of touch in his insanity, until his death.

Luc and the Trousers Drama, and Scabies

YEARS PASSED. THE children were growing up despite the meagre food allowance. And no one was holding hope for a revolutionary change anymore.

Luc could not pull them up. They stuck right at his crotch, even with every effort he made; He could not pull his trousers up an inch further. They were too small for his growing body. Those trousers were for a boy of eleven, when Luc had got to high school, when the Fall of Saigon happened. Luc was thirteen now. He was in year 8, and his school uniforms were too old. The white shirt was tight but not as tight as the pants. He could still button up his shirt without much drama, but the trousers!

His sisters had heard his frustrated grunts every afternoon in the last month or so. Either Kim or Trinh had to come in and help him dress in the end.

"Golly gosh! These blasted pants! How am I going to pull them up?"

Luc said in between breaths. He had been trying for the last five minutes without success, and the effort had left him short of breath and panting.

Kim looked at her younger brother. The pathetic figure of a teenager trying desperately to get into undersized pants that he had outgrown years ago made her want to half-laugh, half-cry. She and Trinh went inside. They had been helping him with this for a few weeks already. The frustration and anxiety at the beginning of the problem had changed to resigned expectation and stoic endurance from the young boy. Poor Luc. He had no other choice but to squeeze his body into the school uniform to conform like everyone else. It was crucial for a thirteen-year-old; he would hate to be any different from his schoolmates. The embarrassment would kill him! It was already bad enough that his pants were a few shades lighter than the normal school uniform because of frequent washing and wearing and being the only ones he had! He had cried openly a few times before when he realised that his pants no longer fitted him. It also left him drained of energy, knowing that he had no choice. There was no alternative. His mother was away on her regular peddler trips to earn a living for a few months and would not be back until next month. They had no money to buy him another pair of trousers, and he knew it.

"It's okay. We'll help you," Kim said gently. She gestured for Trinh to come closer.

"Hurry up, I must go as well! It's almost twelve," Trinh complained but still stepped in. She knelt down, holding the trouser legs tightly for Kim to pull them up past Luc's crotch.

"Why are they too tight? You've grown too fast! Stop growing so fast!" she scolded, wanting to leave for school.

Kim heard her sister's remarks and felt the irony ringing in her ears. Instead of suggesting finding a bigger pair of pants to fit his growing body, her sister was offering a solution that was as impossible as telling time to stop.

"Don't be absurd! Just shut up and hold them down steady, silly bugger!" she curtly reprimanded the younger Trinh.

Then they both gave their attention to the matter at hand. Kim used all her strength to hold onto the waistband and yanked it past the stretch point. She lost her balance and fell backward against the wall, her feet in the air. They all laughed aloud, like normal youngsters having fun, despite the bitterness of the situation. However, Luc could try now to pull his zipper up while his two sisters helped him on each side gathering the openings together.

Kim was impatient now, her forehead sweating from the strain. "Hold still! We can't pull the zipper up if you're not standing still, monkey runt!"

The room was windowless, like most of the terrace houses on the streets of Saigon, where some rooms might not have windows at all. The heat of noon and the exertion of the whole exercise left them with beads of sweat running down their body. Luc's shirt had wet patches on the underarms and the back, clinging even more tightly to his skinny body. Despite his sister's accusation that he had grown up too fast, Luc was lanky and twiggy as a matchstick.

"I'm standing still!" Luc protested at Kim's admonition. He was equally annoyed.

Finally, after many yanks and pulls, their effort paid off as miraculously as Trinh's wish of telling her brother to stop growing and to be able to get inside his pants.

Everyone was happy with the result.

"Bye. I've got to run. I'm late! I'm late!" Trinh shouted, darting off right away.

"There you go for another day!" Kim sighed heavily, not knowing how her brother managed without going for a piss during the day as it was impossible for him to zip up his trousers without help. Poor bugger!

The little kid just had to go without a drink for the entire five school hours and could only relieve his bladder when he got home. Still, he did not want to miss school. Difficult as it was with all the drama of his undersized pants, Luc still tried to squeeze his body into them every day and had survived whole days at school, one after another for another month before his mother shipped him down to Can Tho a few months before their escape. It was a vast relief for the three of them from the day Luc left home. No more school for Luc meant no more pulling and yanking, no more frustration and anxiety for the trio with the "trousers drama," as they called it.

Earlier that previous year, Luc had also suffered from contagious skin rashes over his entire body. In the years 1976–1977, two years had passed since the South had fallen, and many strange illnesses and contagious skin conditions had started to appear. The mysterious skin rash, which affected millions of South Vietnamese, was now quite certainly coming from scabies; but without information and guidance to help them understand, the general population were in the dark. The scabies infestation imported from the Northern soldiers escalated to extremes. The matter was worsened by the scarcity of toiletry products like soaps, shampoo, and toothpaste; they had become so rare that it seemed none at all was available at this stage. At least one or more members of a household were affected by the mysterious skin rash. Everyone was scratching, and everyone was talking about how to get relief from the itch. It was a hot discussion topic in markets, cafeterias, takeaway shops, street stalls, at home, in the classroom, in the office, everywhere!

There were no exceptions. The victims ranged from the poorest to the better off. Worst affected were the children as they tended to scratch more and were unable to stop once the itch-scratch cycle started. Then the more they scratched, the more skin was damaged, with infected lesions spreading over the entire body. To the utter desperation of the whole South, they had no medications to heal it. Antiparasitic solutions, antiseptic solutions, creams, or antibiotics were so rare and expensive that only a few could afford them. Most were old and outdated, the remnants of army supplies or pharmacy stores before the war ended. Everyone was waiting anxiously for their turn to contract the condition, like the inevitable conclusion of a well-known tale.

They were helpless to combat the invasion of the scabies. The whole South was under oppressive control. No one dared to ask for a solution from the authorities. No one dared to request an explanation or assistance from the new communist government, and of course, no help was offered. It was not their concern.

One day, like everyone else, Luc's skin erupted into tiny dots of blisters.

"See these? I got them last night!" He showed them to Trinh.

Trinh looked at those little dots in horror.

"Good gosh, you've got them, Luc!"

It was almost like being sentenced by a judge; the hammer had just slammed down.

"Oh no!" Trinh continued.

"What do I do now?" Luc was as horrified as his sister was.

"Damn, damn, damn!" Trinh ignored her brother's pleading and then turned nasty. "It's because you did not have a shower every day, did you?"

"Yes, I did! But what good does it do anyway? We've had no soap. Smelly ashes in slushy water made my skin so raw!" Luc went red with anger.

They had to use water mixed in ashes, then skim the slimy, slushy solution to use as an alternative to soap, washing detergent, laundry detergent, shampoo, etc. The sulphurated liquid had a certain degree of antiseptic cleansing power and had helped them through difficult times, but it was quite potent to the skin.

"See, so you did not use it, and now you've got these shitty things! Serves you right!" Trinh was angry with her brother for no apparent reason other than feeling devastated by his condition. It was contagious, and everyone was scared of it. She was scared too. At that time, with limited knowledge, they did not know what the mysterious skin disease was, and so they were even more anxious.

"Don't be a nasty, ugly witch! I hope you get them soon, Roly-Poly Trinh!" In his retaliation, Luc used his sister's nickname to tease her as he knew that she hated being called that.

Only half the phrase was delivered before Luc started to scratch involuntarily. The more he scratched, the more blisters popped out, as quickly as pork skin crackling under a hot grill. His once beautiful, transparent, baby-smooth skin was gradually becoming red, inflamed, and oozing with yellow discharge. The ugly dots covered his whole body. It was a nightmare for him and everyone else at home as no one knew how to get rid of them. Many remedies were being spread by word of mouth to try to alleviate the symptoms, and many were disastrous, worsening the aggravation with lethal substances like salt and vinegar.

Every time his mother returned from her peddler trip, she brought home some outrageous remedy to try out.

"Try salt. Rub salt onto it. It might help." A Mrs. A had said, and so the hit-and-miss trials started.

Luc had to grit his teeth and bite his tongue while his mother sprinkled some salt onto the blisters. The searing pain of salt in contact with his rashes was the worst of his suffering. He jumped up and down, enduring the pain in the hope that his itchiness would go away. He needed to make them go away; it drove him insane during the day, at school, every waking hour, and throughout the long, dark night. He would try anything!

"No, no! I won't try it again!" He had cried out testily the second time he was about to be marinated with salt once more as the feeling was almost like being roasted alive. To his relief, after seeing that his condition showed no sign of improving but was even more inflamed than before, his mother stopped that horrible remedy.

"Try vinegar. One part of vinegar and three parts of water. It really works!" A Mrs. B had said.

Mother then tried this, and so homemade vinegar was even more in demand. It stung less than the salt, but the smell was rancid and sour. It dried out the skin even further, and the itchiness that increased tenfold afterward made Luc scratch like a mad dog.

His mother had to shout to him. "Stop it, son! You made it worse. Go have a shower and stay in there until you don't scratch anymore."

"Try crushing some pointed mint leaves with pure alum and make them into a mixture. Then bathe in it for an hour a day until all blisters have gone completely." Another suggestion was forcefully stated, quite sure of its result. It was followed diligently by Luc as it seemed the mildest solution and seemed like a much more pleasant experience.

From then on, every day, Luc prepared his bathing routine like a king, albeit a scabies-infested king. Everyone brought him pointed mint leaves grown from their tiny potted garden or bought from the market whenever they passed by the house. Kim or Trinh had to remember to buy alum and mint leaves when they went to the market for groceries every day. They had a circular tin basin used for laundry washing. It was one metre in diameter and about a foot height and was large and deep enough for Luc to sit in there with his concoction. The rashes were worse around his crotch, and the sensitive area was dense with blisters.

He went about preparing the bathing ritual with the utmost care, praying at the same time that this was going to set him free of this horrifying itch. Sometimes Trinh helped him boil many kettles of water to mix into the warm bath. She stayed in the kitchen, tending to the woodstove and enjoying chitchat with her brother. The mint leaves were crushed in the rock mortar and pestle together with a lump of alum and then poured into the basin for Luc to soak in.

The basin was placed in the open wet area in the middle of the house. He would then decorously take off his clothes, step inside, and immerse himself in the warm mixture floating with mint leaves and smelling pleasantly of an aroma suggestive of chicken cabbage salad, as mint leaves were the main condiment used in that dish. Luc used the duration of the bath as his dreamtime. Yes, he would dream of having a delicious dish of chicken cabbage salad while enjoying the warm soothing sensation from the minty alum water.

The Townhouse

IT WAS EARLY evening. The sun had gone down, and that part of the house was cool and pleasant enough with an occasional breeze. This open sky area was in the middle of the house, allowing air to circulate throughout the whole length; only the rooms next to it had windows. The inner rooms had none, like most townhouses in Saigon.

The glow of electric light from the Phan family, their next-door neighbours, was shimmering through from above, and it was enough to keep Luc company. His house was still in twilight. Mother had asked them to conserve electricity as much as possible and only turn on their lights when it was dark. The common wall dividing the two adjacent houses was streaked with the varied vertical green shapes of slime mould, formed from years of rain pouring down the wall. It had sometimes been whitewashed in the past, but not lately; that was the least concern in the minds of the occupiers at the moment. The appearance of their residence was of minimal importance. Most of the houses and existing buildings in the south were derelict and had been neglected for a few years now. There were other urgent matters to attend to, like food and clothing.

The absence of daylight made the green shapes darker and more mysterious. Some looked like animals, elephants, or horses, and some looked like dancing snakes in Luc's imagination. The top of the wall was laden with mix-and-matched broken glass from bottles. The edges were sharp, rising five centimetres high, as an "optimal" barricade to prevent the intrusion of strangers or the residents of one house to the other. The base was also green with moss. Trinh or Luc used to jump up on the edge of the tank and slide down, scraping off the moss to feed the fighting fish during the summer when the trendy season was in.

The 1.5 × 1 × 1 metre rectangular water tank was built-in, next to the wall and constructed of cement and brick. During the war, it had to be regularly filled with tap water to at least halfway or to the brim, in case there was a siege like the one during the Tet Offensive of 1968. The bottom of the tank was also slimy with green mould, as was normal with stagnant water in sunlight. Sometimes it had to be emptied and scrubbed clean but most of the time it was left there. The water reservoir was a presence as comforting as any other was for Saigon's residents, just like food, rice, and water, the essential necessities for every household during wartime. Even now, though living in Australia or elsewhere around the world, the habit of storing extra food in the house was still hard to eradicate for most Vietnamese. It was rooted deep inside their minds, the fear of having no food or water to live on. The horrifying realisation from past experience that there was no one to turn to for help but themselves was somehow permanent in many generations of the bitter, war-born population, especially Trinh's parents and like-minded people. The pantry had always to have enough food to last at least a month or so in their house, and the habit continued.

It was not only for the fish that the kids used to hop on the side of the reservoir, tiptoeing along the edge to reach up for moss; they also used to have a peek at Mrs. Phan's clock on the other side of the wall for the time to go to school. Their grandfather clock needed winding up. It seemed no one had enough time to do that, and it was easier to peek through the wall. The beautiful green moss was smooth as velvet, and always there as a green plant for Trinh to look at, something that grew on and on without help, lush and fresh, permanently in the tropical weather.

Noise was easily overheard between the neighbours through that open space, including shouting or yelling in heated arguments between the members of the household. Privacy was a privilege in those times. It seemed everyone accepted that space and everything else was shared without question. Common bedrooms were normal with five or six children in one big dormitory room. Crowds were not a concern at all; people were happy to share and lived in harmony despite hardship and encumbrances. Children stayed together in big or small spaces and were content with crude toys or none at all to play with or just enjoyed running around in the open air. They had the company of other children, and that was enough. Interactions between one human being and the next were essential and easily accepted; there was no isolation. Back then, depression was a foreign word. People were trained to readily put up with adversity as much as to tolerate suffering without leaving mental scars. In doing that, they tended to bury or forget the ugly incidents in order to be able to live on. But that is not to say they were immune to grief and sorrow. Their tolerance was just growing along with their misery and difficulty; they laughed bitterly and shrugged their shoulders like bearing another unavoidable burden. They took it all in, and sometimes, they began to believe they received those burdens as their destiny, a testing curse that would soon pass. Quietly and patiently, they were all waiting for it to pass. The influence of Buddha's teaching was prominent in their belief.

However, their acceptance of hardship sometimes turned against them as it could very well diminish their will to fight, leaving them weakened and vulnerable to oppression.

Like most townhouses in Saigon, Luc's was narrow, about six metres in width, and elongated, with five rooms from front to back. There was a semisecond floor section at the back as a dormitory section for the children and a covered patio at the rear as a garage for bikes. The front room was used as a garage at night for Father's car when it was still in his possession, a La Dalat manufactured from the first automobile company in Vietnam in the early 1970s, was his latest one. During the day, it was arranged as a lounge or living room. Then the dining room followed, and next to it was their parents' room. Next was the large spacious kitchen with the high ceiling and the open sky area where Luc immersed himself in the bathtub and in his dreams.

In the kitchen, there was a divan, a prominent piece of furniture that was very much a symbol of a South Vietnamese home. The rectangular hardwood divan was as big as a king-sized bed and was usually made of teak or lesser wood, depending on the wealth of its owner. It was as characteristic a feature of Vietnam as an ao dai. Everything was done on that rectangular piece of furniture, a treasured traditional image for every Vietnamese. Trinh remembered it well. It was converted into a bed at night simply by placing the mosquito net over it. She used to sleep at her mother's feet on that divan when her father was away on his official trips. Its surface was shiny and polished with regular use. Like other Vietnamese families, theirs used the divan as their centre of activity; many would gather around, sitting on its rectangular hardwood surface and talk, eat, prepare meals, debate political issues, confer over family matters, and just about do anything. It was where they sat waiting for the announcement of the surrender from President General Duong Van Minh on that historical day. When that piece of furniture was sold for food and necessities, they all cried as if someone had died. It was as dear to them as a close relative.

There was another common sleeping quarter further back in the house before it ended with a covered patio for parking bikes at the rear. The house was considered large enough and functional for a family of seven children in Saigon at that time.

It was grouped together in a row of townhouses, about a dozen in number, stretched lengthwise across the boulevard and the avenue in District 1, leaving every house on the neighbourhood two entrances, the front and back. The neighbourhood was once a prestigious area, quiet and aristocratic, as the District 1 residential area of Saigon was normally for the affluent, well-to-do class. The boulevard was lined with tall, handsome *Dipterocarpus zeylanicus* trees on both sides. Their straight trunks reached to the sky, with two-winged fruits sometimes scattering down on the breeze, poetic and enchanting in the summer evenings. Their heavy round base acted as a centre of gravity, and sometimes they would spin in the air with the turbulence of the wind, their double wings upright. Trinh used to chase after the two-winged fruit, letting it land upright in her small open palms and laughing with joy with each successful catch. When the wind was strong and turbulent, Hoan, Kim, Trinh, and Luc would run excitedly with the change of season, racing with each other to gather the large dry leaves falling from the sky. They gathered the prominent veiny leaves in separate piles to compare whose was the largest. Later, the piles were combined together with twigs and branches and lit with matches in a pretend campfire. The gang of four would sit around in a circle under the warm glow of fire and wispy smoke and listen to the happy crackling noise of wood catching fire. Sometimes Dien would join in if he were on leave. Then, putting on important airs to debate nonsense or laughing merrily for no reason other than mischievously playing with fire unnoticed by adults, they were happy for a little while at least.

In some parts of the street, further away from their house, the tops of the trees entwined with each other, blocking out most of the blazing sun in the fiery hot afternoon. The boulevard became the much-loved street of most high school boys and girls in Saigon.

The row of townhouses remained dearest in Trinh's memory. Some were twice the size of the others in width, but most were very much the same in their outer design. Most had trellis iron gates or full metal gates of different colours and patterns. Those gates seemed out of bounds to the general public, carrying a distinguished and forbidden air of refined dignity, separating the occupants from the harshness of common life. Like the forbidden gates of the Chinese, they were hardly open, and to sneak a glimpse into the life of those behind was almost a privilege.

That was before the invasion. Now the whole neighbourhood had to blend in with the rest of the South, reduced to one common class, which was the most honourable class in the government's slogan: "Everyone is equal in status."

The Pigs, the Cats, and the Kittens

1977

Most people in the neighbourhood around Trinh's house had to change their lifestyle to get involved with real labour. She had seen the ex-minister of finance from the old regime sweeping up his front yard and picking up rubbish on the streets. The other minister of internal affairs was seen sitting on the pavement talking to the street bike repairer animatedly, showing everyone that "all are equal!"

"Labour is an honourable duty!" That was another slogan of the Vietnamese Communist Party, and Trinh had to remember. Nothing was considered real work without involving toil with hands and feet in mud or soil.

"You must follow the soldiers' example of using all resources for food and necessities!" They were told. Then somehow, peculiar as it might seem, a pigsty or a chicken pen in every house, as proof of adhering to the slogans, was the talk of the entire city. Without available land, Saigon citizens could not grow a garden, and so they turned to raising pigs or chickens inside their cosmopolitan houses. Like the rest, Trinh's mother bought three little mountain piglets, one black and two white, to try and raise. There was a smart black one called Miss Piggy. She became their leader in no time. Their pigsty was at the rear and the kitchen was forbidden to them, but Miss Piggy seemed to know when there was nobody at home. She would lead the whole gang out of their pen and venture out to forage excitedly in the garbage bin. Trinh could not blame them. The family had little to eat, and so did the pigs. Kim usually gave them the prawn or fish heads cooked with remaining food scraps and burnt rice from their cooking disasters. Like the humans, they were hungry all the time.

"No, no, no! Go back down there, piggy pigs!" Trinh would shout to the swine clan, stamping her feet and pointing toward the back. She was about to go to school and was already late as usual!

"Oink, oink, oink." The gang leader looked back at her, curled up her snout, and quickly gave one last shove over the garbage bin to steal a mouthful of food scraps. The others saw an opportunity to attack the pile of rubbish like their leader, and so in they all went. They snorted and grunted with enthusiasm, ignoring Trinh completely and squealing with delight in their sumptuous feast, something different from their meagre daily meal allowance.

Trinh knew that it was futile to scold since they tended to ignore her most of the time, so she had to pull and push Miss Piggy along to the back. "Naughty girl, you'll make me late for school! Naughty! Naughty!" Miss Piggy reluctantly clicked her hoofs away from the mess and followed Trinh's steps. The girl put the gate back on carefully before running out of the back door to go to school.

Miss Piggy would pay attention only to Mac. Mac would shout in his authoritative voice when he got home, once he sighted their appearance in the kitchen, "Get out of here, and go back down there!"

Miss Piggy was as smart as a dog. She would attempt another raid before turning round guiltily, her tiny tail curled up at her round rump, clicking noisily away on her four trotters. The rest of the gang followed suit, clattering their way over the ceramic tiles back to their sty in a hurry.

That period of most Saigon residents living with pigs lasted a year, and it proved pointless with so much cost involved and damage to houses that the Communist Party had to abandon the scheme. It was just one more of the tiresome, unrealistic schemes the Party imposed on all Southerners to engage their minds and forget about everything else.

There were other tiresome schemes like growing vegetables right in the parkland, in the middle of the city, by following another slogan on the billboard: "the People of Communist Vietnam need to learn to utilise all the natural resources." Saigon citizens were amused by various vegetable patches in the midst of their city where flower gardens used to be. Trinh almost ran into a family of chooks in her hurry. Unlike the first day going back to school, she was not surprised to see almost all the farm animals, hens clucking frantically, roosters crowing proudly, ducks waddling about pleasurably, and pigs snorting noisily on the footpaths or running wild in school yards or everywhere in the city.

The little townhouse somehow had enough space to accommodate, at one time, ten people, three cats, nine kittens, and three mountain pigs. The animals were in harmonious existence within their boundaries and endurance, just like the humans. The three cats were scavengers by nature, so no one had to worry about feeding them as much as the pigs. They were called "Grandma," "Mother," and "Daughter," three generations of the same linear cat family that had lived alongside them for as long as Trinh remembered.

Luc used to rush home from school looking for them to give them left over titbits from his snack and lunch. The entourage of cats and kittens would normally walk out of their hiding place beneath the stairs one by one in a long single line. All twelve of them, the three adult cats leading the way, the kittens followed with their tails high, their feline large pupil eyes alert and their pacing gait gentle, walking with their legs moving in perfect unison like a soldier marching, slowly coming toward Luc for the treat of the day. That colourful picture always brought pleasure to everyone's eyes until the day they had to give up all the kittens for adoption.

Grandma Cat was very old. She often lay in a corner, her eyes closed, resting most of the time. Then one day she did not get up when Luc called them out for their dinner with his usual tune of "meow, meow, meow, come on, meow, meow, time to eat." She died quietly in her little corner, leaving Mother Cat and Daughter Cat as the remaining pets of the family. Luc and Trinh buried her in a shallow grave in their small backyard, but it was not long that the dogs smelled her body and dug it up, leaving the hole emptied.

Daughter Cat was a lazy one. She had that kind of beautiful perfect fur in three colours—white, black, and gold. Luc used to stroke her fur and murmur, "What had you been up to when I was at school? Did you miss me at all?" Purring and meowing seductively while waiting for a titbit from Luc, Daughter Cat would just lay there enjoying his attention. Perhaps she thought she was a lady, superior to the rest of her feline clan, refusing to neither hunt for food nor chase after the mice even when they circled around her tentatively at night.

Mother Cat, on the other hand, was an extraordinary one. She was a black and white. She hunted and sometimes stayed very mellow near the saucepans, her eyes closed and her tails waving up and down intermittently, waiting for her chance to steal when no one was looking. On many occasions at night, Trinh witnessed Mother Cat sitting up against the saucepan, her eyes gleaming in the dark full of mischief, the pupils pointing penetratingly, and her long whiskers extending sideways from her cute little black nose. She used her right front paw to dip into the remaining family dinner, bringing it to her mouth skilfully like a human.

Then one day, she brought home a big chunk of steak she had obviously stolen from some unsuspecting family! Kim and Trinh were home preparing dinner for the whole family as usual. Without a moment's hesitation, the girls jumped up and chased after Mother Cat, reclaiming the steak for the humans. The family had meat that evening for a change, thanks to Mother Cat's special skill. Sadly, they could not keep her and had to give her up to a friend who was in need of a cat that hunted. For obvious reasons, Daughter Cat was not an option, and so Mother Cat was given to the family twenty kilometres away.

Luc cried when bidding his farewell to Mother Cat. He whispered to her, "It's all right now, darling. You're going to be well looked after. They have food to feed you, unlike us. We're too poor now to keep you, but we will love you always. Go and live with them. We won't forget you."

The children stood there on the pavement looking after the motorised scooter until it had completely disappeared from their sight before turning inside. Mother Cat wiggled vigorously in the bamboo basket, which was tied neatly at the top, and hung on a hook between the rider's seat and the scooter's control. Her hostile growling and hissing was sad to hear. She was probably disappointed at her owners' betrayal.

It was a month later that Trinh heard a loud thud in the open-air kitchen in the middle of the night.

Lying there in a puddle of blood, both bright and purplish red of fresh and old blood, Mother Cat had returned home. Perhaps she had encountered human scavengers travelling that long distance home and had suffered the injury from the attack but managed to escape and come back to the family. They had nothing to help her with except an ancient-looking bottle of mercurochrome, which had expired years ago and which only had a tiny bit left. She lay there slowly recuperating with this expired antiseptic solution. Her stomach had been split open with a long gash, exposing her intestines, and she had lost a lot of blood. She was alive and well after a week. It was a miracle. In times of crisis, it seems that animals or humans always manage to survive if they still have the will to live.

Mother Cat stayed back with the family, and she eventually had a litter of kittens. Trinh put the kittens in a small cardboard box lined with straws donated by the fruit vendors following her trips to the market. She hid them under the stairs as usual. The tiny wet kittens with their infant eyes still shut looked helpless and fragile. Many nights after that, Trinh often heard the frantic meow calls of the neighbourhood cats. The calls were eerie and haunting in the dark like meandering lost souls trying to find their way back to their bodies. Lying in her bed, Trinh shuddered at the thoughts.

Then one night, the noise was even more disturbing. The meows were more frantic, and there was the sound of fighting in the kitchen. Trinh awoke to see the silhouettes of a few small animals lying on the floor. At first, she thought they were mice as Mother Cat was sitting next to the carcasses, licking her paws as if she was grooming herself without any concern. Then, coming closer, she realised that they were her kittens. Some were in halves, and some had had their bellies torn open, exposing the ribcage cavity without any entrails. Their infant eyes were still shut tight. Trinh stood there in awe, trying to comprehend what might have happened to her kittens. She managed to cry in the end, figuring out that they were all dead after being savaged and eaten. Some cats might have attacked them in the dark of the night, scavenging for food to maintain their survival like everyone else in this trying period.

Secondhand Trading and Uncle Tam, a South Vietnamese Disabled Veteran

IN LINE WITH changes in the country, many prestigious neighbourhoods gradually underwent cosmetic alteration. Trinh could not remember when it had begun, but the clean cemented front yard of her townhouse strip was leased almost all at once to peddlers for daylight trading, the popular market of Saigon at that time. Their front street became a market overnight. Trinh's house was no exception, and the rental income helped bring food to the table for them. It was a relief for Mother, the extras that added to her income from selling trips. It was noisy, with customers bargaining and quarrelling, a real contrast to the elegant facade of just a few years before.

Not many factories were allowed to operate after the Fall. Everything was scarce after three years of minimal production due to the shortage of raw materials. Most were from surplus storage, but the sources were running dry or were out of date already. Saigon had nothing new to offer consumers with every industry at a standstill, and therefore, nothing was produced.

Everything was consequently recycled or repaired and then sold up in Saigon. Everyone had to sell some of their belongings to be able to buy something they needed in return. Their buyers were the new class of citizens, the Communist capitalists, who now had boxes of money after the currency change. All the large furniture was gone, leaving them mostly with smaller items, and so the secondhand trade flourished. Everyone was rummaging through piles of old knickknacks at home to sell them on the streets. Everyone was buying other necessities through secondhand stalls. Each trader had a large tattered tarpaulin or old cloth to spread on the ground to display his or her goods. They were buying and selling everything, from the smallest items such as old buttons, threads, needles, watches, clocks, wrenches, shovels, and nails to world maps, compasses, outdated medicines, and old comic books. It was an endless list of things.

With time, the skin rash disappeared mysteriously as it had come. The people in the South all sighed with relief. The parasitic arthropod Sarcoptes scabiei, or itch mites, somehow died, leaving darkened scars on the Southerners' skin as a reminder of that horror.

Sitting in the warm circular tin basin and sensing his itchiness slowly ebbing away, Luc felt relieved. There was some hope after all. His skin was raw with the scratches covering his whole body. Some parts were inflamed and infected. Malnourishment and wretched living conditions did not help the young boy combat the scabies infestation nor did the lack of medication. It was thanks to pointy mint leaves and alum, the wonderful concoction. Or maybe his immune system just fully recovered. He never knew.

The clanking of metal reverberated in his ears from the front of the house, telling Luc that it was getting late. He looked up and saw the sky darkening above. *Uncle Tam must be clearing away his secondhand goods*, Luc thought. He was a trader of spare parts—everything from automobiles, motorbikes, and bicycles to dish washers and rotor blades for catamarans. He rented a corner inside Luc's living room as storage and the front cement yard to display his goods. Luc called Uncle Tam "Uncle" the way all Vietnamese people call the elderly by terms of endearment: "Uncle," "Aunty," "Sister," or "Brother," out of respect, regardless of their real relationship.

Uncle Tam was a disabled veteran from the previous regime in the South. A short stump protruding from his right shoulder was what was left of his arm. A long, livid scar crossed his right cheek from the eye to the lips and made him look harsh and ferocious. However, he was the kindest man Luc had ever known, even though he used crude language sometimes to mask his gentleness. His skeletal body would once have been muscular in the old days as the shapes and the curves were still there but no longer the bulk. Luc and Trinh used to sit chatting with him in their free time; the two young kids enjoyed listening to the old soldier talking about everything from the past to present.

He was bold and blunt, indifferent to tales the informers were telling about him. As he said, "I am maimed, ugly, and have no-one, so if them spies want to put me into their gaol hole to rot like most of my mates, then let them. I won't need to take care of my own well-being anymore. So there!"

Trinh would giggle at his remarks and tease him a bit. "But Uncle Tam, gaol is no fun, and you won't have kids like us to chat with you. Besides, if someone were looking at you from the left side, then they would see a handsome face and a full figure, not ugly at all! Very handsome, indeed!"

Luc added, "Yeah, Uncle Tam. You had better turn your left side toward people all the time and not let them see your right one. Then the girls will notice you right away. Right, Trinh?"

Trinh agreed readily. "Yeah, do that, Uncle Tam, give them your left side to look at and then they'll swarm all over you and you'll have to swat them away like flies in no time!"

Tam smiled sheepishly like a young boy and slipped into the common accent. "Kiddies! I don't want girls looking at me. So don't you all get excited about it," he scolded, pretending to be annoyed. "Don't be daft!"

Trinh ignored him and continued. "But I saw Aunty Truyen glancing at you all the time when she was preparing coffee for customers, and you smiled at her real cute when she gave you a cup of coffee the other day. So don't go denying all that. We saw it. Didn't we, Luc?"

She winked at Luc conspiratorially. Luc laughed merrily, seeing the chance to have a bit of fun with the veteran. He agreed at once. "Yeah yeah, you two are eyeing each other all the time! I saw it too."

Unprepared for the kids' attacks, the South Vietnamese veteran's face went red. "Nah, nonsense! Go away, kids. You're too young to notice anything like that! Silly monkeys!"

He shooed them away, embarrassed at their remarks. Nevertheless, he smiled inwardly after the kids went inside. They were good kids. He liked them. They were very polite and smart but also very cheeky. He had to be extra careful when Truyen was around, especially with little Trinh, keen observer as she was. He hoped that his affection for Truyen, the young cafe vendor, had not been as obvious as the kids observed. Tam often thought that he was not good enough for her. Disabled and poor as he was, he felt inadequate and inferior. Who would think of having a relationship with him?

Tam was in his early forties. Being a disabled veteran in the pre-1975 period had been hard when he was only thirty-five, but now it seemed hopelessly impossible. After the fall of Saigon, he had no income to support himself as the Vietnamese Communist Party denied any responsibility to ex-servicemen and ex-public servants from the previous regime, including veterans or retirees. He was left to fend for himself like the rest and find ways to earn a living with absolutely no help and no recognition from the new government. For hundreds of thousands of disabled veterans, it was devastating. Many struggled to survive and were often dependent on their families and friends. Tam's darkest days were during the first few years after the war ended when all the resources dried up. He was ashamed of being a beggar on the streets of Saigon, a town in which he had been a hero not so long ago. His days were counted by the hours, and basic meals were unaffordable luxuries. There were times he had to eat from garbage bins in the markets or restaurants and takeaway shops, sharing his meals with the swines. He never knew how he would survive the next day. Each day he woke, his first thought was where to find food. Everything else was irrelevant.

A boom in secondhand trading was a lifesaver to many. With help from Thanh, his sister, Tam managed to make ends meet, and life became much easier for the disabled veteran. He still had to find sustenance one day at a time, but eating from trash and strangers' leftover meals was now in the past.

He used to tell the kids how he was injured in battle. It was during the Tet Offensive of 1968. He lost his arm in the bloody battle of Khe Sanh, receiving a medal for bravery upon his discharge.

"I was a major in the ARVN Rangers [Biet Dong Quan]. Do you know that, kids?" He winked at them then continued. "It was horrific! The fighting was ferocious and the killing appalling. It was the worst experience of my life as a soldier." He paused and then asked, "How old were you then, kids?"

Trinh replied, "I was six, but I remember standing in front of my gate looking out. There was black smoke and fires on the horizon at that end." Trinh pointed in the direction of District 3 where the dense population of blue-collar workers lived.

"There were people running wildly on the streets, some covered in blood. They cried and screamed. Children and mothers were clinging to each other in terror. I was scared, but I still wished I could go out and play like on a normal Tet day, oblivious of the gunfire. At first, I thought it was firecrackers on New Year's Eve, but it was real gunfire and my parents were so upset. Then we were ordered to go to bed without any usual ceremony of a Tet day. I yearned for New Year to be able to wear new clothes, to receive lucky money, or *li xi*, and eat festive food like *banh tet*, or rice cakes, and *thit kho*, or slow cooked pork in coconut juice and fish sauce. And I cried so hard because I knew that was impossible. It hurt so much, but no one noticed and no one paid any attention. And I cried in bed that night.

"Then I was so disappointed when it was just gunfire, bombing, and people running on the streets the next day. There were no firecrackers, no smiling, no wishing of good luck and best of health or prosperity, and no laughter. Just crying and screaming. I only thought of my disappointment, and I didn't care if the children were scared to death out there, away from their homes. It was very selfish of me, wasn't it?" Trinh lamented.

"No, of course not!" Tam rejected the idea. "That's a natural thing to wish for, Trinh. You were just a little girl. You were not selfish. You just wanted to have peace. Didn't we all want to have peace? Perhaps that was wrong from the very start of this war. They always wanted to fight, and we only wanted peace! They were so bloodthirsty, and we were peace-loving people! You see, they won because they meant to advance and fought to achieve their goal, however mean and barbaric. And they attacked, and kept on attacking! We didn't even retaliate. We were only trying to defend. Damn it!"

Tam paused. He looked at them apologetically following his burst of emotion and then resumed in a gentler tone. "Tet was supposed to be a cease-fire period, but the Viet Cong didn't care. They violated the Paris Accord Agreement as they always did. We were taken by surprise, and we lost many important cities to them. More than a hundred cities and many provincial capital cities were attacked, and we lost them initially for a week or two, longer in some parts. Hue, in the central region, and Khe Sanh, near Saigon, were lost to the VC for more than two months. Many districts in Saigon were taken too. The most gruesome, brutal battles actually happened during that major offensive, with bloody fighting, shocking treatment, and barbaric conduct from the Viet Cong, especially the brutal Massacre at Hue. Hue was in their hands for two months, and the killing was horrendous!

"Ah, but the world was not shown that. They only saw the shocks they received from the South on television. It was real-life television! The world thrives on real-life television, and Vietnam war provided that! See, the Communists did not allow journalists to observe their battles, only when they wanted to tell their side of the story. The South with its half-baked democracy always gave out the wrong messages to the outside world. That was very unfortunate for the South, and consequently, we lost. Now, Vietnam's civil war history is based on their version, the Vietnamese Communists' version! We are being buried alive, kids! Just you wait. And believe me, they are going to erase the past sooner than everyone is aware, a criminal act that we have no control over! They are going to rewrite history for their own liking. It's a shame!"

Tam looked down at his stump then continued with a subdued tone. "I think the world began to feel the destruction of war and its ghastly horror in Vietnam from those images on television in the Tet Offensive. They were broadcast around the globe, the atrocious fighting with casualties among both the armed forces and the civilians. It made everyone cringe."

Tam paused again, a faraway look on his face. He was immersed in his tale, forgetting that his audience was only fifteen and thirteen years old. "Changing tactics, the Viet Cong, under the command of their General Vo Nguyen Giap, believed a full offensive on scattered populated towns and places in the South would bring a total uprising and ultimate victory. Hundreds of towns were attacked in the early hours of January 31, 1968, the first day of the Lunar New Year, the Year of the Monkey, those bastards. The most horrific battles of the war occurred and left many unforgettable images with all of us, especially the world out there. The Viet Cong were successful at first because of the surprise factor, but then they lost quickly afterwards. They thought they could provoke a general uprising from the combined force of the people from the South. But of course, nothing happened, apart from destruction, terror, and death, as in all wars."

That was how Tam began the story normally, and the kids always listened in awe, even though they could not fully comprehend the politics in some parts of the story.

He continued. "However, perhaps we lost the war because of winning the Tet Offensive! I know it sounds contradictory, but it might be true. The South Vietnamese government's political manoeuvres were primitive, unsophisticated, and poorly presented. Its propaganda was not as effective as the VC's. It did not understand how the world reacted to the horrendous images of war in the country and the outburst from angry senior military personnel. The shooting of a VC in execution style in front of a camera by General Nguyen Ngoc Loan fuelled the antiwar activists in condemning the South and the war, even though I understood why he felt compelled to act. He was born in Hue, the city worst affected by the offensive. The killings were brutal. His family was there. The VC killed thousands of civilians, armed force personnel, religious leaders, and government officials by forcing them to dig their own graves then shooting them or even beheading the men in front of their family members."

Tam sighed softly. "Ah, but those images were never documented! That was how smart the VC were. They did not let the world know of these atrocities on their side, only their suffering. Very cunning, those bastards. And we, we were naive, or plainly gullible, and had bad leadership. I think we lost because of that," he concluded sadly.

Sighing loudly this time, he spoke again. "It's what I call 'rudderless.' South Vietnam was like a ship without a rudder. The whole country drifted aimlessly in the political war. We did not have strong guidance from our leaders. Most of them were rotten to the core. All but a few were corrupt. It was criminal! We lost because of no proper leadership, not because we did not know how to fight! Damn it!"

Then, realising that he was talking with the teenagers, Tam apologised softly. "Sorry, kids. I didn't mean to swear. Now go along and buy something nice to eat." He gave each a ten *xu* coin and winked at them in an attempt to lift the tone and change the subject.

Reeducation Camps and Tuan, the Lieutenant

IT WAS LUCKY for Tam that his sister had some jewellery left. She sold it to give him extra cash to start his business in secondhand wares. He was to manage this for her, and they were helping each other get food and everything else with the income. Her husband was in what the communists called a "reeducation camp," one of the many thousand camps scattered around the country.

"Reeducation camp, my foot!" Tam spat out disgustedly. "It's a jail that he's in. They do not even have the decency to say it, deceiving bastards!"

Tuan was an army lieutenant of the previous regime, and like most of the prisoners in his country's postwar period, he did not have the slightest idea how long he was going to be in for.

He had said good-bye to his young wife in the morning lightheartedly, reporting to his allocated centre and feigning the belief of going to a job interview. The elation of knowing that he was going to be recruited back into the civil service was high. "Didn't they say so?" Tuan muttered to himself.

A few weeks of disturbing uneasiness had passed after the Fall, and everyone was dispirited and anxious about what was going to happen. Then there were announcements from the new Provisional Revolutionary Government (PRG) of South Vietnam about self-reporting for classification.

"All American ex-employees, personnel of the previous Thieu's puppet regime, and ex-service men of the previous Armed Forces of the Republic of South Vietnam are to report to their allocated centres for re-registration. The PRG of South Vietnam is encouraging voluntary registration and is willing to recruit everyone for his service in reconstructing Vietnam back to its glorious state under the true leadership of the Vietnamese Communist Party. However, if you refuse to come forward, then you will be faced with severe punishment."

"Hah, so much so for voluntary registration! They're so clever with words. Don't you dare not to!" Many had cried out in their discussion of "going" or "not going."

The officials also said, "You are to bring enough food, money, and personal belongings for ten days when reporting for high-ranking armed forces officers, lieutenants, and up or similar."

There were others who were less "important" and who were to be in for three days or so, it was announced.

"I'll be back soon, darling. Leave the boxes of old clothes there for me. Don't bother to tax yourself with them. I'll put them away when I come back home."

They embraced in silence. She tried to put on a brave face for her husband, but inside, Thanh was tormented with weariness. Her gut knotted into a tight ball of apprehension. Somehow Thanh was so afraid. She was petrified of the future and could sense its horror. Tuan was a Southerner, kind and gullible. The Viet Cong were never to be trusted; she had known that from her late father. He often told her so from his experience escaping to the South in the exodus of 1954 after the Division of Vietnam by the French at the 17th parallel. She shared his terror from many unbelievable stories he had witnessed. Thanh wanted to cry, wailing out loud to let this feeling of foreboding spill out of her chest; but she restrained herself. Tuan had enough to worry about at the moment. He seemed so relaxed.

Thanh addressed her husband unflinchingly, "You take care, darling. I'll be okay. It's only ten days. I'm going to count, and it's going to end before I even remember it."

Tuan gently stroked his wife's long straight hair and landed a gentle kiss on her head. "Yes, sweetheart. It won't be long at all. Don't you worry, Thanh. And I'll be back before you know it, baby." Then he held her tighter and said quietly, "Don't cry, darling."

The moment Thanh heard her husband say "Don't cry, darling," tears started streaming down her face uncontrollably, regardless of the effort she made to hold them back. She buried her face in Tuan's shoulder, holding him against her body with all her strength, sniffing in his maleness and repeatedly soaking in his scent and sobbing intermittently in her anguish. Trying desperately to stifle her crying lest it turned into a wail of despair, she was already missing him. How was she able to go on living without him after a so short period of rejoicing in togetherness?

Tuan shuddered involuntarily; he wished he could relieve his wife of her distress by doing something other than just offering vague reassurance. "Please don't cry, Thanh. I'll be back soon. The war's over, the country's at peace, and we're all safe now."

Thanh blubbered apologetically between hiccups, "I'm so sorry, darling. I'm sorry. I didn't mean to be so…"

She could not utter another word and left the sentence unfinished. Then, breathing deeply to regain her composure Thanh stepped away from her husband. She looked up at his beloved rugged, weather-beaten face. She saw his strong, determined square jaw tighten and his intelligent eyes overflow with tenderness for her. She took it all in and stood still, trying to memorise the whole picture, arms hanging lamely at her sides, afraid of moving a muscle lest she start bawling once more.

Tuan turned abruptly, hitched his satchel containing his belongings for ten days onto his shoulder, and walked away quickly out of the door. He did not look back, afraid of being disheartened at the tear-streaked face of his dear young wife and succumbing to the weakness of not reporting. But he had to go. Tuan had pondered the option of not reporting many times, but he finally decided to go forward and start life all over again as a good citizen in a united Vietnam, as everyone else had hoped to do.

Thanh did not know that was the last time she would ever look into her husband's eyes or breathe in his scent.

The Reeducation Camp
June 1975

Tuan was a mechanical engineer before being drafted into the army and was trained in the Reserved Officer Training Academy School of Thu Duc before going to war with the rank of first lieutenant. He had only recently been promoted to second lieutenant and then to lieutenant after the bloody battles of An Loc in 1972, just a few months after he graduated from his army school. Now, after the war ended, he was restless and worried. A young and heroic lieutenant in the war would not be in a pleasant position on the defeated side at all; Tuan knew that. He was in for a hard ride, and he was in some danger from the attention of the Communists. Many times at night, he wanted to tell Thanh that he had to leave her and follow some of his mates into the jungle to form a military resistance against the invading Northerners. The thought of doing something to salvage the respectability of the South Vietnamese Army was burning inside his chest, but in the end, he sadly abandoned the noble urge. He was home after the war now. His wife had him in her arms at last; he could not bring himself to tell her that he had to go again so soon. He would try to be with her for a little while at least, Tuan resigned.

It was only four months after their marriage in early 1972 that he had gone away to battle and had only managed a few weeks here and there together since then. Three years had gone by, and they had hardly had any time jointly as husband and wife. She loved him dearly, and he was lucky to have her in his life. They felt complete being with each other. Happiness had been fragile in the past. Every time he said good-bye to her to go to combat, it was as if they were saying farewell for good. The nightmare that his young wife might have to endure seeing him brought home on a stretcher was torture enough to keep Thanh worried sick. Every time she heard of the death count in battles, Thanh just had to pray. She chanted in her head that she would go through the day as normally as she could and was only relieved when she heard his voice again on the phone.

The life of a soldier's wife in wartime was tragic! At last, no more fighting and no more combats! They needed time for each other. Thanh was hopeful.

However, peace and happiness was short-lived, as always! They only had a few weeks together. Then the new government announced mandatory self-reporting, and the informers around his neighbourhood would not let him stay in peace for sure. They would very gladly point their fingers and drag him out in the open if he did not come out himself. He was famous for his courage in battles, and they all knew about his distinguished service in the South Vietnamese army. He had to go to the reporting centre to avoid all the complications at home.

It was not only that; the new government had promised an understanding and a recruiting scheme to place men back into civil service. He hoped he could contribute his skills to rebuilding the country if they would allow him. After all, the war was over. Vietnam had had this fight for so long. It would be best if peace was actually here. Tuan was trying to believe in the promises; he had to reassure himself repeatedly for his wife's sake. He had to put on a cheerful air for her.

The moment Tuan stepped onto the reeducation campground, he knew that he was in for good. His belief of being treated fairly shattered into pieces. *That was very clever of them*, Tuan thought.

The cruelty of the North Vietnamese Communists was in naming their concentration camps around the country "reeducation camp." Here they would keep millions of former officers in the armed forces like him, religious leaders, and employees of the Americans or of the Vietnamese republic government detained without trials. They were not for criminals because they were not called "gaols," but the primary purpose of the "reeducation camp" was to retrain the minds of detainees into thinking along communist lines and to learn about the Communist Party and their leader, Ho Chi Minh. The term "reeducation" in English is not strong enough to translate *trại học tập cải tạo* in Vietnamese, the mentioning of the latter terms raised hell in the mind of all Southerners. It was nothing relating to education, but literally an attempt at redesigning the mind, or re-programming the brain, clearing away all the "soft-wares", and making over "sinful" or "incomplete" individuals. The hidden horrors in those re-education camps have not yet been exposed to the outside world, even though the stories of many survivors who fled to other countries were shocking and their painful memories might never heal.

In reality, after a few days, Tuan realised that the new government had invented that system to give free reign to their Communist members to punish the South Vietnamese armed forces personnel with slow death, humiliation, and torture to satisfy their savagery and revenge.

"Look at their camp officers!" Tuan was horrified to see that the Party allowed members who were barely high school graduates the roles of camp officers as rewards for their loyal support after the victory. They could not even spell "lieutenant" when Tuan told them his rank.

After reporting to headquarters with name and rank, the officers were categorised and transported to various camps by army buses in the dark of the night for secrecy. The level of security and treatment toward the inmates were already decided by their rank and divisions. Few generals and many majors and captains had realised belatedly that they were in for a nasty surprise, though some had known that they might not see their family again. Looks of alarm and apprehension were exchanged silently. Some were quite calm and indifferent but still sad and sorrowful. Some were in panic and fear. The chill was there in the air even though the temperature was over thirty degree Celsius in the crowded bus.

Then on the first day at the camp, everyone was gathered into small groups of ten or twenty, and they started by telling the officers to write down detailed confessions of their supposed crimes. Each was given a blank notebook and a pencil.

"You are here to confess to the Party your evil and treacherous crimes in the past. Spare no details, and using your own words, you must not try to deceive us. Any attempt of omitting your heinous acts in the war will be punished, as they will be revealed eventually. Take heed and spill it all out, you traitors and enemies of the Vietnamese Communist Party."

Tuan was utterly confused about what crime he had committed, as he believed in his country, the South. He thought his service toward the country was to be drafted into the armed forces and to fight as a soldier protecting the borders and his countrymen. He believed it was his duty as a citizen. He did not betray the homeland he grew up in; he was not a defiler like many of the double crossers who received nourishment and flourished in the Southern part of the country and served the other party unashamedly. They were what he thought fit to be called traitors, and Tuan had done nothing wrong in that context to be named one.

Bluntly, Tuan refused to write anything other than "I was a South Vietnamese soldier. I am living in the South of Vietnam, which is my homeland, and I belonged to the South Vietnam government. I did what a citizen of a country had to do for his motherland in a time of crisis. I did nothing wrong, and I was not a traitor."

Of course, he was singled out, and his life had been hell since then.

He was summoned to their office the following morning and was made to face a primitive trial by three Northern military officers without any defence assistance on his side. His hands were tied behind his back by the guards. The other prisoners were rounded up outside to witness his sentencing. They were squatting on the dirt under the heat of the rising sun. The armed guards were scattered in pairs around the assembly. There was a company of eighty soldiers at least for the two hundred officers.

The background of the interrogating room was decorated with two flags, the two red-blue halves with the yellow star of the Revolutionary Army and the main red one with the yellow star of the Communist Party. The face of Ho Chi Minh in a portrait twenty by thirty centimetres stared at Tuan. It hung high above the flags, an indication that the Communists do not consider their country's flag as a priority but that they worship their leader more than anything else. Beneath the framed portrait was a banner that said "Long live Uncle Ho, our greatest and esteemed leader!"

The officers were all sitting at the rectangular table, their faces grim and their backs to the wall. There were two guards with AK-47 machine guns standing at the entrance; they were young and undersized in their light green army uniforms and were probably eighteen or nineteen at most. The gun they carried had lost its menace as it seemed they were mere boys playing at dressing up and playing soldiers. The anticipation of witnessing the humiliation of a vanquished South Vietnam lieutenant by their higher-ranked comrades was evident in their eyes as youngsters normally were. They were curious as Tuan's reputation as a rebellious prisoner was already spreading through the camp. The young soldiers took turns on guard to watch his reaction as if it were a scene in a violent movie.

The room was bare, without even a chair for Tuan to sit on. He was forced to stand facing them and the red background. There were two other big slogans saying "All dedication and gratefulness toward Great Uncle Ho and the Communist Party" and "Long live the Vietnamese Communist Party" written on red banners with yellow words, spreading across the room. How he hated the face of Ho Chi Minh, their flags, and the madness of his doctrines. The past leader of the Vietnamese Communist Party was evidently influential even now after his death. He had injected into the mind of his followers, especially the illiterate peasants, the hatred of capitalists and Americans. The whole population, approximately forty million Vietnamese in the North at that time, believed blindly in his propaganda in pursuing the advance of communism in the South. He had kept pushing forward relentlessly to take over control of the South until his death in 1969. In his propaganda, he used the bitter history of foreign oppression of ancient Vietnam in the past thousand years, through one thousand years of intermittent Chinese invasion and the last hundred years of French occupation, to instil extreme abhorrence of foreign invasion in the mind of the Northerners and a fair proportion of Southerners. He then proclaimed to his followers that the presence of the Americans on Vietnam soil was oppression and accused the government of South Vietnam of being a puppet authority on which the Americans exerted their influence.

For over twenty years, under his constant fanaticism, leadership, and profound influence even after death, Vietnam had suffered a long and tedious civil war. The whole country had endured destruction, death, and misery instead of advancement and development after the French Revolution in 1954. That was also the harshest blow. The French retaliated against Vietnam for overthrowing its hundred-year rule by dividing the country in half. Instead of leaving Vietnam total freedom to choose which version of capitalism or communism to follow, the French had simply divided the country in half. How could the country be united without civil war? The inevitable outcome was the sorrow of Vietnam and its citizens through bloodshed and carnage.

His disgust in looking at the red background must have shown on his face. The officers were even more vicious. They did not leave him a chance to defend himself but sentenced him on the spot as "an enemy of the People of the Vietnamese Communist Party" for being a lieutenant who had killed thousands of their people in combat during his service in the South Vietnamese Army since 1972.

Of the three army officers, the highest ranking was a first lieutenant about Tuan's age.

The first lieutenant was the one who delivered the verdict: "There is proof that you are an enemy of the Vietnamese Communist Party and the People of Vietnam. You killed our comrades, our people. You betrayed the Communist Party, and you collaborated with the capitalists and the Americans. You are to change your attitude and mental outlook and learn to become a believer in Communism and a worshipper of Great Uncle Ho. Your sentence is final, and the duration of your stay and hard labour is determined by your records and confessions. You have to prove yourself free of all the crimes you've committed until the Communist Party and the People are satisfied with your sincere conversion. Then you will be absolved and granted graduation and freedom."

That was so strange and vague a sentence that Tuan heard it in shocked disbelief. They were playing God, not acting as government officials. He did not know whether it was a joke they were playing on his mind or a sickening way of asserting their primitive notions of human rights.

To admit to their accusations, Tuan had to deny his underlying nationalist principles, distort the real truth, refute his army brotherhood, and disown his ex-government in order to say what he did was wrong. The bottom line was not that he must satisfy them by the sincerity of his confession but that they must satisfy themselves when they were through with him, Tuan believed. How was he to satisfy their specifications without the simplest guideline? When he was given only a blank notebook to write in? His fellow army officers must have felt despaired of having to condemn their own patriotic acts. Or perhaps, it was the single-minded confession that the Communists wanted to hear from the Southerners, that they were all traitors? How was he to prove himself free of his crimes if all he had done was to protect himself and his countrymen in battle? They wanted to demonstrate that the South had had no real cause. They wanted to humiliate the South Vietnam Republic and the whole population of the South so that he and everyone else were traitors in the end.

Sadly, they were gaining ground as time went by since many camp prisoners had to tailor their confessions and betray other inmates for imaginary crimes in order to prove their sincerity, be absolved by the Party, and get out of this horror.

He spat on the floor and shouted, "Damn you and your Communist Party! Fuck your rotten Uncle Ho! You're all primal apes and illiterate stupid puppets who were very lucky to be alive today because I did not have a chance of finishing you off in battle!"

Tuan was silenced immediately as one of the guards brought the butt of his AK-47 down hard against his head. Blood spurted from a gash behind his left ear, and his body collapsed in a heap. The other guard ran forward, thumping his rifle repeatedly into Tuan's shoulders and back in a fit of rage. They all stood over him, cursing vehemently.

"How dare you! Bastard, you're going to hell and back!"

"Insolent traitor! You dare to insult Great Uncle Ho and the Party!"

"You won't live to see daylight, son of a bitch!"

"Stupid! Stupid! Stupid! You're going to eat your own shit. I swear to that!" Dan was shaking with anger.

Tuan realised belatedly that he had touched their nerves by his profanity involving "Great Uncle Ho." They only stopped swearing and pounding him when Tuan had ceased to move. Mercifully, he had passed out. The guards then took his legs and pulled him toward the metal box in the middle of the field; his hands were still tied behind his back. The trail of blood was bright red on the dirt, like the colour of the banner and their Communist flag. They shoved him in, locked the door, and left him there, showing no concern over his head wound.

Some of the officers in the crowd stood up when they saw Tuan's body dragged out of the room. A muffled cry of shock was heard in the silence. The other guards immediately moved forward and pointed their AK-47 at them, ready to fire. Those who stood up were pushed down violently; one was knocked in the stomach with a rifle butt for being a bit slow, surprised at seeing the first victim of violence on the first day at camp.

The officer doubled over in pain but managed to yell, "Damn you savages from the North! Go to hell!" In return for that outburst, he was shackled and tied under their flag pole for a whole day as punishment.

To the officer, his surprise at the level of brutality of his own countrymen did not lessen but increased in intensity as the hours passed. He could not comprehend the animosity and the malice the Northerners showed toward the Southerners. It seemed totally unnatural. He stopped counting the days of his stay as time passed, and his hope of returning home receded into the farthest corner of his mind. It was too distressing to think about it.

Today was another day. With his hands bound behind his back like many days before, Tuan stood in front of a young official, who looked barely more than twenty. The face was typical of a North Vietnamese. The body was malnourished and short through years of jungle fighting. The eyes were small and elongated. The skin was sallow and blotchy due to prolonged periods of hiding in dark places. The lips were thin, and the mouth protruded, with his front teeth exposed as if unable to close his lips. It was even worse as the teeth were yellowish and blackish with tar.

There were bits of meat on his right chipped incisors, Dan realised.

"Marvellous bits of meat!" Dan smiled gladly. For the last few months after the victory of the Communist Party over South Vietnam, he and his comrades were given meat to eat every week. That was the best treat he had ever received from the Party and Great Uncle Ho. In his entire life as a Communist follower, he had never been so contented. The fat goose of the South was the reward in the end. He was grateful and even had the role of commander of this camp. He could not believe his luck when they told him that. He had never dreamt of having this great power in his entire life.

Dan felt very important and proud of his authority, and the power of controlling so many cocky and pompous South Vietnamese officers and soldiers made his head swell enormously. Those arseholes must pay dearly for his suffering over the years.

He rummaged in his left shirt pocket, took out a bamboo toothpick, and reached into the chipped teeth, pulling out a bit of meat between the cracks, observing it, and then bringing it closer to his nose. He inhaled its smell then put the bits back into his mouth joyfully, smacking his lips with satisfaction. He carefully replaced the toothpick back in his shirt pocket for later use. It should not go to waste. Nothing should go to waste. He had learnt that in his life as a Communist soldier in the war.

There were times when he was in the jungle, down in the dark, treacherous Cu Chi tunnels fighting as a guerrilla, and his longing for a decent meal was more than anything he could think of at that time. The impossible claustrophobic living conditions and the fear of death still gave him nightmares now and then.

It was over now. Now it was changing for the Party and for people like him; it was time to enjoy the feast of victory. It was the work of Great Uncle Ho; Dan had to remember that. His Uncle Ho had the insight of persistently pushing forward. Obviously, his clever Uncle Ho had known of the gold mines that the South offered. There were the riches of the fertile land, the food, the rice, the comfort of living, and the various magnificent jewellery and machinery that added many luxurious aspects of civilisation that he and his comrades had never thought possible.

Dan glanced at his watch. The short hand was at number 7, and the long hand was at number 12. It was seven o'clock, exactly! He beamed with pleasures, feeling very smart. Dan was taught how to tell the time by one of his comrades. He loved the look of his watch and the sensational feeling it had given him when he took the Seiko wristwatch off Tuan the moment he had seen it. The day after, he gleefully wrote to his wife living on the outskirts of Hanoi and boasted of having "a wristwatch with no driver and two windows." He meant an automatic wristwatch with date and month windows, a precious treasure that many of his villagers would envy as none could afford such a luxury! His dedicated service to the Communist Party and Great Uncle Ho had paid off at last. Dan felt grateful again.

Reluctantly taking his eyes away from his now beloved watch, he shoved Tuan forcefully between his shoulders and arrogantly ordered, "Kneel and bow to the Communist Party, to Great Uncle Ho, and to me, low-life traitor!"

The routine humiliation had been repeated every morning for the last three weeks. The ten days detention per the announcement had now passed, and Tuan knew that he was in for a long time. He did not know where he was at the moment. His senses were all numbed by repeated torture. They put him in a metal box under the hot sun for increasing durations and reduced his water allowance every day. It was the seventh day consecutively, and Tuan was already weak with exhaustion. He fell over face down and crumpled onto the earthen floor with a slightest shove.

Tuan regained his senses with a dry mouth and a severe headache. He lay still, listened to his laboured breathing, and wondered why. He thought he was having a dream, that he was in a desert and had no water. It was hot. The temperature in the metal box was 45 degree Celsius at least. He was sweating profusely. That did not help with his thirst at all, Tuan realised. He managed to lick the beads of sweat that trickled down his lips. It was salty, but it eased his dry mouth a bit. There was no space to move. *I must be in a coffin in my dream,* Tuan thought. Slowly, everything became clearer. He remembered now. He was sentenced to a slow death, and this was the first day.

Tuan closed his eyes and pictured the face of Thanh in his mind, trying to obliterate the pain. He wished that he had kissed his wife on the day he left home.

Lying in his cell, Tuan often reflected. Ironically, like him, millions of South Vietnamese, indeed the whole population of the South, foolishly believed the new government when asked to report to various headquarters to make self-declarations along with statements of their occupation, position, and rank as well as confessing to whatever crimes they thought had been committed against the Communist Party through the duration of their service for the government of the Republic of Vietnam. Like him, many had willingly stepped forward, and all were tricked into believing in reclassification and recruitment into new government positions. The whole of the South fell headfirst into the trap of the new regime. Like him, they believed in peace, unity, and their ability to contribute to the reconstruction of the whole nation. That belief was shattered by the betrayal of the Communist Party and its treatment of two and a half million South Vietnamese men in its reeducation camps.

The victors kept their countrymen in these concentration camps for indefinite terms without bringing formal charges or conducting judicial proceedings of any kind. They killed approximately 165,000 men in more than two hundred camps in the vicinity of Hanoi and Saigon for over fourteen years after the Fall of Saigon on April 30, 1975.

It was another day as many previous days. His interrogators seemed to enjoy each torture session in the last ten days.

However, they were getting tired of the game; they were not making progress. They were sick of Tuan and his stubbornness. They needed a new victim. He refused to admit and confess his crimes and was still cocky even in his weakened condition. *But his punishment was a good example for the rest of the inmates*, Dan thought. He still served their purpose anyhow.

Dan ushered the other two officers toward the interrogation room.

His voice was chirpy. "Come on, comrades. Let's get it over quickly today so we can enjoy our card game sooner. The bastard is not going to last very long, and he stinks! It's revolting! He's ruining my appetite, and I don't like anything affecting that. Just another round or so, and we're done with the motherfucker! It's strange that he's still alive. He must have come from good stock." He chuckled at his own logic.

Then, looking up to the sunny sky, he said, "It's bloody hot today! We're having chicken for lunch with cabbage salad. The canteen has already prepared the chooks." Smacking his lips in anticipation of the meal, he went in and changed his expression immediately into a mask of malevolence and arrogance.

The guards pulled Tuan out of his metal box by his legs, one on each side, put him on a stretcher, and carried him in. Tuan was no longer able to stand, so they left him lying on the ground.

The first lieutenant was always the first with a stream of hostile words.

His face distorted with rage and his eyes blaring, he shouted, "You son of a bitch! You're the enemy of the People of the Communist Party, of the Great Uncle Ho. How dare you deny your sin and still think you can get away with it?! How dare you refuse to accept your crimes?! Filthy bastard! Scumbag traitor!"

The other followed quickly with more accusations. "You killed our comrades and collaborated with the Americans in the An Loc battle that sabotaged many of our efforts to liberate the South and unite the country in 1972. We've got evidence and witnesses who are ready to come forward to testify. No way you can deny that, you low-life betrayer!"

Dan was the last. "You cunning, bloodthirsty backslider, three of our best divisions engaged in those battles with T-54 tanks, and you son of a bitch prevented us from taking over An Loc!" He kicked Tuan with his right foot, pushing him onto his side.

In a delirium of exhaustion, Tuan heard them mention the An Loc battle and smiled despite his weakness. It was a glorious victory for his battalion and the South Vietnamese Army in April 1972. They had managed to defeat three North Vietnamese divisions, an estimated 36,000 troops supported by *"thiet giap"* T-54 tanks with their humble M-72 machine guns; they were useless against the heavy Soviet tanks unless fired with total precision and a bit of luck. They drove the Northerners back to the border in disarray, their army in retreat, despite greatly outnumbering of Viet Cong over South Vietnamese soldiers.

He drifted in and out of consciousness. In tiny fractions when his mind was clear, Tuan was indeed glad that he was leaving this hell on earth. He was so hot. His lips were parched and bleeding. He had a high fever. His head wound was badly infected, and there were maggots in the yellow pus forming around his ear; some blackened crusts of old blood matted his hair. His white shirt was filthy and smelt of vomit, and his trousers were loose on his skeletal body. The stench of urine and faeces filled the room. Dan had made sure his vow was carried out by ordering the guards to smear faeces on Tuan's face. The guards and the interrogators had to use handkerchiefs on their noses to block out the smell. Their disgust was visible, and they were glad that Tuan was fading. Today was the last day of interrogation. They would carry him back to his bed and leave him there to die. They were done with him. He was beyond help. There was no way they could convert him into thinking as a communist. What a stupid fool!

Quang, the Caretaker

June 1975

QUANG REMAINED QUIET near his bed when they carried Tuan's body into the tent. The stench of death mingling with all the other smells filled the air immediately. It made him gag involuntarily. He put his hand over his nose. The devils did not even have the decency to give Tuan a wash.

"Just leave the fucking bastard there!" the guard said. He almost ran out of the tent before finishing the sentence.

Avoiding eye contact with the other prisoners, they shoved Tuan's body onto his bed then left hastily. There were only three sick prisoners staying back to do light duties at this hour. Quang waited for all four of the guards to leave the tent before he came closer to the bedside. The other prisoners carried on with their work, avoiding eye contact with each other as well. Lately, that avoidance was practised diligently here in the camp. No one seemed to care about anyone else anymore. Only a few weeks had passed and the spirit of the prisoners was already wearing thin. The death of the Lieutenant, as they called Tuan, was a strong example to them to acquiesce if they were to be spared.

The chance for them to get out of this hell on earth was slim enough just being who they were. Becoming rebellious and showing strength of character would seal their fates, they learnt quickly. Torture and death were the final answers for thousands in the reeducation camps.

Quang rummaged in his sack to retrieve a thin cotton shirt. Using it as a face mask, he went over to the bed to examine the body. Out of habit as an army doctor, Quang began to check Tuan's vital signs for confirmation of death. He picked up the right hand to check the pulse then bent down to place his ear over the nose and mouth to hear any sound of breathing. Tuan was still warm, but Quang detected nothing. The life had left Tuan's body some time before he was carried back here. *That was better for him*, Quang thought. No more suffering, while he and the rest of them here in this camp still had to carry on.

The prisoners were denied even a glimpse of light at the end of the tunnel, Quang thought sadly. They were not given a one-year, five-year, or ten-year jail term, but a vague sentence for their length of imprisonment. "Once you have learnt to accept your crimes, you will have graduated." Just like being graduated from university! The simplicity of this formula was disturbing to the prisoners as they did not know how to achieve acceptance. Supposedly, prisoners of war were to be released when peace was restored.

"Ah, but here it was different!" Quang almost said out loud.

He closed Tuan's eyes and untied his hands. The extremities were already bluish, and rigor mortis was settling in. If he had waited any longer, the eyelids might not close shut, and the body might not straighten properly. He pulled the legs and arms out of the defensive crouch that Tuan had adopted when he collapsed. Quang positioned the arms as close to the body as he could. The pitiful body of the lieutenant was so diminished. After days of starvation and ill treatment, it was dehydrated and infected. In many places, chunks of flesh were missing, and maggots were crawling out of the hollow spaces. Quang returned to his bed, took a pair of bamboo chopsticks out of his tin lunch box, and used them to pick out the maggots one by one, placing them into an empty jar. They wiggled their plump bodies angrily in the crowded jar, annoyed at being removed from the feast they were enjoying. The mass of whitish crawling maggots in the jar would look revolting in normal circumstances; but right here, in this wretched reeducation camp, it appeared absolutely right.

It was where they belonged, the maggots and the prisoners, Quang thought bitterly.

After a while of labouring over the disgusting larvae, Quang was satisfied that the wounds were clean and free of them. He stood up and looked at Tuan again. He was trying to dampen his emotion by seeing him as objectively as he could, a skill that he had to resort to many times during his medical practice.

Quang went back a second time to take a small bucket underneath his bed and a face towel with a cake of soap in a box. He walked out to the well, fifty metres away from the tent, and pumped enough water to half-fill the bucket and carried it back to the tent. He wanted to give Tuan's body a wash, to clean the pus and blood in the wounds, and to put on a decent outfit to prepare for the courageous lieutenant's burial. It was a pity the prisoner was denied the uniform of the South Vietnamese Army in burial. It would have to be in civilian clothes.

Leaving only Tuan's underpants, Quang used a small blunt table knife to cut then tear and pull the trousers and shirt off Tuan's body with utmost care; Quang did not want to humiliate the soldier any further. He was exposed enough as he appeared. The prisoners were not allowed to have any sharp objects in their belongings. Quang had to plead with his tent's leader to keep the knife; it was a blunt knife nevertheless. He had shown him that the knife was useless as a weapon but could be used to cut paper or open letters. It was a precious tool to Quang, and he was pleased that he could keep it.

Naked, the skeleton of the Lieutenant was even more pathetic. Quang used the old towel to wipe over the body and then rinsed it in the bucket. The water darkened with blood immediately. He had to use two more buckets before he was happy with the result. It was reasonably clean now, the best he could do with his limited tools, Quang told himself. The Lieutenant smelled more of soap than filth, as he had half an hour ago. He pulled up the new pair of trousers, which he found from Tuan's rucksack, to cover the now-rigid body. A fresh white shirt was placed over his torso. *Tuan was ready to go*, Quang thought. He looked peaceful and free. *Good for him*, Quang almost said aloud again.

He was jerked out of his reverie when a voice boomed over the whole tent. Dan was standing at the entrance, blocking out the sun light. He was very pleased with the death of a rebellious prisoner; a smirk of satisfaction hovered about his lips.

He said spitefully, "It is permissible to bury the prisoner at the far end of the bush away from the main tents, but it is forbidden to put name, rank, or anything to mark the grave, not even a tombstone or a cross. The prisoner was the enemy of the People of the Republic of Vietnam and did not warrant any formal recognition. He must remain nameless in death." He waved his hand to Quang and continued. "You there. Yes, you. You will be in charge."

Quang looked at Dan, trying to keep his expression blank and devoid of emotion, and waited patiently for the next instruction.

"You can ask the others to help you bury him. You understand?"

Quang nodded his head. He did not care to give an audible reply. He was speechless to hear the heartless order not to mark the grave. How could they deny a basic human right like that! Quang was in disbelief.

Satisfied that his order was understood, Dan turned and walked away. Then he hurried back with more instructions. "Remember, no marking, nothing at all on the grave. You will be punished severely if I find some marking on it! You, all traitors of the Party, will all die nameless, anonymous, and unidentifiable. The graves are going to be unmarked, unspecified, unknown to anyone. You do not deserve to be remembered, you cocky bastards.

"All of you, Southerners, have had a life of luxury with good food, butter, cream, and cheese. You lived in mansions while we were fighting underground as guerrillas, cold and hungry like sewer rats. For over twenty years, you caused us to suffer, and we had to sacrifice our lives to liberate you and reunite the country. Now it is our turn to reap the rewards we are due. We are giving you a taste of what we have been through," Dan had stated that on their first day in the camp without any shame.

Nasty bastard! Quang shook his head in bewilderment. The spiteful idiot made sure the South Vietnamese Armed Forces officers were humiliated beyond life. Even death was not enough to placate them. It was a mystery to Quang and most Southerners why they were treated like this. But the answer lay in the resentment Quang detected in Dan's latest ranting.

He had to think of a solution. He could not let that happen. The grave had to be marked somehow. He would think of a way.

Coming back to look into Tuan's rucksack, he rummaged inside again and found a small cross. It was a wooden cross about the size of his index finger, well used and nothing special but the only thing truly personal in his belongings. Quang took it out and pushed it right inside the pants' pocket of the Lieutenant's corpse. He hoped it would make a difference and perhaps identify the skeleton later on when his family had had the chance to exhume the grave and collect his remains. He then used the old grass mat to cover the body.

He went outside. The sun was shadowed by various banks of clouds. There were no distinctive shapes as on some days when Quang could fill his imagination with specific features. Sometimes they appeared as ships, aeroplanes, houses, or even swans, pigeons, roses, and orchids. They enriched his mind and encouraged him in many ways. He used them to alleviate his homesickness, his longing for freedom. They raised his hopes and allowed his imagination to soar towards brighter days. He had to keep his optimism intact, a promise he carried with him always.

Today, the clouds were hideous and irregular. He thought he had a glimpse of the sickle of the Grim Reaper somewhere up there, even in daylight; Quang chuckled bitterly with this thought. That was a shadow of an early moon or late moon, no doubt. There were no birds, no butterflies, and no dragonflies in the sky. He could not find a single wild flower to put on the grave for the Lieutenant. It was a pity. This summer was so harsh. The bush was parched. The red dirt cracked under his feet. It was going to be just the plain earth and him. Perhaps that was better—no baggage to follow the Lieutenant further from this life. The wooden cross from home would help release his soul quickly to heaven. The string of thoughts paraded through Quang's head like verses from a poem. He wished he could be a poet. In a time of tragedy, being a poet might have been very helpful, he reflected. There were no boundaries between dreams and reality in a poetic world.

However, he was just a scientist, a medical doctor, a major in the army, a patriot, and a prisoner—everything but a poet. He chuckled bitterly again.

Back to reality, Quang approached the banana bush with his blunt knife; he had to get strings from the outermost fibre of its trunk to tie the corpse in a bundle. He and the others would carry it to the far side of the camp, about a kilometre away. They would then dig the grave together and bury the Lieutenant there.

That was the first grave Quang was to take care of. The Caretaker was the name they were to give him in the camp after many more graves were lined up at the far side of the bush months and years later. Quang pencilled Tuan's full name, his rank, service number, and today's date, June 28, 1975, in his neat handwriting on the first page of his notebook. While he was relieved that he had the information written down, he still had to mark the grave somehow. Even if it was forbidden by the Communists, Quang was determined to outsmart them. Tomorrow, he would go back and plant the seeds from a wildflower or something there on the newly dug mound. The white hibiscus would do for now; white denoted bereavement in Oriental culture. The demise of the whole country was just at its beginning, and everyone was in mourning; white was definitely appropriate. He put down in his notebook, next to Tuan's details, the name, and the colour of the flower. At least, it would suffice for the time being. There was little else to choose. The bush had few wild plants or flowers, and he had to mask it to make it appear natural. He did not want the guards to be suspicious of his efforts; he had to be careful for his own safety as well. He had to stay alive to look after the graves.

Years later, when he had run out of plants or flowers to mark the tombs, he had to arrange combinations of them, shame-weed with passion-vine for one, or shame-weed with yellow hibiscus for the other, etc. Sometimes there were three or more small plants positioned together on one mound. He drew the diagrams in his tenth notebook to keep track of hundreds of unmarked graves, each identified by his code of plants. It was a duty he felt very honoured to fulfil as caretaker of the memories of the fallen prisoners.

Sue and the Open-Street Bar Trade

THE LAST SECONDHAND dealer had gone home. The street was deserted for a few hours. Then nighttime came, and it became alive again with open-street bars called *bia om*, an alternative to more expensive nightlife entertainment elsewhere in Saigon. These vulgar, raunchy street bars sprang up faster than mushrooms. Overnight or within a couple of hours, a rough construction appeared consisting of a few rickety tables and stools, a partially covered dark corner on the pavement, and a mobile bar unit displaying beer, soft drinks, some fruits, and a juice blender, with some voluptuous women in tight dresses thrown in. All that was needed to get a bia om operating.

These illegal bars were the means for many women to make ends meet. Some were professional prostitutes, but some had been plain housewives just a few years before. There were two and a half million men in reeducation camps, which would leave at least half that number of wives having to support themselves, their children, and their gaoled husbands. It was the seventies, and following Vietnamese tradition, most women in that era had not ventured out to join the workforce but remained at home. The sudden change of role from being a housewife to an income earner to support their husband and family had thrown many desperate women onto the streets, entering the trade of the flesh. Bitter and downgrading though it was, there was no other skill they had known.

Some were able to start small businesses with resources from selling their personal jewellery. Some were capable of weaving their life into society with newly acquired skills and managed on their own in odd jobs. Some moved out of the city to the countryside to start a new life in far rural provinces to save money. However, some were totally helpless and desperately poor! Vietnam had had no social security services in the past, and there were none now. When a person was penniless, then he was truly poverty-stricken. He was empty-handed, with not a cent in his pocket nor a piece of paper or a pen to write with! Two years had passed and those who depended on the handouts of family and friends had to find other ways as the source was draining away. Everyone was struggling to make ends meet. It was impossible to help anymore.

Sue was the first to open the bia om in Trinh's neighbourhood. Her bia om was four doors down the road, in front of the "odd one out" house. The main residential front part of that house was confiscated by the new government after 1975 like most of the vacated houses or buildings in Saigon and the rest of the South during the early stages. The house had been vacant most of the time in the past as the owner was usually overseas. The rear part was designated as the housekeeper's residence, and she had turned it into a domestic childcare centre, which looked after babies and kids whose mothers were working in various positions from shop assistants and secretaries to escort women or even bar girls.

The war and the Americans had turned Saigon into a city with a riotous nightlife, rowdy public bars, and wild clubs, and along came prostitutes or call girls. Further down the track, there were many orphans and abandoned children of mixed races, both black and white Amerasians.

There was a beautiful Amerasian boy among the kids at that place. His name was Mike, and he had stayed there permanently since he was a little baby. Trinh was always fascinated looking at him from afar whenever the nanny brought him out on the street in the afternoon for a stroll. His glamorous and charming mother normally came to visit him in a taxi with gifts and toys once a week or so at first. Then it became less and less frequent until one day there were no more visits. That was the day after Saigon fell. He was around nine or ten when it happened.

His sparkling blue eyes were of the most beautiful colour Trinh had ever seen. The thick lashes and the translucent pearl-white skin with curly gold hair were a most intriguing image at that time to the little girl. He was just like a precious, expensive doll that she wished to have, a special ornament standing separately and aloof from the rest of the common ones on the shelf, so pure and innocent. He was a nice, clean, beautifully clothed, and properly looked after little boy until the day his mother abandoned him. She must have escaped with one of the US soldiers at the time of crisis and must have totally forgotten about her Amerasian boy, or perhaps she was unable to come back for him in time, Mike often reassured himself of the more appropriate explanation. His nanny was stuck with the abandoned boy after a long period of nonpayment for his keep and no news from his mother. He had remained there ever since. She had a kind heart and was unable to do otherwise but let him stay.

Without his mother and with the turn of events, Mike had turned into a street kid who had to grow up by the rule of nature, which was "survival of the fittest."

Trinh often watched him playing on the pavement of their street with the rest of the other kids. Tall and big among the smaller boys, his features had not changed much, even though his fair skin was now darkened from many hours on the harsh, sunny streets. *How would he be able to blend in with his blue eyes and golden hair,* Trinh pondered? It was impossible to dye both the colours to brown to avoid attention, regardless of the fact that his language was just like any Saigon street kid, a common alliterative rudeness in fluent Vietnamese, swearing nonstop in every sentence with four-letter words. She was so disappointed and sad hearing him swear the first time. Her once precious and expensive, pure, innocent doll had gone forever. The beautiful ornament had fallen to the ground and sunk gradually into the disturbing, violent world of hatred, the hatred of Americans and mixed-race ethnic population in Vietnam under the Communists.

It had not been pleasant for those Amerasians in the pre-1975 period, but it was now a hundred times worse postwar. The traces of American blood in their appearance were quite clear regardless of their fluent Vietnamese, and everywhere they turned, they were the odd ones out. Majority of them were rescued in time by the Red Cross Society or the American Authority during the last days of the war, but regretfully, many were still left behind to live in a hostile environment. They were not being accepted as citizens but considered to be the rock-bottom class in a racist society. Citizens were divided into many hierarchical classes. From top to bottom, depended on the category they were in, the benefits and treatment by the authority would range from best to worst. There were the members of the Party from the longest to the shortest duration of membership then the precandidate members of the Party who were the next in line. Those precandidates were sieved through family history of non-involvement in the ex-government through periods of political studies of Communism and personal labour achievements before being accepted as true members. Then there were the normal nonparty member citizens who were the general public and then the pre-1975 Southern citizens who had connections with the ex-government or Americans, and those would have no chance of getting into the governmental system or public service or higher education.

During the eighties in Vietnam, the resume played a vital role in a person's life and education. Kim had to climb the ladder gradually with diligent political studies to become a precandidate of the Party in the hope of gaining entry to university. She was in year 12 now. Their family, which included Dien as an ex-soldier and their father as an ex-government officer, had too many negative factors. She had to prove to the Board of Selection her devotion to the Party before being granted advancement in her study.

The family often teased her as a mole, and they would often say, "Hey, careful! Kim is here!"

She had to have class after class of political studies and examination after examination just to be a precandidate.

Then there was the ethnic race of the highland areas and, last of all, the Amerasians, who received the worst treatment in the already-biased government. Sadly, they were ostracised by the authority and the general public with the term *con lai*, which meant "mixed-race." Not only were they forgotten by the outside world, but the fraternal side of their blood also refused to acknowledge their existence or did not try hard to rescue them. They had to struggle to survive in their mother's land in which love and affection were hard to come by, as the mother was sometimes ashamed or even regretted having borne her own con lai. The interracial relationships between Vietnamese women and American soldiers were never looked on favourably in society.

Three years had passed. In 1978, Mike was a little boy of twelve. With his American blood, his nanny was reluctant to enrol him in the public school system under the new government after he finished his primary school, and there was no way he could afford private education. Besides, everything was under the tight control of the Party, and privatisation was unheard of at that time. So Mike stayed out of school and enjoyed his freedom. In the morning, he collected cans and bottles, tin bottle caps, and sometimes cigarette butts for recycling. In the evening, he helped Sue in her bia om business to earn his keep. Sue was one of the bar girls in the pre-1975 era. The riotous nightlife with quick cash and the lifestyle of a bar girl with only rudimentary principles ended abruptly when the war ended, leaving Sue with no other alternatives to earn her living. After lying low for a few months and using all her meagre savings and staying out of the watchful eyes of the 30th-April spies, Sue ventured out in a refreshment stall business on the street veranda with the last of her cash, trying to restart her life.

Her attempt to be a modest woman in a modest gig did not last very long as many male patrons who stopped by at her corner had got wind of her reputation as a bar girl in the old days and started to tempt her back into it. There was a frequent visitor, a Comrade Vinh, a 30th-April Communist, who pushed her further in that direction every time he stopped by for a chat and a drink after work.

"Oh, come on, Sue baby! We all know where you're from. I'll help you out with your business, and we'll share the profit, honey."

He continued. "Get the young chicks to work for you, darling. You're too old to work anymore." He chuckled at his remark and then continued. "All you need to do is be a manager, and I'll get you your clients. Other comrades are quite willing to taste the forbidden fruits of Southern girls. They've got the cash and the tools but not the joint to rest their gizmo!" He laughed uproariously with this last statement, thoroughly enjoying the dirty tone of it.

Sue was only thirty-four, but in those times, women over thirty were considered old maids, especially in her trade. She still had her rugged beauty, crude as an unkempt garden but oozing with raw sex appeal and suggestiveness.

She put down a chilled young coconut in its raw green outer shell, with a recycled miniature colourful umbrella and a recycled straw inserted in the small opening. "But Comrade Vinh, don't you think that's prohibited? Bia oms in Saigon?" Sue gave Vinh a smirk. "You sure have guts! And hey, how dare you think of me as an old maid!"

Vinh chuckled. "Oops, sorry! I didn't mean that as an offence, babe. Old maid as you are, you're only fit for me, darling. And don't pretend to be naive, honey pie!"

He could not resist patting her plump behind playfully when she turned around and said, "Of course, it's forbidden by the Party, and it's against the virtuous teaching of Uncle Ho! He was a disciplined bachelor all through his life. Did you know that? Ah, but our comrades need to unwind and enjoy their rewards now after so many years of war. Don't you think?"

Sue chuckled inwardly. *Disciplined bachelor, my arse!* He sure had fun with his women in secret, and they all turned up dead corpses after he had pumped enough larvae through them!

Vinh waved her closer. "Sit down. I want to talk real business with you." He shamelessly brushed his right hand over her left breast smoothly, pinching the nipple lightly in a quick motion through the tight fitted blouse.

Sue started and gripped his hand hard then pushed it away with all her strength in disgust. His hand fell against the side of the table and made a cracking noise. The table tipped and almost fell over, but Sue managed to stabilise it in a quick reflex.

Scattered on the pavement were a rickety bamboo table and four equally rickety stools for her patrons to sit on; they were placed a small distance from her booth. Most patrons just stood around her refreshment stall or, as drive-by customers, stood on the kerb with their motorbikes. Business was slow lately. Sue had realised that being in a decent and honest trade was hard work. Besides, there were many bia om hangouts sprouting up everywhere recently. The trade of the flesh had been quiet for a while because it was under the watchful gaze of the new government, but now it began to flourish due to much demand. Many Northerners and 30th-April Communists were establishing themselves after three years of control and acquiring large amounts of money through bribery. Now they were looking for ways to spend their cash. *Yes, who else but the Communists with money to spend after a few years of robbing the*

Southerners' valuables and properties as well as businesses and jobs, Sue thought bitterly.

"Fuck!" Vinh yelled, holding up his right hand. "Ouch, ouch! Nasty bitch! Hey, but you liked that, didn't you?" He leered at her provocatively, looked at her hardened nipples, and gave her a wicked smirk.

Unaffected by the commotion, he said, "It was meant for the comrades' entertainment, honey. Believe me, you won't regret it. I'll protect you, sugar pie. I'll tell the district security comrades to leave you alone. Just fifty-fifty, and the business is yours!"

"Half?" Sue grimaced, avoiding his flirtatious move and angry with herself for letting him get away with it. "That's a lot!"

"Nah, it's nothing. Considering, that is more than fair, babe. Look, I've got to give them half my share already. See, so that's a quarter for me, a quarter for them, a quarter for you and a quarter for the girl. Brilliant! I don't think you can find another deal like that, sugar plum."

He leaned forward and gave her a pinch on her behind when she stood up to clear the coconut shell, quickly forgetting her strong reflection a moment ago. Sue ignored the bastard's lecherous gesture and threw the empty shell in the garbage bin forcefully after taking away the straw and the miniature umbrella. She put them into a plastic basin containing some murky water, rinsed them briefly, and then placed them on the shelf for reuse by the next customer. It was a practice that was normal with everything in Saigon at that period. Everything was recycled and reused, even needles and syringes, without the slightest knowledge that it was the perfect way to transmit infectious diseases or hepatitis.

Sue warned, "Hey, next time take your dirty hands off my private property, esteemed comrade! It's not for free! Besides, your Great Uncle Ho might turn in his frozen bed and thump you for having more pleasure than him!"

Vinh laughed at her jeer and stood up. "Here, stop collecting small change and start on real business soon, darling. Think about what I proposed. Don't leave it too long. Otherwise, I'll give it to sexy Linh down the road. Then you'll have no chance, even if you'd given me a free, on-the-house satisfaction for my pleasure."

He gave her the note to pay for his drink, laughed aloud at his own remark, and then left. His fat belly shook with the motion as he heaved himself over his motorbike and turned the engine on noisily.

Dirty bastard! Sue's face went red with embarrassment and anger, "I'll bite it off if you dare give it to me, honourable comrade!" She sneered at him, stressing the last words sarcastically.

"Anytime, sweetie! Anytime!" Vinh guffawed. His small eyes narrowed to a slit, and he smacked his lips lewdly. Then turning his tone into a serious note, he continued. "All for the good cause of the Communist Party and the Great Uncle Ho! You are losers, and we won, remember?"

The arsehole, the vulgar creep! Sue shuddered at the image and the bitterness of being treated as a call girl sank in painfully after Vinh left with a filthy gesture.

In the end, she agreed, even with the thought that the greedy son of a bitch was taking half of her profit just for being named as her protector! He was a real pimp. He was nothing but a filthy scumbag! But never mind. She knew how to skim it. She was smarter than that.

Sue gathered a few other old acquaintances and then began the new service for the comrades of the Party. Then once her business boomed extensively, Sue started to go around the neighbourhood, recruiting young wives of reeducation camp prisoners or war widows for her fresh blood in the trade. Many women just had to accept the offer as there was no one else helping them to earn a living, and sadly, there were no other sources of income.

Anh, the War Widow

AFTER A FEW turns deeper into the labyrinth of shanty dwellings farther off the main street, Sue poked her head through the front louvre window. The room was empty and sparsely furnished. There was a shrine with a photograph of Anh's deceased husband on a shelf with an incense burner in front of it. A glass of water stood forlornly in place, the only offering to the spirit Anh could afford instead of the more extravagant sweets or fruits.

Seeing no one, Sue rattled on the iron trellis door. "Open up, Anh. It's me, Sue."

Anh got up slowly from her bed then walked tentatively to the door and opened it a small crack. "What is it, Sue? I'm not very well. Can you come back later?"

Sue ignored the lack of welcome in her greeting and pushed the folding door harder to one side, walking right in. The only furniture in the three-room abode was a single divan of simple mango wood in the furthest room; a thin, battered grass-leaf mattress was laid on top of it with a pillow and a thin sheet as a blanket. The faint light shone through the louvre window, illuminating the inner room that had a small ceramic tiled bench in a corner, a cooking nook just 150 × 50 x 80 centimetres without any cupboards or drawers, a basic three-point clay stove, and a little snuffed-out chunk of partially burned wood still inside, saved for the next occasion. On top of the simple clay stove was a watery rice congee in a saucepan. There was black soot all around the saucepan and up the walls. There was not a chimney in sight; the nook was not designed with a ventilator for this cooking method. Saigon had recently turned back to primitive cooking fuelled with wood fires, coals, or even paper. Some wet green wood would certainly fill the place with choking smoke that stung the eyes. A jar of coarse greyish salt and a small bottle of cheap salty fish sauce were standing nearby. The toilet and shower cubicle was a walled-off rectangular corner with a flimsy curtain for privacy. Pitifully, the door must have been taken off its hinges and sold off recently for food and necessities. Everything seemed to have its own value in times like this. Ironically, privacy was worth much less. The adjacent area was set up as a wet section for washing up and laundry, with a tap extending from the wall and a bucket under it. The floor was sunken by ten centimetres to prevent any splashing of water over the edge. This was a typical dwelling in a communal apartment building and was of the standard size for a small family unit with no children.

Anh had been Sue's best friend since primary school. However, their life had little in common after the age of twelve, as Anh had managed to finish her high school and marry a marine while still in her teens; she had been a child bride of eighteen. Sue was out earning her living, helping her mother as a vegetable vendor at the local market; her education was cut short prematurely after primary school. Then her mother passed away suddenly, and Sue was forced to become a bar girl when she was just twenty. For over ten years, the two lost contact. Anh tried to avoid gossip from neighbours about her association with a call girl when Sue turned up in her outrageous outfits with short skirts and revealing tops. Nevertheless, their friendship was anchored in their childhood and, like most, continued into adulthood and was destined to last a lifetime.

Anh became a young war widow just a year before the Fall of Saigon, and this turn of events brought them together again. The two lonely women had to find the means to stay alive in a Communist world in which they were largely ignored. They belonged to the two most detested classes of citizens—one a war widow of the now-defunct South Vietnamese Armed Forces, and the other one an ex-American call girl.

Sue had helped Anh where she could and ever since. She knew that Anh's furniture and personal jewellery were being sold off to keep her alive, even including the bathroom door. Anh had been living on watery congee and plain salt or fish sauce for some time. Her health was deteriorating with such a poor diet, leaving her weak and frail. The war widow's pension was cut off immediately after the new government took over control of South Vietnam.

Anh had tried to manage on her own for a couple of years, but it had now come to an end. There was not a single item left in the house that could be sold. Down to the smallest item, her kitchen utensils, clothes, even her late husband's used marine bath towels had gone to the secondhand market last month. She was not clever enough to start a new venture, knowing that she would fail miserably if she tried. Anh was also timid and cringed every time a stranger looked at her, when their gaze taking in her beautiful face and gorgeous body. It made her tremble with fear. Despite her poverty, she had retained her delicate beauty and grace.

"You are so thin now, Anh! You just look like a young child, honey!" Sue declared, seeing how much weight her friend had lost.

Sue placed into Anh's hands a packet wrapped in two layers, old newspaper on the outer and banana leaves on the inner side, tied neatly by banana strings. It contained a cup of boiled rice and a piece of pork belly with poached duck egg slow-cooked in fresh coconut juice and fish sauce, a delicacy that Anh could hardly afford these days. She licked her lips, inhaling the aroma of pork and rice and swallowed her saliva discreetly. Anh suddenly realised that she was hungry after all; she had had nothing in her stomach except a bowl of watery congee and salt since the night before.

"Here, Anh. You'd better eat this while it's still warm. Geez, you look terrible, honey." Sue could not resist her remark then she untied the banana strings, removed the outer newspaper, and pushed the packet toward her friend. The exposed contents in fresh green banana leaves shining with pork fat looked delicious to Anh.

Anh glanced at Sue, tears streaming down her face. She was lost for words. The comfort of knowing there was someone in the world who cared was already nourishment for her body and soul.

"Why, Sue? What about you? Did you have anything to eat today?"

Anh knew that everyone was trying to manage in truly basic living conditions each day, from breakfast to lunch to dinner. Having eaten enough at the end of twenty-four hours meant another day struck off the calendar. Let tomorrow come and then worry about whether it may include a meal of some sort.

Sue nodded. "Yeah, I've had my dinner already. You eat, Anh. I worry about you every day. You can't live like this anymore."

They both went over to the cooking nook and squatted down on the two little wooden stools, the only furniture that had not been sold. Anh hesitated, not wanting to eat in front of her friend and reveal her obvious hunger. Her little remaining dignity was all she had left of her pride, and Anh was certain that she would devour the packet of rice and meat like a hungry dog after tasting the first mouthful.

"I'll eat later, Sue. How's your business?"

"Very busy lately, darling. The bastards are spending like mad. The comrades really adore gorgeous Southern girls, you know. They're holding wads of cash like stacks of newspaper and are ready to throw it away on drinks and girls. The thieves! Of course, they are robbing the South without a hint of remorse, and now they're ready to indulge themselves."

After a brief moment of searching for the right words, Sue gave up and commented, "You look terrible! Come and work with me, sweetie."

Anh smiled weakly. "I know you care for me, Sue. I'm very fortunate to have a friend like you. I don't think I can cope without your help." She shook her head. "But what can I do? You know I'm useless in many ways."

"You can help me with my bia om joint, Anh."

Then she corrected herself immediately, sensing horror in Anh's large round eyes. "I mean you can come and help me with the general duties there. Not as a bia om girl, baby. I love you like a sister, and I would never allow you to do that, honey."

Anh was immediately sorry for her spontaneous reaction a moment ago. "Oh, Sue. I didn't mean that at all. But you know I'm very shy and uncomfortable in the presence of strangers."

"Yeah, right! Silly girl! You can't avoid that any more. Just look at yourself. I bet you haven't looked in the mirror for ages, have you?"

Sue stood up abruptly and went inside the bathroom. She brought out a hand mirror and, as if to prove her point, pushed it toward Anh. "Look at yourself, Anh!"

Anh took the mirror and turned it away, not daring to look at it. She knew she was very thin and her eyes were dull and lifeless. She was afraid to see their blankness staring back at her.

"You must pull yourself together and get out there. I promise you I won't let anything happen to you, Anh." Sue sat down next to her friend again.

Anh put her hand gently onto Sue's shoulder and said, "Yes, I know you care for me, Sue. And I know I must go out and work or do something, but I'm a coward. I haven't the energy or will to do anything. I'm sorry I worry you so much!"

Sue stood up, the stool tumbling behind her. "Yeah, you're damn right! I don't know why! It must be bad luck that our paths crossed, Anh! Why am I your friend? You're as pure as a spring fountain and as sweet as an angel, and I'm a lowly prostitute! But here we are. The two of us must find a way to get out of this shitty hell. We mustn't let them bury us alive, Anh."

Suddenly she was angry, not because of her friend's reluctance to fight for her existence but for the circumstances that had brought them together. They were helpless, and their welfare was utterly ignored. Somehow, Sue could not resist feeling responsible for her friend, for no reason other than their childhood connection. She knew she had her limitations. She was a woman as much as Anh.

Anh burst into tears. "Please don't be angry with me, Sue!" Her soft, pitiful pleading made Sue even angrier.

Sue knew that she had to be tough, tougher than most to weather the storm. She could not cry as she wanted to. Keeping her voice steady and without emotion, Sue coaxed, "Don't be absurd, silly girl! I'm not angry with you but at myself for not being able to help you more than I could. I must insist that you get out there and work with me tomorrow night, Anh. Think carefully, girl. That's the best I can offer, and you'll hurt me deeply if you don't turn up. See you at six o'clock. Be on time."

Sue left her dejected friend and walked out of the house quickly, avoiding any response from Anh. She knew she was betraying her closest friend's trust. She knew there was nothing Anh could do but reluctantly become a bia om girl, eventually.

Sue's first bia om was in District 3, not far from the high-rise communal ghetto where she lived. Those high-rise communal apartment blocks were courtesy of the Americans, who provided housing for homeless families after the Tet Offensive in 1968. They were centres of dense population with the low-income and labourer classes in Saigon where Sue found most of her old "colleagues" in this neighbourhood. Following the trend of the country at that time, they brought the trade of the flesh to the level of the street bar or street prostitution to provide services for the comrades whose wives and family were still in the North.

The illegal aspect of the trade did not deter many other ex-bar girls from launching their own business along the streets because that was the only trade that thrived. After a while, District 3 became a rowdy, debased area, and that attracted corrective action from the new government. The magnitude of corruption and bribery was on the rise in every direction among the Party members. The prolonged civil war had buried most of their youth in the jungles, and now they were out making up for lost time. The authorities received protection money from most of the bar owners who were warned before any raids. A clean sweep was in operation to satisfy some high-ranking Party members and to see that there was some corrective action at least.

With the periodical raids from the police, Sue and the rest of them would move their street bars from one district to the next. Legal action from one district security bureaucrat in his territory would mean bribing the next district security comrade who would go on to receive protection money. The bia oms moved from district to district. They were a thorn in the side for some but a golden egg in the hands of others. The authorities ignored the problem until they received urgent orders to move it further along to the next district around Saigon, a merry-go-round situation that was impossible to eradicate until the late 1980s.

Bribes and outright possession by force were then the practice. Only Northerners had cash and power, and they were taking literally everything from the South to the North. From small necessities like soap, sugar, rice, meat, fruits, and even a small baby doll to larger items like a Seiko "no-driver with two window wristwatch," an electric fan, a bicycle, a radio, a cassette player—all were riches to those treasure hunters, and now including Southern girls and women.

Mobile street bars forced by police raids to migrate to other parts of the city were now set up on the front pavements of Trinh's neighbourhood. Trinh was often frustrated by the constant commotion outside her place. The young girl of fifteen used to sit in her front room and study at night. Despite the noise, she had to concentrate intensely to block out the sordid activities around her. However, there were times she failed. The unavoidable sounds reverberated through the locked wrought iron gate, filling her ears with revolting exchanges between bar girls and their clients.

One late night, when everything had quietened down, Trinh jumped in horror to hear the whisper of a rough male voice through the small openings of the iron gate. "Come on, baby. Come closer, and I'll show you how you'll lose your virginity with my hard tool."

Trinh shook with fright and rage, unable to move. The shock of hearing those dirty words paralysed the teenage girl. She did not dare to look up even though there were a good five metres between where she was sitting and where the voice was coming from. Her heart was thumping fast and loud in her ears. She choked with emotion and could hear screams in her head trying desperately to get out. The eerie silence was very still in the night except for the disturbing heavy breathing through the cracks.

The man laughed aloud, satisfied his joke had frightened a young girl. He moved away from the gate and left, still laughing.

Mike, the Amerasian Kid

Today was his lucky day. It was bright and sunny.

And look! "Wow!" Mike exclaimed softly. The boy was excited. There were so many cigarette butts and tin bottle caps scattered haphazardly on the ground in the vicinity of the bars. They were his bonus income. Last night must have been a busy night for the sisters. *It was no doubt that the Party comrades had one hell of an enjoyable time with their pocket money,* Mike thought. The fag ends and tin bottle caps were littered on the cement ground in greater numbers than on previous days. Some cigarettes were hardly smoked at all, with a good bit still left on the ends.

"That's extravagant!" Mike muttered, shaking his head in disapproval.

Those guys must have been in such a hell of a hurry to get in or get out of here that they had extinguished their smoke prematurely, Mike thought and chuckled to himself. His young mind strayed to the images of coupling between the sisters and the comrades in the dark corners of the street bars, and that made his whole body tingle as if thousands of ants were crawling on his skin. With the curiosity and rising testosterone of a growing boy, Mike used to peek through the flimsy curtain when the action was in full swing. He was always eager to approach the makeshift tents when the grunting noises and sounds of bodies thudding against each other in the limited space could be heard from afar.

Only two nights ago, Mike had poked his head into the tiny cubicle to see the back of a kneeling man, his head bobbing up and down in his ecstasy, panting and whispering, "Oh, honey pot! Sweet heaven! I love you, baby!"

In the small tent, the prostitute was perching dangerously on a rickety bench, her knees wide apart and her musty odour filling the enclosed space as the humid tropical evening increased its intensity. She looked up as though on cue when the curtain was drawn apart, and opened her mouth in astonishment when she recognised the Amerasian boy. Glaring at him, she shooed Mike away, silently mouthing the words, "Get out of here, cheeky bastard!" Then she closed her eyes again and went back to her chore.

It was one of her best nights. This man was particularly fond of her, and thankfully, he was gentle with her. The other clients were usually very rough and demanding. Their carnal language could range from a gentle coaxing to extreme vulgarity. "Oh fuck it! Open your legs wider, stupid bitch! What are you waiting for? I don't have time to stand here and wait! Hurry up! Heave your big arse up so I can get to you, silly tramp!"

What a life! She often tried to shun her thoughts when dealing with crude and foul-mouthed clients, obeying their demands perfunctorily and getting on with it as quickly as she could. Sometimes, she still flinched with the rawness of it all, even now it was already two years since she first began her trade. Although she had thought it impossible from the start, her shyness and dignity had rapidly worn thin. But of course, a veteran's wife had no life in the new communist world, and she had no choice. It was a lazy way to explain it, she knew. They always said there were other choices. *Like becoming a comrade's mistress*, she thought amusedly. Perhaps that was better: ignoring a jailed husband in reeducation camps and burying the past to get on with a new beginning. *Ah, but this was going to pass,* she often reassured herself. There were always "buts" in any situation, and she had to believe in them, the "buts" and "ifs" of life. She was going to regain her dignity and to become a wife again if her husband was released from the reeducation camp. It should not be too long. How she wished that he were here now to help her bear the burden of life. But she knew that he was bearing a different ordeal that was a thousand times harder in his reeducation camp. She should not compare. Other times she just closed her eyes, her mind drifting out of the tiny cubicle, and thought of her children and their dinners, praying that they would never question her source of income.

Then the man stood up abruptly, breaking her line of thought. He wiped his mouth with the back of his hand before unzipping his fly hastily and thrusting himself roughly into her. He shuddered and went limp in a fraction of a minute, panting heavily. It was over before it had even started! She wished it were longer; she had almost gotten there! With a twinge of shame, the prostitute felt herself regretting the short-lived copulation. She thought she could have had her day at least. Oh, the irony of it all, the normal physiological needs of a woman! She wanted to shout it out. She needed to be loved and to love. They did not even allow her that when visiting her husband in jail. She wanted to be a woman, to be feminine again so much. It was so hard. Life was cruel. Tonight, she pondered why she was more emotional than usual. *It must be the moon,* she thought. It had brought out the loneliness in her. She wanted to cry, but she fought it down and put on a waxy smile as the man zipped up his pants before pushing a two-dong note into her hands as he departed.

In 1978, an average monthly salary for a blue-collar worker was around twenty-five dong and for a white-collar worker or professional, thirty-five dong, barely adequate for life's necessities. With enough clients, a prostitute could earn fifty dong a month and afford to feed her family as well as saving for a monthly visit to her husband in his reeducation camp.

The woman stood up and pulled her dress down. She reached for her panties and slipped them on then went out to wait for the next customer, dropping a fifty xu into Sue's box on her way, a share fee for the boss. Xu was the cent monetary value in Vietnam as the dong was to the dollar.

Mike's miniature penis perked up and hardened involuntarily by what he had seen. The boy was amused and tried to push it down with his hands, but it was stubborn and stayed erect. This erotic glimpse with its suggestive movements and language were more than sufficient for his tingling sensation to last a good half hour into the night. Back then, long before the digital revolution occurred and pornography was still a subject out of reach for young boys like him, sex was a mystery. Many young boys and girls did not even have a chance to understand the changing phases of puberty, and the subject of sexuality was heavily taboo in society. Information was hard to get, and for a poor street kid like Mike, it was impossible. He had no chance to get his hands on books or magazines; those were luxuries beyond his reach. This free "feast" was a real bonus to the growing teenager.

His fascination with the penis heightened his curiosity. The boy looked for opportunities to rekindle that erection during his rounds in the evening with the street bar women. Alternatively, just to listen to the whispering was enough to get his young mind racing; and just by thinking of it, his skin instantly prickled with goose bumps on his arms and legs. Perhaps it was his mixed American blood. Mike often wondered if his arousal was unusually early for his age or if it was normal. Was he an alien as they often teased him? He had no way of knowing. He was on his own, a poor and neglected Amerasian kid in a Communist world.

His mind drifted away from the dirty reminiscence and back to his piles of cigarette butts. Mike hoped Uncle Ba would give him a fair amount of cash for these. Uncle Ba had a tiny glass cabinet sitting on an obscure spot on the pavement selling loose cigarettes. Back then common people could only afford to purchase a single cigarette at a time. Those who had even less money would get recycled tobacco, which was collected from the half-smoked butts. Ba would amass the leftover tobacco leaves from those discarded butts then hand-roll them into clumsy, coarse cigarettes with week-old, recycled newspaper. The crispy, yellowish paper that seemed to belong to the last century came in very handy. The tobacco-addicted blue-collar labourers were his main customers. They had no choice. Pall Mall, 555, Winfield, or any brand name tobacco was practically out of their reach; even any of the local products were still too costly for them with daily incomes of barely one dong a day for a meal or two for themselves and their families. Little kids like Mike kept Ba's business sustainable.

Mike was glad with his pickings today. He could think of a nice, scrumptious dinner tonight, a dish of broken rice and a piece of succulent barbeque pork rib for a change after all. He would bite into the crunchy skin and savour the sweet, greasy taste of fat, which was rare to come by to feed his growing body. His good old nanny could only give him a corner in her kitchen to sleep at night, the size of a single mat, but nothing else. The thin mat made with a certain palm leaf, woven in intricate and distinctive homely patterns, was dear to him, and he kept it closely with him as the single possession reminding him of his mother. He was very careful with it and afraid of any wear and tear he might cause. It had been more than three years, and his mother's face was now only a dim picture. He wished that he could refresh the image of her face somehow. Mike had forgotten much of her features as his memories of her came primarily from his heart. He was very young when she left him, and there were no photos or anything from her personal effects for Mike to keep. There was nothing except that thin palm mat where the two of them used to lay together for an afternoon nap when he was a little boy. Every morning, he rolled it up ever so carefully, tying it tightly in a bundle and hiding it in a corner, making space for the tiny kitchen.

He was no longer a little boy, and Mike noticed that he was growing up fast. His body was bulging out in many places. It was only last month that he used to have his shower with other kids his age at the communal water pump a few streets down in District 3, completely naked and free of any pretended dignity. They stood under the spray of the pump, plainly in public view and happily scrubbed away without any shame or shyness as if in the total privacy of their own bathroom. He used to enjoy his time at the communal water pump when the kids were friendly to him, splashing water over each other in childish games.

But that was then. Now, Mike had a few hairs sprouting down there, and he refused to join other boys anymore to have showers at that communal pump. He waited until late at night after returning from Sue's Bar. Growing up as an orphan was lonesome. Mike had trained his mind to stay neutral about any attachment he felt for anybody, including his feeling for Sue, even though he was grateful for her generosity towards him. He was afraid of being left alone again, and he tried to look at Sue only as his employer. His pay from her was for his expenses; small as it was, it gave him more choices in his daily life. Meals were his main concern, and it was only luck if he had enough to eat, day by day. If he could get a small boiled sweet potato or a piece of cassava or a handful of sticky rice with palm sugar and peanuts for breakfast, it was lucky for him. The last choice was only possible if he had a bit of extra cash. His typical lunch was just plain congee and half of a salty boiled egg, and dinner was what was left over from the meals of Sue's customers. His regular feast for a while was boiled rice and gravy without the meat itself. He used to wish he could have a thin slice of that roast pork on display to remind himself of a forgotten taste. Plain and simple meals were cheapest, and that was all he could afford after his daily pay from Sue for helping her around the place as a general bus boy. His scavenging of cigarette butts and tin bottle caps served as an extra income for an occasional luxury, like a taste of real meat or an occasional ice block. After every three or four days, if he collected a substantial amount, he would bring them to Uncle Ba to exchange for cash.

There were other poor kids in it as well. Like him, they were scavengers, joining to form gangs on the streets to protect their own interests. Mike was a loner as his Amerasian appearance made him an outcast among the Vietnamese boys. However, he was territorial and had fought strongly for his ground. What belonged to Mike started from Sue's bar and extended in a one-hundred-metre radius in both directions. The other kids were not bold enough to fight Mike, even if they joined forces. He had the fierce determination of a real fighter when it came to his chief interests.

Today, Mike was wearing cotton board shorts with an elastic waistband, old and grubby, even a size bigger than his already large body; they were grey-and-charcoal-checked. His feet were bare, his toenails were blackened with dirt and grime, and the heels were thickened and cracked with deep lines. His upper torso was also bare; the pale skin was pinkish from prolonged exposure to the sun but was stubbornly refused to tan. There were freckles on his pink cheeks, and the golden locks had changed to wavy sun-streaked light brown. His hair was shoulder-length, not from choice but from infrequent cutting. His eyes were still blue but a shade lighter, not as deep as before.

Mike suddenly noticed a boy busy picking up the "goods" in his territory. He yelled, "Hey, fuck off! Go away or I'll smash your skull, scumbag! Those are mine, shithead! Don't you know, stupid idiot!"

"Fuck you, American-trash arsehole," the boy shot back, still holding a handful of tin bottle caps. Stuffing them hurriedly into his satchel, he darted away. He stopped after a fair distance and poked his tongue out at Mike, taunting him and mouthing the words, "Your mother's an American's whore."

Mike dashed up, his right hand forming into a tight fist. He chased after the kid for a short while as a warning then returned to protect his territory. Forget it! He could not waste more time than necessary. His time was more valuable than that; and besides, Mike got used to the insults, becoming immune to them over the years. He had been called nastier names, and they did not make him wince or tear his heart out anymore. His stomach was more important, he realised.

Sometimes he would show them his American cowboy blood by daring them to a kick boxing fight that used fists, elbows, knees, shins, and feet in a full-contact combat. The boys, ranging from twelve down to six or seven years old, would gather around the cement footpath after school and divide into two groups, one on Mike's side and one on his opponent's. Each boy bet five xu on the winner. Whoever won received the whole lot, and the winner would shout the group to some sort of treat. At first, Mike always won. His ego and his eagerness to show off his power gave him strength and energy. Eventually, the boys refused to bet on the other party anymore but solely on Mike. Mike learnt that he had to pretend to lose now and then to lure them into betting, and so he prearranged with his opponents to let them win and share half of what he collected. The kids enjoyed the games, and Mike enjoyed showing off his boxing skill as well as having some extra cash to pay for his luxuries. An ice-cold lime sorbet after the game with the kids was the highlight of his day.

"Come on, American-trash boy! You can do it!" the boys on his side all shouted excitedly.

The other boy's team was equally rowdy. "Show it to him, Kinh! Don't let the son-of-an-American's-whore beat you!" Then they all laughed uproariously, clapping their hands with the excitement.

Kinh was sweating; he was four years older than Mike and was of the same build. He had tried to land a few punches on

Mike's left shoulder repeatedly, but the boy ducked away expertly on the second attempt, retaliating with a nasty left-handed elbow jerk to his chin.

Kinh yelled out in pain, "Fuck it! You nasty bastard! I'll get you for that!" He snarled at Mike, one hand still holding on to his bruised chin.

Mike laughed sarcastically; his practised manoeuvre had paid off at last. That should teach the bastard for trying to punch him real hard in the first place, even though they had already made a pact before. They were supposed to playact, with Mike agreeing to let Kinh win this time. The older boy had promised to play soft! Cheating swine!

Mike strutted in a circle, exhibiting a cheeky arrogance. "Yeah, motherfucker! Come and get me if you can!"

Standing in the outer circle, the other kids laughed and cheered. They always enjoyed the fight as Mike was becoming more adept with his moves; his kicks, punches, elbows, and blocks were so natural that it was as if he was a born fighter. The two boys eyed each other, and Mike nodded his head; he knew that Kinh was already tiring and wanted out. That was the signal. Mike danced on his feet again; he wanted to show off his kick to the crowd before a prearranged knockout. Kinh came closer; his breathing was laboured, and the pain on his chin was worsening. The American bastard must have cracked a bone. Kinh was furious. In his hand was a sharp stone that he had concealed in the pocket of his shorts, a strategy that Kinh had planned in case Mike failed to let him win. The older boy was tired of Mike's strength. The two boys slowly moved closer, cheered on by the spectators.

"Yeah, go for it, Mike!"

"Hit him hard, Kinh! Don't let the shithead win again!"

Kinh dashed out with his backhanded punch this time. Mike had seen that coming and could have avoided it easily, but he pretended not to so that Kinh would have his revenge. Unexpectedly, the sharp stone tore into his right cheek and opened up a gash. At once, bright red blood started flowing through the wound.

Mike was surprised by the pain. He swore, "Oh fuck! Cheating bastard!"

He staggered backward. The pain was not anticipated. While it angered him, it boosted his resolve, giving him a surge of energy. He stood up immediately. However, Kinh did not let Mike regain his stance and pounded him twice more on the skull with the sharp stone, using all his strength. The Amerasian boy was defenceless. More blood spurted out, dripping down onto his bare upper body. Kinh was incensed with rage, as if the sight of blood stimulated his adrenaline. He slammed Mike into the ground, whacking him a few more blows before standing up triumphantly. This time, it was he who strutted around proudly like a peacock.

Mike did not move; his pitiful body slumped into a foetal position. He lost consciousness shortly afterward. Kinh must have hit him hard when he fell to the ground. The other kids were silent now as they realised they were witnessing a real bloody fight; and some younger boys had actually run home, terrified by the sight of injuries.

Some stayed back and cheered on, "We won! We won!"

Then they all left the scene laughing and happy with the loot, with no concern for the wounded boy. Mike lay there in a heap not far from his nanny's place. He did not know how long he had been unconscious, but he awoke slowly with a familiar voice in his ears.

Sue shook Mike lightly by his shoulders, her voice heavy with concern. "My goodness, Mike! What on earth happened to you, son?"

She patted his forehead and felt his warmth and was relieved that the boy was still alive. His bloodied head caked with dark red stains frightened her. The street was dark now. In line with the power-saving scheme from the new Communist government, many streets in Saigon were pitch-dark without any lights in the evening, and that made it even more favourable for the open-street bar trade.

Mike was dazed. He could not get up. The wounds to his skull must have bled a fair bit, and the metallic rusty smell of dry blood filled the air. His cheek was tender and swollen; Mike put his hand over it, and he could feel the deep laceration there.

"Fuck it! Fucking son of a bitch!" Mike swore under his breath. He did not want Sue to hear.

He replied, "I had a fight and fell to the ground. Nothing to worry about, sis. I'm okay."

Mike tried once more to get up, but he was hit by extreme nausea and dizziness and had to lie down again. He reassured Sue, "I'll be okay. You'd better started opening your business soon, sis. I'll join you in a few minutes."

Sue looked at Mike, her eyes filled with tenderness toward a good kid who had had a poor start in life. She knew he was wounded and might not be fit to work tonight, but she had no choice.

She agreed finally. "Okay, Mike. You get up when you can, boy."

Mike knew that he had to report to Sue as soon as her bar opened. He usually helped her time the men in between visits to the "copulation" cubicle and counting the beers. The men had to consume a certain amount of beer per hour to give Sue her profit. Mike just had to bring out more beer and clear away the empty or half-empty bottles to keep the cash flowing in. He had to tally the bills and collect the payments. Mike was smarter than most kids his age. Perhaps that was nature's way, the law of survival in the human jungle: the harder the life, the smarter or wiser a person becomes.

Mike would have to survive his ordeals like the rest of the population of South Vietnam in those years.

Truyen, the Café Vendor, and Rural Oppression

PLACING AN OLD army tarpaulin on top of his pile of secondhand wares as a last gesture, Tam said, "Bye, Truyen!" Then he looked at the sky and added as an afterthought, "I'll be back tomorrow morning if it is not raining heavily."

Truyen was waiting for him to lead his wobbly bike out before she closed the iron gate. "See you tomorrow, Tam!" she called with a bright smile, the corners of her dark lips curving up charmingly. "I don't think it's going to rain tomorrow!" Truyen rejected his forecast like an experienced meteorologist.

She was the firstborn in her family of six girls, a typical number of siblings in the Vietnam of the time. Traditionally, Truyen had to help her parents bring food to the table and look after her younger siblings. Because she could not leave to seek for her own happiness when her family still needed her, she missed many chances in her prime when suitors asked for her hand in marriage; the price she had to pay for being a dutiful daughter. On top of that, like the majority of young women in the difficult postwar period when most Southern men were in reeducation camps, she had limited choices. Unless Truyen was to get together with a Northerner after the war, which was her last option, she would stay unmarried. An attractive woman in her early thirties with traditional Vietnamese looks, Truyen was petite and slim. Her oval face, long straight hair, warm almond-shaped eyes, short flat curving nose, and full dark lips added to her pleasant and graceful manner. Her dark brown skin was the result of a hard rural life in her childhood as she had spent most of her time working in the rice field under the harsh sun and operating a coffee stall on the pavements of Saigon.

Like millions of the most recent migrants from rural areas flooding to Saigon to find jobs, which were scarce in their hometowns, Truyen was shy and timid. Saigon was established only in the early 1950s, but its reputation as the "Pearl of Southeast Asia" was well-established by the sixties. The city's residents were seen as sophisticated and stylish but also considered shrewd by some, the classical stereotype of city dwellers by which most peasants would feel intimidated. After her move here, she became a vendor in one of the regular cheap coffee stalls that sprouted up everywhere for the common labourers during the last few years. Truyen was able to compensate her family for the extra income that rural life could not provide now.

She had moved her coffee business from District 3 to District 1, into the front of Trinh's living room three months ago due to the popular demand for refreshments here from the secondhand traders. After Truyen was introduced by a friend, Mother agreed to let Truyen use a quarter of the front of their house and collected rent from her.

Truyen's family was from the rural southwest region of Rach Gia, three hundred kilometres from Saigon. After the Fall, like most rural peasants and the rest of the country, they had to struggle hard to survive under the new Communist system. With two hectares of wet land, they were able to live comfortably before 1975, if not extravagantly. The annual income from harvesting rice and raising a dozen pigs was enough to afford a pleasant life. It was not easy then, but the family was happy and content with their productivity. They were independent, enjoying little luxuries affordable to them through the income from working hard in the fields. The girls all attended school and helped in the rice paddy in their free time. Two of Truyen's sisters were boarders in the city of Can Tho, roughly a hundred kilometres away, attending university there before the war ended. Their parents were very proud; it had not been easy to raise children and give them an education back then. It was impossible now.

When Saigon was lost, everything fell into chaos. Along with freedom, their dreams for the future had vanished. The peasant's simple lifestyle was gone, and the straightforward logic of their existence was destroyed. They were as confused and lost as the rest of the population, if not more so. What had belonged to them before now belonged to the state. They did not understand why and had no protection to shield them from the vicious treatment. The further away from the capital cities of Hanoi and Saigon, the more savage was the ruling from the Party. Each province had its own overlord, and each overlord imposed his own rules over his peasants. The rules from one province could be totally different to the next. In fact, there were no set rules or protocols in government policies. Local rules and state rules might be contradictory, leaving the citizens to face roadblocks in dealing with the authorities. There was no cooperation between central offices and local offices, and jurisdiction was an issue. No authority believed he should be under the control of another, and sometimes, they hated each other. Matters were resolved on the mere whim of an arrogant politburo or a committee of high-ranking party members, among whom the most highly educated might be just high school graduates. They were given positions in the management of the state as their reward for being long-time party members and guerrilla fighters during the war, regardless of their ability to govern.

Not long after the Fall, copying Mao's practice in China, the Vietnamese Communist Party started the policy of collectivism. All rice harvests from each individual family in the village or the whole province were collected in one big local mill for the state to repay foreign debts during the war. It was compulsory, and severe punishment would be imposed if the peasants did not obey. The politburo of each region had the right to search their farm and storage area anytime on only a rumour of holding back from their harvest. In those times, South Vietnamese people often dreaded the nights. When darkness fell was the time a knock on the door meant harassment and captivity. Lacking the capacity for self-defence was the worst fear. Being visited by the Party politburo after dark in the post-1975 era was for the Southerners worse than being visited by them during the war.

"I don't believe it!" Binh declared, the leader of the rural division of Rach Gia to Truyen's father, Lam.

Lam pleaded, "But this year's harvest is all there, esteemed officer, sir." He added the respectable addressor "sir" quickly to please Binh.

He knew that the officers all desired to be addressed as "sir" or "madam" in situations like this. It made them feel important and magisterial. He was almost eager to bow low, in a sort of kowtow like greeting a monarch. Lam would gladly try it all if he could avoid a nasty confrontation with the Party politburo. Lam was shaking. He wished that he were transparent and could be swallowed beneath the ground to escape the animosity so clearly displayed on the face of the Party leader.

Put a Northern Communist into a uniform and he would show you how to obey his orders, Lam thought regretfully. Even the guard had addressed Lam insolently like a beggar, without much concern for his seniority. Yes, Lam mused, even a guard could have shown some power over any person entering his realm of authority. Ironically, Lam reflected, it was contradictory to their doctrine, which boasted equal rights to everyone; the farmer class was especially considered the revolutionary class that helped solidify the Communist Party during the war. If he had any rights at all, Lam felt helpless.

"Bullshit! You low-life peasants! How dare you lie to the Communist Party and to the Great Uncle Ho. The harvest was supposed to be equal or greater than last year!" Binh shouted.

Binh loved the way Lam addressed him. It gave him ego satisfaction and brought to the surface his power complex.

Standing up, his face blue with anger, Binh swore, "Fuck it!"

These stupid peasants! They had ruined his day. This was the limit! He had promised his mistress an expensive piece of material for her new ao dai this coming Tet, and one after another, they had come in to tell him that their harvest was down to 60 percent compared to last year. How was he to report the grand total to his senior Party members? He had planned to pocket at least 10 percent as per the previous year, and now this was even less than expected. Damn it! He had already boasted an increase in productivity to the politburo of Ho Chi Minh City and an extravagant gift for Hanh, his mistress who was twenty years his junior. The realisation meant a certain reprimand from the centre and a reduction of his allocated bonus in the total harvest as well as a substantial loss.

"Don't you stupid peasants know that the order from Party is to make sure your devotion to the Communist Party and Great Uncle Ho is carried out through your labour and rice? If you fail to provide the expected quota, then your devotion is under question. No doubt, you're harbouring antigovernment activity by keeping some proportion of rice to give to criminals. That means a severe punishment from the Party! Don't you idiots realise that at all? You're not going to get away with it that easily. I'm giving you a week to cough up the rest of the harvest. If there is none after the specified period, then you and your family will receive nothing for this year, you understand?"

He glared at Lam and the rest of the farmers.

"Don't ever think you can hide anything from the Party, you fool! Every farm is going to be searched extensively. And you will be taken into custody and fined heavily if I find you are lying to me!"

Lam and the others had no opportunity to protest. They were timid little mice waiting for the disastrous blow. Lam had learnt from his previous experience that it was better to say nothing. The overlord had already sent out a decree, so the more he said, the worse his situation would become.

This was the hardest part. But they all expected that. Of course, he and many of the farmers hid part of the rice harvest away for their family use. The Party only returned one-tenth of their total harvest or a certain amount proportionately to the number of family members. The rest of the value of the harvest was transformed into state coupons for purchasing other necessities in state stores like meat, poultry, oil, sugar, salt, and other sundry products.

Lam was sick of the system. This year, he had decided to cultivate just enough rice for his family to consume. Bugger the state and their greedy Party members; he was not going to be their slave any more. He did not want to see the fruits of his labour and that of his wife and the girls go to Binh and his mistress for free. Enough was enough! Let them come and search his farm. He was keeping over a tonne of rice for their annual use, barely sufficient for his family of eight.

Similarly, many farmers were beginning to feel frustrated by their ill treatment and the ill-gotten gain of the Party members. They followed Lam's example. The following year and many years after, the South experienced a shortage of rice that had never happened before.

Hoan, the Communist Soldier

WAR ERUPTED AGAIN in the country between Cambodia and Vietnam, leading to the Southerners' horror of seeing their sons being forced to enlist in the Vietnamese Communist's Army.

Hoan looked up from the crude wooden table. There were a few scratches here and there on the blackened surface, but the smoothness of the old wood was pleasant to the feel. Contrasting with its crudeness was the beauty of the heavy mango wood, ageing gracefully and shining with the natural varnish of sweat. Its surface glistened as if from the tears of people it had witnessed during the years. Its four legs gleamed from long hours of endurance, and the entire body glowed with the warmth from human contact. The beautiful shine was only possible with years of use. There must have been countless number of people sitting around the rectangular table time and again, discussing the stories of their life, crying through bad news, and laughing with good news. Hoan had no doubt about that.

Separated by an extended arm's length, his mother's tired and weary face appeared across the table in front of him. They were in the camp canteen. The thatched hut with its uneven, red earthen floor was packed with the weary faces of visitors and the anxious young faces of the new regime army recruits, the *bo doi*.

Hoan was about to enrol in university, if his resume allowed, but the new government requested all young men to be conscripted in the army when they finished high school. Hoan had just turned nineteen, a few months after graduating from high school in 1978. Although he was a son of an ex-government official and the younger brother of a fallen as well as an ex-soldier of the previous regime, Hoan must fulfil his duty as a soldier first. His father, a retired director of the department of finance in the former government, had tried to make plans for Hoan to dodge conscription, as he knew the fate of these so-called "soldiers-on-condition." Young boys of the south were herded into the Vietnamese Communist Northern army training sites scattered along the highlands of the south, previously the old headquarters of the Southern army, to learn quick-fix combat tactics, a mere three to six months of crucial basic training. Those new conscripts' most daring warfare approach was carrying unloaded guns on their shoulders and marching around the training site. On the battlefield, nevertheless, only ammunition or army supplies were what were allowed; and as a result, many of Hoan's friends had fallen like flies in combat. They were defenceless targets on the bloody ground of Cambodia in the brief Vietnam-Cambodia war between December 1978 and January 1979. For obvious reasons and as a precaution, many were not allowed to carry loaded guns or any kinds of weapon lest they rebel and fight against the Northern platoon leaders in those early times. Of the total 150,000 to 200,000 soldiers in this war, two-thirds were young boys who were primarily descendants of veteran Southerners or ex-government officials or just peasants and Southerners. They were obviously not fully trusted after a mere two and a half years since defeat as well as being forced to enlist.

Hoan reported to the recruiting headquarters of his home in District 1 in Saigon after several attempts at delaying. His family received a formal letter every fortnight and a personal visit from the communist party political bureau every week asking for his enlistment. Everyone was jumpy every time there was a knock on the front door. His mother and sisters had tried to conceal his whereabouts whenever they had to answer these queries, and finally, Hoan gave up. He could not put his family in the spotlight any more than necessary. Members of the Communist Party political bureau could exert their authority in a nastier way than just showing up in front of his door. They could search their house without a warrant and put pressure on everyone to get to Hoan. His family had already had several warnings and might face the heavy penalty of being forced to move out of Saigon to live in some remote territory. Hoan would have had no chance to return to a normal life if that happened. He would have to stay a refugee living on the outskirts of society or change his total identity in order to get back into society.

In the end, to avoid complications, here he was. Let destiny rule his life. Whether he would be a survivor or a goner after this war depended very much on his fate. Hoan was resigned. His half brother, Sam, had sacrificed his life; but his other brother, Dien, had survived the previous war. And so would he, Hoan believed.

His training camp was in the vicinity of Long Khanh, a remote high mountain jungle far from the main town, public transport, and everything else. Seeing his mother and his sister today was a surprise. Hoan did not expect it so soon as everyone was only allowed one visit every month. He had already had one two weeks ago.

He smiled awkwardly at his mother, walking hesitantly toward her from the canteen's entrance, not sure of the purpose of this visit. He was afraid of anything out of ordinary these days.

The thatched hut was separated from the main unit by a double barbed wire barrier. There were two guards with guns at the gate; exits and entrances were only allowed with permits. There was a long tedious process to get the permit.

Without ceremony, Hoan asked quietly, "How much did you have to give them this time, Mother?"

Chi looked at her son; the camp had not transformed his childlike features as much as she had feared. The once naïve-looking, handsome boy was still unaffected in his demeanour by the harsh army training. The darkened skin and the gaunt face in Northern army uniform was a betrayal of her sense of security, Chi reflected. She was still not used to seeing that Viet Cong uniform on Hoan and still had flashes of apprehension looking at it now from years of seeing graphic news on television from the fighting period between North and South. Her husband had lost his own son, Sam, a few years before the war ended, and her first-born son, Dien, had been a soldier in the Eighteenth Battalion of the South Vietnamese Army. His headquarters used to be somewhere in Long Khanh as well. It was also where their rambutan plantation was located, a long-gone possession that they did not dare to reclaim in fear of being branded capitalists, an added sin in their long list of sins. The enemy uniform of just a few years ago was now worn by her second son. *How peculiar that was*, she thought sadly!

Chi answered softly, "Erm, not much. And we can afford it. We had to come to inform you, dear."

After the Fall of Saigon, travelling was not an easy thing. Going to places required permits from various departments and going from one office to the next. First, his mother had to get a permit from the political bureau in his family unit group followed by District 1 back home. In order to travel to Long Khanh, she had to request a visiting permit from his army training headquarters to see Hoan. As this was outside the ordinary allowable visits per month, his mother had to bribe more heavily than normal. She discreetly reminded Hoan in her letter that when he received the order to see his training officer for the permit to meet his family, he had to promise a gift either on his return or downright offer cash bribe in exchange. That was the way the country operated now. Chi sighed. Every stop along the route required payment, from the busboy to the guard to the officer to the director of departments to the prime minister of the country. The list went on.

They sat down on the table without hugging as hugging or kissing in public was not the usual form of expression of affection for them. They were all shy in showing their love toward one another. Hoan playfully hit Trinh's head softly as a greeting after smiling broadly at them. He was so happy to see them both. He longed to go home; he badly needed to be back in his familiar surroundings. He needed his family. He was still a young boy.

Trinh was sitting beside her mother, her feet dangling loose on the same mango wooden bench, whose surface was as smooth as the table. It was almost regal in its simplicity, a real contrast to the makeshift thatched hut and uneven earthen floor. It had the feel of antiquity. The rest were just plain pine wood, young and rough. Her eyes were keenly taking in everything. The air was acrid with smoke from various nearby campfires behind the barbed wire. The sixteen-year-old girl was delighted at being allowed to accompany her mother on this trip. Oblivious to any degree of nervousness or anxiety from her mother, Trinh was glad to have a day off school and get away to the countryside, a rare treat these days.

Her curiosity increased with the activities in the camp. Glancing beyond the guarded gate, Trinh saw groups of young men like her brother busy preparing lunch. Open cooking fires were everywhere in front of each large corrugated dwelling. Darkened skin and bodies hardened with training made them seem more mature-looking, but upon those bodies were thin and haggard faces on skinny shoulders. There was never enough food. Hoan had said so in his letters home.

Trinh caught sight of two young recruits carrying a large saucepan, a metre high and blackened with soot, toward the open fire.

Following his sister's eyes, Hoan said in answer to her glance, "The camp's having meat today. It's a once-a-month treat."

A fifty-kilogram mountain sow had been delivered that morning from the local butcher to cater for two hundred people. On average, a growing boy of eighteen in the army training camp was allowed 250 grams of meat and bone per month, or just 50 grams of meat per week! The bones were scraped clean and polished off without a minute trace of meat when the recruits finished with them. Some even broke out in a fight for the bones with marrow; that most nutritious fat and protein was amazingly sucked empty by any man. *They had to be strong to fight with all their might if need be, to survive, and to return home*, Hoan reminded himself. No wonder the gate was guarded day and night. Who wanted to stay?

"So are you going to miss it today because of our visit?" Trinh asked, worried for her brother.

Hoan shook his head. "Nah, I wouldn't let that slip away, no way! I told Woody Ben to keep my share for me. Remember him? Ben, tall and lanky—"

"Yeah, of course, I remember him! Where is he? Which crowd is he in?" Trinh stood up from her bench, leaning forward and pointing toward the groups behind the barbed wire.

Hoan turned to look, squinting, moving from side to side, and trying to single out his friend in the crowds. The sun was very bright, reflecting everything like waves floating in the air. Trinh could almost see the rays of light piercing through the pointed bamboo leaves from faraway bushes at the right-hand side of the camp. *They could have burst into flames, those bamboo bushes, if they waited long enough for the sun to sear the leaves,* Trinh thought wickedly.

Woody Ben was one of Hoan's favourite friends. He had acquired his nickname after the Fall of Saigon. His family was selling wood as a means of income. Trinh was friendly with many of her brothers' friends as she was considered a mere child, unlike her sister Kim, who was just two years older but whom the boys regarded more as a potential date. This made Kim even more timid when they were around. Ben was shy also; he had a boyishly handsome face on a thin, lanky body. He used to come to her house on a motorbike, which in Trinh's eyes at that time was a real luxury. Kim had not dared to be around Ben much as Trinh guessed Ben was besotted with her sister, and obviously, Kim had a hunch as well.

With Ben around, however, Trinh was eager to ask for a lift here and there without fear. She was delighted to sit on the back of his motorbike, holding boldly onto his body whenever she had a chance for a ride. Ben never refused; he saw that as a way of asking Trinh questions about Kim and so leaving Trinh even more ground to pester the older boy. An answer was bartered for an exchange of treats for every question. Ben did not mind, and so Trinh had the pleasure of seeing Ben to satisfy her whims.

Hoan pointed toward a tall, thin young man with a distinctive straw hat and said, "There he is, holding a smoke in his hand, standing against the big gum tree. See him?"

Trinh moved nearer to her brother. Her eyes followed his finger, and she saw a familiar face among the strangers. Woody Ben still looked like a poet from a distance, his mind drifting somewhere above the clouds with the body language of a thinker. *At least his feet were on the ground,* Trinh thought amusedly. Perhaps he was thinking of her sister. Kim was supposed to come today too. As only two travel permits were allowed for her mother and Trinh, it was a pity. Otherwise, Ben would have had an opportunity to come and gaze at Kim for a while. Hoan returned to his mother's side. Trinh left them alone, remaining quiet while her eyes still wandered in every direction.

Through the murmur of conversation from every table came the clicking noise of chopsticks and chewing. The young recruits were enjoying the treats brought by their families.

Returning her attention to her mother and Hoan, Trinh caught her brother's reply.

His voice was soft, but he enunciated clearly, "Yes, I understand your instruction, Mother. I will wait for your letter. Don't worry. I will do my best."

Chi looked carefully at her son again. Her eyes brimmed with tears. The Northern army uniform was still strangely out of place. The AK-47 standing in the corner was even more out of place to her. Eyeing it, her skin tingled at the sights that brought back unpleasant memories.

She nodded her head, speaking softly as well. "I know you are capable of that, Hoan. Just be careful and please do not tell anybody else. Keep everything strictly to yourself, son. And destroy the letter once you have read it please."

Reassured that they understood each other for the planned escape in the next few weeks, Chi reached down into her large bamboo knitted tote bag containing the special lunch she had brought for them and pulled out some small parcels wrapped in fresh green banana leaves. She urged her children, "Have lunch with us before we have to go back. The last bus for Saigon is leaving at three o'clock. We can't afford to be late." Chi could not help but add, "You're too thin."

Placing Hoan's much-loved meal of boiled rice, roast pork, and cabbage wraps on the table, Chi repeated, "Come on, children."

Hoan's eyes widened with excitement at the feast lying in front of them. All the while away from home, his mind was full of imagined aromas from the cooking his mother used to do at home. Without further prompting, Hoan picked up a pair of chopsticks and busily helped himself, placing a thick chunk of roast pork quickly into his mouth. His right cheek expanded with the size of the meat. He chewed on it a bit then moved to his left cheek and chewed a few more times, his usual chewing habit, then swallowed it hastily.

"There's never enough food here," Hoan said in between mouthfuls. "Never!" Hoan repeated his statement as if giving them an explanation for how quickly and hungrily he gulped down his meal. The lunch went by without much small talk. Trinh only had a little, not that she was not hungry but seeing her brother gaunt and thin, she knew that he had not eaten decent food during his stay here. She wanted him to have as much as he could, and so did her mother, Trinh thought. Chi was busy putting pieces of meat and this and that into her daughter's and son's bowls instead of her own throughout the meal.

It was well past noon. The sun was still hot and glaring in the open field. There was not much shade over the red, dusty ground, and only a few small hibiscus bushes were among the banana trees. In the distance were the shadows of hills and mountains that looked to Trinh's eyes as if they were sitting at the end of the horizon, far away and enormous. Trinh wondered if she could ever come back here again.

Gathering up their belongings, they said good-bye to Hoan. Her mother's eyes welled up again.

Trinh looked away, trying not to see his brother's sad face and quivering lips.

"Bye, Hoan. See you when I see you, okay?" Trinh managed quietly, looking down to the red earth beneath her feet.

"Bye, kid. See you soon." Hoan ruffled her hair and looked away, avoiding eye contact as well.

Chi murmured, "Take care, son. I'm praying for your safety every day. Don't disappoint us, Hoan! Please! Promise me!"

"You must promise me!" Mother said forcefully.

"Yes, I promise, Mother. I will be safe," Hoan replied with conviction.

They left the thatched hut through the guarded gates, leaving Hoan behind to wait for a letter with a signal from the family to escape the camp and join them to flee the country.

Woody Ben and the Cambodian War

"HEY BEN, HOW'S your lunch?" Hoan asked.

In his hand was a tin of *thit cha bong* (dried shredded pork), the precious animal protein that everyone was dying for in the camp, packed tightly in an old Guigoz powdered milk tin that his mother had given him. The Guigoz tin was a phenomenon that every household in South Vietnam possessed with pride and used extensively as a container in the sixties to eighties. The powdered infant-formula milk marked families as upbeat and trendy in those times as it was mistakenly being considered as much more preferable than breast milk.

Hoan knew that in order for him to have this half a kilo tin of dried meat, his family had had to skimp on their daily portion to provide him with special treatment. His mother had wrapped the tin in layers of old tattered newspaper as Hoan had instructed as he did not want any of his mates here in the camp to get the impression that he had anything special, especially meat. It was shameful, Hoan had to admit sadly. There had been many occasions in the previous weeks when food was stolen from other recruits, and now everyone was holding tight to their supply; most was hidden carefully or disguised in different forms of containers to avoid being taken. Not many recruits had a family that could afford to visit them or bring them supplies. For growing boys of eighteen or nineteen, the meagre meat ration of 250 grams per month was never enough to satisfy their need. Some had fallen into the obsessive pattern of rummaging through their roommates' supply. Hunger had taken over their sense of morality, and there was no choice but to obey the demands of the stomach, sad as it always was in history.

Even Hoan had shared with his two friends a looted bread roll brought back from Saigon that a mate had hidden in his sack. They had divided the twenty-centimetre-long bread roll equally between the three of them while the owner was being punished severely for breaking out without a permit. After enduring a hundred rods and a whole night of standing upright near the flagpole, cold and hungry, he returned to his bed in the morning exhausted and boiling with rage on finding that his precious bread roll with bacon, liver pate, and salad had disappeared. The delicious aroma had given away the hideout, and so it had gone quickly into the empty stomachs of the boys. In the end, Hoan and others managed to find a packet of instant noodles with half a dozen dried shrimps as a compensation for the poor guy, though it was much less tasty.

Ben looked at Hoan as if that was the silliest question asked, "The lunch? You're asking me about the lunch? It's fucking good! There should be more of that if it's what you mean, Hoan! You must've had a triple good lunch yourself by the look of your deliriously happy face!"

Hoan chuckled at his friend's banal swearing. If there were something he learnt fast in this training camp, it was the foul language. Hoan had rarely sworn before at home, in fact not a single word, but now he picked up the habit readily and used it extensively. It was a way to mollify the exasperation that most of them carried as extra baggage in their life and had no other choice but to let it out through profanity.

"Yeah, twice this month already. I'm getting fat! See here?" Hoan flapped gaily at his expanded belly as proof. "Did you manage to save some lunch for me?"

Then he mimicked his friend with his foul language. "Hey, stop fucking swearing or I won't tell you anything."

"Yeah, right. What's there to tell, and why should I do you that favour, Hoan? Saving some lunch for you! Are you a royal, Hoan?"

"Don't you want to know how my sister's doing?" Hoan teased lightheartedly.

Ben's face turned red immediately; he was still a shy boy after all. He tried to cover his embarrassment by quickly asking, "Your sister, the cheeky little monkey who talks nonstop and laughs at everything?"

Hoan swore. "Bullshit, you know very well which one I mean. It's no use pretending, because I've heard you calling her name in your dreams while you were scratching your hairy balls, Ben!"

"Is that so? I thought I was calling your darling baby's name and fantasised having her as my girlfriend in my sleep every night, Hoan!" Ben retaliated triumphantly.

Hoan jerked up his unloaded AK-47 and playfully pointed it toward Ben then pressed down on the safety catch. "Bang bang, I shoot you down even in your dreams, Ben. Don't you dare think about her!"

Then as an afterthought, he added, "Besides, she doesn't even know that you exist on this earth, mind you! Her heart is already filled with my image. You haven't got a chance, shy boy."

Ben playfully punched Hoan in the stomach in a defensive attack and asked jokingly, "So how's the other sister then? Did you ask if she missed me?"

"Kim was supposed to come today, Ben. But it's Trinh who came instead. She said to say hi to you and said that you still look like a dreaming poet, even in bo doi uniform."

"Yeah, this fucking bo doi uniform, how did we manage to be in it?" Ben said solemnly.

The cheerfulness had evaporated rapidly from the two friends with the mention of their situation. Ben continued angrily, "I only care for cigarettes now, not a fucking poem!"

Woody Ben swore even louder, as if it gave him more relief for his bottled up emotions. The trap he and his friends were in had no opening, and the prospect of the future was frightful to them all. The war with Cambodia was coming closer every day. They were going to be the first to march to the frontier, no doubt about it, Ben often mused. His swearing masked his fear and frustration, and it had increased in intensity lately.

"Got one dong, Hoan?" Ben pleaded in a quieter voice.

He needed a smoke urgently. Headquarters had given him a letter telling Ben of his transfer further south, closer to the border. He had gone in before Hoan, and so his training was considered over. Even though they had not fired a single blank or a real bullet in training, this was it. *Time to get real*, Ben thought, frightened. He did not want to tell Hoan yet, lest his friend be alarmed unnecessarily.

Hoan turned sideways, shielding himself from Ben and picking out a one dong note in his bundle of five hundred dong new currency his mother had given him for the planned escape. He gave it to his friend.

"Here, go easy on the cigarettes, Ben."

Ben turned and walked away to the canteen to get his smoke. Hoan was relieved. Hoan did not want Ben to know that he had a whole half a kilo of dried meat on hand. He would share some with Ben and his other friends eventually, but later; and only after he had divided it into smaller containers, his way to deter the craving, showing them that there was not a lot to be shared. Pitifully, that was the survival instinct of the needy. In order to sustain the long days and nights in this training camp, Hoan had to scheme. He just had to, Hoan reassured himself. There were days when he was starving and had looked with yearning eyes at Ben, lying next to his bed in the same dormitory, having a banquet on just a packet of steaming instant noodles and the tiniest dried prawns. Hoan had drooled, his stomach growling hungrily and his nostrils flaring to inhale the delicious aroma occupying the entire space. Ironically, in normal circumstances, that would have been considered a very simple meal for a down-and-out. He had stood up immediately when Ben was about to discard the remaining soup in his bowl, and gathering up courage that had seemed impossible before, he muttered, "Don't, Ben. Leave that for me. I'll have it please."

Ben looked at Hoan, hesitantly. He was not sure of what to do. The packet of instant noodles was just barely enough for him, and what was left in the bowl was muddy soup and a few dried shallot flakes without anything solid. In the end, he moved away reluctantly to let Hoan have access to it and said in a regretful tone, "Really, Hoan? I didn't know you were hungry too."

Hoan shrugged his shoulders unceremoniously then carried the bowl carefully with the remnant of his best friend's leftover meal to his quarters and poured in the cold boiled rice from his last share. Hoan sat down gulping every grain of rice and savouring the soup to the last spoon in the bowl. It was enough to satisfy his hunger pangs. The most delicious instant noodle soup with boiled rice Hoan had ever eaten!

It was a meal Hoan would never forget as long as he lived.

Those were destitute periods in between visits, Hoan remembered. He was lucky this month with the extra supply and surely had enough to last till the end. Even with stingy measurements and contriving to share frugally, Hoan still ran out of his food supply by the third week. Then he had to rely on his friends' generosity or scheming disposition, just like they had to rely on his earlier. They were Woody Ben and Glassy Ben, two of his high school mates who shared the same fate with him in this journey.

⎯⎯⎯ ✪ ⎯⎯⎯

It had rained for a whole week; the monsoon season had just started. The red earth became soggy, slippery clay. The days were miserable with stuffy humidity, and the nights were chillier in the misty mountain air. He had no more money and nothing else in his bags. The daily meals provided by the camp canteen of diluted porridge and dried salty fish or mixed sweet potato chunks in old, broken rice were inadequate to keep the chill out of his emaciated body. Hoan wanted to go home. He felt so lonely and lost in this unfamiliar environment; it was only his third month, and Hoan already dreaded the time ahead. The cacophony of toads croaking in the long dark hours of hungry nights did not help. He lay in his wooden trench bed listening to this discomforting sound and wondering about his future. Hoan missed Tanya, his high school sweetheart since year eleven. They had been courting for two years before Tanya and her family disappeared. He had been heartbroken and had wandered the streets of Saigon looking for their lost memories. He had succumbed to be conscripted into the army when her letter arrived telling him that she was now in America. His dream of seeing her again seemed hopeless at the time. His first love seemed short-lived and left him empty inside.

Finally, Hoan drifted into a broken sleep, the sound of his stomach growling in concert with the toads' croaking echoing in his ears like a sad, unmelodious lullaby.

"Hey, wake up! What the fuck's up with you, Hoan? It's past eight o'clock already!" Woody Ben shook Hoan's shoulders vigorously through the thick mosquito net.

The sun was shining through the open windows; the corrugated dwelling was hot and humid already. Ben's voice was as if coming from a dream, and in his grogginess, Hoan did not know where he was. The heat and lack of sleep made him even more confused.

Ben shook him again, showing more concern. "Hoan, get up! Are you okay? Today's our turn to dig. Better we start early. Otherwise, the rising sun will roast us alive." His voice was gentler.

Hoan bounced up and out of his dreamlike state in an instant. The dreaded task they had today was to dig a cistern to use as a toilet facility for the whole camp then fill up the old one with the dirt they had dug up. There were ten or so partially covered tents built on top of the holes, creating simple structures from tree trunks and tin roofs, which were used as toilets for the whole camp. They were located further into the jungle. The red clay was as hard as a brick in the dry days but softer to dig after the rain, even though it could become very sticky. They had no choice but to work in the latter conditions.

"Oh shit! Why didn't you wake me up earlier, Ben? It's getting late!"

Hoan bolted out of bed, hurriedly put on his rubber sandals (the Viet Cong sandals that made headlines in the war), and went out with Ben to a row of ceramic urns, some covered by wooden lids and some bare, to wash his face. He reached up a pole to get the shiny hollow coconut shell to use as a pail. It had a long bamboo stick through its upper opening and extended to form a handle at the other end. The shell was smooth and brown, showing grains of lighter colours throughout. It was beautiful in its own natural way.

He stepped onto the raised platform constructed of the wooden trunks of gum trees, bound together with small gaps in between, four poles high in the corners and about three to four metres square. It was used as a wet area and also as a kitchen bench for cooking preparation and washing up dishes, doing laundry, and for general use. They did every chore standing up or squatting down on a small stool, also made of sticks. The platform stood next to a well so deep that Ben and Hoan used to dip their head in and sing some silly tune to hear the sound mysteriously echoing back to them. The well was half-full today after many days of rain, but most of the time, it was so dry that a rope of twenty metres was needed to get some muddy reddish water from it.

There was no toothpaste but a jar of greyish salt to use instead. Hoan dipped his toothbrush into it and quickly went about his routine. The taste of salt had no resemblance to the Colgate minty toothpaste he used to have before the Fall of Saigon, but it did the trick wonderfully by killing some bacteria and refreshing his mouth somehow.

"Oh my, are you going to enter a beauty contest, Hoan? Hurry up!" Ben urged. "Don't be so fucking slow! We won't be able to get done today, Miss Universe!"

"Shut up!" Hoan splashed some water toward Ben in response and stepped off the platform. They strode away quickly carrying shovels, buckets, and a bottle of water in their hands. "And stop swearing!"

The sun was high, and the heat was already strong. The air was muggy and humid. It was very quiet in the jungle; the gum trees were standing still. There was not even a breeze to rustle the leaves. No birds chirping, no insects calling; those had been captured and eaten by hungry men, women, and children throughout the entire country.

The pair walked in silence for five minutes before Hoan broke out, "I'm going to desert soon, Ben."

Ben turned round to look at Hoan and shot out a series of exclamations. "Oh shit! Get real! Oh my god! I knew it! You've been acting fucking strangely in the last few weeks!" Then he added, "How?"

Hoan looked around to make sure they were alone before answering, "I don't know yet, Ben. But I must somehow. My family's going to escape."

"Your family? Everyone?"

"Yes, everyone!" Hoan heard his friend draw a deep breath.

He felt very sad, but somehow glad at the same time. Leaving his friend behind, alone in his ordeal, was something that made Hoan sick at heart, especially knowing of Ben's affection for his sister Kim. The feeling of loss that Ben would face when Kim had gone would perhaps equal his own when Tanya had disappeared a few months ago. His mother had instructed him to keep it a secret, but Hoan was so struck by his friend's loneliness that he just had to share with Ben. Hoan could not leave without saying good-bye to his closest buddy. Ben would have felt betrayed, even though betrayal was happening everywhere in the country right now.

The South Vietnamese were facing a disturbing period during 1975–1978; it seemed they no longer trusted each other. Some families were hiding secrets between members as one son or daughter could have become an informant and brought the whole family to destruction. The son or daughter was a new member of the Communist Party and hoped to gain a step up by being an active informant about any serious plot. Fathers were wary of their sons and avoided talking about the fighting period before the Fall of Saigon, lest they were branded rebels. Teachers were afraid to tell students too much in case they were branded capitalists. Mothers were reluctant to share intimate thoughts with daughters in case they were branded filthy and defiled; either that or vice versa.

But Hoan trusted his friend, and it pained him not to.

After his revelation, they worked in silence digging a large deep trench as a toilet for the whole camp. Hoan did not know what else to say to Ben.

Ben decided not to tell Hoan he was moving out to the battlefield next Monday week. He did not want his friend to worry for him.

The next afternoon, Hoan left camp after persuading the guard to let him out to buy some cigarettes for both of them. Hoan left the guard with his watch as collateral, a precious possession in the mind of the Northern soldier. A watch, a radio, and a bicycle— those three were the most wanted items in the postwar period. Hoan took up his courage and just walked out of camp. He did not dare to run nor quicken his pace; he hitchhiked and walked home, pretending to be on leave whenever anyone interested to ask. Even in his desertion, he carried his AK-47, albeit without ammunition, on his shoulder for the whole trip; and that added some sort of protection miraculously. The bus driver and other passengers eyed him warily, thinking he was a Northern soldier.

Ben and Hoan did not say good-bye to each other. It was not until half a year later that Hoan got news of his friend's death in the Cambodia-Vietnam war in 1978. All Ben had was a mere two days in combat.

There was never an official death count, but it was estimated at fifteen to thirty thousand casualties in the Vietnamese army with more than thirty thousand wounded and more than a hundred thousand Cambodian civilians dead during the decade of war between Cambodia and Vietnam during 1977–1989. The figures excluded the famine that killed more than half a million Cambodians between 1979–1980 after the fall of the Khmer Rouge and the horrendous Killing Fields of two million deaths that reduced the population figure of Cambodia in half.

PART 2:

THE SEARCH FOR FREEDOM

The Second Currency Change

The Planning
May 2, 1978

THREE YEARS HAD gone by. During the last few months, Trinh noticed hushed talks in the back of the house between her mother and her brother-in-law, Mac, late in the evenings and in the small hours of the mornings.

They decided to organise an escape for the whole family after his agonising, failed trip with his wife, Giang, and their eleven-month-old daughter in late December last year. He was left behind together with many other men and was angry at the inefficiency of the people involved in coordinating the escape. They were supposed to join their wives and children who had been hoisted onto the ship moored offshore earlier that night. There had been a miscalculation in the time taken to move all the men on board from the smaller dinghies to the ship. It left without half the men, for lingering any longer would have jeopardised the entire escape by drawing attention from the coastal patrol police.

Mac had returned home alone in the morning in the very early hours, and woken all of them by his sudden reappearance. He had travelled back home after spending the dark, suspense-filled night hiding in a thatched hut near the shore. Together with the other men left behind, cowering with fear and apprehension, he had to wait until the coast was clear again to leave. If caught, he would be charged with attempted escape, and that would mean torture and imprisonment for an unknown term. The chance of getting out of gaol and breaking away again would be much harder. However, quick to assess the damage, Mac returned home and reported to work immediately as if nothing had happened during the night. Exhausted with anxiety and traumatised by the incident, he was relieved at his narrow escape from the coastal police.

Trinh looked at him sitting quietly in his bedroom at the rear of their house for a brief moment before getting ready for work. His eyes were red, and his face was haggard with tiredness. She felt a pang, knowing that he was so worried for his wife and daughter on board the ship and moving further and further away from him every minute. *He might not see them again*, Trinh thought sadly.

Looking up from his sorrow, he waved his hand and motioned her closer.

"Giang and Kate have gone. I hope for their safety. I am okay," he said and smiled awkwardly, trying to hide his weariness. "Aren't you about to get going for school too?"

She nodded and swallowed the lump in her throat then hurried out of his sight to avoid the melancholy feeling in the air.

Mac had returned to work and started his planning almost immediately. He and Mother had chosen their rendezvous at Ninh Kieu Market at Can Tho, a popular port for most escapees. They decided to outsmart the system by using the regular port, doing the expected at an unexpected moment.

The previous currency "liberation dong" in the South was volatile. No one believed in its value after the first currency change in the South following the Fall of Saigon in September 1975. The bank notes could be turned into useless paper trash overnight by the unexpected change of currency. Eighteen-carat gold was used instead; and gold nuggets, each weighing approximately 37.5 grams, were the main medium of barter for most large transactions. The gold was divided into smaller portions as leaf of one-tenth or one-twentieth nuggets for ease of use as well.

Through a labyrinth of introductions and contacts, Mother had established rapport with the politburo party members or coastal guards on various occasions in preparation for the escape. With sufficient reward, the other organisers would bribe their way by giving the authority large amounts of cash or gold nuggets to ensure their smooth operation and secure the hours of boarding on the departure date. The authority would turn a blind eye, and the escapees were supposed to be protected during those particular hours, or so it seemed. However, there were cases where the party members or coastal guards or both could turn treacherous and arrest them if the price were not enough to satisfy their greed. Both parties would face harsh punishment if discovered. Alternatively, if either party turned whistle-blower on the other one, then the whole operation would be aborted and mayhem would result, unless even more bribes were offered. There were so many stakes involved that trust had to be part of it. Ironically, the trust that came from joint clandestine adventures was normally a two-edged sword. Neither party was able to seek justice if it were betrayed.

Chi knew how peculiar and how irrational it was to plan for the family to escape regardless of the uncertain outcome, but it was what Vietnamese people did during those years. Desperation was another word for it as what else could they hope for in the future? Dying out there at sea or suffering right here in their own house was very much the same; the living conditions and the suppression were far more than they could stand. Escaping meant they might have a chance to breathe in the air of freedom again, and to escape was the only solution they could think of then. They just wanted to get out of the country, away from the Vietnamese communists, and that was enough, regardless of arriving anywhere else.

During that extraordinary period, Chi was prepared to leave everything behind, even her own life and the lives of her beloved family, just to gain the precious freedom that was taken away from them. She was prepared to risk it all and take a one-way ticket to reach either a safe haven or, for some unfortunate souls, horrific hell.

However, there are profits to be gained in destruction as always. The exodus had provided riches for people traffickers who reaped enormous fortunes by charging each person five gold nuggets per head. One gold nugget had enough cash value to effectively sustain a family of five to six members with enough food for a year. The traffickers and their accomplices were comrades in high positions in the Communist Party, who had enormous power to impose any law or stage any coup anywhere at any time in the South. They had the authority to grant "visas" for the Vietnamese boat people in their semiofficial modus operandi. They were inadvertently the culprits driving many South Vietnamese boat people to their deaths.

Without the courage and boldness to plan the escape, Chi knew that her family would never have a chance. They were living on a day-to-day basis only by her modest profit through trading in the stretch of territory from Phan Thiet and Saigon, a route of three hundred kilometres. Chi became a frequent traveller, managing to feed her family during those difficult times. She could never have saved enough gold nuggets to afford the price of escape for her family of eight. The only chance was to plan from scratch with two other distant relatives for each of their own families to escape together, and Chi and Mac had managed to organise it with limited finance. In fact, they had used every penny for the preparations to purchase the boat, fuel, compass, food, water, and other necessities.

The time for the departure date was set for approximately three months after the commencement of the operation, the shortest time possible to prepare and strike without raising suspicion. There was no time to lose. They had no choice but to let their fate be determined by luck. The boat could not remain idling at the mooring for very long without being noticed. After many nights of deliberating about alternatives, they decided to take their chances and would just board the dinghies by nightfall at Ninh Kieu Marketplace on May 15, 1978, D-day. Their bet was all or nothing for a glorious jackpot, out of the country in search for freedom or a total loss, empty-handed. This was it. They hoped that the time was right when the South was still in the turmoil of the second currency change.

Their escape was scheduled two weeks after the second currency change, and the latter happened on Tuesday, May 2, 1978.

A few days before that historical event, Mac was curious to notice that many party members working in his office suddenly decided to purchase everything available in the state department stores, from large notable valuable items like bicycles, radios, and watches down to smaller items like sugar, rice, fish sauce, and so on. The stores were almost empty by Saturday. Even though the quality of many items in the stores was not as high as in private trade, every long-term party member seemed to be determined to acquire them all. Through his observation, and by instinct and sheer luck, Mac went out to purchase gold nuggets that Sunday with most of his cash. It struck home to Mac when a total curfew was announced on the Monday night, followed by the second important event that once again shocked the whole South. The second currency change was to take place the next morning, and the inside information was given to long-term party members beforehand as previously!

"Twice within three years!" Mac was shocked but not surprised.

He was shocked at their attempt to rob the South of their wealth the second time, but he was not surprised at their malicious intentions. He knew the purpose behind this historical event was to maintain total control of the people of the South, snuffing out any rebellious endeavours and pursuing a foolish determination to abolish capitalism as well as reverse their uncontrollable rate of inflation. It was very clever indeed, the cleverness of the cold-blooded criminals. Once more, the rate of exchange was five hundred old liberation dong in the South for one new united Vietnamese dong, meaning fifty thousand old liberation dong to change to a total of one hundred new united Vietnamese dong. The government decreed that each household was allowed to change a maximum of one hundred new united Vietnamese currencies, regardless of how much they had in their possession, as happened before at the first currency change, but only half of the amount this second time.

During that time, with regard to the new united Vietnamese dong, the average blue-collar factory worker received forty net per month and white-collar classes like teachers, engineers, architects, doctors, etc. received an average of fifty to sixty-five net per month. The Communist government considered that a household should only possess one hundred in cash; a mere two months' wages irrespective of how much they had saved! Even if a household had one million, five hundred thousand, or fifty thousand cash in old currency, they would only receive a maximum of one hundred in new currency in return. The rest of their cash would be useless by the next day. It was appalling. There was again no compensation, no consideration, and no explanation from the government for their action. The citizens of Communist Vietnam simply could not have that surplus amount in their possession. It was against their policies!

Mac was angry and sad for his people. *It was pure robbery, an act of barbarism in the history of Vietnam, or perhaps in the history of the world,* Mac thought. Only the Vietnamese Communist government could have managed to inflict upon its citizens such treatment, the Party that had its own method to suit its doctrines and condemn its citizens on its path! He was so glad that he was leaving. Dead or alive, Mac could not bear to coexist with them any longer.

"After boarding the dinghies discreetly from the river port, we will be carried to the main boat waiting near the mouth of the bay. The plan is to try and dodge the coastal border observation station and quickly get out to international waters or the high seas as the first step, then to try to get to the nearest neighbouring coastal region and hope for the best," Mac explained to them during the family meeting.

They could not afford to bribe the port, but Chi still had to ask the Nink Kieu station ferry chief to hire dinghies for them.

"Please accept this one-tenth leaf of gold as our token of thanks, Mr. Man. The date is Thursday next week. Please make sure you have enough dinghy operators around the port between 6:00 p.m. and 10:00 p.m. to cover our boarding." Chi put the leaf of eighteen-carat gold in between the sticky rice cakes wrapped in coconut leaves and discreetly handed it to Mr. Man, the station chief. This was not the first time she had to bribe him. However, due to the final escape date, this was the most difficult time of all. Previously she had more cash. The whole country had had the second currency change thirteen days ago, and they could not buy enough new currency in time. What luck it was that Mac had bought gold nuggets before the dramatic change, and Chi had a few gold nuggets left to use for the last bet?

"How many of you are going to be here?" Mr Man quickly pocketed the gold leaf and peeled a rice cake to eat. He chewed noisily; the string of beige coconut leaves trailed a good metre from his hand. His chubby fingers were short, and he had a gold ring on his little finger, a thick gold chain on his left wrist. Helping people to escape seemed to be ludicrously prosperous. Each time an escape was about to take place, he and his mates netted a substantial amount of gold leaf each. There had been a continuous flow of business ever since last year, and it was increasing in frequency. They had a rendezvous on almost every second day at Ninh Kieu Marketplace.

"There are going to be around fifty of us. I need you to hire six dinghies with rotor operators to bring us to the main vessel moored out there, sometime after dark. Please allow them to do the rounds for us. Thank you so much, Mr. Man. We won't forget your kindness. You'll be rewarded even more after we're safely out there," Chi reassured him, playing on his greed.

"Okay, leave it to me, Madame Chi. I'll take care of everything. Don't you worry!" He threw the palm leaf wrappings on the ground and walked away.

During the peak two years of 1978–1979, desperate South Vietnamese were impelled to take to the sea in groups of fifty to a hundred, two hundred, or even larger numbers in crowded boats. No matter what size and shape their boats were, whether seaworthy and reliably constructed or not, the South Vietnamese were willing to test their chances by boarding the vessels and taking to the sea. Their rationality was overwhelmed in their sheer determination to get out of the country and get away from the ruthless suppression imposed upon them by the government. The people were appalled at how brutally they were treated. They felt there was no hope for a change for the better, and they saw the government as rotten to the core. There were no other alternatives but to leave. Everyone knew that a change of government was impossible under the "democracy" of the single-party system.

The exodus was a historical event that sent shock waves across the continents with over a million South Vietnamese fleeing their homeland. It was also horrifying to realise that the sea became a mass grave, with approximately half a million deaths at sea, making an approximately 60 percent of survivors who reached land safely.

D-Day

May 15, 1978

TODAY WAS D DAY. Trinh got up the moment Mother touched her lightly on her shoulders. She had slept fitfully and was waiting anxiously in the darkness for the signal. Kim was already up as well. The sisters averted their eyes from each other, avoiding all communications that might break the thin layer of calmness each tried to display.

It was five o'clock in the morning. The air was cool with a touch of dampness like most early mornings in the rainy monsoon season. A few noisy scooters were passing the house, invading the stillness of the empty streets, which would be flooded with traffic in a couple of hours. Light was scarcely visible outside when Trinh peeped through a little hole in the rustic iron folding doors.

She was ready, out of bed, and quickly dressed in a simple outfit like a village girl with black satin pyjama pants and a white peasant blouse, the almost identical outfit that most of the girls and women in their group were wearing that day.

"Oh, I'm so excited!" Trinh told Kim. "But I'm scared too."

Kim nodded her head. "Yeah, me too."

Trinh then left her sister alone and walked to the front trellis door. Pressing her nose against its little holes, she breathed in the fresh air of the early morning. She was not allowed to open it yet, but she loved the crisp, clean oxygen in the air now without smoke and fume later from traffic pollution. Trinh hated the smell as her nose was very keen. Making a ninety-degree turn, she looked eagerly at the old cuckoo clock hanging on the wall of her family lounge, waiting for the time to depart. *That clock had been there ever since she could remember, something from the house that she was going to miss,* Trinh thought. Mingling with the sadness of saying goodbye to the house she had been living in for an entire sixteen years and the unforeseen adventure of getting out of the country was an unexplained butterfly feeling in her stomach. The family had been planning this escape for almost half a year.

Today, she was about to embark on an adventure! Excitement was very much in the young girl's mind at that time. The dangers at sea and the unknown fatalities of many other boat people were meaningless to the sixteen-year-old girl. After three years under the Communists, she was relieved to be leaving the country.

"Are you ready, Trinh?" Mother asked.

"Yes, Mother. I'm ready,"

They were the first group to leave. Kim and Vy, her other sister, would be next. The family was divided into groups this morning to go to the station to catch a bus to Can Tho, the rendezvous, where they would be meeting again to board small dinghies to the larger vessel further out. They left their house in pairs starting at the crack of dawn, then at half hour intervals. Mac was the last to leave. Trinh's older brother, Dien, had already gone to the rendezvous two days ago. Luc, her younger brother, had been disguised as a busboy on the boat since last month. Hoan, her older brother, had boarded the boat a few months ago. Her father had also been on board as a boat keeper since the day they had bought the vessel. This was a one-off chance. If anything were to go wrong, the whole family might be left homeless and could not return to Saigon to live.

"Yes, Mother," Trinh repeated, seeing that in her preoccupied state of mind, Mother did not hear her reply.

"Here, carry your own bag. Take good care of it." Back to her senses, Mother then handed Trinh the small bamboo-woven hamper.

There were not many things in it, just some of her clothes. Trinh swiftly slipped her small address book inside. Mother would not be pleased as they had to avoid suspicion at all cost. She had moved most things down to the boat previously in her many trips during the organising period.

Mother had already booked a familiar motorised rickshaw to bring them to the bus station. He was waiting outside with his motor running noisily, which made Mother wince for fear of being noticed too much. The motorised rickshaw was a rear-engine-operated open vehicle, with the driver's seat on top of it behind the passenger seat. He stepped down from his high seat with the steering handlebars on top of the engine and made a gesture to help Mother carry our bags, but Mother waved him aside dismissively. They hopped onto his vehicle, trying to get clear of their house as quickly as possible.

Trinh looked at her house for the last time, trying not to cry. Her excitement in the early hours was replaced by her anxiety of saying good-bye to everything she had known all her life.

The midmorning of April 1975 when she had witnessed the Fall of Saigon was still fresh in her mind. She had stood there in silence, eyes wide in shock, with many others in front of their house. The impact of seeing the bicoloured red-and-blue flags with the centre yellow star of the Vietnamese Communists, once their enemies, so close to home was frightening. The image of the flag flying on the North Vietnamese army tanks, which looked strangely unfamiliar from afar, then approaching menacingly, was still vivid in her mind. She could still see the painful, disbelieving looks of many adults. They were swiftly exchanged for a blank, emotionless stare toward the parade of victory from the North Vietnamese Army. The impact of the shock in that first few hours was made even more unnatural by the peculiar silence in the air.

All that had left an unusually powerful image, disturbing to a young girl. Three years of cruelty had passed since then. Trinh was so glad to get away today, to escape to the free world. Her once-beloved country was no longer a dear place in her heart. School was not the place for a young mind to learn new theories and practise common science. Most time was spent on political subjects and on mimicking the phrases of Karl Max, Lenin, Mao Tse Tung, and Ho Chi Minh like parrots. Grades were based not only on how smart you were but how well the student absorbed the political propaganda, and without an A or B in the latter subject, there was no chance of gaining an A or B overall. From kindergarten kids to university undergraduates, all had to pass this stage before being able to gain places in school or universities. She was so sick of being told what to worship and of learning fabricated history that even a young child had found hard to believe.

A few droplets of dew from the dense foliage of trees along the kerb landed on her hair and startled the girl. The motorised rickshaw carrying Mother and Trinh passed her high school. It brought her mind back to the present. The young girl was awash with emotions. Her small body was not yet fully developed. Her face was round, and the jaw was strong, with short tapered hair around the neck. She sat beside her mother, sharing the same narrow seat. Young as she was in appearance, Trinh had matured more than her age in other aspects. Sweet sixteen, the most acclaimed stage of a maturing young woman, was lost in her life. The carefree, lighthearted moments were scarce. Laughter was mingled with bitterness, a kind of black humour. There were no candles and flowers to celebrate this coming of age but images of war and the brutal reality of daily life to deal with. There was no doubt that her virtue was as pure and crystal-clear as a mountain spring, but there were sad thoughts and harsh, hurtful images in those troubled years that lingered longer than necessary.

She changed her position slightly and glanced backward all the while the rickshaw went past the entire length of her school. The tall, iron gates were locked, looking forbidding and austere. The high wall stretching along the perimeter and facing the street divided the worlds into two: theory and practice. The school had an air of mystery at that moment as the trickle of light in the early morning was not enough to penetrate the darkness, and that also left an impression of indifference. She felt sadder. Trinh wanted to look closely at her high school for the last time. She wanted the rickshaw to stop so she could come near the gates. Everywhere she looked was for the last time. She was leaving the country for good. She wanted to memorise the streets, the trees, the leaves, the background, the surroundings, and her friends, her people. She would like to keep everlasting pictures in her heart.

Her schoolyard was a sweet memory in her heart, but even the subjects that were taught there were strange to her after the Fall of Saigon. Her school was not as dear to her as she remembered it in the past. But she remembered the same dear tiny leaves from tamarind trees, yellowish in colour, falling, falling on the ground on windy days. And there were jacaranda trees with early blossoms of reddish flowers, bright in the summer sun and scattered about the paths. They were the two most popular trees found in most schools of the south. Oh, how she wished to see her classroom for the last time! It was on the first floor looking directly down at the main assembly area, almost on a straight line with the school flagpoles.

Damn! Trinh suddenly recalled. She had forgotten to return the schoolbooks! It was the last week of school, and Trinh wanted it not to be noticed that she did not return the books earlier in fear of being discovered. As ordered strictly by Mac and her mother, she was not supposed to disclose their secretive plan of escape to anyone else. Trinh only told four people, her closest best friends, and repeatedly asked them to keep it a secret for her. See, she did not tell the whole class, of course! Trinh reassured herself that she had obeyed her mother in some degree. She could not resist giving Lan her fountain pen, Xuan her diary, Oanh her handkerchief, and Thao her book of pressed flowers as souvenirs. The girls had cried together and whispered their farewells a few nights before.

"You're so lucky, Trinh. I'm going to miss you."

"Please write to us as soon as you can and please be safe! Don't worry, your secret is secure with us. Right, girls?"

They all nodded in agreement.

"Be careful, Trinh. I've heard many sad stories. I'll pray for you!"

"Oh, I wish I were you! Your family is so lucky to be able to organise their escape. Everyone is wishing the same thing."

"Don't forget to write to us, Trinh, please!"

For the entire time of organising the trip, they did their best to divert suspicion by going about their normal daily chores without any deviation in their activities. Trinh still had to queue for necessities with coupons and ration books as before. Although the time spent queuing under the scorching sun was very long, Trinh had felt as if it went faster. She did not feel as frustrated when she went home empty-handed after one or two futile hours fidgeting in lines and was told that there was nothing available for her.

She was going to escape. The girl started to daydream about the new life she was going to live. She would not have to queue for food anymore. She would be able to read her books and listen to her music as before. She would be free of propaganda, of absurd communist idealism, from restrictions on movement and speech, and of being under the control of her stomach! Oh, how she would love to be herself! She had to pretend to follow doctrines that went against her beliefs for the last three years. She could stop her play-acting once she was out of Vietnam. She would return to her true self in the free world.

Freedom was the dream of many boat people who tried to escape and were ignorant of probable death. They were very naive, Trinh realised that now. After so many years had gone by after the day her family stepped onto the small boat in search of a new life, Trinh always wondered at how simply and easily many of them, her family and others, thought about their escape. In her mind, it was as if once they got away from the Vietnam coast there would be a welcome party waiting with open arms to help them reach their goal, showering them with love and attention! Trinh thought of the open sea as literally as mild and docile as a giant river. How foolish of her!

Mother held her hand lightly, pulling it to her lap, as if to stop Trinh from fidgeting about.

"We're almost there," she reassured Trinh softly, her face serene, as if empty of thoughts.

Poor Mother; she was a figure of strength and femininity all in one. Trinh knew that her Mother was as anxious as she was, and she did not want to disturb her for fear of falling apart.

Chi breathed deeply and steadily, keeping herself from shaking with anxiety. Her hand entwined with Trinh's, the youngest of her brood of seven, and she was grateful for the body warmth emanating from the girl's closeness. The innocent face of her young girl, unaware of the danger ahead, touched her heart like a sudden throbbing pain. Looking away to dampen her feelings, Chi told herself to be calm. There was too much at stake to lose if she were to panic now.

Chi's decision to leave the country was reinforced after her oldest daughter, Giang's, escape to Sydney, Australia, a direct journey from Vung Tau. She missed Giang and her granddaughter, Kate, dearly. It was the first time ever that Giang, the eldest of her children, was away from her. She was so far away. Chi sighed quietly. The thought of not being able to see the two of them again in her life was so unbearable that Chi had agreed readily when Mac started talking about escape for the whole family. It was a risk she had to decide on alone as Chi had become head of the family ever since her husband lost all interest in the devastated country and his surroundings after the Fall. He became reclusive and left Chi to manage their lives.

The sun was beginning to show its presence, glaring at her, heating the misty air, and increasing the humidity rapidly. The streets were noisier and busier with traffic when they got closer to the bus station. At her feet was the small nylon hamper containing some food for them on this short trip. Most of the journey preparations had been done a few weeks before, and everything was already aboard the boat.

"Watch where you're going, bastard!" a pedestrian growled angrily at the driver, his index finger pointing aggressively as he swirled around avoiding the motorised rickshaw at the sharp turn. The driver quietly mouthed a "Fuck you!" in response before slowing down completely to a full stop at the busiest section of the station. Chi pulled out a wad of bills to pay him generously but not overgenerously, to avoid raising the suspicion of the busybody onlookers. They were staring at them, curious at the two women who were tentatively stepping out onto the kerb.

They were different! Chi thought resignedly. It did not matter how much she tried to blend in to become a peddler like every other woman; Chi knew that she looked strangely out of character. Her voice was as soft and clear as a young girl. Her delicate skin was a betrayal to all the disguise she put on. Her language was polite and gentle, the kind that street vendors never used. They often had to ask her to repeat what she said and laughed amusedly as if hearing those words for the first time.

"What did you say? Say it again," One would ask, and another one would mimic Chi's voice. "I beg your pardon." Then they would roar in laughter uncontrollably.

Chi remembered the beginning of her life as a peddler. She had become a traveller going to places along the highways from the southern point of Ca Mau to the high land of Phan Thiet, a stretch of six hundred kilometres that Chi had never dreamed of travelling alone in her previous life. With the help of her cousins, whose truck was a means to transport goods of various kinds back and forth between those places, Chi joined them and was able to bring food to her family by doing a similar exchange. Her trip was once every two or three weeks, and she had to live in the vehicle among the goods. The women had a tiny corner inside the truck, just big enough to stretch out to sleep at night. The men used the bottom of the vehicle as shelter in the dry season. In the rainy season, all four of them had to scramble into the limited space available. The stench of those sweaty men and the humidity in the confined space were the worst that Chi had to suffer in those longest nights. She was hardly able to breathe. Her hands and feet were calloused from carrying heavy baskets of goods containing rice, sugar, and fish sauce, and walking long distances in her sandals. Her skin darkened from many hours of harsh sunlight but retained its delicate softness, as Chi was always careful in concealing her face from damaging UV rays. The change in appearance of a once beautiful, elegant, and street-shy woman was subtle, but Chi knew that her life had changed for good.

A woman in her midforties, Chi had never ventured out of the door without her husband at her side before the Fall of Saigon. She had never handled anything more than keeping the house and raising her children dutifully like an Oriental woman of her time. A much-protected wife and mother of an affluent family, Chi was totally aghast at being thrown into dealing with almost everything in this new life. Chi realised that she had to adapt and had gathered all her courage, becoming a street vendor whose profit was just barely enough to keep her children safely at home with enough food and necessities.

"Are you hungry yet, Trinh?" Chi asked her daughter.

Trinh was looking in fascination at the activities around the station. People were everywhere. Mother had emphasised many times at home in the drill before the actual trip that she must keep an eye on her belongings all the time, especially at the station where pickpockets and snatchers were quick to strike. Food stalls were selling a variety of cakes wrapped in dark banana leaves in many shapes and sizes. There were attractive steamed white pork buns, offering a delicious aroma and causing her stomach to growl hungrily. It was seven o'clock now. She had been up at five and did not eat well at all the dinner before in her agitation at the coming adventure.

"Yes, Mother. What can I have?" she asked softly, not sure if she was supposed to have anything from the stalls but wishing that she could.

Chi smiled at her daughter, giving the young girl encouragement. Trinh beamed with pleasure, happy at the thought of having a treat at this trying time.

"That one?" She pointed toward the pork bun stall, opening her eyes wide and waiting for her mother's approval. She could not wait to hold one of those soft, fluffy white buns in her hands to feel its warmth and inhale its delicious meaty flavour. Chi nodded then hurriedly went after the girl as Trinh sprinted to the stall at top speed even before her mother's nod completed its movement.

The Bus Trip

"WE'RE GOING TO get out of the country at last!" Kim whispered.

"Oh, I love the suspense! It's stimulating!" Trinh rolled her eyes upward, stretched her arms against her sides, and pretended to give her body a free fall backward for a moment then breathed in deeply, steadying her balance. They both giggled quietly, easing their tension a little.

They could not risk being discovered and were very jumpy, but they were excited at the same time. The apprehension of travelling to Can Tho and dodging many inspection stations to reach the rendezvous was electrifying. They had never been in a situation like this before, unlike others who had failed after several attempts and ended up in jail. Careful planning and all, James Bond's style or not, how plain it was in the end! Because, even though they had started the journey separately from home, leaving in groups of two in half-hour intervals by different transports, they all had ended up on the same bus, travelling the same route.

In hindsight, Trinh smiled at the simplicity of their thinking at that time. An acute observer would have guessed that there was something unusual going on. Coincidentally, without knowing it, and despite efforts to pretend to be peasants going about their normal daily lives, more than half the passengers on that early morning commercial bus were going to be on the same trip and had the same goal: escape to the sea! Out of the total fifty passengers, thirty were in the plan. The bus was bringing them to Can Tho, a provincial city a hundred kilometres to the southwest of Saigon as the departure port. They all looked out of place and were shy in their outfits, with the clean, pale skin unmistakably typical of city girls and women, not the harsh weather-beaten, dark leathery skin that most peasants had.

Mother sat a few rows in front with Trinh. Kim and Vy were at the back. They pretended not to know each other or any other passengers on the bus. Every time the bus stopped at an inspection station, Mother began to worry. Before it came to a complete standstill, Mother turned and eyed the sisters silently, discreetly signalling for them to stay quiet by putting her finger to her lips.

"Don't talk, Trinh," she whispered, firing a string of successive "don'ts." "Don't look at them, the guards, or the officers. Look away or down at your feet. Do not let them see your face. Don't let them suspect anything, child. And don't fidget about." She squeezed her hand lightly in encouragement. None of them had obtained any permit, and if caught by the inspector without the official paper, then they would all be doomed.

Trinh nodded her head quietly and snuggled closer to her mother, wishing they had already arrived. Sitting in the crowded bus, they had passed two inspection stations already. It would take at least another three hours at this rate. Trinh sighed heavily. The guards were looking for escapees and peddlers with prohibited goods. Since 1978, when the exodus of boat people began, travelling had become even more challenging than before. Travellers had to obtain permits to go distances as short as a kilometre if he or she was to stay overnight at that destination. Similarly, unless with an authorised permit, transporting anything was prohibited by the Vietnamese Communist government after the war ended. The smuggler was considered a black market peddler, even for as little as five kilos of meat or ten kilos of rice. So much so for rules and intricate patterns of authoritative layers of the Communist System; however, with bribes, everything was possible!

The profits from exploiting the escapees and black market peddlers attracted the guards and officers at every inspection station. With the pretext of reinforcing security measures and collectivism, the authority at each local station had enormous power to terrorise the travellers. Their eagerness to earn extra income from solicited bribes or confiscated goods encouraged them to be vigilant in their duties.

Luckily, their bus passed the last two stations in peak-hour traffic. The line of vehicles waiting for inspection seemed to Trinh about a kilometre long, and the guards were so busy they were waving vehicles through to speed up the process. Their bus dodged inspection by sheer luck, a relief for all of them. However, at the last station, they would have to be searched. Trinh knew that and waited in apprehension when the bus slowed down to a full stop.

"Everyone, get off the bus for inspection," the young driver's assistant yelled at the top of his voice over the chattering of his passengers. "Leave all your belongings on the bus, folks."

This was going to be a big test! Trinh thought. Would they be all right? Would they be able to avoid the guard's suspicion? How would she cope if she were in jail? Who was going to visit her if all their family members were caught? Would her friends know? Who would write to her? Mother squeezed her hands and signalled the sisters as previously, jerking Trinh out of her scenarios. She had put on a mask of calmness, and Trinh heard her mantra chanting under her breath. The passengers got slowly off the bus. Many showed their nervousness clearly; their eyes fluttered, and their steps wavered. Some girls were clinging tightly to their mothers. Waiting for her turn and having something to occupy her mind with, Trinh counted roughly fifty passengers on the small bus. The majority were female. Some were middle-aged, some were over fifty, and there were a few young women and teenagers like Kim and her. Trinh then made a quick calculation in her head. Only the three old men among them, with the driver and his assistant, brought the percentage of males to females to 10 percent. *Perhaps most men were still in reeducation camps*, the girl reflected.

"Come on. Hurry up, folks! We haven't got all day!" the middle-aged driver urged, yelling from his front seat. He was getting impatient. His bus was behind schedule, and he hated that. He boasted to his passengers of always being on time. "Damn it! No time for me to visit my mistress before going home tonight," he mumbled to himself. Bloody hell!

All the passengers were edgy. Chi knew that it was not because they had something to hide but because there were no rights or laws to protect them. Their fate depended very much on the whims of the local officers and guards, the ultimate arbiters of the law. Anyone wearing a uniform or displaying a badge was enough to terrify people. Local rules and state rules were sometimes only remotely related; a permit carrying a stamp from one town might be meaningless in another. That terrified people still more as uniforms could transform the wearers into God-like figures at any time, any day. Consequently, the fear of authority was indescribable. Anyone could be accused of a crime at any time without a chance of offering a legitimate defence. That feeling of terror from authority stayed with Chi and other Vietnamese in her generation for many years later on.

Trinh noticed that a pretty young woman, two rows down from her, was reluctant to leave the vehicle. She was looking uneasily at the two large hampers underneath her seat. A small child perched skilfully on her hips, leaning to one side. Trinh could also see that she was flustered; her steps were slow and her face ashen. The little boy was whimpering softly. His feet were bare, and he was wearing colourful home-sewn boxer shorts that were much larger than his skinny chicken legs. The fading cream shirt was crudely sewn, with the last two buttons missing, exposing his big belly and prolapsed belly button. The distended belly was out of proportion with his bony ribcage, an indication of threadworm infestation, playing-detective Trinh deduced. Ah, but the prolapsed navel might also be the result of excessive crying from constant hunger and neglect, Trinh concluded with satisfaction, observing the mother and child.

"Hurry up, woman!" the driver urged, jerking mother and child down the steps. She was the last one to get off the bus. Her collarless cotton blouse was plain grey, with sewing on square pockets on both sides. Her black satin pyjama pants were now charcoal from many washes and wears over the years. On her feet was a pair of black thongs with dark grey straps, the heels wafer-thin. She was wearing a conical palm-leaf hat on her head and a grey chin-strap that matched her blouse with part of her hair showing under the hat. Overall, it was the typical dress of the peasant in this part of the South. Even though her clothes were plain and showed signs of wear and tear, the young woman still looked tidy and self-respecting.

The young guard in the light green army uniform, carrying an AK-47 on his shoulder, was standing next to the inspector ready to board the bus. The inspector was a middle-aged man, his uniform was of the same colour as the guard's, with two yellow stars sewn onto red fabric on either side of his shirt collar. He stepped onto the vehicle without a smile, a small baton held behind his back. On his feet were the open-toed rubber sandals, typical footwear of the North Vietnamese Army, showing chipped fungal-infected nails that were black and deformed. His face was cold and harsh, as if being friendly would not show off his power or create the fear he wished to instil. He walked slowly toward the back of the bus, poking into hampers and luggage beneath the passengers' seats.

"Whose hampers are these?" Suddenly, his voice boomed. He motioned to the young guard to pull out the two large hampers belonging to the young woman with the little boy. He was very pleased with his detection. Ah hah, he would show them who was in charge here. Three years had passed since he was stationed here, and still he could not shake off the inferiority complex he had with Southerners. They always made him feel small just by their gaze. How peculiar that was!

Never mind, at last there was something here today, he told himself. The whole morning, up and down, there had been many buses without any reward, and he was not amused. Damn those cunning Southerners! They were getting smarter every day. They knew how to hide their goods and cheat him. It was harder to catch them now, stupid low-life peasants! But look at these hampers! Beneath the tattered clothes and bunches of sugar bananas were the treasures he craved.

Prohibited goods were meagre amounts: ten kilograms of rice; one kilogram of pork, two kilograms of brown cane sugar, twenty or so loose cigarettes. That was enough to be charged as a profiteer trading in prohibited goods and for the goods to be confiscated on the spot. The offender could face severe beatings and days, weeks, or months in detention without trial. Few might escape their fate by bribing officers. However, the bribe might be more than the value of their goods, and so some peddlers just preferred to abandon them to avoid beatings and detention.

"Whose goods are these?" He repeated his question, his voice booming louder this time, several decibels higher and even angrier.

No one dared to speak up. Mother held Trinh's hand tightly, the dampness of her sweat made their grip slippery and clammy. But Trinh did not try to break away. She was afraid of any movement that might draw attention to them. She leaned against her mother for protection and peered through the gaps of the crowd. Mother understood the woman's dilemma as she had been caught under similar circumstances a few months before with five kilograms of rice brought back home for the family in Saigon. Luckily, she was released on the spot as the driver had befriended the inspector on many occasions before. He was her cousin and had helped her out, with bribery, of course. However, she knew that was a narrow escape as she could have faced the same misfortune as this young woman.

"Where did you find them, comrade officer?" The driver stepped up and asked tentatively. He wanted to get on with his trip and get out of here as quickly as possible. They were late already, and he did not want to be held responsible to his boss.

"At row number 10 in the middle seat. Do you know who they belong to, driver?"

The driver hesitated, holding his breath for a split second before pointing his index finger to the young woman. He had made up his mind. Worse luck! He felt very sorry for her, but he also had his job to do. His family was dependent on him, and he could not delay the bus a moment longer. He needed to find a culprit quickly to clear out of here. There was no time for him to sympathise with anyone.

After the driver identified the young woman, her face turned as white as a corpse underneath her conical hat. Her whole body shook uncontrollably, causing the child on her hips to shake with the movement. Sensing something terrible was going to happen, the boy started wailing with fright. She tried to calm her son by whispering into his ear, albeit unsuccessfully, as she was already terrified herself.

"Hush...don't...cry, son. Don't...cry, baby," she choked.

Sensing his mother's distress, the child bawled even louder with all his might. The woman put her son down on the ground, almost throwing him off her hips as if unable to bear her burden any longer. However, she threw herself down onto him, wrapping him back into her arms and immediately regretting her prior action. Helplessly, she glanced at her wailing son, lost in her sorrow, not knowing what to do next. She then looked up at the officer, tears flowing freely down her high cheekbones.

"Please, highly respected officer. Please, take whatever you desire, but let me go. I have three other children at home, and they have no one else to care for them. Their father is in a reeducation camp, and I'm their sole carer. This is my first time. I swear, I'll never do it again. Please, please sir. Be kind and be generous. Let me go. Please don't hold me back. Don't put me in detention. My children will be so scared if I am not home with them tonight. I'm so desperate to earn some money for the family. That is all I have. Please take it." She hesitated then continued decisively, even knowing that she had no way to repay the loan for the cost of her goods. "Please take them all but let me go. Please!"

Still kneeling on the ground with her hands clasped together, she begged him and cried harder, bowing her head, kowtowing on the ground in a pitiful gesture.

Indifferent and unperturbed by the wailing figure on the ground, the inspector walked toward her, using his baton to flick the hat off her head. The chinstrap caught, making him repeat his action. It was comical regardless of the woman's dire situation, and some kids sniggered, making him even more furious. In the end, he jerked her hat off forcefully with his hand and trampled on it irritably.

"Damn it! How dare you trade goods without a licence? It is unforgivable, and you even pretended to be a mother with children! You ought to know that the transport of food is prohibited, especially rice, meat, and cigarettes. You're bringing them to the rebels, aren't you?"

After barking his string of charges, releasing his temper satisfactorily, he looked carefully at the woman.

"Whoa, whoa! What we've got here! Good golly, she is a pretty one! This is getting better!" He muttered under his breath, feeling his excitement building.

It was promising! He could have done something here to ease his tension. It had been a while since he had a woman for a victim. Smacking his lips, he inhaled deeply, thinking he could smell her pungent aroma, anticipating the pleasure the woman would bring. Then imagining his fingers circling around her nipples, he was delightedly aware of his hardening penis rising in his trousers. Without a moment to lose, he turned to the driver and gave him the signal for the bus to move along without the woman, her son, and the hampers.

The young woman turned frantic. She cried and begged even louder, knowing that her fate was sealed for the meagre amount of food in her possession. The prospect of punishment she had to face was horrifying. The woman gathered the boy tighter into her arms as if she could use his undernourished, pitiful body as a buffer, protecting her from the terrifying experience she was about to endure. She would have no money left to purchase a ticket home to her family after her interrogation session with the guards at the station and their bribes. She would probably have to trade her pride to be able to return home tonight. The young woman stared desperately at the departing bus; her eyes followed its trail with anguish. The passengers on board had not dared to interfere. Everyone averted their gaze and was very glad that it was not they who had this bad luck.

In the bottom of her heart, Trinh knew that they had the woman and her child to thank for their escape.

The Rendezvous:
Ninh Kieu Market place and the Departure

THE BUS ARRIVED at Can Tho without any more incidents.

Immediately after getting off the bus, Chi went to see Mr. Man again. She gave him five new Vietnamese currency notes from her pocket as discreetly as last time and then walked back to the market. The sisters were hanging around the market stalls, pretending to look for things to buy. The noise of bargaining and bantering between the shoppers and hawkers was as deafening as in most marketplaces. There was confusion in the air as they were trading in new currency and the conversion made the bargaining harder. Even though official trading was in state-operated stores, the quality was usually poor. With more cash in hand, the black market was the better place to buy goods.

"No way! You're not going to sell that for ten! Too expensive!"

"Why not, Madame Hue? It's a good piece of material. See, pure silk from the maker of silk in this province. You can get a beautiful ao dai tailor-made from it."

Trinh was listening to the woman with a Northern accent dressed in a colourful miniskirt and orange blouse. She was short and plump. The skin on her bare legs was dotted with various dark scars, which resembled the spots on a Dalmatian's fur, and Trinh could not help giggling softly at her comparison. On her feet was a pair of wooden platforms, a good ten centimetres in height, very fashionable at that stage. Her shoulder-length hair was permed in tight curls. *She needed something to counter the spherical shape of her entire image instead of those curly locks,* Trinh thought. The comrade was obviously a high-ranking party member who had gained enough power and hard cash to be able to alter her image and afford luxury. The typical outfit of a party member, the simple peasant uniform and rubber sandals, was replaced by the fashionably trendy look. Scars from mosquito bites and scabies rashes from years of jungle fighting were still visible, marring the impression. Poor posture from the uncomfortable high platforms did not help. She stood with her behind jutted backward, trying to keep balance.

The bargaining between the silk merchant and the comrade was loud. Everyone in the market was looking and listening to their bantering with interest.

"Ok, five hundred to one, then five equals one cent, ten cents equals fifty, Gosh! It's complicated!" the merchant calculated aloud, trying to make a clear picture of old dong and new dong. "I'll give you ten cents discount then, and that's a very good discount, believe me. You will never get a better piece of material like this anywhere in this province. It's pure silk and has a beautiful design. Look at the lily and its leaves, exquisite! Everyone is going to be jealous of your ao dai, Madam Hue. Get it now and you can wear it at the coming Moon Festival." She chanted her sales talk like a well-trained parrot.

"No. I'm not going to be fooled by your information. There are many stalls around here that could offer better value for money than you do," Comrade Hue curtly rebuffed her.

"Oh, come on, Madam Hue! Give me the benefit of the doubt please! Name one price for today's sale. Yeah?"

"Six new dong. That's my final offer," Comrade Hue bargained down heavily, trying to converse in her head the value of new dong and old dong like the merchant and hoping she was not robbed blind by this crafty woman. It was all so confusing!

"I swear on the heads of my children, I only make ten cents profit with 8.70. Please be considerate. My family would have nothing to eat with anything lower than that."

"6.50 and that's it!" The madam walked away, the sound of the wooden platforms clicking distinctively on the bamboo floor of the market.

"Oh, please don't walk away so fast. Here you are! I am not making any profit today. Indeed, I am losing, but I am giving it away to mark the first sale for good luck! Good on you, Madam Hue. You've got yourself a bargain," the merchant trailed on. "My children just have to eat plain congee tonight. Ah, it's better than nothing, I guess!" The merchant sighed theatrically.

That concluded the sale, and the comrade was pleased with her purchase. After that delightful exhibition, Trinh lost interest in the market. She trailed behind her mother anxiously, observing everything but seeing nothing. Her mind was too preoccupied thinking of her friends. Time seemed frozen at one moment then accelerated at lightning speed the next moment when the boarding hour struck. They had to wait around the port from late afternoon until dusk to board the small wooden dinghies; each was about six metres in length and one and a half metres in width. They looked flimsy to Trinh's eyes even in daylight. A strong wave could have capsized each one easily. There were half a dozen different ones to carry the women, children, men, and young boys to the bigger vessel moored out at the harbour's mouth.

It was a dark night, the kind from which the escapees had chosen. Due to the shortage of energy and the conservation scheme, there were no streetlights on and the port was pitch-black. Trinh held her mother's hand tightly. The dinghy operators were hand-paddling into shore as quietly as possible. There were indistinct whisperings behind her. Trinh could not distinguish any noise except the thumping in her chest. She told herself to stay close to her mother and just looked ahead through the darkness without thinking.

"Come on, quickly."

"Just a maximum of ten on each dinghy. Don't worry. There are more coming in, and we're coming back."

"How long?"

"Fifteen minutes, in and out," the operator lied smoothly. It would take at least three quarters of an hour to get there and back, but he did not want to cause panic among the escapees. He wanted to pick them up and leave them at their boat then go home. He was only paid a small amount for this operation. It was risky, but the trip was worth a hundred times his normal fare.

"Hurry up. Don't just stand there! Get in the water and walk closer. We cannot paddle the dinghy further inshore. It might get stuck, and it's going to be harder to push it out!" Another operator pressed on impatiently. They were all nervous and eager to get out of there as quickly as possible.

"Take off your thongs. Get in the water, Trinh. Raise your bag high, child." Mother pushed Trinh in the water toward the dinghy. The group started to plod forward, following Mother's action.

They did not use the public jetty as the station chief had alarmed Chi belatedly of their breach of security with the coastal guards. Then there was confusion within the groups as Chi had told them to gather around the jetty. They were all ready and waiting for the dinghies to come and collect them as instructed, and then they had to walk hurriedly back to the market in darkness.

"No, it's not here. We have to go back to Ninh Kieu Market. Hurry, everyone!" Chi whispered.

"Why?" someone queried in a hushed tone.

"Are we in trouble?" another one asked. Then the others started to panic.

"What happens?"

"Why isn't it here?"

"My brother was told to wait here. Are you sure?"

"Are we going to be caught? Oh my god! We're doomed!"

"Shssh, are you crazy? Talk more quietly!" someone reprimanded in the dark.

"Are you certain that we're not going to board the dinghy here?"

"There's a change of plans. There is not much time to stay around. We have to be quick. Otherwise, the guards will change shift, and I will not be responsible for your safety."

Chi took up her bags and signalled for her daughters to follow, ignoring the rest of the group. She was not responsible for any of them anyhow. They were the families of her distant cousins, her partners in the operation. Chi only had to look after her family members, and the girls were all here. That was all she should worry about, Chi reassured herself. That was what had been agreed upon; each person had to care for his or her group's safety.

Lucky for them, the beach near the market was shallow and tapering offshore. There were faint kerosene lights shining in some of the shops and motels about fifty metres from where they were. However, there was no electricity and no streetlights. All the better for the escapees as they were more confident moving about in darkness. Trinh went in with her woven bamboo-leaf bag held high as instructed by her mother. The water was cool, and the river mud was slimy beneath her feet. It was stinky with rubbish floating on the surface. Damn, she had not taken off her thongs as told by Mother, and the suction from the mud and water had broken the thin straps. She heard the snap of one strap after another when she attempted to lift her feet, and her thongs were jerked off her feet in the end. The movement tipped her off balance, and her bag fell from her grip.

"Oh, Mother! My bag!" Trinh cried out in a hushed whisper, alarmed.

The bag contained her address book. She could not lose it. Without thinking, she shook her hand free of her mother's and went hurriedly after the bag. The girl could not move as quickly as she thought against the resistance of slimy mud underneath her feet. She looked on sadly and saw her bag drift away with the current.

"No, Trinh! No! Leave it. Come back here!" Mother whispered in the darkness. Her voice was hoarse with fright. Her daughter's silhouette was so small and seemed so far out of reach.

The bag went further and further away. Its shape disappeared and reappeared in the distance and the dark, following the waves. Sorrowfully, Trinh realised that she could not rescue her bag and started to retrace her steps. To her horror, the currents pushed Trinh away from the dinghy, and the river mud glued her bare feet tighter to the spot. It was harder to walk than before. The effort pushed Trinh's upper body forward without moving her feet at all, and she lost her balance completely. She fell facedown into the river. Immersed and panic-stricken, Trinh swallowed several gulps of water and tried desperately to stand up again. Behind her, people were pushing on, leaving her to cope with her own predicament. In the darkness and fighting for their own survival, they were ignorant of what was happening to anyone else. Then someone nudged her side accidentally in passing and submerged Trinh in the river once more. She swallowed several more gulps of stinky water and started to panic, her feet slipping away. She managed to get up eventually and was too frightened to know what to do next. In her fear, the girl was disoriented and lost all sense of direction. Her bladder was released involuntarily in her horror. She could not move. She wanted to cry, but she did not dare for fear of making too much noise. She held her breath and closed her eyes to force the fear down.

"Hold on to my hand," a familiar voice whispered in her ear.

"Oh, thank you!" Trinh felt alive again. She could breath normally now, and started to unclench her fist.

It was Vy, her sister. Trinh steadied her body against her sister and was relieved to have someone so dear to hold on to. The sisters slid against the currents to go back to the dinghy, and then both climbed up onto it. It rocked dangerously when they were hoisted on. Silent passengers were sitting side by side on the wooden planks on the little dinghy. They were glad that the incident was over. The two operators were at both ends, ready to row away with their paddles.

"Silly girl! Don't you ever do that again!" Mother scolded angrily, and she held Trinh's hand tighter than before. Their hands shook slightly, and she was panting as if she had just run a long distance. Trinh peered through the darkness at her mother. Though her features were well hidden, Trinh could tell that her mother's eyes were glistening with tears. Trinh was so sorry and felt an overwhelming sense of relief that she was now together with her mother.

Chi searched for the faces about her and was thankful to see that all her girls were on the dinghy. The tightness in her chest a moment ago with the small incident was enough to remind her of her terror of losing any of them. At least they had completed the first step of their journey. There were going to be many steps to follow, and none would be any easier. But they could do it, Chi repeatedly told herself. There was no going back now.

The dinghy was paddled out by hand for a fair distance alongside the mangroves near the riverbank to reduce noise. Then after passing the last of the inlets, one of the operators started the rotor blade engine to move with greater speed toward the boat. Everyone was quiet. The suspense was almost palpable. The wind was stronger than earlier, and it was high tide. There was not a star in the sky and the night was dark, but Trinh could see silhouettes of other dinghies moving against the currents and joining the group. There were three dinghies carrying women and children on this side of the port. The men and young boys were on different groups boarding the dinghies at a different jetty. They were approaching the main boat and more were moving in.

Their journey in search for freedom had begun.

The Sea Voyage

THE NIGHT WAS still dark. After being lifted off into the bigger vessel, everything went blurry. Trinh continued to hear indistinct whispering and confused chatter. The girl was holding tightly to her mother, still recovering from her fright. They stepped down together into the boat's cargo hold below, and then Mother released her hand from Trinh's grip and pushed her gently down onto the bench.

Starting again with her string of don'ts, she said hoarsely, "Sit here and stay put. Don't make any noise and don't go anywhere. Don't say anything! Understand, child?"

Trinh nodded her head, unable to utter a word. She was wet, barefoot, and shivering. The peasant blouse was muddy. A few snap-on buttons were undone, leaving her blouse partially open. Blasted buttons, they never stayed in place; they were poor-quality, recycled ones. Trinh gave up after trying to snap them back together all the time during the night. Her black pyjama satin pants were ripped from the hems to the knees on both trousers. The flimsy material was not able to stand rugged wear, especially when wet.

"I'll be back. Don't move. Remember, don't make any noise!" Mother left her there and disappeared onto the upper deck, her faint silhouette moving away in the dark.

After a while, Trinh realised Kim was sitting next to her. Kim must have obeyed Mother's instruction to stay close by her side all the time. Both were quiet and tired. It had been a very long day for them, and the ordeal was not over yet. They were not safe until the boat was out at sea in international waters. The guards might spot the boat and gun them down in the morning if they were still in sight when dawn broke.

Trinh closed her eyes and curled up on the bench. The young girl could not care less. She was wet, cold, hungry, frightened, and exhausted. She just wanted to go to sleep and hope that when she woke up tomorrow, the sun would be there for her.

Chi went looking for her sons, Hoan and Luc, and was relieved that they were there, sitting in a corner with their father. Nguyen spotted Chi, and they nodded, acknowledging each other before Chi dashed away again. She had to make sure all her children were on board. All the dinghies were departing and going back to the shore. The last escapees were safely hoisted onto the boat.

"Are you all right, Vy?" Chi asked her second daughter.

"Yes, Mother. I'm all right. And you?" Vy answered softly. She did not dare to look Mother in the eye.

As if sensing something wrong, Chi suddenly asked, "Where's Dien?"

Vy hesitated, as if searching for words, before answering quietly, "He's gone back on shore in one of the dinghies, Mother."

"What?" Chi uttered in astonishment.

"Dien what?"

"He's not on this boat, Mother. I could not hold him back," Vy said lamely.

"Oh no! My Buddha! What a fool!" Chi felt her heart skip several beats and felt about to faint. But she told herself to be calm and strong for the rest of her family. She staggered back to the below deck and would deal with that later, but not now.

Dien had decided to go back because he did not want to leave his sweetheart behind. Vy realised that her brother was a romantic soul, and it was his first love. He stayed in Vietnam and married her a few months later.

Day 1

Trinh was awake and feeling dizzy. The boat was rolling, and everything was upside down. She closed her eyes again, and everything was spinning in her head. Nothing helped to take away that gross feeling. She had lost track of time. She tried to sit up, but she vomited immediately on the cargo floor. The stench of vomit was strong. There were many people lying against each other like sardines in a can. She was not the only one vomiting right next to where she lay; several others were doing the same. It was smelly and stuffy in here. It made Trinh vomit again and again until she passed out completely.

Many times in her twilight zone, Trinh vaguely remembered a silhouette helping her sip spoonfuls of water and keeping her hydrated.

Day 2

The next time Trinh opened her eyes, she could not sit up at all; she was weak with exhaustion and thirst. Her lips were parched and cracked, and she could not breathe. It was stuffy and unbearable. The stench of vomit, human bodies, rotten cassava, and sweet potatoes was overpowering in the crowded cargo hold.

Trinh recognised Vy, and her sister gave Trinh a little sip of water in a small cup; but the girl threw up immediately, even if there was nothing there. Trinh could taste the bile in her mouth. Kim was lying next to her, but the older girl seemed better and able to hold down the sip of water successfully. Trinh closed her eyes again and wished that her torment would just go away when she woke up.

Day 3

Trinh could feel the fresh sea breezes on her cheeks. In her semiconscious state, she smelled the ocean, and that brought a smile to her face. It was wonderful, and she felt at peace. She opened her eyes fully but shut them quickly again as the sun's piercing rays were directly above her. Trinh came to full consciousness. She was lying on the upper deck, and it was a beautiful sunny morning. Instinctively, Trinh tried to snap her blouse buttons back on as that was the last thing she remembered, those blasted buttons. Ah, but someone had changed her into a T-shirt and a normal pair of trousers from the pile of clothes Mother brought down to the boat long before the trip. Thank goodness for that. And miraculously, her nausea had passed! She inhaled the sweet, fresh air into her lungs, letting them expand fully and filling every alveolus with pure oxygen. Trinh could almost feel its atomic movement travelling from her nostrils to the bottom ends of her lungs' alveolar sacs, just like swallowing a first sip of water in an empty stomach and sensing its flow. Trinh was relieved that she was alive! Alive and breathing! She could not believe it! Her endurance test had ended. There was a time when she had just wished to die; it would have been much easier.

Mother came to her, and she smiled too. The girl was weak and dehydrated, but she had come round at last. They had rescued both Kim and Trinh from the lower deck after two days and three nights at sea. The boat was out in international waters, running at maximum power just when dawn was breaking out.

The captain was chatting animatedly with her brothers. "We were damn lucky. I was scared shitless going past the coastal guard station with the noisy and ancient engine running during the night. It was deserted as far as I could see. Otherwise, we would easily have been caught. The speed we travelled at!"

"How fast was it, captain?" Mac asked.

"Ten knots! And the engineer was certain that he could get the boat up to fifty knots with two engines running! What a load of bullshit!" The captain shook his head at the lies.

He repeated, "We were damn lucky!"

Day 4

Trinh recovered her strength quickly in the next few days; being youthful was an advantage.

She was fascinated by everything. This was her first sea voyage, and the sea was enormous. There were clear skies and water in beautiful shades of blue, from indigo to dark to cobalt to azure to baby blue. It was an extraordinary sight and was tranquil with white, fluffy, peaceful clouds above.

Her family's boat was small—fifteen metres long, five metres wide and with a hull as round as a ball. It was a cargo barge that used to transport sweet potatoes, cassava, and water chestnuts along the Can Tho river and had been crudely modified by laymen to carry fifty people to sea without the slightest knowledge of what a sea vessel's requirements were. The naval captain had been released from reeducation camp a few weeks before and quickly recruited by Father through his connections to join the escape. He was horrified on seeing the state of the boat in the morning under the sun, but it was too late for him to turn back.

The people's life in the cargo hold below now became his sole responsibility. He had to bring them safely to shore.

Sitting at the bow, he kept muttering, "We need to keep faith and say our prayers, folks! I'll be glad when it's all over! Yeah, I'll be damn glad!"

There was desperation when they stepped onto the boat to get out to sea, but it loomed larger everyday when they could not see the shoreline, any shoreline would do. They had been floating aimlessly for three days, and land was nowhere to be seen. There was only the peaceful water and the sky. However, at times, there were angry skies with boisterous dark clouds and a ferocious sea ready to swallow everything in its path, exerting its power over meaningless lives and sudden death.

"Wake up. Shush! Wake up, but shush." Hoan shook Trinh's shoulders, waking the girls.

It was night. In her grogginess, she was reluctant to open her eyes. "Why? Go away!"

"Mother and Father want us to go onto the upper deck together. Wake up and hurry." Hoan added, "But don't make any noise. We don't want to wake the others."

Hearing the seriousness of his voice, the girls came to a full alert. The boat suddenly rolled to one side when Trinh was trying to sit up. She could hear the rain and the *spit-spat* splashing of waves against the sides of the boat now. Then she realised the constant downpour from the darkened sky seemed to increase in volume suddenly and the waves were angrier in the short time since she awoke. The change was swift. The windows on both starboard and port sides were brimming with water as the boat rolled with the atrocious sea. Waves were splashing over the sides and water was already over her feet when Trinh stepped out of the lower deck. The water kept rising rapidly.

Kim was beside her. "There's a big storm out there, Trinh. " She was in awe.

Both mounted quietly to the upper deck where all their family were already huddled. The captain was at the steering wheel, and his family were gathered in a corner as well. The rain kept pouring down in torrents. The intensity of the downpour made the water droplets cutting onto Trinh's face as sharp as the scratches of an angry sea monster. She ducked her head down, trying to avoid them, but they pounced on her back as equally painful. The sisters were holding hands tightly and moving along the rail toward the rest of their family.

"How many of us here in the boat, Mac?" Trinh heard the captain asked. His anxiety was audible.

"About fifty, fifty five," Mac answered. "Why?"

Not knowing what else to do, they were all standing in the rain holding on tightly to the rails and waiting for it to stop. It seemed impossible to them that it might stop at all. In the meantime, the riverboat kept rolling sideways and up and down like a lone, floating tiny egg in a giant boiling saucepan. Mac and the captain decided to gather their families here but leave the rest out of it in fear of causing panic.

"How many water tanks do we have?" the captain continued. His hands were busy controlling the boat.

"About twenty. Why?" Mac was puzzled.

The captain hesitated then sighed. "Forget it then. I was about to tell you to empty all the water in the tanks to turn them into floats. However, there're more of us than them. So forget it, Mac. We just have to pray harder for the storm to stop or we'll all go down with the boat. There's not much choice for us," he concluded.

Then he said, "Just go down there to the engine room and tell them to turn them all off. We have to let the boat float along the waves and ride with the storm. Can't do much with its size and shape and its engine, but let the Almighty decide our fate."

Before the captain finished his sentence, the engine suddenly started to roar louder. The boat lurched dangerously sideway and almost capsized.

"Oh no! No! Stop it! Stop it now! What an idiot!" the captain shouted angrily.

"Quick, Mac. Run down there and tell him to kill all the engines now, all of them! Stupid fool! What does he think he's doing? Getting us down to the bottom of the sea?"

After his outburst, the captain returned to his calmness and concentrated on his steering wheel. He looked up and out and around him in weariness. How he wished it were over.

The angry sea monster scared the hell out of everyone for a brief period of less than half an hour, then it left them. Constant rain was still pouring down from the dark sky, but the real danger had passed. It was tamer now, and it had no interest in the group of pitiful boat people anymore. It was satisfied with its game.

Day 5

Miraculously, the storm stopped at dawn. The sunrise was as beautiful as ever. Slowly ascending from the horizon, its powerful rays shone brilliantly down its subjects without prejudice. The water was as clear and blue as before. The sea was a mask of tranquillity. The waves were gently splashing against the boat in friendly caresses with no trace of the violence of a few hours ago. The only evidence was the water in the lower deck. They had to use buckets and everything they could get hold of trying to get rid of it. Many had slept right through the storm without realising the danger at sea and their possible fate. Who could have thought of its capability in changing its facade from tranquillity to maliciousness in just a fraction of time?

"It was only thanks to the calmness of the captain and his professional manner in dealing with the situation that we survived at all. Just imagine the state of panic among the passengers and the state of the boat last night. It makes a frightening picture," Mac told Nguyen and Chi, shaking his head in disbelief at their luck.

"Without his skilful manoeuvre in letting the boat roll along with the waves, we could have ended at the bottom of the sea right now!"

The day was tranquil again, but later that night, they encountered another storm. However, this time, it was not as ferocious as the last. The sea monster had scared the boat people enough from last time, and this time, it was just to tease them a little bit in its creative game once more. Hoan did not wake the girls to come to the upper deck as last night, and the captain was as skilful and composed as before.

So they survived one more day.

Day 6

"Hey, there's a boat!" someone pointed to starboard.

"We're safe. We're going to be rescued!"

"Hurray! We're safe!"

"Hey, everyone, we're going to be rescued!"

Many were looking toward the approaching boat and eager to be rescued as they believed.

"It's a Thai fishing boat," the captain, sitting high on his control wheelhouse chair, said quietly to Mac. He then slid off his gold bracelet, ring, and necklace, pushing them into a crevice beneath his seat. It turned out that the captain had seen it coming but thought nothing could be done to prevent it. The passengers were men, women, and children weakened by the voyage and not equipped to fight against invaders. It might turn into a violent bloodshed if they resisted, and it was best to let them satisfy their greed.

Mother heard the exchange between Mac and the captain, and she saw what he did with his jewellery. Intuitively, she did the same with hers, hiding it on top of the roof. Then she whispered to the girls, using the only tactics she knew. "Don't look at them, and stay behind me all the time. Don't let them notice you at all. Understand, girls?"

Trinh was puzzled at first. Were they not going to be rescued? And she was about to ask but was hushed by Vy.

"Shssh, don't say anything."

The Thais were muscular and lean. Their dark skin was tanned like charcoal. They jumped onto the boat and started yelling in Thai, which no one understood. At first, some passengers rushed forward, ready to greet them; but they stopped midway when the pirates started taking out their hatchets and knives. They were stunned by what they saw and stood paralysed with fright.

The pirates started to rummage into people's belongings and yelled out more Thai in heated voices, gesticulating to people's necks, arms, and fingers for personal jewellery like necklaces, bangles, chains, watches, or rings.

The passengers on board silently obeyed. They were hurt and felt betrayed. It was a first encounter with humans after many days at sea, and they had thought they were going to be safe at last.

"Arrh!"

Trinh heard a girl scream in terror, and she turned to see one of the Thais reaching at the girl, pulling the gold necklace off her and making several buttons of her blouse snap open. He was just a young boy of eighteen or so. His naked upper torso was covered with tattoos. A figure of a naked, voluptuous girl was on his right bicep, so when his muscle moved the girl seemed to dance around. A cobra was on the other bicep, and crossed swords with a large skull were on his back. On his chest was some transcription, the kind of writing similar to Khmer script or Brahmi in ancient Indian; it could be his name or it could be anything. The girl started to cry hysterically. Her hands crisscrossed in front of her chest; her blouse was fully open.

The girl's father rushed forward, and her mother quickly stepped closer, pulling the girl toward her, away from the pirate.

Mother held Trinh's hand tighter, pushing Kim and Trinh behind her back, as if shielding the girls from sight.

"Step closer here, Vy," she told Vy. "Sit down behind me. Don't stand up like that." She panicked.

The boy mumbled something then turned around, looking at their alarming faces. Then he walked away hurriedly to the upper deck and joined with his gang. The girl's necklace remained on the floor, and its gold aura was visible on the dirty timber deck. He did not pick it up as if it had almost turned him into a devil and he had to run from its evil influence.

They were fortunate again, as it was in the early days then, when the Thais were fishermen who sighted Vietnamese refugee boats by chance and were opportunistic pirates, but meant no harm to human lives. It was only a few months later that they became real terrorists, who raped, tortured, and robbed refugee boat people in outrageous atrocities that remained ugly scars in the minds of many survivors.

The Thais left after taking most of the valuable belongings and jewellery with them. In exchange, with the little bit of humanity that remained, they gave the refugees some oil and a few cans of fresh water and pulled them a little closer inshore.

That taught them a lesson to be cautious of approaching boats. That same afternoon, they encountered another Thai fishing boat with a similar scenario, but this time there was nothing for the pirates to loot. They were angry, and in revenge, they pulled the refugee boat further out to the sea, leaving them there without supplying oil or water. Their boat was running low on both essentials, and everyone was exhausted by their situation now.

———— ✪ ————

Day 7

By luck, they arrived safely on land after a week at sea.

The last time they had encountered another boat, everyone was indifferent. They were sick and tired of being robbed, violated, or pulled away to sea.

However, this time they had a pleasant surprise. Their boat was fortunate to come across a group of Malaysian yacht club members near the island of Bidong. The tourists—generous, kind, and wealthy—intercepted them and towed them back to their island. They let the boat people came on shore to visit their holiday cabin and gave the refugees a real feast with ham, cheese, chicken, meat, breads, fruits, cakes, and biscuits, and, most of all, water. There was even Coca-Cola!

"Look! I've been given this!" Trinh showed the Coca-Cola can to Luc, beaming with pleasure.

"It's not fair! I want one too," Luc protested.

"I think they give everyone a can, Luc. Go over there and get it."

By the end of the seven-day voyage, everything was running out—food, water, and oil. Their boat relied on the benevolence of the people they came across, even the Thai pirates who robbed them the first time. Their boat had been running out of water a few days ago, and they had already had to drink water from the bottom of the large tin container, which was muddy and reddish in colour with iron residues. The taste of the soda can was exceptionally sweet. Not only did it quench the young girl's thirst, but it gave her a taste that she had not come across since 1975. The new government had cut off trade relations with the United States after the Fall of Saigon. Anything to do with America was banned and completely taboo in the country.

It was the best meal that Trinh had ever eaten in her life. Everything tasted deliciously good. Even the water was sweet, fresh, and clean water, not muddy and reddish with iron residues in the tank that she had to drink in the last few days. They devoured the food awkwardly.

Receiving food and a can of Coca Cola from one of the Malaysian tourists, Trinh did not know what to say as she did not know many words of English, except phrases like "Thank you very much," "It is very good," "Yes," and "No." The kids even joked between themselves, Hoan, Kim, Trinh, and Luc: "If they ask you questions and you can't catch what they're saying, just reply with one yes and two nos if feeling negative, or with two yeses and one no if feeling positive!" Then they laughed at their silliness when practising their answers, pretending to be very smart.

"Thank you." Trinh tried so hard to enunciate the words clearly that the Malaysians smiled at her effort.

After feeding them with a generous amount of food, the tourists gave them the rest of the supply and a few cans of oil and then showed the captain the direction of the refugee camp.

Sated with a delicious meal and feeling lighthearted at the prospect of being nearer to land, the boat people were grateful for their fortunate encounter. Their boat went out for a few hours before they saw land again.

"Ahoy! There's the island!" someone shouted.

"It's land! It's land. Come on, everyone! It's land!"

"Oh my god! We've arrived."

"We are here!"

"We are safe now!"

Some others rushed onto the cabin and joined in the chorus, but most of them remained quiet. They exchanged looks of concern as the boat had been pushed and shoved away by the Malaysian authority twice when approaching the shorelines yesterday and the day before. After giving them more water and oil, the coastguards even fired several shots in the air to frighten them and shoo them away quickly.

"I hope we're accepted here!" Mac worried. "I don't think I can go on any longer!"

"It's the right spot. The kind Malaysian tourists pointed this place out, I'm sure," the captain reassured him.

Then the captain was perplexed when he heard shouting in Vietnamese from the shore.

"Stop the engine. Smash it!"

"Scuttle the boat!"

"Smash the hull!"

"Punch a hole!"

"Crash the boat! Sink it."

"Yes, sink it! Quickly! Otherwise, you'll be pushed away."

"Come on! Do it now! Scuttle the boat! Don't just stand there!"

"Hurry up! Do it quickly!"

The captain then realised the message was to destroy the boat so they would be rescued rather than being pushed away again for trespassing as illegal immigrants.

"Ahoy down there! Stop the engine!" he yelled to the lower deck while still holding to the steering wheel and keeping control of the rolling boat.

"Mac, go down below and tell them to crush the hull, quickly," the captain ordered. Then he repeated, "Tell them to stop the engine immediately, the silly buggers!"

There was shouting on the boat to the lower deck to crush the hull. Suddenly, Trinh felt humiliated and embarrassed, hoping they were not to be pushed away like beggars again. She felt so small, so belittled, wishing she had not left her country. She was reduced to a nobody, without pride and with no country of her own to return to, a stateless person. She cried silently, surprised at her emotions. She should be glad that they reached land safely. Instead, she felt very much like a refugee. She was just one member in the group of disparaged and pitiful people arriving in their odd-looking boat, appearing ridiculous and pathetic, wide-eyed in shock and with dirty hands and feet. That moment of humiliation mingled with the joy of landing on shore stayed with her for years after. Trinh was sure every refugee had a similar feeling until proven differently. Then the joy overcame that moment of humiliation with shouts of jubilance from people on the boat and on shore.

"Everyone, lie flat on the floor with your head down and your hands above your head, please," a Malaysian coast guard ordered.

They were checked for weapons and allowed to disembark after. Some were immediately reunited with brothers, sisters, family, and friends within the crowds. There were indescribable feelings with cries of happiness and of grief when telling the news from home. The cheerfulness was there after an incredible journey, but there were also heavy feelings in their hearts. The realisation that they were now out of danger from the Communists was beyond ecstasy, but it also came with the realisation that they might never see their country again. That last insight filled them with foreboding.

The Hut and the Vegetable Pond

Pulau Besar, Malaysia

WALKING ON THE hard surface of the land after having been on water for a week was a strange sensation at first. Trinh felt the earth moving in waves as if she was still at sea and about ready to fall when on her feet for the first few days on shore.

"Hey, do you feel the earth moving?" Trinh asked Luc, giggling at the strange feeling.

"Yeah, it's weird!" Luc extended his arms sideways as if trying to balance himself walking on a tightrope.

"It's as if we're still on water," Kim joined in.

"Yeah, it's really funny! I have to lift my feet up, one step after another, and place them down carefully on the ground with each step," Hoan added.

"Like a robot!" Luc laughed.

Then they reached the hut and entered it in silence. The children tried to stay calm even though their excitement was shown clearly on their faces. Their eyes twinkled, and their noses twitched liked rabbits about to enter a den full of lettuces. The primitive thatched and timbered hut was given to the family for a minimal amount of bartered exchange from the previous occupants.

The average period for boat people to wait for a permanent settlement in the third country was three months at that time. However, there were many who had to wait for years and years if encountering complications with their application. Without any means to purchase a private hut, each new arrival or family shared an area in the large common one, which was built by United Nations High Commissioner for Refugees (UNHCR), with other families. By having some cash for a private hut, the individual family was better off than the rest. They had more privacy, of course, the sacred privacy that the refugee longed to have after having none back home. There were about twenty common huts and at least five hundred individual ones scattered around the island. Those who had come earlier had built their huts nearer to the beach, and later arrivals had to go further inland. Some families with enough manpower and skills and who owned their boats had dismantled and used the planks and timbers from the boats to build their own huts. Some had the cash to purchase raw materials to start from scratch. With a stroke of luck, Trinh's parents had known the previous occupants of this hut, and they left it to them for a minimal amount when departing for settlement in the United States. They only had to stay in the common hut for a day and then moved to their own hut the very next day. It was one of the few huts built by the earliest groups to arrive. Being on a corner of the main pathway leading to the front beach, the family had the advantage of hearing gossip from people walking by. It was only six by ten metres in dimension. There were two large timbered platforms built along the length of the hut used as common dormitories for the male and female members separately.

They did not have many belongings except some bamboo-woven bags of clothes and some kitchen utensils that were used on the boat. Hoan and Luc dragged the bags along and put them on the dirt floor in the kitchen. The simple open-air kitchen was right at the back of the hut; on the log bench was a three-point makeshift stove. Once more, they had to use woodstoves here.

"Back to primitive life, folks!" Hoan declared grandly, looking about him.

"Hey, I thought we'd said good-bye to woodstoves and wood smoke for good!" Trinh exclaimed, eyeing the kitchen.

"Faint chance, that happening! Here we are again!" Kim said, and they burst out laughing despite the circumstances. It was a good, humorous laugh that showed their true happiness, and it jingled in the simple thatched hut liked Santa's bells at Christmas, unlike their black humour back home.

"Never mind about that! I am happy! We are here! Yippee!" Trinh declared and giggled happily. She almost toppled over when she tried to inspect the stove, still wavering from her steps.

"Yeah, we are free!" Vy agreed. She was the quietest sister in the brood, and her statement always carried substantial weight for the whole group.

"We're here and we're happy and free as a refugee!" Hoan sang aloud in his silly tune.

"Yeah, happy and free as a refugee!" Luc chanted after his brother, and then the boys started locking arms and dancing in a circle.

"Oh, shut up! Silly boys!" Kim admonished. But she laughed merrily at the same time.

They giggled, laughed, sang, and danced.

Then the lot of them ran excitedly to the back of the hut and walked around, checking out the neighbourhood. It was strange that they had ended up in this place so far away from home. After a week's journey at sea, arriving on the island was still a dream to them.

"It was land at last!"

Nothing could describe their relief as the boat approached land. Nothing could be more precious than seeing something apart from the sea after a week or two of floating aimlessly. They were still nowhere, it was not their final destination, but the journey had almost ended. They had reached land safely at last.

Now, the family even had a hut to stay in.

"Hi!" Trinh nodded to her neighbours opposite.

"There are so many kids in that house! There are more kids than ours," Trinh whispered to Luc.

"There are a hundred of them!" Luc agreed. "Fifty boys and fifty girls!" And they giggled together over their silliness. Their happiness lingered on for many days afterward, and they laughed about everything while settling in the camp.

Outside the hut, leaning against the thatched partition and facing the path, was a small rectangular logged table with seating for six and two connecting benches on both sides, also made of logs. They used to sit around that table and talked about everything happening in their life during this transitional time.

But the most wonderful possession they had in the refugee camp was a vegetable pond.

"Look! We even have a vegetable pond!" Walking around the perimeters of the pond and looking down into the green shoots below, they were amazed at seeing the familiar bok choy vegetable from back home.

"How cool is that!" Luc was counting the steps, trying to measure the size of the pond.

They had inherited a two-by-three-metre bok choy pond from the previous occupants as well. It was dug down a step to collect water and turn the ground into a muddy patch, and situated farther towards the back of the hut. For many days afterward, they realised that was a real luxury in camp, a real treat! A vegetable pond that the family was able to use as a source of greens was a godsend as the refugees had hardly any vegetable supplies. Some of them had to venture out into the woods to look for edible greens to supplement their main diet of canned food and instant noodles. The bok choy garden thrived on, soaking up recycled running water from the kitchen and a shower cubicle. Water from the washing up, from the washing, from showering, and from all the family's use was drained through a small trench leading to the pond. Regardless of the unhygienic practice of using recycled water for their pond, they were grateful for its produce. The pond was a miracle, a wonderful dream. It kept regrowing endlessly with new shoots of bok choy throughout their stay at the camp. The more they cut the stems and the leaves, the faster the shoots regrew. The family was never short of vegetables in their meals.

They all called it "our incredible and miraculous vegetable pond."

To add variety, Mother also planted some other greens collected from her walks in the bush and forced the children to eat them as a fresh salad in homemade organic vinegar from fermented ripe bananas. They were *Peperomia pellucida* or peper elder, with shiny, fleshy heart-shaped tiny leaves. Trinh often chewed them tentatively, then spat out the weird looking greens with their hairy tentacles along the stems when Mother was not looking, even with her mother's forceful statement: "Eat these, they're good for you. They make you grow taller."

"Supplies! Supplies! Food is coming!" Luc yelled at the top of his lungs, running back from the beach.

They had supplies of sardines or tuna cans, instant noodles, flour, sugar, salt, soy sauce, fish sauce, and monosodium glutamate as their main food. Fresh fish and meat were occasional treats. The coming of the supply boat always brought happiness, an event that heralded guaranteed joy rather than the approach of other refugee boats that might bring shocking news to the camps.

"It's your turn to queue for supplies, Hoan!" Even though they still had to stand in line for food, they knew that it was only temporary, and that cut all anxiety and weariness down to nothing.

"It's no use trying to get out of it this time, soldier!" Trinh commanded with feigned authority.

Curiously, to Trinh, the three-month period in the refugee camp was the happiest one in her life. Primitive as their living conditions were, they had their freedom. Sitting around in a circle, with or without a guitar, they could stay singing and talking into the night with other refugees, debating about anything that they could not freely discuss before. They often joked about the term they used to "do their business" regularly every morning. "Have you been to Ho Chi Minh's mausoleum yet?" They would laugh hysterically at the childish joke, satisfying their childish revenge.

Friendships and romance were rapidly formed in the camp overnight and ended rapidly as one party might be accepted by the Americans and the other by the Australian Embassy, and so separation or heartbreak was often heard about. There were crimes of burglaries, robberies, and rapes. Murders and stabbings happened between jealous parties and over power struggles. There were babies born with happiness, but there were also babies born with heartache as the result of encounters with Thai pirates. Overall, a refugee camp was a minicountry governed by volunteers who came and went at intervals and typically was at times quiet and peaceful but at other times chaotic and full of turbulence, and as unpredictable as the sea.

The boat people would be screened at first by UNHCR, which recorded their name, date of birth, and fingerprints before giving them the refugee status. Then each family or adult was given an application form to fill in the country of their first choice. Then they all had to wait in turn for being interviewed by the immigration officer. There were successful applicants, but there were also a number of rejected cases, and so the waiting period in between having been accepted or not at all was incredibly terrifying. With Giang and Kate, who were already in Sydney a year ago, they were all trying to apply for Australia as their final settlement. Trinh's family was divided into five units. Her parents, Trinh, and Luc were in one, as the children were under eighteen. The other adults, Mac, Vy, Hoan, and Kim were separate as individuals. They were all very anxious about the prospect of being rejected and divided but hoped for the best as always.

United States of America was the safety net for all who were not accepted anywhere else. Good old USA, which offered the door to those poor refugees as the last resource.

Trinh remembered the Australian immigration officers were always wearing shorts and casual clothes when visiting the camp, unlike others. They laughed when Trinh answered their question, "What do you know about Australia?"

"Kangaroos and the Opera House!" Trinh declared, feeling very clever at that time.

The sea, the beach, the sun, the hut, the bush, the crimes, the romances, the tragedies, the heartaches, and the frequent trips to "Ho Chi Minh's mausoleum" in the bush with at least two or three companions for safety reasons were unfading memories for the refugees, even if they were later to become a governor or a nuclear physicist! It goes with the saying: "Once a refugee is enough for one's whole lifetime."

The Refugee Camp

1978

"Hey, there's a boat coming," Luc said. They were standing on the hill overlooking the beach.

Trinh put both her hands over her eyes to shield them from the sun's glare and asked excitedly, "Where? Where is it? I can't see anything."

"Look over there! There, there! See? Look on the right. Can't you see it now?"

"Oh yeah, I can see it now. It's only tiny."

"It's coming closer!" Luc jumped up and down with his discovery.

Then he ran toward the beach. "Hey, everyone! There's a boat coming ashore."

It spread rapidly, and the rest of the camp was shouting excitedly with the news. It was midafternoon. The sun was strong and high still. Its glare was bright, reflecting light on the white sandy beach. The waves were splashing in gentle languid movements, quiet and good-natured. The sea bubbles spread lazily onto the wet sand and disappeared below its surface, going back to the ocean to restart another cycle. Yesterday the surf was rough, with gusts of wind, violent and fierce, echoing the howling of the sea that churned hearts. That kind of weather made the adults look out to sea and worry.

"Let's hope the boats out there survive unsettled seas," Trinh heard her mother whispering at night, pleading to the wind and begging it to protect desperate boat people. "Let them come safely to shore. Please let them have a chance. Please!"

It was like that every time, and every time a boat or trawler came ashore, the whole refugee camp came alive. Noise broke out everywhere. Footsteps were heard from every direction. Children and adults, young and old, they were all rushing to the beach and standing there in eagerness, waiting for a glimpse of hope. Running in bare feet, bare chests, or in just an open-shirt, boxer shorts, and thongs, the men and boys led the race. The rest, young girls and women in tattered clothing and battered footwear, were not far behind. Most of them were still skinny as muscles needed time to grow slowly with the food in camp, but overall, they looked healthy and alive, a real contrast to the shocking images they portrayed to the whole world when being rescued. Racing to the beach to welcome the new arrivals, the appearance of the crowd might look depressing, but deep down in the hearts of those people were pure happiness and hope.

They hoped to see and to recognise a familiar face among the new arrivals, that of a friend, a cousin, a sister, a brother, a lover, a wife, a husband, a mother, a father, or even anyone from their hometown. They were all longing for a loving touch in this foreign land. Anyone, anything, the delicate dear connection that linked them to the homeland they had left behind. As slim as it might appear, that chance of reconnection helped bring warmth to their hearts and provide stability at the time when everything was slipping away from them like quicksand. The refugees were clinging tightly to that sheer hope every day, a flimsy thread linking them to the life they once knew that now seemed so out of reach. The Vietnamese are not travellers by nature. Living at the same town where they were born or at the same address for generation after generation is the norm, and they rarely leave their place of birth unless something forces them to. Added to that, their desperation of not knowing when their homecoming might be was heartrending and indescribable; as at that time, it seemed like an impossible situation. They were crossing the border illegally and branded criminals with severe punishment if caught. It was an irreversible outcome.

They risked losing their families, their homes, their properties, and everything, including their lives, to escape. There was only a thin line between happiness and despair or safety and death, either of which could be the boat people's destination. They could easily stumble on either side by luck or ill fate and bask in glory or wallow in despair. The refugee camps for the Vietnamese Boat People in the peak periods of 1978–1989 were places packed with stories of tragedies and heartaches. According to UNHCR, there were roughly 750,000 boat people who landed on shore alive. It was also estimated there were 450,000 to 500,000 people who died at sea. The death toll was 40 percent of the total number. The figures were daunting in hindsight, and it seemed impossible to believe. Of a total of approximately one and a half million Vietnamese refugees who arrived safely in the promised land, about half of that number were refugees in the Orderly Departure Program (ODP) initiated by UNHCR in the late 1979, and half were boat people. Of those 750,000 to 800,000 boat people who finally settled in their third country, many had suffered great loss, catastrophe, and overwhelming injury to their body and spirit. That staggering number shows the desperation of Vietnamese refugees who chose to flee their homeland by crossing the sea in primitive, small boats, which was clearly extreme. Danger of death was irrelevant to them. They simply desired to get out of the hellish environment they were trapped in; they had been pushed to the limit. This expatriation was entirely out of character, and many had never experienced it before in their lifetime.

It was a phenomenon. Their compulsion to take to the sea in droves created an unusually strong impact on the outside world.

Then, after the ordeal of surviving the sea, this transitional life in a second country so foreign and so far away from home was very unsettling to most of them. Their homesickness was so overwhelming that some even thought of returning and facing criminal charges. Their conflicting emotions were full of turmoil that they could not understand.

It seemed there were more and more boats coming in since June 1978, just a few weeks after Trinh and her family arrived at Pulau Besar. It is a beautiful island in the coastal region of Malaysia, approximately thirteen kilometres from the mainland. The nearest town is Terengganu. The stretch of land was virginal and picturesque with strikingly clear blue water and a fine, sandy beach, which had the shape of a pregnant woman lying on her back. There were fountains, little hills, rivers, and ponds on the island that added to its beautiful and tranquil landscape. The island had turned into a refugee camp with the influx of hundreds of boat people coming in every day in the period from 1978 to 1979. The exquisite scenic island had become the refuge for approximately eight thousand boat people at one time. When that maximum quota was reached and the island was overflowing with thousands and thousands of refugees coming in daily, the camp was forced to close. The refugees were transferred to a larger, adjacent island called Pulau Bidong. At its peak, this latter camp housed forty-two thousand boat people, making it one of the largest refugee camps during 1980–1989.

Without the Vietnamese boat people, the beautiful white beach would be just as peaceful and serene as a holiday resort. However, looming over the sandy beach were the carcasses of refugee boats in various sizes, colours, and shapes. Mostly were painted in blue and green, and they looked odd and very out of place. Some even had their names still proudly etched on the bow. Bleached by the sun, the paintwork was fading slowly, but the letters and numbers were still visible. The MT259 must be from My Tho and CT3671 was from Can Tho, and so on; they were obviously just litter for disapproving lovers of nature. However, they were saviours to the Vietnamese. These fishing boats or trawlers, which had normally been used for trips around the coastal regions only, were scarcely equipped to sustain a rough sea voyage for longer than a week or for storms longer than an hour. That was the sad explanation why many boats had sunk to the bottom of the Pacific in small storms with winds as mild as sixty kilometres per hour or less. The lucky ones arriving ashore had had extensive damage to their hull where water had seeped in through the cracks and would surely have sunk if not rescued in time. Now, many parts of their structure, mostly the planks, were being used as construction material in camps and were slowly being taken away, leaving the pitiful carcass naked on the sunny beach. The unusable remains were left there, unclaimed by the boat people, and stayed as reminders of their fearful experience.

Those who escaped safely with their whole family—parents and children, husband and wife—were privileged. They were grateful and blessed. Even though they longed to reencounter a familiar face, anything at all to bring them a moment of reminiscence of the old life they had had was enough. However, the feeling was intensified for those who travelled alone. The loneliness and insecurity of these people was excruciating. They were hoping to see someone who would bring them snippets of news from home, of loved ones left behind that they might not be able ever to see again. Even though fleeing from their birthplace was the obvious move, they had left with broken hearts and broken pride. Until they had been accepted for final settlement in their third country, they were stateless citizens with nothing, the true meaning of "I was nothing but a refugee," as Pearl S. Buck noted.

Kim sympathised with some of the girls travelling alone in the camp. Many boys and girls eighteen years old or even younger left their family to take their chances on the rough seas by themselves as their parents could not afford to accompany their children. The cost of getting out of the country was substantial, and many had to scrape their last pennies together to finance just one or two members of the family. Parents hoped to give their children a chance of beginning again, even if it might mean danger and death.

Kim understood and felt the unbearable longing for a reunion with loved ones from those less fortunate young people. Their faith was sustained by searching for faces whenever boats arrived. They needed the assurance to gain strength and confidence in order to stay alive and go on.

"Are you coming, Kim?" Trinh asked her sister, ready to run off herself to the beach.

"Of course, but wait a minute. Let me find my thongs."

Kim reluctantly abandoned the book she was reading and hurriedly put on an old pair of thongs. The book, *Tu Luc Van Doan*, was a precious copy that Kim borrowed from the camp library, one of many prohibited books that the Communists had confiscated or burnt during the feverish days after April 30, 1975. Some thoughtful boat people had brought it along with them and left it here at the camp. The refugees were lucky to have the chance to read it again after three years of longing for something old and romantic in sophisticated literature. The language was a total contrast to the crude language of the Communists in their relentless themes of fighting, killing the Americans, and liberating the citizens of the South in all their books, poems, and essays. Vengeance seemed to be the core of their literature, transcribed into ugly words with which they had tried to poison the South in schools and everywhere else. Albeit the new government's intention of eradicating the entire cultural heritage of the South, many books, songs, and poems of pre-1975 were kept hidden and exchanged secretly between the Southerners back home. Kim and Trinh, and all of the refugees, were delighted to reread those old titles and enchanted to relisten to the old songs.

Kim put the book down in the corner, and together, they ran to the beach. Trinh wore her special knee-length flowery dress, which everyone said was more appropriate for her nickname, Roly-Poly. She had turned into a chubby girl of sixteen, growing quickly out of her tiny shell in just a short period of breathing in the fresh air of beaches, the sea, and freedom, but still not very tall! The lack of nutrition from her early childhood had shunned her growth a fair bit.

"See, you do not eat Mother's tentacle vegetable and you stay short because of that!" Hoan often admonished her jokingly.

Kim had on her dark pants and plain-coloured top. She felt the eagerness of welcoming the new arrivals as much as the rest of the camp; perhaps someone she knew would be coming. Perhaps someone from her high school would join her here to ease the pain of her homesickness. Even though the eighteen-year-old girl was devastated to leave her high school friends behind, she still understood the grave implication of what real devastation meant to other less fortunate people. She felt lucky every time there a boat came in, considering the voyage they just had taken. Her family was safe and intact. She was protected and secure in her environment. She was on land.

The sisters arrived at the beach when the crowd was already dense. People were milling together, and talk broke out animatedly among them.

"Good gosh! Did you see that?"

"Holy shit! A pitiful sight!"

"Yeah, the girls on stretchers? They're barely eighteen, nineteen! Poor things!"

"Were they dead?"

"I'm sure they wished they were!"

"Poor girls, they were as lifeless as corpses!"

"Body and spirit, they were beyond help!"

"The girls and the women on board were gang-raped repeatedly for days. Fucking bastards, the Thai pirates! I swear!"

"How could they be so cruel?"

"They're bloody animals, of course! That's why!"

"Why didn't the men try to do something? There were men on board, weren't there?"

"Hah! The boat went off course for days, and they had no more food and water. They were all weak with exhaustion. The men could not even stand up! The fathers of the girls were beaten senseless when they tried to interfere."

"Besides, I've heard that the boat was raided three times, and the last time, the fucking animals could not find anything more valuable than exhausted human beings. So they decided to feed the girls and women, give the men and children water, and towed the small boat alongside their vessel for their barbaric pleasure," someone said angrily.

"The bloody bastards only released the boat after two weeks of enjoying the gang rape!"

"Is it real? That's incredible!"

"It's shocking! It can't be real!"

"Yeah, it's real! A sad truth of sickening human behaviour, but it's real!" The man shook his head in disgust.

"You meant, the boat was robbed three times, and the last time, the pirates decided to rape the girls and women instead?"

"Yeah, robbed three times by three different groups of pirates."

"On three different days, they were intercepted one by one, and some even thought that they were being rescued by the second and then the third encounter, only to realise that it was the pirates again and again!"

"How horrible that must have been for them! I feel sick!"

"They only released the girls after seeing that they were dying and of no use to them anymore."

"Unbelievable! I can't fathom that cruelty at all!"

"How was it possible? The pirates, how do they know of refugee boats?"

"I think the pirates are sending signals between themselves when they sight refugee boats. Or they might have heard of the loot gained from other pirates and are now better equipped for the treasure hunt."

"It's so easy for them. We are, the boat people, I mean. We're their easy target. Hungry, thirsty, lost, gullible, and exhausted, they only need to push and shove, not even a knife or a gun to threaten us."

"Yeah, our boat was attacked twice. We were very fortunate, if you called that fortunate, being robbed only twice! At that time, they were merely fishermen who smelled the gold from refugee boats and got greedy. They only came on board with knives and hatchets, which they use for scaling or chopping fish. We were already out to sea a week and so confused at the vastness of the sea. At first glance, we were glad that we had come across some human contact in the ocean and we were ready for them to come and get us. We waved to them and were quite happy. Only when they stepped on board with their weapons, primitive as they were, did we realise it was too late. They only took our valuables but did not harm the girls or women." Mac was among the crowd, and he shared the family experience with the throng.

"What month was it?"

"Around May 1978."

"Did you fight at all?"

"No, it took us by surprise. We were shocked that there were pirates out there. We were so naïve! We thought that once we were at sea, we would be rescued and no harm would come to us at all!"

"Of course, that seemed to be the same for most of us. No one thought that there were worst dangers than Communism!"

"Obviously, the phobia of Communism outweighed the risks. The destructive force of the sea is meaningless to boat people. We just wanted to get out, regardless of the consequences. It's madness!" Mac concluded.

"But they weren't violent, were they? The Thai pirates you mentioned, I mean." Someone turned the conversation back to the Thai pirates.

"No, they weren't violent then. They were harmless fishermen, just greedy, but not cruel. Not harmless as harmless truly means. They were barbaric and avaricious, the way they mugged us. But you know what I mean!"

"I wish they were only interested in valuables, and they would leave the girls and women alone!"

"They weren't caught or punished at all, and so they continued to do whatever they wanted, man."

"It's getting worse because they've gained so much from their hunting trips, and the greed has now turned to lust as well. Thai fishermen were so poor. One successful scoop was worth more than a decade of fishing. The temptation was too much to resist."

"I wish the authorities could do something to prevent it!"

"It's too vast for policing, the whole Pacific Ocean! Besides, which authority and which country will carry it out, this police work?"

"The UNHCR is trying to do something about it, I think."

"Yeah, the atrocity of the crimes is too evil to be ignored."

"The UNHCR are investigating the problem, interviewing the victims to try and pinpoint the areas and the culprits. But it's vast. The sea, I mean. It's impossible to search and patrol the whole Pacific Ocean. Besides, the cost for that kind of operation is huge. They only have limited funding. The refugees are already a burden, what with feeding, housing and settlement—"

"But the crimes are beyond the scope of human suffering!"

"It's true, I know. There are bound to be more offences if there are refugee boats floating around the sea. We can only hope that the refugees know how to avoid those monsters and arm themselves to ward off the attacks."

The sisters were stunned with the conversation they overheard. There were more and more boats coming in with horrifying stories of pirating and raping. They had been waiting to greet the new comers in dread and suspense lately because almost ninety-nine out of one hundred boats coming ashore had been raided. Half of that number had seen rape and violation or killings and kidnappings. The price the boat people had to pay for their freedom was very dear. Nonetheless, Kim was amazed at the influx of boats.

"Where are the girls now, Uncle?" Kim asked one of the adults. She used the term "uncle" as the customary way to address an older male with respect.

"They are in the sick bay tent waiting to be transferred to Terengganu. They are in real bad shape, kids."

"Do you know them?" another adult queried Kim.

"I don't know. I might go to the sick bay and check, Uncle."

"Be quick if you want to. The ambulance is coming soon to take the girls to hospital."

"Okay, thanks, Uncle." The girls ran off immediately.

Kim was curious as well as feeling dejected at the girls' predicament. They were as young as she was, Kim reminded herself.

The sick bay tent was crowded with onlookers. It was a small square thatched hut, partially enclosed on two sides by timber and palm leaves. It was ten by ten metres, with a room at the back for discreet examination and an open plan in front. The dirt floor was raised a fraction higher, and there were benches along two sides and a high bench for the examination of minor ailments and injuries. There were people waiting patiently on the bench as usual.

The sisters had to force their way forward to get closer. Being bolder and smaller, Trinh managed to propel herself to the front and got quite close to the figures on the stretchers, which were placed on the examination table. Covered by thin coloured blankets, the two small, still bodies with their eyes closed, were a sad picture. Their battered faces were swollen and bluish. Some of the blood was still fresh; it was oozing from the wounds and forming a trickle down the throat of one of the victims and formed a puddle on the ground between her legs. She opened her eyes wearily, just in time for both Trinh and herself to recognise each other. In that moment of astonishment and recognition, both were horrified at the circumstances. They were speechless with embarrassment at their situation.

"Oh no! Oh no!" Trinh cried out involuntarily after an instant of silence. She stepped forward.

One of the healthcare volunteers in the tent held her back.

"Don't disturb them, kid. They'd had enough, don't you see?"

"But I know one of them. I know her." Trinh pointed toward Mai. "Please let me see her," Trinh pleaded with him.

"Really, is that so?" He thought for a brief moment then continued. "In that case, you can come closer and try to comfort her, kid. She's a loner, escaped all by herself." He added sorrowfully, as an afterthought, "Tell her to hold on, okay?"

"Thank you, I will," Trinh replied perfunctorily and hurried to the stretchers. The girl did not understand the implication of the volunteer in telling the victim to hold on to her life.

"Hey, is...that...you, Mai?" she asked the girl hesitantly, wishing that it were not.

"Is...is that you, Trinh?" Mai whispered her question. Her voice was weak and slurred. Her breathing was laborious. Trinh had to lean forward to hear.

"Yes, it's me. It's Trinh. You...eh..." Trinh did not know what else to say. She abandoned her sentence. "Kim is here too. I'll go and get Kim. Wait here," she quickly added.

Trinh turned around, looking for Kim in the crowd behind her. She did not realise the stupidity of her statement when asking Mai to wait for them, as if the victim would have had enough strength to stand up and walk away, as if all the pain and agony would have disappeared and she would become normal again. She waved urgently for Kim to come closer, mouthing the words, "Come, quickly!"

Kim tried to push her way to the front. *Trinh must have seen something*, she thought.

"What's up?" she asked with a little frown.

"It's Mai. She's in there," Trinh murmured.

"Which Mai?" Kim asked, and then a horrible realisation came instantly. "No way! Mai Huynh? From Gia Long High School? My friend?"

"Yes, your friend, Kim. Go and look for yourself. She looks really bad, so bad." Trinh shook her head in bewilderment; her voice was shaky with emotion.

"Are you sure?" Kim was reluctant to believe her. She stepped tentatively closer to the stretchers. She was afraid to accept the fact. Her heart sank with Trinh's revelation.

Back home, Kim remembered Mai as a beautiful girl with the slender proportions of a model. Her hair was silky and straight, cascading down her back like a flowing river. Her eyes were full of life, and her voice was vibrant with energy and ringing with optimism whenever the girls met. Her parents were once wealthy and educated. Before 1975, both were lawyers who were now unemployed as the legislative system was obsolete in the communist Vietnam at that time. The new regime closed down law school immediately and put in jails magistrates, judges, and lawyers with terms according to their duration of service for the previous government. Being the only girl in the family and being as beautiful as she was, Mai was her parents' treasure. She was

314

elegant and sophisticated in her manner and in every way. Kim thought of her as the pure, innocent image of an eighteen-year-old girl brought up in an affluent lifestyle.

Now, looking down at the girl on the stretcher, Kim was shocked and disturbed.

"Oh no! Oh, Mai. Why? Why must it be you?" Kim could not resist exclaiming.

Her eyes immediately filled with tears. Kim reached for her friend's hands and held them tightly. She felt inadequate and hopeless. She was incapable of doing anything to relieve her friend's anguish. Mai's hands shook uncontrollably in Kim's grasp. The girls locked eyes for a moment. Kim felt the pain, the shame, the humiliation from the look on Mai's eyes and wept harder.

After a while, Mai started. "I was so scared. I'd never been so afraid in my life when it happened. There were a dozen of them standing around onboard. Most were young men in their early twenties. Some wore unbuttoned open shirts, showing dark skin shiny with sweat. One of them had tattoos all over his arms and back. I kept seeing his tattoos. They kept returning to my head even though I tried not to. There was something like a figure of a naked, voluptuous girl on one arm and a snake was on the other, and a large skull was on his back and a pair of crossed sword. On his chest were some writings. His hair was long, shoulder-length and straight, untied and messy. He looked directly at me, eyeing my body up and down. I tried to divert my eyes immediately, and I wanted to be smaller, much smaller, to be out of focus, to disappear out of that scenario. And that was all I could remember. Everything else was so wrong after that."

"I...eh...I don't want to think anymore." Mai could not say another word than just that before sobs broke out of her chest like a dam breaking. She gasped for air between her moans

Trinh joined her sister and her friend. The three girls cried together openly with tears streaming from their eyes. Trinh used the back of her hand to wipe them away constantly without success. They were unstoppable, much as the grief and sorrow, which continued to come their way.

The descriptions from Mai fitted in with the tattoos on the same Thai boy they had encountered at sea. It seemed he had succumbed to the devil inside him and went along with greed and evil deeds after all.

Sydney, Australia, and East Hills Hostel

End of winter, 1978

THREE MONTHS HAD passed. The children were not enjoying their frequent trips to "Ho Chi Minh's mausoleum" as much, but they got by.

"Listen, everyone!" Mac walked hurriedly into the hut, carrying a letter in his hand. "Great news! We're all accepted by the Australia's government. We're going to leave next week for Kuala Lumpur by road then to Sydney by air as soon as the paperwork's done."

"Hurray! Yippee!" Trinh and Luc jumped up and down, clapping their hands at the same time. "No more instant noodles," they chorused. Instant noodles were the main diet in refugee camps along with canned meat, and after such a long time, they were fed up with the taste of both.

"It's my first aeroplane trip! Yippee! Ee, ee, ee! It's my first flight. Aye, aye, aye!" Luc sang his silly tune with joy.

"It's everyone's first, Luc. None of us has travelled by air before. I'm so excited," Trinh corrected her brother.

"Yeah, how nice to be able to get on a plane. We're going to fly." Hoan was excited too.

The whole family gathered, and as they speculated about the trip, they quickly realised they had no proper clothing for the flight to Australia, a distance of 6,611 kilometres from Kuala Lumpur. Everyone was worried they'd be boarding the plane wearing their usual rags. Giang, who reached Sydney last year, was over the moon on hearing the news her family was going to be in Australia soon. She had managed to send some money so they could all buy some new clothes. They had spent three months in the refugee camps wearing hand-me-downs from friends who had left to resettle in other countries. The clothes they had arrived in from Vietnam were now completely worn out, so Giang's money arrived just in time.

"Sorry, kids! You will just have to wear your thongs on the plane. There's not enough to get everyone a pair of shoes," Vy told them regretfully, having just paid for everyone's new clothes.

Even in their excitement, they left their hut, the miracle vegetable pond, and the refugee camp in tears. Their long journey was finally coming to an end with resettlement in Australia.

Landing safely on the runway on a cold winter's morning, the Qantas flight had successfully transported its complement of refugees from Kuala Lumpur to Sydney's Kingsford Smith. Then, after the cabin was sprayed with disinfectant by customs officers, the weary boat people were ushered towards Australian customs.

"What are they spraying for?" Trinh was curious.

"Dunno, us. Perhaps we're too stinky, especially you, Trinh!" Hoan teased.

"No way, I think it's you and Luc and your smelly feet," Trinh retaliated.

"They're spraying to get rid of germs. You're full of germs, Trinh," Luc added.

"Everything is so nice and immaculate!" Kim was in awe, changing the subject. They were walking out into the customs area now.

"Shush!" Mother was stern. Authorities and their representatives were always frightening images to her.

"Children! Behave yourselves." Father was being serious too.

"Your right index finger, please." The interpreter put her right index finger up for the group to understand, translating the custom officer's order.

"Your left index finger, please." This was the second time they had to go through this.

The procedure had been done initially back in the refugee camp while preparing their IDs for the UNHCR's records. "Your fingerprints will be in the international fingerprint library. No chance of being incognito now!" Father had said.

Now, Mac joked after they were through customs, "There you go! Whatever you do from now on, stay out of trouble or they'll catch you easily, Trinh! There's no way out! Your fingerprints can be easily retrieved. No chance of escape! They'll pull you in like a stray dog! So behave yourself!"

They all laughed nervously even though the thought of performing a criminal act in Australia was the furthest thing on their minds. But the knowledge that detailed personal records could come back and haunt them brought cringing memories from back home.

Giang and her daughter, Kate, came to the airport to meet them and followed them to their hostel. They cried and laughed together as if in a dream.

"It was only a year of separation, but it seemed like a lifetime," Mac said with tears of joy when reuniting with his wife and little girl.

"I am still dreaming, am I?" Giang asked no one in particular in between her crying, laughing, hugging, and kissing everyone one by one.

Mother could not say anything as her tears streamed nonstop down her cheeks.

Then the group was directed to board two buses leaving the airport for East Hills Barracks.

Settling into the bus and looking through the windows, Trinh was fascinated by the red-brick-and-tile terracotta houses, seeing them for the first time, "They're different to our terrace townhouses. They're on one level, and the bricks are not rendered."

"Yeah, everything is so neat and nice. There's a garden in front of every house too, and so many trees, flowers, and grass. It's fresh and colourful!" Kim agreed.

"They look strange…foreign." Trinh smiled, knowing that she did not make much sense.

"But there're not many people around, are there? It's quiet, and the streets look deserted. Where are the people?" Trinh was puzzled. In the past, back home and especially in the refugee camps, she was always surrounded by crowds and noise.

Leaving the dense suburban area to the remote suburb of East Hills, the bus entered semibushland with patches of yellowish dry grass on either side of the road.

"Oh no! Are they taking us to the state's new development sites like the Viet Cong? They're not, are they?" Mother cried out in fear. She was scared to death of the Viet Cong new state developmental sites back home as being sent there almost meant a death sentence, far away from civilisation where one would labour for no reward.

"It can't be, Chi," Father reassured her. "There're houses along the route. See, there." Father pointed to occasional homes here and there on either side of the road.

Chi smiled weakly and forced herself to believe her husband. "Yeah, they're nice people, Australians and their government. They're not going to harm us, I hope!"

Then she fell into silence until the bus came to a full stop at East Hills Barrack. Father did not say anything else; perhaps he was not quite sure either.

Looking up from her reverie, Mother sighed with relief. "Oh, there're buildings here after all. We are in civilisation! There're power lines and flower beds and gardens!"

Stepping out of the bus into the cold wind of August, the group was shocked at the change in weather from hot and humid to the colder temperate climate of Sydney. It was not only that; the flimsy material of their clothing and their bare feet meant they all felt the cold.

"Brrr, it's so cold!" Luc blew out his breath, fascinated by the cloud of condensation flowing from his mouth like smoke.

"Look, look! I'm smoking!" Delighted with his ability to make it happen, he put his index and middle fingers in front of his lips as if holding a cigarette. Then, swaying with the motion and circling an O with his mouth, he blew rings of condensation like a regular smoker. Tapping his fingers on his imaginary cigarette, he pretended to flick the ash before inhaling again, entertaining the family.

Trinh copied her brother, both of them happily absorbed in this playacting like grown-ups with cigarettes in their fingers.

"Yeah, it's…brrr…cold," Kim agreed in between her chattering teeth.

"Nah, it's not cold. It's freezing!" Hoan corrected, jumping up and down on the spot and rubbing his hands together to keep warm.

"I've never felt this cold before," Trinh spoke between her make-believe smoke clouds. She pressed her body closer to Vy, trying to steal her sister's body heat.

Huddling together, they shivered in their flimsy tropical outfits, sandals, and thongs. The sun was shining and bright, but its mild heat was not enough to penetrate the cold air.

"It's winter in Sydney. Just like being in the fridge, only ten degrees outside, I think. Of course it's cold," Vy explained to her siblings.

"My feet are going blue," Hoan said, wiggling his toes.

"Keep moving. Walking up and down might help, Hoan," Vy suggested.

They were standing outside the reception area of the East Hills Barrack Hostel waiting for their admission to allocated rooms. Numerous buses had disembarked more than a hundred refugees on to the hostel's grounds. Most looked lost, untidy, and pitiful, a contrasting image to the clean, neat surroundings and the clear blue skies of Sydney.

Then they all cried out with oohs and ahhs when being ushered inside the hostel's heated dining room, away from the chilly wind outside.

"Welcome to East Hills. My name is Bill Murray. I'm the manager here. Lunch is ready, and my staff will be serving you." He nodded towards a row of uniformed staff standing behind him before continuing. "Just get yourselves comfortable at tables over there and help yourselves to plates, cutlery, and food at the counter. After that, you are free to go back to your rooms and have a rest or get acquainted with the hostel's grounds. Dinner will be served between 6:00 p.m. and 7.30 p.m., breakfast from 7:00 a.m. to 10:00 a.m. and lunch at 12:00 p.m. to 1.30 p.m. I wish you all a happy stay here. If there's anything you would like to ask, please do not hesitate to do so. Thank you and enjoy your lunch." The interpreter translated the hostel manager's announcement.

The group was in awe of the formal introduction as the foreign aroma of beef stew, chips, boiled and mashed potatoes, peas, and carrots filled the dining room and tantalised taste buds. They quickly dispersed away and looked for a table to sit down at. Some had found friends from back home and joined in excitedly. Some were bold enough to act like they had been here before. Some were timid and shy, not daring to initiate a move until encouraged by the social workers.

"Yum, I smell food!" Hoan smacked his lips with eagerness.

"Yeah, yum yum, no more instant noodles!" Luc declared, repeating his wish before leaving the camp.

"Wow, it's so nice in here, so clean!" Trinh said, looking around with wide eyes.

"Children, go over there and line up for your lunch," Father said. "Go collect your plate, knife, and fork and let the staff know what you want to eat. Now, go on. Don't be shy!"

"Hurray, we're going to eat our first Western meal!" Trinh declared, hurrying to the counter with the rest of them.

"Geez, look at you two greedy pigs! How are you going to finish that?" Trinh said with astonishment, looking at the pile of meat on Luc's and Hoan's plates.

"Easy, just watch us!" Then they dived in, attacking their plates with gusto and soon returning for a second helping as big as the first.

"You two are real refugees, aren't you?"

"Of course, we are! There's no denying that, is there? So what? I'm not ashamed of that," Hoan said in between mouthfuls.

"Yes, we are boat people and refugees. And no, we don't deny that. We're proud refugees, if there's anything like a proud refugee," Trinh said, and they all laughed with her.

It continued like that for several weeks, and as they became tired of the canteen's menu repetition, they returned to two-minute Maggi instant noodles, longing for their familiar earthen meals with fish sauce and bok choy.

"Haha, who said good-bye to instant noodles forever?" It was forbidden to cook in their room, so the instant noodles became a simple alternative to hostel meals.

The rest of their first afternoon was spent in their warm cosy rooms on their beds under thick blankets. The excitement that followed their long journey and a filling hot tasty meal had made them drowsy until all of a sudden they were jolted upright by an urgent knock at the door.

"It's the charity people! Come on, get up! They're here. Hurry." Luc charged in with the news. He was staying in a different room with Hoan and Father. Mother, Vy, Kim, and Trinh were in the next room. His nearsighted glasses crudely attached by wires were delicately balanced on his nose and ears. Luc was so glad to retrieve his broken and trodden-on glasses on the upper timber deck when the Thai pirates had left their boat after hoarding many valuables from them the first time. Back in the refugee camp, Luc had skilfully repaired them and had been able to see once again. The little boy had no other choice, of course!

Following Luc's announcement, they were walking out slowly in single file: Luc and Trinh first, then Kim, and Hoan. Father and Mother were at the back. Timidly standing beside a large bin on wheels and huddling together and shivering in the cold, they were waiting with eagerness until the ladies urged them to pick what they needed.

Returning to their room, Trinh stood proudly in front of the mirror. "Look, they gave me this jumper!" She examined her image, enjoying the wonderful warm sensation of her newly acquired woollen top.

"It's yellow! It's bright, and it's nice!" In all her life, Trinh had never felt so glad as the joy she felt receiving her first set of warm clothing from the two ladies at Saint Vincent de Paul on her first day in Sydney. She was also grateful for their caring heart and generosity toward a little person from the other side of the world.

The piles of secondhand clothes in the bin disappeared quickly. Each refugee was allowed to choose a jumper, a jacket or cardigan, a pair of trousers or skirt, a shirt or a dress, a pair of shoes, socks, and a nightie.

"Hey, I've got a complete wardrobe!" Trinh beamed happily. "Except shoes, none of the shoes are my size. But never mind. I can still wear my thongs with socks." The clothes were oversized and well-worn, but they were perfect and new to her. And most importantly, they were giving her the warmth she wanted more than anything else.

"Aren't they kind?" Kim was glad too. They had enjoyed rummaging into the piles of secondhand clothes and choosing their first winter outfits in Australia. Arriving from the tropical heat of over thirty degrees Celsius to a mere ten degrees was a big difference, and wearing the wrong clothes made it even worse.

"Yep, we're here, and we're lucky!" They often had to remind themselves that to shoo away the melancholy from their aching heart and from their homesickness.

"It's real now. We're so far away from home. There's no turning back, is there?" Trinh asked Vy.

"Don't think of it, Trinh. We have to step forward now, one step at a time. There's no turning back. Be strong, girl!"

"But I miss my friends, my school, and our house," Trinh said softly. "It's so hard."

It came to Trinh now that, after almost forty years, that was perhaps the best thing for them as refugees of the eighties—being unable to turn back. It became the strongest force propelling them forward to achieve what most of them had achieved in the shortest time possible. It had been a rocky road for all, but they had reached their destination safely again, on shore this time.

Recently, an Australian friend of hers had commented that he was surprised to see the Vietnamese so proud that they were refugees or boat people of the eighties. To some others, the need to conceal that fact might be necessary to keep in line with the level of becoming outstanding citizens by many of them in society today.

"You guys talked about your suffering and hardship of those early times without showing any scar or grief. It's wonderful to see many of you emerge from a tough start to embrace life with optimism and openness becoming successful professionals or merchants. Within forty years, the Vietnamese community in Australia had risen from scratch to become a well respected, well regarded, and affluent community with many considerable achievements succeeded by humble and unpretentious people." He added, "I take my hat off to them for that, I must admit!"

Her chest had swelled up with pride hearing the comments.

"Yes, we received but we also have returned," Trinh told him proudly. "I was at a cheque handover meeting on Tuesday, January 20, 2014, at the Vietnamese Community Centre in Cabramatta as a representative of Australian-Vietnamese Health Professional Associations in NSW (AVHPA-NSW) to witness the presentation of $95,000 Australian dollars. It had followed the remarkable effort by our community, a mere population of 120,000 in total in NSW, to help the people of the Philippines after the devastating Haiyan Typhoon. There were many refugee camps in the Philippines back then, and they had shown us their tremendous support. We wanted to give back what we could."

Trinh added, "Also, it was only last month that the community raised $165,000 AUD for the NSW Bush fire victims. Then the Victorian Bush Fire in 2009, Saint Vincent de Paul Society in 2010, to mention only a few." Trinh smiled broadly, feeling like a strutting male peacock displaying his magnificent tail again. She had not felt like that for ages.

One Dollar, Hyde Park, and Dymocks Bookstore

1979

"HERE, A DOLLAR for you, Trinh!" Mother gave her a crispy one-dollar note, its edge stained with cooking oil from her fingers.

"Thank you, Mother." Trinh beamed with pleasure, holding the note tightly in her hands. She could not wait to get out of the small crowded caravan, run to Dymocks bookstore and spend her one-dollar note.

"And this is for you too, Luc." Mother also gave her brother the same.

Ready to bolt away, both glanced at each other and gave out silent signals. They had been inside the small caravan for the whole morning busily helping their mother handing out boxes of Vietnamese fried rice and cups of springrolls through the caravan's window. The caravan parked on a pedestrian walkway near the famous Archibald Memorial Fountain of Hyde Park sculptured by Sicard, a French artist, to commemorate the association between Australia and France in the First World War. The fountain became their second favourite place in the park whenever they were there helping their mother with her food stall. Their most favourite place remained Dymocks, the giant bookstore on George Street, Sydney, even if they could not pronounce its name properly in those days. Once a week, they were given a dollar for helping Mother, and they could not wait to spend it on books.

"You two can have a break now," Chi said, releasing them from their duty at seeing their eagerness clearly shown.

"Hurray, thanks, Mother," both chorused and darted out of the van swiftly.

"Let's go, Luc," Trinh shouted.

"Yeah, let's go," Luc echoed, then both ran to Dymocks in a hurry before their allowable break time finished.

The giant bookstore in those days was always crowded with readers staying around reading books or browsing the aisles, fingering one item after another. Trinh loved being in here, she felt so much at home. There were walls and walls of beautiful books in every category on display for her to touch and admire. At first, she did not dare to take them off the shelves but walked slowly around them, looking at them longingly for a feel. Stacks of books were neatly exhibited that astounded her. There were rows of the adventures of Tintin by Herge, their beloved cartoon character from back home, in colourful illustrations. Trinh stood there mesmerised.

Then one day, her brother approached from behind and whispered, "Take it down. You know you can take them down and look at them freely without being asked to purchase them."

"Really, are you sure?" Trinh was surprised. "You're not pulling my leg, are you?" her brother was renowned of playing practical jokes on her many times in the past, and it was best to be careful.

"Yep, believe me. I saw many of them doing the same, taking books off the shelves, reading them, then putting them back on, and walking out of here without anyone stopping them or asking them to purchase anything," Luc reassured, nodding his head toward the patrons in the bookstore. "See them there?"

Trinh was glad that her brother had been observant, and she was eager to take her first Tintin book off the shelf, *Explorers on the Moon*, and absorbing in it fully for the entire lunch break. That began their frequent trips to Dymocks every time they were around this part of town. Then the brother-and-sister's collection of Tintin books materialised from a dollar bonus on Saturday or Sunday working with Mother.

"Look, it costs ninety-nine cents, Luc," Trinh said.

"Yeah, we can afford to buy it."

"Shall we?" Trinh hesitated.

"Why not? We still have a dollar and one cent left. We can get a burger, an ice cream, and a can of Coca Cola for our dollar," Luc said.

"Okay, I'll go there and pay."

"Here is your change. Thank you." The cashier gave them a one-cent change.

They had spent their whole one-dollar-a-week extravagantly as rich kids, accumulating the books one by one until all the titles sitting proudly on their desk.

After their joined cartoon collection, Trinh went on saving her money for her next purchase. Meanwhile, she continued standing in the aisle reading *Gone with the Wind* by Margaret Mitchell, her first novel in Australia, whenever she was at the bookstore. It was several months before she had saved enough to purchase it together with an *English to English Oxford Dictionary*. Trinh had given up using her *English to Vietnamese Dictionary* as the explanation in the entries confused her even more with the complication and contrast of the English and Vietnamese language. Even though the thickness of the novel, almost five hundred pages, was intimidating to her English's vocabulary and grammar at that time, Trinh had determined to get it. Having the book in her possession, she had spent hours and hours reading word by word with a notebook and a pencil on the other hand jotting down each vocabulary and its meaning in her quest of literature reading. By the time Trinh reached the end of the book, all the pages were thumbed many times over and over. She had to return to the pages after trying to understand the meaning of each word patching up the phrases. And the cover was almost torn apart. That book and its film with Vivien Leigh and Clark Gable remained in her memories everlasting images of the American civil war and its brutality until now.

Their anticipation of the weekends to go to the Archibald Fountain and Dymocks Bookstore was their highlight every week even if they had to help Mother most of the time with her caravan food stall.

"$1.00 for a container of fried rice or three springrolls," the handwritten sign hanging on the front of their counter read.

That was a huge step for Mother to take, venturing out in a food stall, considering her timid nature. After a few months of settling in with a new life, Mother was quick to start her business adventure with one of her old friends, Aunty Na. Everyone in the family all gave her a hand. Back then, it was genuinely considered everyone's business and responsibility, helping with the family without thinking of rewards or wages. Chi was as excited as all of them were. Their first interaction with the whole new world of Sydney and its residents was through a brand new endeavour. Aunty Na had managed to get a licence selling food in Hyde Park and had given Mother a loan to buy an old caravan together. She had come to Australia as an exchange student well before the war ended and been granted a permanent resident status after the Republic of South Vietnam was abolished on the world map.

When all paperwork had been arranged and the caravan was scrubbed clean ready for business in the following week, they were all in euphoria. Afterward, their weekend was full of activities. Starting on Friday, they had to prepare everything for the two-day trading in the park. The night before, for the spring rolls, they had to roll them in improvised filo pastry ready for frying on trading days. For the fried rice, the dicing of carrots, ham, onions, and spring onions were done. The final steps were completed inside the caravan during business hours. The excitement continued when they were all piling up into an old bright-canary four-door Datsun 180B on early Saturday mornings before dawn and arriving to the park without a scratch. All eight of them emerged out of the car refreshed and chirpy as innocently as only refugees could be, as if that was a perfectly normal thing to do. Those days, seatbelts had not been in effect. Not many police patrols were on the roads, and refugees were like matchsticks in that as many as eight could all fit in a sedan easily. Not to mention that sometimes they had to stow the caravan from its parking place to the park if Aunty Na was late. It was amazing the Datsun was able to manage its task miraculously; it was a good old, reliable Datsun 180B or 200B that the Vietnamese refugees loved so much. Each family had at least one in their lifetime in Australia back then.

Hiccups were sometimes encountered. Then they all had to push and shove the heavy, encumbrance caravan by foot with the Datsun in front when its machine refused to cooperate. But they were all happy to do it, and they sailed through the challenge as their boat had passed over the small storms, and they climbed over a road hump one at a time. Business would be open as usual regardless of any hiccups, and everyone had his or her task throughout the day. It was always hectic.

"Hurry up! Where are the springrolls? Customers are waiting!" Aunty Na would shout over the noise in Vietnamese.

"Don't just stand there, Luc!" Mother would say. "Pick up the springrolls and put them in cups, son."

"Okay, okay," Luc replied, reluctantly turning to his task and picking up the springrolls by chopsticks. He was watching the throng through the caravan's window with fascination.

Vy would try to speed up her frying, and baskets of hot springrolls would arrive for Trinh and Luc to hand out to Aunty Na in cups of three.

"Hey, pick yours at your side, Luc," Trinh protested. They were always in competition, comparing which had done more than the other had.

"Hey, speak for yourself! Cheater!" Luc was not pleased.

"More, more! Quickly!" Aunty Na urged. "And stop arguing, children!"

"More springrolls, Vy!" Trinh pushed.

"I only have one pair of hands!" Vy would shout back, counterattacking the pressure coming her way.

"Get Kim to help you there," Mother would command while busily frying rice in a large square electric pan.

"Fried rice, more fried rice, quickly!" There was more shouting.

"Put more rice in the electric cooker, Trinh. We need them fast." The lunch peak hours were always the worst for those inexperienced kitchen hands and cooks in the crowed caravan.

"Excuse me, I think the springrolls are uncooked." Occasional complaints would come back at them with the still red raw meat inside.

"Oh, sorry. So sorry, let's change them for you. Please wait," Aunty Na would skilfully reply, then she would shout toward the back in Vietnamese, "Slow down, everyone. Make sure the meat is cooked, Vy."

"See, you asked me to hurry up. Now you want me to slow down!" Vy accused.

However, the rice escaped criticism most of the time even though in their haste, it was half-cooked as well. But no one had noticed or thought that was the way Vietnamese fried rice was supposed to be!

In any case, Aunty Na came to their rescue every time in dealing with customer's complaints. Her English was a hundred miles ahead of them, newly arrived refugees. They all looked up to her as their most trusted guide and often listened with deep respectful awe when she started her conversation to English-speaking people.

"I wish one day I can speak like that!" Trinh told Kim. "If one day I can whisper in English rather than speak loudly with difficulty every word then I can classify myself as an Australian!" she declared with conviction, believing her statement wholeheartedly, as if mastering the language would be the final step in the transformation of her whole being.

To her, at that time, and perhaps until today, speaking English was a vast mystifying process. All the twists and turns of the tip of her tongue in "the," "thin," and "thirteenth" words caused her problem, and the phonetic accent of the English vocabulary was much in contrast to her Vietnamese monosyllabic and clearly pitched words. She often stressed on a wrong vowel or spoke in a monotone, and it would end in the frustration that no one could understand her.

"I don't get it! Why can't they understand me? I thought I was speaking very clearly!" Trinh would often complain to her sister, still very upset at the recent incidence.

"I asked the man, I would like to buy some ve-*get*-ables please." Instead of stressing on the first *veg*, she had tried to pronounce it monosyllabically as ve-*get*-tables; and of course, it was a totally strange, nonexistent English word. "Then he said, 'I beg your pardon. What would you like to have?' a fruit vendor would ask, trying to be helpful."

Trinh was retelling her story.

"Some ve-*get*-tables, please," she repeated. And seeing a puzzled expression on the fruit vendor's face, she would add, "Any will do." Trinh would feel puzzled as much as he did.

"I don't think I have what you asked. Sorry!" He shook his head and shrugged his shoulders, unable to decipher her request.

By now, Trinh would get angry with herself and the fruit vendor and feel awkward by her inability to get a simple message across.

"Clearly, he refused to understand!" she concluded.

"Yeah, they do not understand our English. I often have to repeat. I wonder why!" Kim agreed, readily shaking her head. "You're not the only one, dear. Don't worry about it. I went to the supermarket today asking an assistant for an air freshener, and I had a similar reaction, Trinh."

It was Kim's turn. "Do you have a la-*ven*-der air freshener?" Kim was bold enough to make her query.

The assistant pondered for a few minutes then asked, "Say it again?"

"A la-*ven*-der air freshener," Kim said clearly, enunciating each syllable very proudly.

The assistant's brows knitted together for a little while then repeated her request with a smile on his face. "Do you mean a *la*-ven-der air freshener?"

"Yes, of course! A la-*ven*-der air freshener! Thank you!" Kim was glad to get what she wanted in the end. Bugger if it was *la*-ven-der or la-*ven*-der; they were all the same to her, and they were spelled exactly the same anyhow.

Even her favourite bookstore, Dymocks, gave her the trouble of pronouncing it right!

Pointing and gesticulating was their main tool in complementing their lack of language skill. Hoan got home one day and told everyone how he got his chook by flapping his arms about and clucking as a hen at the butcher.

His friend would laugh and said, "Nah, that's easy! It's how you get eggs that much more complicated!"

"How?" Trinh was interested.

In those days, not many things were on display when a customer would just pick up and pay for whatever he or she had wanted at the cashier. They had to ask for the items, and it was always their dilemma in shopping for their groceries and meat if they did not want to employ an interpreter to go along, as of course, the names of the items often were not in their head.

"Go get me a glass of ice coffee then I'll tell you," Tu ordered, enjoying his chance of having her attention.

"You! An exploiter of labourer!" Trinh declared before walking inside and brewing Tu a cup of coffee.

"Here, how you do it. Watch me." Tu used the slender teaspoon to stir his coffee before gulping in large mouthfuls. Then he stood up, flapping his arms and clucking about as a hen while at the same time bending in half and pointing his fingers to his bottom mimicking the sound, "*Phewt, phewt.* You know, *cluck, cluck. Phewt, phewt.*"

The whole group would laugh uproariously with this ingenuity of gesticulation.

"Lucky that you went into the right store! They might bring out chicken manure if you're not careful!"

Their caravan food stall and Hyde Park adventure lasted half a year, providing enough money for Mother to contemplate the idea of moving out of East Hills Barrack. Still, Trinh remembered clearly the day Mother opened her first savings account in order to receive money from the government welfare support. Nervous and timid, she was queuing in line at the main office in the hostel, still very much in awe from the experience with the authority and their arrogance back home. The Australian bank clerk was sitting on the desk with the necessary paperwork. His foreign look did not help one bit even though there was an interpreter sitting next to him.

"Please give me your ID, and I will help you fill out the forms. But you have to make a small deposit to open your account, Mrs. Chi," the interpreter instructed.

Chi gave the interpreter her refugee permanent resident paper with her fingerprints imprinted as her sole ID at that time, then she was more nervous looking at them.

"A small deposit please, Mrs. Chi," the interpreter urged.

Chi was quite embarrassed. "Oh, but...but...I've got nothing to give you!"

"Just a small deposit will do, Mrs. Chi. It's a procedure to get your account running," the interpreter coaxed, thinking that Chi did not want to pass on her cash same as many others who had had a bad experience with their loss before.

Chi stammered. "Erm, I know, but—"

"One or two dollars will do." The interpreter was losing patience.

"Eh, I don't even have that. I'm sorry!" Eventually, Chi had to admit the truth. Her face reddened.

The interpreter was helpful seeing that Chi did indeed have no money. "Oh, okay. Can you borrow from somebody? Your welfare support will be deposited into your account after a deduction from the expense at the hostel in the next few weeks, Mrs. Chi."

"Oh, thank you. Yes, I guess I can try. Of course!" Chi was relieved to find a way out of her dilemma that in her embarrassment she could not think of the solution. Chi hated to have to borrow if she could not repay.

"Kim, Trinh, quick! Run around and ask anyone that we know for a dollar or two for me please, children. Tell them that I will repay them as soon as the welfare cheque comes. Please hurry, kids."

At last, Mother had her dollar to open her first savings account. She had borrowed from a friend of the family, and now she was operating her first business adventure in Hyde Park, selling Vietnamese fried rice and spring rolls, getting her dollar to work.

To save on cost, Mother, Vy, Kim, and Trinh used go to Flemington Market by train to buy the necessary ingredients. They walked a long distance of two kilometres from East Hills Station to the hostel, carrying large bags of carrots, onions, and meat to East Hills Barrack at Voyager Point. It was always a big ordeal for the women. Sometimes, Hoan and Luc also came along. They divided the carrots, onions, meat, eggs, and rice into smaller bags, and the entourage of strange-looking people parading the streets caused a stir among the locals.

"Look at them!" Some were pointing at the group, fascinated by the new batch of refugees recently arrived from Asia and who looked and acted so odd in everything.

"They are using umbrellas! How peculiar!"

"Yeah, funny kind of people! How could they use umbrellas in this kind of weather? Silly!"

"Where were they from? Martians? Aliens?"

It was sunny and warm in an early summer day in December, the kind of weather that Australians used to love to sunbathe in the era of undetected sun damage to the skin. Looking at them shielding their faces and bodies from the sun seemed very weird to the locals.

Trinh knew they were uncharacteristic and odd in every which way and often wished if she could blend in without being taunted at. How was it possible, she often asked herself? She wished if it could be done effortlessly by peeling off her idiosyncrasies layer by layer to make her appearance normal in their eyes.

"They're laughing at us, Kim." She nudged her sister and whispered in her language, glancing at the girls their age standing at the station, afraid they might overhear their conversation. She did not know that the sound of her language was odd too. But when they talked in Vietnamese, heads turned toward them and sometimes ridicules came along.

"Ching chong ching chong. Ding dong ding dong."

She often heard that mocking tune directed back at them and was shy of not knowing how to reply in English. She thought she was very proud of her mother tongue, and Vietnamese language was the core of her origin. What was wrong with it now that they made her feel ashamed of speaking it?

"Why are they taunting us like that?" she asked Vy. Trinh often had many whys to ask her sisters.

"Because we came from a very different background, Trinh. We're from the East and they're from the West. Our cultures are many oceans apart. Our features are Oriental, with slanted, almond-shaped eyes, jet-black straight hair, golden skin, and not with large blue eyes, curly blond hair, and white skin. We are standing out in the crowd. Our philosophy, art, religions, principles, concepts, and values are like chalk and cheese to theirs. We are simply different."

"How different?" Trinh was clearly puzzled. She did not think that her coming to a foreign country could bring so many obstacles in every direction.

"To start with, our religion is based on Buddhism and theirs on Christianity. The list is endless. We believe in reincarnation, and life is a journey for us. Everything happens for a reason. Things come around, and you reap what you sow. Our future is based on what we do today. Their future is unknown or predetermined by God, and it has nothing to do with their deeds. We tend to coexist in a family environment or as a whole, and they believe strongly in individualism. We are introverted, and they are extroverted. We tend to wait for things to happen. They are acting to make things happen.

"Heaven and earth, we tend to think of that as an eternal recurrence. For the Christians, they tend to think of themselves as elements in the universe. Their existence is with their service to their God or material matters to make life better, and everything has its beginning and its end.

"There are weaknesses and values in both cultures, I think. However, as we are mystifying to them as they are to us, that makes us a threat to them in every way. People tend to be nervous of the unknown. When they could not understand the other party's behavioural patterns then they're incomprehensible. Simple as that, I think. Just make sure that we do not erect a wall shielding or isolating us from them. Then they will see that we are not impenetrable as they think we are now."

"Will they be able to understand us if we try to explain to them one thing at a time? As we are trying our best to understand them every day now, aren't we? It's not easy for us too," Trinh asked her sister.

"Yes, it's that way because we are immigrants. We are new arrivals. It's their homeland, Trinh. I'm sure if it's the other way around, we would behave similarly. Don't be too upset. They'll come to accept us and our philosophies if our behaviours are not invasive to their cultures. Time will tell. Be patient and be good." Vy smiled at her last phrase. "We'll let them understand us."

Garlic and Fish Sauce

"ARE YOU GOING to do it?" Trinh asked her sister. Rolling her eyes upward in a gesture of befuddlement, she repeated her question. "Are you, Kim?"

"What do you think? Shall we? It's our way, isn't it? Can she do anything to us?" Kim paused a few seconds in her wondering and then came back with more determination. "What can she do to us anyhow? Are you game enough, Trinh?" she challenged her younger sister, trying to mask a trace of nervousness in her voice.

"Yeah, I'm game. Why not? If it comes to the worst, we don't have to open the door!" Trinh whispered, a little frightened and a little excited. She was in awe of what her sister was suggesting they do.

The pair were standing in their kitchen and looking toward the front door with apprehension. In Kim's hand was an old aluminium frying pan with stubborn greasy stains on its sides and a loose handle that rattled when the older girl put it forcefully down on the electric stove. Yes, they were going to fight, and Kim meant it. A couple of fresh garlic cloves were sitting cosily on the plastic chopping board next to the stove. About a dozen small fish were draining in the colander by the sink, and some of their remaining scales sparkled in the light reflecting through the kitchen window. The sisters were about to fry their fish for the family dinner tonight. The teenagers did not mind this daily task of preparing a meal as they had often used to do it back home. But after they moved here a few weeks ago, into the uppity suburb of Top Ryde, they dreaded taking the special step of frying garlic in oil before every stir-fry dish in their cooking method.

Their family of eight was happily settled in a three-bedroom flat on the third floor of a four-floor apartment building, following the suggestion of a friend of Giang's. Debbie and her husband had moved here in 1975 after their escape from Saigon on a ship, which landed in Darwin. Giang had stayed with them while waiting for the rest of the family to arrive from the refugee camp. There were very few boat people around this part of town, and Debbie had persuaded Mother to come along with them when their family decided to leave the East Hills Hostel to venture out into the real world.

"Please move to Top Ryde with us. We would love to have you as our neighbours. We will help you guys in everything we can, like shopping, moving around, getting here and there, doing this and that. Besides, it's a very nice place I've found for you, just across from our building and we can drop in on each other whenever we feel like it. You're going to love it. There's a high school nearby. Trinh and Luc can go there. Very nice area and beautiful people around."

After gathering all her courage to move out of their temporary first residence, Mother had not known anywhere else to turn. It was all the same to her—strange places in a foreign country barely six months after their arrival—so she agreed readily. The move was easy. A few garbage bags containing some of their clothes were all they had, most of which were old secondhand clothes and shoes given to them by St. Vincent de Paul Society. Debbie had a Ford wagon, and they all got in together. All nine people and some garbage bags fitted in easily as they were all tiny and skinny! Their language skill in English was as meagre as their possessions was, but the odd family of Vietnamese boat people had dared to venture into a suburb just twelve kilometres from Sydney and had hoped to blend in without knowing the effect of their idiosyncrasies. Their culinary Oriental custom of using garlic in almost every dish inadvertently brought about disaster in their first attempt to start a new life in a Western society in the 1980s. Little did they know that Australians were not used to exotic cooking methods. Adventurous recipes or aromatic spices were unheard of at the time or unpopular and most of them despised garlic and its smell, considering it as intolerable or antisocial.

The sisters experienced their first intimidating encounter with the upstairs neighbour on day one. What a shock to the teenagers. One afternoon, carrying on their task as usual, the pair were jovial and chatty after a day at school. Kim was in her matriculation course in Granville Technical College, and Trinh was in year 11 at the local high school. Everything was new and mystifying. Sometimes it could become terrifying, and they were all very shy and very timid. They were struggling to stay afloat with everything so different and peculiar coming in on them from every angle. Trying to speak English was hardest of all as they were often frustrated at their inability to get their message across. Coming home in the afternoon was relaxing. They could switch to their mother tongue animatedly, speaking Vietnamese with each other at last, happy in each other's company in a familiar setting where they felt they belonged.

On that day, the pair had prepared everything, and it was Trinh's turn to cook. As usual, she threw a couple of pressed raw garlic cloves into the hot frying pan and used a spatula to mix them around. To her disappointment, the garlic browned quickly in the overheated oil and turned it to charcoal.

Looking over her shoulder, Kim commented coolly, "You're burning the garlic, Trinh." Then she helped her sister by pouring the diced pork into the pan. Immediately, an acrid smell of burnt garlic in hot oil and light smoke was circling in the small kitchen, looking for a way out. Kim went to the windows and opened them wide to let the smoke out while Trinh sprinkled a spoonful of fish sauce and sugar into the pan to taste. The distinctive fishy smell blended with garlic and caramelised sugar quickly rose upward and escaped through the windows, out into the open air. What a horrible aroma! The pair did not know that it would be the start of a battle between them and the neighbour upstairs. On top of occupying an overcrowded unit, having mismatched furniture, wearing secondhand clothes and oddly outdated shoes, displaying Oriental features, and speaking in haltingly accented English, now came garlic and fish sauce. What a combination!

Just when Trinh was about to pour some more fish sauce into the pan to taste again, they heard frantic knocking on their door. They were even more surprised when a woman's voice on the other side started yelling in English, "Open the door! Open up!"

Her knocking grew louder and more demanding every minute. Glancing at each other, the sisters were frightened by the urgency of the woman's voice. Knowing that they had to speak English to whoever was on the other side made it worse.

"What happened? What did we do?"

"What is it?" They were whispering in Vietnamese.

"Why is somebody yelling at our door?" Trinh asked her sister, a little quiver in her voice. "What does she want?"

"I don't know. What do we do now?" Kim was equally frightened.

There was some more banging, and the woman shouted louder this time. "Open the bloody door, you fools!" Both sisters stood still, not knowing how to react. The pan was still simmering on the stove, and the aroma of garlic and fish sauce kept filling the flat. They could tell that the woman was losing patience as she kept banging on urgently.

"What are you cooking in there? It's disgusting! Come upstairs and smell it yourself!"

They exchanged eye contact. Both were reluctant to move toward the door, seeing that the person was angry. Even with little English, they could understand that she did not like the smell at all. They were puzzled by the situation and could not fully comprehend her anger and frustration. Cowering with fear in their kitchen, they wondered what was wrong with their cooking. That was the normal way they cooked back home, and they thought they could do the same here. What disaster had they caused?

"Why is she angry with us?" Kim whispered.

"How are we going to speak to this person?" Trinh asked her sister, also whispering, afraid that the stranger on the other side of the door might overhear them and charge in. Nobody else was home but the two of them; one was eighteen years old and the other just turned seventeen. In the end, both agreed to approach the door and open it together.

Hands on her wide hips, red face puffing with short breaths as if she had run a marathon, the woman fired a string of sentences in rapid English at them once the door was open, leaving the sisters even more frightened. Trinh stepped closer to her sister, using Kim's body as a shield to block out the stranger's angry face and body language. They could pick out a few random words in her vocabulary that indicated she was upset and threatened to inform the landlord of their filthy habit. "It's disgusting and smelly what you're cooking in there! How could you eat something like that!"

Kim apologised softly, "I'm sorry. We're sorry. Er, sorry." She did not know what else to say. It was as much as she could do to muster all her courage to speak for the two of them. The woman fired some more lengthy sentences in English before stomping off upstairs, her long skirt billowing in her wake. Trinh wondered if she might step on the hem and slip off the stairs, fall facedown, and break her nose at any moment. She looked on disappointedly when nothing happened and the woman disappeared around the curve.

That was the first time. After debating for a short while, they thought the culprit was the fish sauce.

"It must be fish sauce that made her so angry with us. Perhaps we shouldn't use too much next time," Kim concluded. They thought they had found a solution to appease their neighbour. Of course, they were worried sick and nervous about what had happened.

"Perhaps we shouldn't open the windows," Trinh suggested.

After that, they made sure that all the windows were tightly closed before starting to cook their meal, preparing their ground as if launching into a battle. Soon they realised it was also the smell of garlic that triggered the antagonism.

"Have you closed all the windows yet?" Kim asked.

"Yes madam!" Luc would click on his heels and salute like a sentry.

"The bathroom too?" Trinh insisted.

"Of course! All is clear! Just count on me, generals! The Woman will be pleased, trust me!" Luc reaffirmed. In their whispered discussions, they had nicknamed their difficult upstairs neighbour as the Woman ever since.

Confident with the all-clear, Kim tossed a couple of garlic cloves into the hot oil for a fried rice dish. To their puzzlement and horror, even with all the windows closely shut, there were steps running hurriedly downstairs and more banging and yelling as before, and then more sincere apologising.

"Sorry, very sorry! We're sorry!" Vy smiled sheepishly and uttered the well-learnt phrase.

As a last resort, Vy followed Debbie's suggestion and bought a can of super strong lavender air freshener in a nearby supermarket, and everyone thought that would solve their dilemma for good.

"Surely this will eliminate all odours!" Vy declared with conviction. They were all very tired and nervous with banging and yelling every time they were about to cook their dinner. It must end somehow.

How futile it seemed. The distinctive garlic aroma was difficult to mask, and it escaped upwards, inevitably creeping into the Woman's nostrils. The law of physics did not help by letting vapour rise upwards, not vice versa! It was sheer bad luck that they were living a floor below their difficult neighbour, and there seemed nothing they could do except stop using garlic and fish sauce in their cooking. It was a simple solution, but they could not think of it then, because it had always been their way before. They wished there were different ways to cook without offending their neighbour, and they did not know any other but their traditional method. It was all because of garlic, with its history of use for seven thousand years and its heavy influence in Oriental culinary recipes!

Until today, when they decided to go for broke! Stubbornness had arisen in the girls, and they wanted to test themselves with the challenge. They were still scared stiff and shaking with fright every time they heard the frantic knocks and their hearts still jumped out of their chest in anticipation, but they had made up their minds.

Dreading it just as much as ever, they decided to remain silent behind their door, refusing to open it and avoiding the abuse that they did not fully comprehend.

"If we're going to do it, just be quiet and don't answer the door. That's all, Trinh," Kim told her sister.

"She'll come down soon enough if we're going to do that, I know!" Trinh said.

"So what? Let her knock!" Kim declared stubbornly.

As soon as the cloves of garlic hit the frying pan, the girls expected the usual banging on their door and they waited patiently. The aroma of garlic was whirling upward through the kitchen window, and as if on cue, they heard footsteps running hurriedly down the stairs. *Thump, thump, thump. Knock, knock, knock.*

The sisters smiled defiantly at their daring act, but they lacked the courage to open their door to confront their difficult upstairs neighbour.

High School and Sausage Rolls

1979

HALF A YEAR had gone by, and so many changes had happened.

Trinh looked at herself in the mirror and did not like it at all. Her school uniforms were all wrong. Her white shirt and burgundy skirt were homemade. Her brown shoes were not the same as the other girls. They were of a different shade and style, cheap synthetic shoes that her mother bought at the local shoe store on a 50 percent discount. Mother also managed to get some white cotton and burgundy polyester fabrics at the material shop after a short debate on how much it cost to buy Trinh and Luc uniforms for their high school. It ended up that girls' uniforms were easier to tailor than boys'. And here she was, clad in an entire outfit that looked odd to her; even her shirt collars were too big, and her skirt was too long. Just to complete the picture, her schoolbag and her lunch box were secondhand and cost fifty cents each from the weekend market at Rockdale.

Mother was prompt. She spent a whole day on Sunday cutting out the uniform templates in old newspaper and sizing them against the fabric, then started her project by working on them with an old Singer sewing machine, also bought at Rockdale Market last Saturday. She cried out with joy seeing the famous brand that she used to have back home, and obviously, she could not resist buying it. Even with her shyness and limited English, Mother struck a bargain with the seller, and it went home with her that day for five dollars.

"How much?" Mother pointed to the Singer.

"Ten dollars for you, dear," the man replied, eyeing Mother bemusedly.

"No, eh"—Mother put up four fingers in the air—"yeah?"

The man laughed. "Nah, too cheap! Six dollars, no less, honey!" He also put up six fingers to Mother, helping her to understand.

She shook her head and put up five fingers again. "Okay? Yeah?"

The vendor smiled and said, "No, no, no. Six, it is!"

Mother hesitated then turned her head and pretended to walk away, even Trinh knew that she wanted it very much. *But her mother had learnt the art of bargaining since she was a baby,* Trinh thought.

The vendor shook his head for a fraction of a second and then nodded at once. "Okay, here you are! Five for you, sweetie! I haven't sold anything today. Consider yourself lucky!"

Mother neither cared nor understood what he said, but she was pleased with her purchase as it was something that reminded her of home. That evening, the dear, ancient machine was creaking away as she pedalled forward and backward, racing to finish her project. It was late at night, after the last buttonholes were done by hand on both items, when Mother triumphantly gave them to Trinh, beaming happily at her results. The girl was sitting nearby waiting patiently at her mother's side for hours, eager to try on her new uniform.

Her excitement depleted quickly like a deflating balloon as soon as she looked in the mirror, saddened by her oddity. She pleaded with her mother, "Please make the collars of the shirt smaller and the length of the skirt shorter for me, Mother, please?"

"Why? What nonsense! I think they look perfect, darling." Mother stepped in front of Trinh, as if shielding her daughter from the image she was looking at, and tried pressing the shirt collars down and pulling the skirt up, nodding her head with satisfaction at her tailoring skill.

Then looking up to observe her daughter's pouting lips and unhappy face, she coaxed gently, "Just wear them tomorrow as they are for the time being, Trinh. It's not easy to alter them at this stage, and it's late already. You need to wear them, and I'll redo the whole thing after a week at school, darling. Give me time. I'll do it. I promise," Mother assured.

Trinh nodded her head and told herself to be pleased. She must see that her mother had made the greatest effort for her to blend in at the new school. Examining the skilful buttonholes, each beautifully embroidered carefully by her mother's hands, Trinh sighed softly. *The collars might be too big and the hem might be long, but she must be proud of her buttonholes,* Trinh thought. No one at school had their shirt's buttonholes embroidered by hand for sure! Last week, on their first day, Luc and Trinh went to school in their casual clothes, outdated and old but neat and clean. They walked up under the staring eyes of the entire assembly. They could sense that they were a phenomenon, two refugee boat people recently escaped from Vietnam with limited, accented English that sometimes no one could understand, now attending Murray High School. The timid pair was introduced briefly to the English as a Second Language (ESL) class with the rest of the immigrants and then separated into different year groups.

Trinh did not know how she managed the school hours without being able to speak the language. She was dubbed "the talking machine" back in Vietnam as the girl who could talk about anything nonstop. Here, she was timid and lonely. *Her popularity and her confidence had stayed there as a punishment for leaving her country,* Trinh thought.

"No pains, no gains," someone had told her that. "You've got to sacrifice something to be able to gain something. Get used to it!'

It seemed that she had to get used to having the pains more often than necessary, Trinh thought. She missed her school, her classroom, her friends, the tamarind and the jacaranda trees in the schoolyard. The teasing from the boys back home whenever Trinh appeared late to class with her odd-looking uniform patched with many squares of "hi-fi speakers and TVs" on the hem, as rags were nicknamed then, never caused embarrassment to her. She was confident enough to shrug her shoulders and walk with her head high in front of them. She was a top student and a daughter of an ex-government official there. Although her status no longer existed in the Communist world, Trinh was proud of herself, wearing rags to school or else. She was considered "a rich girl" with the more hi-fi speakers and TVs a person had on his or her hem. However, it was different here. Here, she was a refugee, and her idiosyncrasies were her embarrassment.

"Hi," a girl in her geography class would say to Trinh, trying to be friendly. She pointed to her chest. "Rebecca."

"Hello," Trinh said in return and doing the same as Rebecca. "Trinh." Then they both fell into an uncomfortable silence, not knowing what else to say.

Trinh often sat in her classroom, her mind wandering out of the windows and thinking about her school or any other things but not the subject at hand as she could not understand a word from the teacher; they were all mumbo jumbo to her. The girl sitting next to her was very helpful. She would point to Trinh the particular chapter in the book they were studying. Trinh would go home every afternoon and look into her dictionary for almost every word in an attempt to decipher her textbook. It was confusing patching the meanings together as each word had more than one interpretation. She often ended up crying in frustration trying to understand it all.

In her high school years, sometimes Trinh wished she could afford to have a sausage roll for lunch more often. That wish stayed with her until now, as there was not many occasions then, she was granted freely. They had little money, and their lunch box contained normally homemade sandwiches. How peculiar that was, but at that time, a sausage roll, the very symbol of an Australian snack food and simple as that, seemed to be Trinh's most wanted item. Perhaps all she wished for was acceptance.

Public Housing and University

TRINH PLODDED THROUGH her high school years miraculously and moved on.

———— ✪ ————

"What time are we going to start?" Trinh asked.

The evening was cool with an occasional breeze disturbing the yellow hibiscus bush at the corner. Sipping hot jasmine tea with an air of sophistication, the young adults were sitting on the grass outside Trinh's house. They were discussing their plans for the upcoming midautumn or Moon Festival event. The warm and pleasing acoustic guitar sounds blended in with the gentle rustling of leaves, creating an enchanting atmosphere in the spring evening.

"Look at the moon, shining and almost perfect!" Trinh added.

"Not too late so the kids can march with us, of course!" Tu said, stopping his music for a while.

"Say, 7:00 p.m.? Not too early either because we want to light the candles in the lanterns, don't we? It has to be dark outside," Luc said.

"Yeah, the idea is for the kids to sing the song of "Tet Trung Thu" and parade with brightly lit lanterns around the neighbourhood," Kim added.

The song of "Tet Trung Thu" or Moon Festival is the Vietnamese folklore song that children used to sing while marching with their lanterns around the neighbourhoods back home.

"We want them to learn the song first, don't we?" Trinh asked. "But I don't remember the whole song. The first part of the lyric is easy, but I forget the latter part." She smiled sheepishly.

"Oh well, it's not too hard. I can write them down for you. But they can always repeat after us, or we adults can sing as loud as possible," Quan said. In those days, printers and computers or word processors were not as common as now. Most documents were typed and photocopied or handwritten. It was a laborious process that modern technology had helped cut short and turned into a simple procedure. Now, it was almost taken for granted.

"Who is in charge of buying moon cakes?" Nam asked.

"Ty is. But Kim and I are buying the lanterns and candles. So far, we have eighteen kids and twelve of us. We don't have enough money to get one lantern each. It has to be shared unless someone is going to cough up with some more cash!" Trinh smiled at her last comment.

They had pooled some cash for the planned expense from their few savings, hoping to create an event that introduced the kids to the Moon Festival and refresh themselves with some back-home nostalgia.

For thousands and thousands of years, the Shang Dynasty from the early tenth century BC had celebrated harvest time during the full-moon period of August or the eighth month of the lunar calendar. The tradition started on the fifteenth day and lasted for a few days afterward, and continued to be honoured by most Oriental cultures well into modern times. They also believe that the brightest and most beautiful moon happens at the same time. Hence, Tet Trung Thu, or Moon Festival, is celebrated during this beautiful full-moon season. It falls during September or October of the Gregorian calendar. There are many myths explaining the meaning of the Moon Festival, and to this day, anyone with an imaginative mind could just make up their own beliefs. Traditionally, squared moon cakes are specially made and consumed during the festive season. The shape of the cake was believed to complement the symbol of fertility in Oriental culture. A square and a circle are signified as a successful birth of a healthy offspring and a fully recovered mother, respectively. Therefore, during the Moon Festival, it also provides an opportunity for young couples to ask for a blessing. There are also mythological characters associated with the moon. One was the beautiful immortal moon goddess, chi Hang, whose ancient admirer, chu Cuoi, could only catch her silhouette once a year during a full moon in August, when he forever dreamt of a reunion with his undying love. In modern times, the Moon Festival become the Children's Festival in Vietnamese culture, celebrated with brightly lit various shaped lanterns ranging from the natural living creatures like fish, rabbits, butterflies, bees, mice, to boats, houses, and even mythological objects.

"Hey, I can almost see the moon goddess floating around charmingly up there in her beautiful flowing dress, and her forever thousand-year admirer chu Cuoi sitting on a tree stump, totally spellbound looking at her, wishing, wishing, and wishing," Quan said excitedly.

"Yeah, yeah, yeah! That chu Cuoi looks very much like you, Quan!" Trinh replied. "You have so many crushes on so many moon goddesses that you'll end up like him if you're not careful! Always a secret admirer looking from afar without her noticing at all!"

355

The teenagers and young adults of the Bonnyrigg Housing Commission Complex were boat people arriving in Sydney at approximately the same time, and ending up in the same area a few years later. The public housing complex catered for at least a thousand families. At one time, most of the residents were Vietnamese boat people of the 1980s; the youngsters were quick to recognise the need to connect. Friendships were formed easily as they were sharing the same difficult start and the same longing to speak their mother tongue in the still-brand-new environment, where the English language remained a major struggle. They were thrilled to be surrounded by people of the same cultural background, and their bare living conditions hardly bothered them at all. Having their companions and living in a house with front and backyards, a lounge, a kitchen, a dining room, and bedrooms to share between two persons only, not four or more, they were happy and content. Their compact circle included more than ten families whose kids were mostly university undergraduates at Sydney, NSW, or Macquarie universities or the University of Technology. Some were also high school students.

The group used to come to Cabramatta train station together every morning to travel to university. It was almost a social event as there could be twenty of them in one train compartment at one time going to Lidcombe, Regents Park, Redfern, or Central Station. Then, scattering to various faculties—general science, engineering, architecture, computer technology, law, art, nursing, pharmacy, dentistry, medicine—the children of the housing commission residents or other similar places were emerging from the lowest socioeconomic background to become professionals of the future. Mixed with the hardship was a carefree feeling of camaraderie, helping them to sustain the days ahead and to sail through university to reach their final goal. They embraced their freedom wholeheartedly, savouring the delicious taste of peace and stability without having to worry about the danger of war and its ugliness. The youngsters were never a concern for their parents; they were rowdy and mischievous perhaps, but they grew up gradually without overstepping any unlawful boundary. Shortly after they left Bonnyrigg, it was upgraded and transformed into a new community by the Public Private Partnership Project, which was absorbed by the NSW Housing Department in the 1990s.

With his savings from various odd jobs and from his parents' allowance, Tu purchased an old Volkswagen Beetle 1960s model for a mere fifty dollars. Ironically, he had to pay eighty dollars to tow it to his house and managed to fix its engine back to life! It was, however, a prized possession with many jealous admirers. He used it to drive his brothers to the station. His house was just two hundred metres from the backdoor of Trinh's house, separated by the park. Normally, Trinh and Kim had to walk and catch a bus from Bonnyrigg to Cabramatta station; then Trinh would go to Redfern, walking another half an hour to Sydney University to start her day. When Kim finally reached Central, she had to catch another bus to NSW University. Every day, the trip took one and a half hours, each way. Since having his old sedan, Tu was more popular among the group, and now had the two sisters sharing the ride to Cabramatta station as well. Even though the good old Beetle refused to cooperate sometimes, and they all had to push it to start, they were delighted at being able to cut short the first part of the trip, saving them at least half an hour every morning.

"Quickly, we're going to be late again," Trinh urged. "Last time, he went off without waiting for us, Kim, and we had to chase after the car. Remember? That cheeky devil! He doesn't want to make it easy for us. He turns it into a cat-and-mouse game if we are late. Hurry up!"

"You can run over there first and stall him then I'll catch up, Trinh." Kim was hurriedly making their sandwiches. Using a butter knife, Kim spread a thin layer on the sliced bread then placed a piece of ham, some cheese, and tomatoes on top before wrapping it hastily in the plastic wrap. She then threw it towards Trinh and quickly started making another one.

Trinh cupped her hands to catch it, but the sandwich landed on the floor. "Hey! Lousy thrower!" she protested. She picked it up then ran out of the house as fast as she could toward Tu's house, nodding her head and yelling, "Bye, Mother!"

"Hey, lousy catcher!" Kim shouted back. She hurriedly went after her sister, carrying her sandwich in her hands and echoing, "Bye, Mother!"

Chi waved her hands dismissively and shook her head disapprovingly then went back to her mountain of pattern pieces. It was always hectic with them in the morning, regardless of how early she tried to wake them up.

"Wake up, wake up! It's seven o'clock already. Hurry or you'll be late again!"

Ignoring her mother, Trinh would not open her eyes and try to steal another ten minutes without looking at her watch, knowing that her mother usually woke them at least ten or fifteen minutes earlier than the said time. Routinely, she then knew that Mother would go to the kitchen, turn on her Singer industrial sewing machine, and start her day labouring at the pile of pattern materials. Lying in bed, Trinh would wait for the next wake-up call to come from the kitchen, enjoying her exquisitely golden extra ten minutes. Then she would listen again to the churning of her mother's sewing machine as the final kick before bolting upright and dashing to the bathroom to wash her face, brush her teeth, and change into jeans and a T-shirt. In a record time of fifteen minutes, Trinh would be out of the door by 7:25 a.m. and running toward Tu's house, a sandwich in hand and a bag over her shoulder. It was the same frenzied race against the clock for both Kim and Trinh every morning. The earlier their mother tried to wake them, the more they dragged their feet.

"It's a no-win situation here! I really wonder why! You girls are hopeless!" Mother would shout in frustration one day. They would be bolt upright at her first call for the next few days, and then everything would return to the rush and chaos again when the heat died down.

When Trinh was leaving her house with the sun bright and high in summer or gloomy and dark in winter and when she was returning home in twilight or in the dark, her mother's position would be very much on the same spot, glued to her stool in front of her sewing machine, toiling away until 7:30 p.m. every evening. During those twelve hours when they were away studying, her mother would be at home trying to make their lives better and utilising her skills as a home machinist. Sometimes, her mother would cry out in frustration that she had not understood the instructions given to her and that the whole batch had been spoiled.

"Oh, dear, I did not change to a different thread for the hems and now they all have to be undone and redone!" Mother said sorrowfully.

Then they would all stay by her side after school trying to help, unpicking the threads one by one for her to redo the whole order and doubling her time and effort. Sometimes, their assistance was needed too if she was falling behind.

"Oh, do we have to?" Luc would say. He was eager to be out with his friends; he was going out with a local high school student.

"Can I watch *Happy Days* now and help later this evening?" Trinh would try to bargain.

"Don't cheat, children!" Kim would sternly reprimand with an authoritative voice. "You guys have to do your bit before going off anywhere!"

"Come on, if everyone lends a hand we'll be finished in no time," Vy would say, and that was the final word for all. She would then give a "don't mess with me" look!

On most weekends, they would help Mother turn the newly completed clothes right side out and fold them neatly in place, ready to be picked up by the contractor. Regardless of complaints or protests, they all joined in. Her mother's mountains of pattern pieces emitted a fine dust, which settled in every crevice of the house when she was doing overlocking or industrial sewing. Its churning noise remained in Trinh's mind all the time they were living in Bonnyrigg. The little house with enough space and garden for everyone was dear to her memory.

Kim and Trinh had the front garden for their flowers, the first flower garden in their life. They attempted to grow roses, azaleas, daffodils, carnations, and other varieties that seemed exotic to them. Some thrived and some died, but the sisters were enjoying their flower garden as much their mother was with hers.

Mother had her back garden, with which she was equally delighted. Within a couple of months, she managed to turn it into something similar to the one back in her country home with her herbs and plants. She asked everyone she knew for seeds or young tropical plants and all Vietnamese mints, such as spearmint, pointed leaf mint, heart leaf mint, then lemon grass, banana, sugar cane bushes, and chilli, paw paw, mango, longan, and guava trees along with numerous other plants and herbs. Walking past a garden and looking at its plants and herbs, Trinh would know if the home's occupiers were Vietnamese. Her mother's garden was very much the same.

The garden kept her mother busy and filled up whatever time she had left in her day. She would rush out to water them, pick up dead leaves, mulch the roots, sort her dispute with the caterpillars and snails, or just admire the vigorous green shoots and the fruits of her plants; all of it was justification for her hard work.

"I don't have time to feel homesick. That's the best way," she said.

"I don't want to have any idle time. I want to move forward to the future and not dwell in the past because if I turn my head I will have to remember. And it's painful to remember. My heart skips several beats if I start to remember. Perhaps I will have the courage to reminisce about the past when everything settles down, when I don't feel an aching inside for the wish to return home, but not now. Now I'm haunted by that frightful thought— that we could not stand being away from our homeland and only wish we hadn't left. I can't breathe sometimes if I let my mind drift back to those memories, of the house we were living in, of your grandmother's face the last time I was saying good-bye to her at the bus station. She could not cry, and I could not weep as much as I had wanted because we could not risk exposing ourselves. She was standing there holding her emotions intact and watching me leave, not knowing when or if we would see each other again. It's extremely difficult. Ah, I must forget those sentimental feelings," her mother concluded dismissively.

"We're here, safe and sound. I'm grateful to Buddha and the Almighty who blessed us with luck throughout our journey. I've vowed never to forget the day we left, but I have also vowed that I will not be dragged down by such desperation again!" She often told them that when they asked her to slow down.

Trinh went to Sydney University during her stay at Bonnyrigg, and the university was a dear place for Trinh to remember where she met a group of thirty or more Vietnamese undergraduates. They normally gathered around the Wentworth Building for lunch or a general catch-up. After a few years of high school, somehow she passed her Higher School Certificate (HSC) to enrol into a bachelor of pharmacy course. It must have been her math, Trinh was convinced. Her four-unit math course definitely had bailed her out.

Once, during exams season in university, Trinh brought in a cassette player and started her dance classes in the basement of the Fisher Library, teaching cha-cha-cha, tango, bebop, and similar steps, in between her tedious hours of studying for examinations.

"You're a daring girl, Trinh!" one of her friends would comment.

"Ah, but I've got students!" she'd say and smile.

She was playing her style of music, and half a dozen of them would gather in the remotest corner of the library and follow her dance steps, enjoying a few carefree moments in their student life.

Those years went by pleasantly, but with the same difficulty of communicating in English. She often had to use a dictionary to translate her text. It then took her triple the amount of time to understand the context before having to memorise them for the tests.

Sometimes her reply was odd because she could not get their meaning.

When someone asked, "Hi Trinh, how are you going?"

"I am going by train," Trinh would reply.

"No, I mean. How are you going?"

"Yes, I am going by train," Trinh repeated, feeling very smart about her answer!

There was another time when a preacher started asking the crowd after his session of *The Origin of Mankind*, "So, in answer to God, where do you come from?"

"I come from Vietnam." Quickly and proudly, she would try to speak loudly.

Her English had not improved a lot since the day she was confronted by a staff member in the East Hills Hostel asking about her skin condition. The server came to her table and said something to Trinh that none of them could understand. Luckily, one of the staff was a Vietnamese. She approached their table seeing that they needed help.

Listening attentively for a while, she explained to Trinh gravely in Vietnamese, "Have you eaten chicken in the last few days? If it was in a box, then you must go and see your doctor immediately because you are not allowed in the canteen!"

"Oh, dear, why am I not allowed in here? I don't think I had any chicken in a box at all!" She was afraid now at hearing the words "not allowed."

"But you must, because your skin has erupted in a rash, and you must stay inside your room," the Vietnamese lady said.

"But no, I'm sure I did not eat chicken in a box. Whatever chicken I had was from here. The canteen was the only place I had my food. So how come eating chicken in a box prevents me from eating in the dining room?" Trinh was clearly puzzled and terrified. "How am I going to have my meals then?"

"We'll bring your meal to your room, dear."

At this, Trinh reluctantly walked back to her room, feeling confused but less nervous of being starved to death because of her trouble of eating chicken in a box.

In the end, fortuitously after being examined by a doctor, it dawned on her much later that she had chicken pox. It was contagious, and she had to be confined to her room until her skin had cleared up! The Vietnamese lady had got confused with the condition of "chicken pox" and translated it as "chicken in a box"!

Her English continued to be limited during her first few years at university in both speaking and writing that when she was asked to write a paragraph for a classmate in the yearbook she did not know how. Struggling with it for weeks, she finally submitted her contribution. Lucky for her that it was anonymous and no one would know who was writing for whom, but her heart sank with shame when someone posted her paragraph on the community wall with a comment, "How could someone with bad English like this be allowed to enrol into this course?"

But then, Trinh was the first in her family to graduate with a degree. The timid, non-English-speaking refugee had gone through her years of study with a dictionary and her textbooks hand in hand and came out of it successfully.

Chi was so proud of her daughter. Looking from afar, her chest swelled up with pride, and she could not help crying seeing a small figure of her little girl on the high platform receiving her bachelor of pharmacy degree from the dean of her faculty from Sydney University.

Trinh became a pharmacist-in-charge of a large pharmacy a few years later, but she often encountered confrontations like, "No, I'd like to speak to a pharmacist-in-charge please! Not a shop assistant!" when presented herself to the customers. Her diminutive figure and innocent childlike face masked her authoritative duty for many years afterward.

Thanh, and the Lieutenant's Exhumation

1985

TEN YEARS HAD gone by. The expatriates were moving along with changes in their life overseas as well as the remaining population in the country.

"Thank you, Dr. Quang. You're very kind."

Thanh bowed her head to the old prisoner, showing her gratitude.

Quang used to be as wiry as a dry stick, but now he looked plump. The dark skin looked mouldy with patches of whitish flakes and the yellowish tint of jaundice. His gait was slow, and he walked with small shuffling steps like a baby who had just accomplished its first steps but was wary of taking long strides.

It was beriberi and vitamin B12 deficiency catching up with him, Quang thought. His resilience in staying healthy in both mind and body was wearing thin. It was time to get out of here or, like them, he would suffer the same fate.

The old prisoner waved his hand dismissively to Thanh. "It's nothing. I wish I could have done better, but that was the best I could do. His was the first burial I had to prepare, and they called me the Caretaker ever since. I am very sorry for your loss and the lengthy suffering you had to endure waiting for his return. He died only a few weeks after being transported here. His death was a shock to us all. He was lucky in some way. He did not suffer long."

Thanh nodded and swallowed the lump in her throat, trying to believe the doctor. She spoke in short sentences. "I didn't know about his death until a week ago. They sent a letter informing me where to find his remains. They didn't even explain. A very impersonal letter was all I received—so cold and indifferent. I had tried to trace his whereabouts for years, but they moved the prisoners to the far north or scattered them in places where no one knew or cared. I was kept waiting in vain."

She paused for a while and looked around her as if searching for something familiar in this strange, desolate camp. Thanh was not sure whether to continue confiding her anxiety to this stranger or to keep silent with her bottled-up frustrations of the past decade. The old prisoner sensed her hesitation but remained motionless. He did not want to push the young widow in either direction. *Let her choose whether to confide,* Quang thought.

Thanh steered her gaze away from the mounds of red dirt like undulating waves in the ocean and then resumed. "I guessed there was something very wrong when he did not write or contact me somehow, but I did not want to give up hope. One week then one month then one year, and it went on for a decade. Would you believe it? I had to wait ten years before knowing his fate."

Thanh paused again, this time looking for words, her fingers touching the brim of her straw hat. "I can't describe how much I prayed. If only I could have known why there was no news from him. But I guess I survived those long ten years with a faint hope of reunion. If I had known of his death from the beginning, I might not have had enough courage to continue living until now. Whether that's good or bad, I don't know.

"But at least now, I have an answer, even if it is of the worst kind. It's the unknowable truth that is so frightening. I cringed every time a letter arrived at the door. I was terrified to receive any news, but I also wanted to know. It's a complicated feeling. I guess it was similar to your going through this indefinite sentence. The tunnel was so dark and never-ending. There wasn't any light at the end, was there? There were times I wanted to give up, to be gone from this miserable life. But then I thought of him, of not knowing where he was, whether he was alive or dead. Then I gathered all my courage to go on. I did not want to be dead when he was still alive. If you know what I mean, I did not want to cause him any more grief in his life of little happiness and joy. It's very difficult. There were rumours, of course. They haunted me during the nights and filled my days with pain and anguish, those rumours. However, there was never a definite answer from the authorities. They gave me nothing to rely on but a vague statement saying that he was 'being reeducated' whenever I asked about his welfare. I had no address to write to him. No news had been received from the day he left. It was maddening. My state of mind was so uncertain, but they didn't care. These were the ups and downs! For me, living is an inexplicable experience. Death is easier to understand. If you know what I mean." Thanh continued her narrative in short bursts of emotions.

They were standing at the cemetery. The little mounds were in neat rows. There were hundreds of them—little waves in an ocean of dry land. Some had a single plant in the middle, some had bushes of different wild flowers on top, some had small hibiscus plants in various colours along the perimeter, and some were covered with different kinds of grasses. There were weeds or passion vines. They looked confusing to onlookers, but to Quang, they had a pattern only he could understand and decipher. They were his codes to differentiate the names and ranks of the deceased prisoners. He had taken his responsibility seriously since the first burial, and by doing that, it had helped him survive the long years of imprisonment. He had a goal to pursue. With a mind to combat the condemnation of the South Vietnamese Armed Forces personnel to unidentifiable graves, Quang had devised that scheme to outsmart the authorities.

His handwriting got smaller and smaller as he ran out of notebooks or blank paper to jot down as much information as he could for the records. The subsequent notebooks in the following years were from recycled paper as crispy and yellow as if it had been in existence for the past hundred years. That was how strange it seemed. The prisoners' existence was so far into the past that the years were moving forward in chunks. What was supposed to be a few weeks or a few months in reeducation camps became almost a decade or more for some prisoners. Some had returned to earth for re-incarnation of a better life. Quang wished them the best.

Thanh pulled her straw hat down a bit further to cover her entire face. She wanted to see nothing else in this sorrowful place. Thanks to this little man, the graves were well looked after, but they were still dismal. Sighing softly, Thanh lifted her gaze, nevertheless. She could not find any tombstones and was puzzled by it.

"Why aren't there any headstones, Dr. Quang? Where is Tuan's?"

Quang was smaller and slower than he used to be, his muscle mass now replaced mostly by oedematous tissue from lack of vitamin B12. His plumpness was a falsified appearance of weight gain. His coordination was stiff from muscle weakness and dyskinesia. However, Quang was still alert and sane. He had witnessed psychosis, bipolarity, and mental disorders among his friends throughout the years with increasing alarm. Poor diet without meat, fish, and legumes had badly affected the health of the prisoners. Many had died from malnutrition coupled with torture and depression. The prisoners had to eat whatever they could find to supplement the lack of protein and vitamins, especially B-group vitamins that were essential for the formation of red blood cells, DNA, nerve cells and the maintenance of other functions. Severe deficiencies would lead to deep depression, paranoia and delusions, memory loss, poor muscle coordination, difficulty in walking, oedema, and fatigue; the list went on and Quang had known that. To deal with this, he forced himself to catch field rats, birds, or any live animals that he could trap for extra nourishment. He tried to encourage the inmates to preserve their energy by drinking plenty of water, chewing, moving slowly, and getting as much sleep as possible. They were hibernating, he would tell them jokingly, waiting for a new era. The more active the prisoners, the quicker their energy and nutritional reservoir became depleted. After two or three years, the damage became irreversible if left untreated for a prolonged period.

Initially, the prisoners were able to manage with the rats and birds. Those unfortunate animals were abundant at first and easily caught when they ventured too close to their tents. The ill-fated rodents or birds were lifesavers to those poor souls who later on ate anything

When the rodents and birds became scarce after hundreds of thousands of prisoners in reeducation camps had consumed them, the reptiles and insects were their next targets. Their survival was practically depending on that ability, and the ecosystem in Vietnam was unbalanced for decades after because of that, Quang was sure. *On the other hand,* Quang thought amusedly, *the consumption of the reptiles and insects helped rebalance it somehow.* Without birds and field rats as predators, those reptiles and insects could upset the protection of harvests. Geckos, lizards, cockroaches, spiders, caterpillars, snails, millipedes, praying mantis, and grasshoppers—anything that moved—became their main source of protein. Quang witnessed the saddest sight of his life at two prisoners fighting over a dead gecko as tiny as his thumb. The desperate need for sustenance had destroyed their integrity and reduced them to animals fighting for survival. Their minds only focused on one thing: how to alleviate their hunger. There was no more pride or dignity—just something, anything to eat and how to survive the day, one day at a time.

"They, the 'esteemed comrades,' did not allow a headstone for any of the prisoners," Quang answered as a matter of fact.

"Oh, so how do you know which tomb is Tuan's?" Thanh's eyes widened in disbelief.

"That's the one. I planted a white hibiscus on his grave, and he was the first I buried. I am sure that's the one." Quang pointed to the white hibiscus bush farthest from the rows.

"Oh, thank you, Dr. Quang. You are so kind." Thanh repeated her gratitude.

"You certainly need help to exhume it, Ms. Thanh. Even though they were all shallow graves, you still need strong men to dig them up."

"Yes, I know. I have already asked for help. They're arriving soon. Thanks for your concern and kindness. I don't know how to repay you, Dr. Quang," Thanh spoke softly.

"I've got to go back to my duty. They're releasing us slowly now. My turn is soon. They informed me last week. If you'd come a week later, you might not have met me, Ms. Thanh."

He took a deep breath. "I'm one of the last prisoners here. I don't know how I managed it, but I have survived throughout the last decade. I outlived many stronger, younger men and stayed sane until the end. It was either luck or sheer determination. I'm not sure." He shook his head, almost not believing himself.

Suddenly, with a quick reflex, Quang placed his foot over a moving cricket. Without taking time to think or rationalise, he picked it up and popped it into his mouth, chewed then swallowed quickly, raw and all, out of habit. Then he said, "Good luck and best wishes for your future, Ms. Thanh."

Thanh was speechless witnessing the old prisoner's action, but she managed to say in the end, "Thank you, Dr. Quang. I wish you all the best and please stay healthy and strong. After this ordeal, I am certain that your resilience will enable you to endure many more years of hardship even though I truly wish that your life will be much better in the future."

"Yes, I hope so too. There is the Orderly Departure Program (ODP) initiated by the United Nations High Commissioner for Refugees (UNHCR) to rescue people like me. The 'esteemed comrades' have been very kind to let us displaced citizens leave the country for good. We are considered debilitated, sickly, second-rate, and a burden for them in every way," Quang said bitterly.

They bowed their heads to each other in the customary farewell. Quang turned and walked slowly toward the tent, feeling relieved and glad that he was able to help Thanh find her husband's grave. That was his sincere wish for the Lieutenant.

During the 1980s, the Vietnamese government reattempted to normalise the relationship with the USA. It attempted to make fewer demands for postwar reconstruction aid and show a readiness to improve humanitarian issues. The two countries restarted negotiations in softer terms and language than initially. A full account of Americans missing in action (MIA), including the return of any remains, was required before any normalisation could be effected by the US. Hanoi could not account for more than 2,400 MIA in Indochina. No concessions were made on either side, and the progress was slow or nonexistent for some time. The US continued to enforce trade embargos with relations at a stalemate. It was not until 1985 that Hanoi allowed the US to excavate B-52 crash sites in search of MIAs and return the remains of a number of United States servicemen between 1985 and 1987. With these efforts to improve the relations, Hanoi also allowed the US to make visits to some remodelled reeducation camps during that time.

The only known fate of prisoners was their unmarked graves. Only when there was information released by escapees who arrived in the United States about the brutal treatment in thousands of reeducation camps in Vietnam were investigations begun by the United States government. Those forgotten prisoners were released in the end through the intervention of the outside world. Or perhaps in the end, Hanoi was tired of keeping hundred thousands of sickly prisoners that were by now pitifully harmless. The UNHCR also started the ODP, or Orderly Departure Program, for the prisoners and their families to migrate to various countries.

In exchange for Hanoi's cooperation in matters concerning cases of MIAs, in 1994, the lifting of US trade embargos was effected with the formalisation of relations, resuming in 1995. After over two decades, diplomatic relations between the two countries were finally restored. During that time, Hanoi started to dismantle thousands of reeducation camps, the last prisoners were released in 1989, fourteen years after the Fall of Saigon.

Thanh remained at the graveside until Quang disappeared from her gaze before stepping closer to the white hibiscus bush and kneeling down. She placed her hands on top of the mound and whispered, "I am here, darling. I've found you. It's far too late, but at last we have our reunion." Unable to hold them back any longer, she allowed her tears to flow freely.

Some hours later when the gravediggers had finished their work, Thanh went over and collected the bones, placing them in a sack. Her hands shook uncontrollably. Her feet went weak, and she had to squat on the red dirt with the heavy remains in the cloth sack. The sun had gone down completely. Darkness began to fall. There was little light except the faint illumination from the far distance in the tents. Thanh wanted to leave. She must finish her journey and hurry out of here before her strength evaporated. Thanh paid the gravediggers their agreed fees with a small bonus, thanking them wholeheartedly.

At first, she was in doubt whether the old doctor was coherent and had pointed her to the correct grave to dig. The mounds all looked similar without any headstones. However, she burst into tears when one of the gravediggers picked up a small wooden cross among the remains. The red dirt clinging tightly to the small object made it bulkier in size. She had to scrape it clean before her cross reappeared. It was unmistakably hers. That saddest of mornings, they had parted and said good-bye to each other, confident it would only be a few weeks' separation. Then, before the bus carrying the prisoners and Tuan accelerated further away, Thanh had found the old wooden cross in her bag. She ran after the bus and gave it to him through the window. She remembered whispering to her husband, "I want you to keep it as a symbol of faith and a reminder of me, darling." Their hands had entwined for a brief moment with the cross in between.

Thanh sobbed quietly and walked slowly out of the camp, her lone figure casting a vague silhouette in the barren surroundings. The wooden cross was now lying in her palm covered with dirt and the residue of Tuan's soul, if any.

Mike, the Amerasian, in California

1989
California

MORE THAN A decade had passed, and many dramas had been unfolded.

—— ✪ ——

"Hey, watch where you're going, son of a bitch!" the man yelled, his Californian English reverberating in the hot summer sun. Jamming his foot on the brake, he poked his head out of the car's window and pointed a finger at Mike angrily.

Mike stood still, frozen in the middle of the boulevard. In his hands was a box loaded with meat and groceries. He did not know what to say to the Californian, dumbstruck by his inability to speak the language and by his astonishment. Mike turned and stared blankly back towards the driver for a few moments then silently resumed his walk to the other side of the road. The man shook his head and shouted, "Idiot!" Then he accelerated away in his polished Jeep Wrangler.

"Fuck you!" Mike managed to mouth the words belatedly before the Californian disappeared from his sight.

Jaywalking was a big deal here. Mike had been warned many times by his boss, and if he was fined, then it was entirely his fault. Mike kept forgetting. His mind was not as sharp as it used to be. He got confused very often with everything happening so fast around him.

"Bastard, what's all the fuss about?" Mike shouted angrily in Vietnamese when he got to the other side of the road.

Back home, he could just walk down and cross the street anywhere he liked without any fuss. Motorists would know what to do. He did not even have to wait for the traffic to stop. They would weave their motorbikes around him skilfully, dodging many pedestrians in the middle of the traffic flow as if it was the most natural thing to do.

Mike was annoyed but not taken aback by the man's language; even though he was not sure of the meaning, he clearly understood the implication. He wished he could fire back a string of abuse in his own Vietnamese. He was embarrassed and frustrated in his tongue-tied state. His English was not good enough to embark on a fight. Ironically, the unfriendly tone had been familiar throughout his life, back home in Vietnam and right here, in Santa Ana, where he was supposed to feel welcome and accepted. It made Mike ponder about his existence here. He looked to the right then to the left and wondered if he could ever feel welcome anywhere.

He was feeling tired and homesick. He was still very alone, here or there or anywhere!

Everything here was so neat and tidy. The air was crispy and fresh, even in the summer sun. The pavements were clean and evenly paved. He did not have to watch his steps in case he walked right into a puddle or even fell head down into an open drainage hole in the middle of nowhere. Where was that familiar smell of blocked sewage, rotten garbage, and muddy puddles along the streets? That smell was his reassurance, and he loved it. It reminded him of his motherland. Although he was an unwanted Amerasian in the postwar period, it was where he had spent his childhood. He had grown up as an Amerasian cowboy on the streets, but he was in control of himself. He knew where he was and who he was, no matter if he was on the bottom rung of the social ladder. He had an identity. He was hounded and mocked at, but he was himself. And he thought that he knew who he was.

Ah, but here he was, in America now, at last! Mike laughed hysterically. This was where he had been longing to be. His feet now touched the soil of his father's homeland. And whether it was true or not, his American features had guaranteed him a seat on the plane over here. It was lucky for him that his blue eyes, brown hair, snub nose, and fair skin were obvious for the assessor to classify him as an Amerasian. Mike chuckled at the thought that if his unknown father had been Mexican-American or Hawaiian-American, then his chance of migration was doomed. The racial features would be indistinctive and could have blended in with his mother's Vietnamese blood. It was nearly impossible for those poor souls to prove themselves unwanted Amerasians to the US ambassador, except by the fact of being street kids all their life. For his entire childhood and adulthood, or for almost a quarter of a century, Mike was an outcast living on the brink of society in Saigon, waiting to be rescued, to be accepted as a normal citizen. His dream was now realised, thanks to Father Joseph, a Vietnamese Catholic priest who had come scouring the streets of Saigon looking for boys and girls and young women and men like him.

Miraculously, after years of being neglected, Amerasians in Vietnam were under the spotlight after a few American tourists recognised the remarkable features of a high number of street kids in Saigon who were vendors selling cigarettes, chewing gums, and lottery tickets. In 1982, the Amerasian Immigration Act offered top priority to children of American fathers, not only in Vietnam but also in Korea, Laos, Cambodia, and Thailand, to migrate to America. However, this important legislation granted immigration privileges only to the Amerasians, leaving a huge flaw in the process by not allowing mothers and half siblings to immigrate. They expected the Amerasians to dump their family ties, and because of that, not many Amerasians benefited from this legislation.

Fortunately, with the Orderly Departure Program (ODP) established in 1979 by an UNHCR initiative, following an extraordinary number of refugees fled the country every month, the Amerasians in Vietnam had finally been noticed through many channels. Many had been settled in America by this program as refugees rather than through the Amerasian Immigration Act in the latter years.

It was only in September 1984 that the US announced that over a three-year period, the Amerasians would be coming home, and the Amerasian Homecoming Act was prepared. This law took effect on March 21, 1988, and it stipulated that Amerasians born in Vietnam between January 1, 1962, and January 1, 1976, would have until March 1990, to apply for an immigrant visa. This was a two-year program classifying Amerasians as immigrants but also granting them refugee benefits. It was more than a decade after the war ended, far into the late eighties, before they were rescued and repatriated to their fathers' land. Even though many actually had no idea who their fathers were, ultimately they were much more welcome there. A belated welcome seemed inappropriate then, when most had already suffered cruelty and discrimination throughout their growing years. Migrating to the US in their early adulthood was another real test for those poor souls whose education was inadequate and whose psyche was damaged over the years.

Here he was, in America. Mike exhaled heavily, reminding himself again. He had been rescued from his ordeal, and his wish had been granted in migrating to California. Instead of feeling jubilation and joy, Mike felt uneasy and dejected. It was a strange feeling. Mike had never felt this alienated and distant before. His life had been poor and pitiable while growing up in impoverished living conditions where meals were meagre and undernourished. Being treated badly and trodden on more often than he could remember, Mike always tried to overcome his endurance. He had always wanted to belong. Even though he was sneered at by almost everyone who managed to force inferior status on him by his being born an Amerasian, Mike thrived and determined always to move forward. There had never been a day that Mike wanted to give up fighting for his ground and his needs. He always woke up with a goal to achieve for that day and objectives to look into during the week. Those things kept him going. He had never felt dull; poor, and penniless as he was but life always had an upbeat rhythm, and he had his street friends.

Now, after having arrived in this promised land, after many years of waiting, he felt depleted, like a hot air balloon that had risen to the maximum height and now descended quickly for a crash landing. What was wrong with him? Strangely, Mike almost forgot what it was that made him long to be in America. It was a dream that seemed to grow bigger and bigger as he was getting older. Ah, the things he wished to have! It must be those, when food and shelter was the main focus in life, when he longed for a proper meal and a decent place to live. However, it was far too late now. Those things were not as important to him as he thought they would be now. He had got by and survived the toughest years during the postwar periods, in the years after a shock peace. He had been broken and mended. He had been wounded, and he had nursed himself back to life. The scars were there, deep and ugly, reminding him of his ordeals; but he was alive, nevertheless.

If he had been rescued in 1978, Mike would have felt much happier. That was the worst time in his life—when Mike began to understand life as a growing teenager, when he was vulnerable and unsure of everything. Mike remembered the bowl of cold rice with watery tea that was his savoury meal at Tet in that year. The Year of the Horse, that was. It pained him the most, as Tet is to celebrate lunar New Year when traditionally everyone is supposed to have what he wishes for. He was a twelve-year-old boy who was lonely and missed his mother terribly at the time when family gatherings and festive activities are the tradition for the first ten days of Tet. He had curled up in a corner of his nanny's kitchen, lying on his only possession, a thin palm mat with an intricate and homely pattern that was very dear to him, the only connection Mike had with his mother. She had left him in a hurry, or she had left him with no other choice. On the other hand, she might probably be dead on the way back looking for him during those chaotic days; Mike never had a chance to know. Mike wished he had known her choices. Whether she was forced to leave him in a time of crisis or whether he was of no importance to her, Mike desperately wanted an answer on that New Year's Eve. Other kids might have wished for better things, but Mike only wanted to seek his mother's love and approval, even if he was abandoned in the end.

That was when Mike would have appreciated his father's homeland. Now, it was too late, a lifetime too late. Mike was a twenty-two-year-old man in a new country without a real purpose in life. Now, when he had enough food to eat and a place to stay in, Mike felt restless. In this land of bountiful richness and opportunities, Mike was still very much a beggar. He still needed love and affection. He was still a lonely person, and his role had not changed that much. He had no formal education and no skills, and he had lived on the streets far too long to appreciate any differences in living conditions anymore. Fourteen years had gone by since he had been abandoned by his mother and ignored by his father. Those important years of growing up had marked a strong impact on his soul—when he had to learn to detach himself from any emotional attachment, and when he was so afraid of being hurt again.

He still did not know who his father was, but Mike did not regret that fact. It was already a scar that had no further potential effect on his toughened body and soul. Who cared that he was here now?

Back in Vietnam, his American racial features had marked him as a reminder of the enemy of the new Vietnamese Communist regime, although Mike had never known his father. *Con lai* or "American bastard" was the term they used to refer to Amerasians like him, the lowest class in the Vietnamese hierarchal society. It did not bother him after a while. That was how wonderfully the human mind operated; the level of tolerance increased with time. He survived splendidly along with the other outcasts.

When he was a little boy, Mike did not wish for toys, but he used to wish he lived in a proper dwelling in which a family was supposed to be together, with all the things that meant happiness and sharing. He used to stand looking through the school gate wishing that he were behind it rather than outside of it. He used to listen with fascination at how the schoolboys his age complained about their homework and wished he had that kind of commitment. Mike had ceased going to school at the age of nine when his mother left him during the Fall of Saigon. He longed to be accepted as a Vietnamese, not an American bastard, even though his fluent Vietnamese was of no value now in America. His strong American appearance had hindered his acceptance in a biased society where interracial relations were looked down on.

Here, Mike reminded himself often, "I'm an American, not an Amerasian anymore." At least here, his racial features blended in splendidly. Mike appeared normal until he started to speak.

"Hey, what's wrong with you? Speak English, man! Are you dumb?" Some of them would say to him, surprised at his inability.

"Fuck you!" Mike would be boiling with rage, and he would retaliate with the banality that he caught on to quickest.

Here, in Santa Ana, Mike became a labourer in Little Saigon, doing odd jobs here and there. He still could not speak English as fluently as his appearance suggested, as his daily language was Vietnamese among the Vietnamese community. They often referred to him as, *thang My lai,* which is Amerasian in Vietnamese, instead of his name, a habit that was hard to eradicate. It seemed that Mike never had a chance to escape his fate.

The Morning After

July 2011

MORE THAN A quarter of a century had gone by like the blink of an eye. The young girl had grown into a mature woman. Throughout the years, many things had changed and she was broken and mended.

The clanking noise from the council garbage truck at dawn echoing from the street woke Trinh in a state between alertness and drowsiness. Between the two phases of twilight zone, Trinh dutifully searched her memory to see whether the garbage bin outside had to be collected. Then she felt happy and relieved that it had been, and she came to total wakefulness. She reached up to grab her mobile phone on the night table and was disappointed looking at the time; it was just past five o'clock in the morning. The darkness had not dissipated as happened with most of winter days. Curiously, on almost every Monday morning, she had this sort of occurrence as a punishment for her forgetfulness.

Lucky for her, this time she was still able to stay in bed with the knowledge that her duty had been fulfilled and the garbage bin was out. Phew, what a relief! Other times, Trinh had to sit bolt upright and jump off the bed, rushing with all the speed her legs could muster to charge after the garbage truck, hurriedly pulling along her bin in time to empty its contents for that week. On the other hand, perhaps that part of the household chores had never been registered as her duty. Normally it belonged to the man of the house. Trinh was not out of the habit of letting someone else do it, or so it seemed.

Forgetfulness was one of the traits coming with age, and just like macular degeneration, hers seemed to come along earlier than expected. The discovery of that ill omen from a routine eye checkup with the optometrist yesterday was still fresh in Trinh's mind.

Some spots of light had started to filter through the curtains. They were in a shade of pastel yellow mingling with bouquets of huge dark chrysanthemums in the centre of large green leaves, scattering here and there with small blue roses. Still lying in bed, she closed her eyes and tried to recollect the images of flowers and leaves after a few minutes of concentration. To her disappointment, what she could see with her closed eyes was just black and white, a plain darkness. Her imagination must have tricked her with the white image void of all colours! The human mind seemed to be unable to fabricate colour images with closed eyes in wakefulness. Regardless of how many times she had tried, they were just black and white. How sad it would be if she could not recall her colourful environment the day when she lost her sight? What if everything was plain black and white, like old pictures of a century ago?

With this thought, she turned her head to observe her ten-year-old son, who was lying next to her as the comfort that she treasured most till the time he would decide to move to his own bed. Using all her effort to take a photographic memory of his features into her eyes before closing them again, she tried to recall his face. Lucky for her, this time, as a reward of her concentration and will, she was able to flash back to his image momentarily in her darkness. Perhaps this was due to the most recent memory that her mind had collected just then, but if she had to remember some other faces she had not seen for a while then she knew it was impossible. Memory of faces was also very fragile if it had not been refreshed from time to time. She had to start collecting them now and wished that the images she cared to keep could be refreshed daily.

Knowing that it was futile going back to sleep, she got out of bed and switched on the lights in the dining room to see that Cadbury, her Border Collie with its usual habit, was already sitting patiently outside the French window. Her nose was glued against the pane; her intelligent eyes followed her owner's movements, mesmerised! It was not long ago that she was only a tiny pup, chubby and round with a smooth brown chocolate coat and was as cute as a bear cub. Trinh bought her as a Christmas present for Eddie, but naturally, she had become Trinh's companion ever since. Her tail wagged in increasing momentum with her owner's approach. The moment Trinh let her inside gently patting on her head, she lay down immediately, her entire body pressing heavily on Trinh's feet as a reassurance of togetherness. Satisfied after a few pats, she changed her posture, lifting her paws in the air, belly up, confidently waiting for a rub. Her face lit up with glee. Their routine cuddles every morning, preceding the usual walk, were always the highlights of her day.

She then followed Trinh's every step and obediently sat down, tail wagging frantically, unable to hide her excitement when Trinh reached up to the hook behind the door to get her leash. She was going for a walk! With Cadbury's leash firmly in her hand, Trinh walked out into the damp cold air, breathing in deeply and glad that it filled her head with calmness, though she was still apprehensive about the recent discovery. With the lingering thoughts at dawn and the warning from yesterday, she attempted to reconstruct the surrounding scenes like when she first woke up.

Trinh put each bush, each tree, and every flower into perspective as if one day they would not materialise in her sight.

The Jamaica bushes, one cream and one pink, in someone's garden were blooming with elegant flowers. Many were strewn on the ground, some petals brown and discoloured, their fate as pitiful as most discarded flowers, a sad comparison with their luckier companions still proudly perched on the branch. There was a whole bunch of sugar bananas with many green budding hands growing against the fence. The owner had placed some protective nylon over it to preserve its growth hoping the bitter cold wind and frost would not prevent them from blooming into full maturity. Regardless of his attempt, she still saw a small unripe bunch lying on the grass in a far corner. Some kid must have had it down just for fun of meddling around. A rose bush had only bare branches now, naked of any stunning blooms. The wattle trees with various bouquets of freshly blossoming, tiny, golden flowers proudly brightened up the gloomy winter sky. Orange and mandarin trees were growing wild on the council land, their branches laden heavily with big, attractive, bright coloured fruits, many littering the bare ground, waiting in vain to be picked up by passers-by. Unfortunately, no one was interested, leaving them to rot. A guava tree standing illegally on council land was also showing some midget, underdeveloped fruit, their growth stunted in the cold weather. A flock of herons, legs as skinny and long as ballet dancers, were gliding gracefully down the grass like fairies descending from heaven and inspecting the earth for places to land. Their elongated elegant necks and black thin, pointed beaks added to the effect of fineness and austerity in their look. In contrast to them, the grey pigeons were waddling about, good-natured, plump, and homely as contented housewives, with necks that disappeared completely under the thick layers of feathers.

Again, she tried to put all these images in her mind, using the photographic memory she was so proud of, in an attempt to reconstruct them with closed eyes. In the darkness and as best as she could, sadly, what she saw was devoid of all colours; all shades of pink, green, blue, yellow, indigo, etc. disappeared! It was a strange sensation, as if her world had become black and white. What if one day she could not differentiate any colour and all the scenes, the wonders of nature had blended indistinctly? If all faces and features had gone blurry, then how was it possible she could describe them as effectively as she had seen? Trinh knew that her memory would fade with time without images.

Still, filled with gratitude, she realised that at least she was lucky to be able to see things as clearly as they were at this stage.

The Remnants

September 2011

More than one month passed, the weather had changed suddenly in the last few days. It had turned back to bleak, rainy, cold wintery days since yesterday. When Trinh awoke, that lingering bleakness added to her-not-so-bright-mood, and she started the morning with a heavy and melancholy state of mind. Her sadness was only intensified today. Perhaps the weather had given the signal for her feelings to come forward, or perhaps the suppressed emotions needed to escape sometimes, regardless of rain or shine! After a cup of coffee, she felt brighter. The sun was high and brilliant; the air, however, was still very cold and crisp for a spring day in metropolitan Sydney.

Oddly, the sun seemed to play an important factor in regulating her mood.

She often joked with her customers, "If you have to go on with a divorce and it's winter, just hang on in there. Give your partner a truce and tell him to wait until summer or a warmer season then resume the course of action. You see, when the glorious sun is up, it keeps you company in the lonely days after the divorce. It's much easier, keeping depression at bay!"

The women pondered this action plan and laughed together.

"However, research on seasonal effects on suicide rates suggests a lower rate in winter than in summer or spring, as opposed to popular belief!" Trinh added.

See, Trinh was only using the weather as an excuse for being dismal.

Today was Fathers' Day. Her children had been with their father since yesterday. The unit was quiet; even Cadbury was not making any noise outside. The unit was usually quiet these days. When was the last time she had a house full of voices? Trinh had to downsize from a five-bedroom house to a two-bedroom unit recently. So many things had changed with time, and she often wondered when the happiest time in her life was.

"Ah, there must have been some happy times!" Trinh said aloud to the empty unit.

On the other hand, perhaps happy times were only transits in her journey through life. They were scattered here and there, marking the trail at some significant points as memorable stops or rare scenic lookouts. Perhaps she was in a hurry and only focused on getting to her final destination without realising that the final destination was actually the end, or frighteningly, death itself. Then she would miss her chance of finding those memorable scenic lookouts. If she was not enjoying these stopovers along the way, then there were scarcely happy times to remember before reaching the predictable end! Her journey had been eventful, with many dramatic moments up till now. Trinh promised herself to be more attentive to these transient moments, as time was so valuable the more it passed her by. Her childhood's memory was scarred with the war, the escape, the refugee camp and migration, study. And then busily came the marriage, kids, and work, the whole business, everything!

"Ah, the usual priorities!" Trinh muttered again, wondering if she would like to change her order of priorities or if she were happy to leave them so. Now, sometimes looking at her teenage sons and young people their ages and seeing their carefree attitude in life, Trinh often wondered what it actually felt like. She longed to have that similar feeling as she had never a real chance when she was at that age. Her teens had gone missing in her life, or so it seemed.

She had started her book after the shock of discovering her eyesight was deteriorating faster than normal. The more words she put on these pages, the more she was afraid that time was running out. Day in and day out, so much was happening, and her book was still in its first few chapters. With suffering, death, and sorrow plaguing her family lately, she found tears were easily shed with little warning. Occasions like Father's Day, Mother's Day, Christmas, Tet, and New Year's Day were the hardest.

"You disappeared for twenty-two years, Trinh!" a friend had declared. He used to be a kid among the "one-hundred-kid" neighbours at the refugee camp back in 1978 with her, and he had graduated as a general practitioner shortly after her graduation as a pharmacist at Sydney University.

"I've been hibernating." Trinh laughed with her answer.

Her journey of life was divided into many parts. The turmoils of the first quarter ceased for a while then reentered in the third quarter, leaving the second quarter with some sort of normality such as marriage, pregnancy, and children. That second quarter had ended by a divorce, letting her reclaim her old self again after a usual period of mourning for a broken family.

"We are facing a difficult time as a broken family, and you all have to help me as much as I will continue to look after you," Trinh remembered telling the children during her time of heartache.

"Then who will look after you, Mammy?" her eldest son, Sean, asked.

Tears had flown down her cheeks with that innocent and caring statement. How she wished they never had to suffer any damage from a broken family!

"You guys will look after me, of course!" Trinh managed at last.

That had been more than ten years ago: her family had since recovered and made amends.

Then recently, Trinh had a look at a photograph taken a few months ago with her siblings and her mother, and given it a name: the "remnant of my family" and realised that with a big family like hers, what remained was still substantial, even though the number had dwindled down a fair bit.

She had begun her regular morning walk with that echo of the name, and then tears started to well up in her eyes without any warning. They continued to fall down her cheeks as innocently as they appeared, and no apology was needed.

Leaving them free rein for a little while, Trinh then tilted her head to look up at the clear blue sky as if using gravity to oppose their flow. To her astonishment, the bursting green shoots of trees, bushes, and flowers and the enchanting chirping sound from unseen bellbirds began to engage her, nudging at her awareness. From that moment, Trinh realised her sadness had no foundation. Life is full of beauty and wonder, with togetherness and living things, but also with separation and death. It was this fact that she must accept and become acquainted with.

Another time, she had found in a very old box an audiocassette tape. The date written on it was September 5, 1981. Amazing how thirty years had gone from her life like a flash! The tape was about a Father's Day gathering with her family, consisting of Father, Mother, Mac, Giang, Kim, Luc, Kate, and her. The voices that belonged to those unseen faces appeared to be very young, innocent, lively, and full of spirit. Her father had passed away around this spring time. His was her first experience of death in

Australia nineteen years ago, and then only last month, Mac had gone: the second. These two close ones were only voices now, like memories echoing from the unforseen world of an audiocassette tape. Mother loved Mac dearly for everything he had done, and his failing health and his death from liver cancer had devastated her. Seeing both of her daughters, Giang and Trinh, changed their status to become a widow and a divorcee in just a few years had drained her emotions.

Yesterday morning, Mother had blurted out the minute she sat down at the table, "I swear, in my next life, I'll never bear daughters whose zodiac sign is a Tiger!"

Then, as an afterthought, she sighed and added, "That next life's still not here yet, somehow! It's not as easy as I'd thought!"

"Hmm, is that so, Mother?" Trinh looked up from her morning cup of coffee and gave her Mother a chuckle to disguise an aching heart. She understood from deep down in her being that her mother was feeling for both of them, her sister, and her, bearers of the sign of the Tiger.

"Do you know that in our traditional Asian horoscope, the Tiger is a strong and independent personification of the twelve zodiac signs: fiery, powerful, and successful, with an eventful life, but usually lonely at heart. Not in terms of material means. On the contrary, it usually brings wealth or an affluent lifestyle to that person. But in terms of loving relationships between a husband and wife, it is a sure sign of separation, of a broken marriage or premature death, a guarantee of tears and grief. In short, the bearer has a glamorous and dramatic life whether she likes it or not!" Mother started her narrative apologetically.

"Years ago, in ancient times, before a marriage proposal was put forward between the two families, the groom-to-be's side had to be certain that the expectant bride was not a Tiger. They might very well cancel the whole thing without a second thought if she was! These days, such dramatic scenarios rarely happen, but this belief is still very common. Somehow, most things that happen to female Tigers often have dark forebodings. Either it is the result of remarkable coincidence, or ominous conjecture plays an important role. In any case it is still a mystery!"

"You and Giang are both my Tiger daughters," Chi softly concluded her narrative.

Yet her mother had declared she already decided in her next life she would not produce daughters whose sign was the Tiger. She could not endure seeing her children suffering turmoil after turmoil in her lifetime. Trinh felt so sad hearing her declaration. She had wished to be able to spare her this everlasting grief, most of all from her side, or at best when she was still in this life! It was a wish that was beyond her ability to fulfil, but of course, a wish nevertheless!

Her mother was a very energetic, unselfish, and caring person. Trinh was so proud of her. Without her, the family would not have had a chance to be here. She had masterminded the escape with Mac, and they had landed safely in the beautiful and free country of Australia. Trinh continually marvelled at her keenness in bustling around the kitchen, cooking dish after dish for them, busy doing something most of the time. She rarely stayed idle and constantly looked for things to do, folding clothes neatly in piles even though moments later it was being dishevelled by one child or another once the piles left her care.

Her cataracts had been operated on two years ago, and now her eyesight was ten times better than Trinh's.

"Could you thread the needle for me, Mother?" Trinh gave her a tiny needle. She had to ask her mother to thread it for her whenever she had to mend something for herself or for her sons. Then her mother would gladly take the task out of her hands and finish it herself, seeing how clumsy Trinh was.

"Of course, and I can see minute things now," Mother would proudly say, "even the tiniest specks of dust!" Then she would use her bare hands to wipe the table's surface as proof of her excellent eyesight.

These last few days, Mother was noticeably less mobile and rarely left her room.

"Are your knees playing up again, Mother?" Trinh asked.

"Yeah, this time it was the left one, not the right one like last year!"

Watching her mother walking tentatively, one step after another in slow motion, around the house had filled her heart with anguish. Trinh had felt her pain as much as her mother felt it for herself.

Chi's physical well-being had been defeated by her years. It showed the signs of heartache and sorrow following another death in the family. She had outlived them miraculously and had endured great pain in losing both. Chi had aged noticeably. Twice within a year, she had suffered the agony of burying her son, Dien, and her son-in-law, Mac, from the same cruel disease of liver cancer, an ominous cancer from Hepatitis B plaguing the majority of her people and leading to a high number of deaths. The awareness campaign is being raised in an effort to halt the curse in the community.

Within a few years, Trinh had become experienced, skilful, and adept in dealing with the dilemma of a couple's separation, someone for her sister to lean on. Even though their circumstances were entirely different, the result was still the same. Giang was now alone and grieving. Her lifelong companion had departed from this world, leaving her with emptiness, a giant void that seemed impossible to fill. She was suffering from a brutal loss that was inescapable by the karma of fate, and Trinh had suffered from loss through choice. It was not entirely her choice at that time, but as her life had progressed further along, it became an obvious release for her self-being. Trinh had been very much in shock then, like her sister now; but as time moved on, Trinh had moved on successfully with it. Trinh had given Giang her excellent practical tips for easing the pain of a lonely woman, the last thing they had expected! They had been so confident and ever-so-efficient with their future planning, true to the characteristics of the Tiger, with everything ending neatly from every aspect. So when things went wrong, the shock was very real!

"Listen to Buddha's teaching. Live your life at its own pace. Don't rush forward even in sorrow and sadness, Giang," Trinh had said, trying to convince her sister.

"I know that it seems impossible at the time and sometimes the need to cry was so overwhelming that I found it hard to resist the temptation too. Like you, I'm wondering if crying is the best therapy for the soul to seek solace for the pain it is enduring. Or perhaps we are wrong in assuming that the best way to deal with pain and sorrow? Should we ignore them totally? Should we pretend that they do not exist and go on empty-minded with a carefree attitude as we always appear to the outside world? Or should we look at them as objectively as we can and wait for our body and mind to heal with time? Which way would be best? To cry our heart out and empty its sorrow lightening the burden that life normally inflicts upon every soul? On the other hand, would it be better to gather all pain and sadness, put them in a sealed box, and place it carefully in a locked cupboard into which we might look now and then just to check whether the box was still there? With luck, one day we'll open it to see all the pain and sorrow has vanished or decayed with time!"

Giang was quiet, leaving Trinh with all the talking.

"Talking about a box that contains sorrow and sadness, I've got one given to be from a newly acquired friend, and I named that box as such. In that box, beautifully decorated and softly covered by feminine pink satin, were three crystal angels whose purpose was perhaps to help me push away any undue weariness in life and to continue my journey peacefully and determinedly along the way. I jokingly told my youngest son, Eddie, that the box contained my dilemmas and each angel represented one of them. Meaning that I have three worrisome, unfinished to-dos to tackle, considering I am already three-quarters done as one is more or less out of the way." Trinh smiled. "See, everyone has his or her own dilemma to deal with at any period of time—love, hatred, loneliness, jealousy, teens, health, career, etc. It's how you deal with it. Time is magic, believe me! I've been there, and nothing beats with the clock. It's moving and washing everything away slowly and effectively, believe me."

Trinh smiled then continued. "Don't rush forward. Tackle one thing at a time. Then after a while, everything will be solved, and your sorrow and burden will eventually be less and less. Believe me, Giang." Trinh smiled again and hoped what she said was true.

Giang was twelve years older than her, a full circle of the twelve zodiac animal signs, and while fate had dealt them a similar situation and their hair had lost its youthful shine, their age gap appeared less.

"Strange as it is, I'm now happier. If living independently, peacefully and coming back to being my own true self is the meaning of happiness then it's a happier outcome, despite occasional loneliness now and then. But it's rewarding," Trinh had reassured Giang and laughed, lifting the sombre feeling.

Nevertheless, Giang had had the same forlorn listlessness that a separated person experiences from the loss of years and years of companionship and habitual presence, as Trinh had in the past. Her grief was insurmountable as their marriage had been a close one from the start, an extraordinary thirty-seven-year bond that was now fast becoming unusual in this hectic modern life.

These last few weeks had drawn them closer than before. Trinh often wondered what peculiarity life had bestowed upon them: four out of five women in the family. Her mother, Giang, Vy, and she were now single women.

"I was a widow when I was sixty, and now, it's the same with Giang," her mother said.

There was an absence of men in her mother's life.

"Your father was also a Tiger and rarely stayed at home. He usually wandered around the country either through the demands of his occupation or later because of his adventurous nature after retirement. He led a glamorous life when he was young, very much true to the prediction," Mother would repeat her story to Trinh.

"Your older brother, Dien, came back after the war, but determined to stay back in Vietnam when all the family escaped; and now he has gone."

Hoan had come with them but decided to migrate a second time to the United States only two years after arriving in Australia. He had followed his heart to marry his high school sweetheart when he was in his twenties. Her father with his habitual urge to travel had not stayed long at home just as before, even though the distance from his homeland was eight thousand kilometres away. The latter part of his life ended in loneliness with years in a nursing home after a series of strokes. Her little brother, Luc, had remained her mother's closest son ever since.

Her colleague had remarked, "Somehow, strangely, there are only women left in this world! It's a puzzle where all the men have gone!"

Another added, "Either they're gay or they're all married! Pity!"

"Ah, it's true, isn't it?" Trinh agreed.

She was surrounded with single women who had lost their men along their journey or had not been able to find one.

"Wait a minute. There are married women whose loneliness is comparable to being single, as their men often seem lost in their own alien world, leaving wives emotionally abandoned and confused," another would say.

"You see, maybe I should try now to solve the puzzle of where all the men have gone, and save the world population from an increasing number of single women. Do they all bear the Tiger's ominous foreboding of marital separation, in death and in loneliness, after all? On the other hand, independent, self-sufficient women have perhaps frightened all the men into hiding as a result. Men are afraid of feeling redundant, I'm sure," Trinh added.

"Just stay helpless and dependent or even ignorant and stupid then they will come back and be your heroes, dear." Trinh laughed at her own joke.

"And as for being a Tiger, the coincidence seems quite extraordinary that all three women in my family have all suffered greatly from the cruelty of life. My half sister, Betty, the eldest, had an aneurysm and passed away unexpectedly just a year short of turning forty. I still clearly remember her exaggerated fear of getting close to the historical mark of the big Four-O and as destiny had kindly or unkindly granted her wish, she never reached the four-decade milestone."

Trinh continued. "Thirty-four years ago, forty was considered very ancient. She was also born in the year of the Tiger, two full zodiac cycles ahead. Beautiful, elegant, feminine, and sophisticated, she was very much my idolised sister. Her life was also a dramatic one with tears and laughter mingled together. She was an optimistic person, come whatever situation, however tragic. Betrayal, romance, and separation concluded with her premature death after her short but eventful life."

"Would there be a sound explanation apart from the astrological aspect of her zodiac sign? I truly wonder!" Trinh confided to her friends.

Whatever the explanation, her wish was still the same: that of sparing her mother from further anguish. Her mother's box of sorrow and sadness must be empty, and she must remain happy, purposeful, lively, and strong in all her remaining years. Trinh loved her dearly, and the events of late made her realise sometimes a little too late to express her love, which appeared to have lost its personal touch.

A Farewell Encounter

A FEW WEEKS passed. The family was in mourning for the loss of their loved ones, Dien and Mac.

— ✪ —

The hint of a sunset still lingered on the horizon, but light was fading fast like most evenings in early spring when Trinh stepped out of the flat in Carravale. Cadbury was pulling hard at the leash as usual, eager in her excitement to reach the freedom of the field further into the reserve, to run off her pent up energy. Trinh pulled her up shortly, jerking the leash back to get her attention, "Easy, Cadbury, easy! Slow down, girl!"

Turning her head slightly to one side, the dog gave Trinh a backward glance as if acknowledging the command; but the youthfulness in the year old pup overtook her willingness to obey, and she kept on striding ahead of Trinh as if pulling on a sledge. Trinh smiled and shrugged her shoulders, putting one free hand up in a gesture of defeat in response to a comment from a stranger. "You better run, girl! She is too strong for you! That dog is a working dog. Don't you know that she has to gallop in the field for hours before she gets tired?"

The evening was damp with the rain earlier. The air was cool, and there was still an occasional current of cold wind. Trinh had on her raincoat, serving also as a windshield, to be on the safe side as there were many times Trinh had been caught unexpectedly in a sudden down pour during her walk, getting home soaking wet and cold. Sliding the set of keys into the left pocket together with her mobile phone, Trinh carefully zipped it up using one hand, the other busy holding Cadbury and at the same time trying to catch up with her dog by half-running, half-striding toward the car park. Accustomed to their regular path, confidently trotting ahead, she led the way. Reaching the sign that said "Off-leash Dog Area," Trinh bent down and unhooked her dog. Dashing off like a dart, Cadbury ran past her owner who was walking way too slow for her liking.

This was the first time Trinh had been for a walk without listening to music or doing her vocal exercises. Trinh had not known what it felt like to have her mind empty, a total blankness, no thinking, no musing, nothingness; leaving her concentration and her eyes their absolute appreciation of the beautiful scenery of nature before her in the fading light. Trinh was enjoying all this divine clarity, with no action except the rhythm of her walk in the damp fresh air of spring with its various natural fragrances. The scents of blossoming flowers, of growing buds, of green grass and wild bushes filled the space with amazing fullness of life. It was peace of mind and stillness of thought that added to the wonderful sensation that made Trinh so much aware of being alive. Buried deeply in this trance, the abrupt ringing of her mobile phone startled her, in time for Trinh to notice that darkness had already fallen with the shadows of trees and bushes transforming into mysterious shapes. Unzipping the side pocket of her raincoat, Trinh took her phone out, answering without looking at the caller ID, her voice hoarse. "Hullo!"

Kim's voice was soft at the other end. "Are you all right? Where are you?" the voice of her immediate older sister, now in Canberra, was always soft. Sometimes Trinh had to strain her ears to listen to her talk.

"Oh, hello! I'm walking in the park with Cadbury," Trinh told her, clearing her throat.

"Really, at this hour? It's quite late already. How come you are walking this late?" Kim expressed concern and added, "Is it dark there yet? It's already very dark and cold here. How are you?"

"I finished late at work today, and there was still light when I first started out. But it's not too cold here. I am okay, quite calm," Trinh reassured her sister, knowing that she was worried for her safety.

Kim continued. "Don't forget to bring your kids' birth certificates down so I can go straight to the consulate on the day to get their visas in time for you to bring home on the weekend. Good that you feel okay." Kim sighed softly on the other end. "It's so quick. Seven weeks has passed like a flash!" Her voice was laden heavily with sadness. The visas were for their trip to Vietnam in December.

Trinh was to come down to Goulburn tomorrow to spend a week with Giang and to stay for the seventh week commemorative ceremony after death, *that tuan*, for Mac. In their Buddhist beliefs, the spirit was still in limbo, wandering the earth for seven weeks seeking ways of redeeming their soul or attaining enlightenment. They were not completely gone and at times still being seen by close relatives and friends until this seven-week period was over. Every week a formal ceremony with chanting and praying was conducted to assist their enlightenment on this earth. Week seven marked the end of their earthly existence, when their after-death presence as flimsy shadows or ghosts would be gone forever. Trinh was not sure if this belief arose from the needs of close relatives and friends to alleviate their grief for their lost loved ones through a thousand years of religious practice or through experiences of the living in witnessing some chance encounter. However, the mention of Mac led her wandering thoughts toward his time with her family as her brother-in-law in past years.

Mac became part of the family when he married her sister, and this connection had been a part of their life for those thirty-seven years. To her and to the rest of them, he was more her own dear brother than a brother by marriage. He had done much more for them than a real brother could have done, helping Mother support them with food and necessities, when they needed them most after the war ended, when Mother and Father no longer had the means to provide them. He assisted Mother to mastermind the escape by boat for the whole family. Without his available capital, the whole trip would not have materialised. He helped Mother ease the burden of raising the rest of the young kids when the country was devastated and almost every source of income depleted. Food and necessities, even the very basics like sugar, coffee, milk and soap, and shampoo and toothpaste were scarce. Even with inflation out of control and outrageous prices, sometimes they were hard to come by. Lucky for them that after a short six months in reeducation camp, Mac was released and was allowed to return to being assistant to a deputy in chief for District 8 in Saigon. His training was recognised by the new Communist government, as he had only been newly appointed as vice deputy in chief of the same district one short year, before the war ended. The shortage of staff and specialised, qualified personnel had forced them to recruit many previous fresh-faced officials from the toppled government. His employment was the only official source of income; he was then the main provider for many of them, his family, and his wife. Mother was very grateful for his generosity in sharing the major part of her burden at that extremely difficult time in Vietnam, when it was a crime for anyone to show their wealth and selfishness was a popular belief.

All in all, Trinh's memories of him were mixed with sweetness, bitterness, danger, joy, tears, and laughter. They had shared with him his experiences from the days of his youth, full of authority and control before the war, to the whole voyage on the little boat seeking for freedom. Then, lastly, the days he was bedridden, weakened by cancer of the liver, until the final hours, minutes, and seconds in the hospital.

Trinh still remembered vividly the first time visiting him after he was out of the ICU, after he had endured an operation and miraculously come out of it alive. He had given her a radiant smile that was full of life and hope, ready for the long and tedious road to recuperation in front of him. His spirits were high and in great contrast to his sad appearance before he went in for the operation. He must have thought he had already won. Trinh could not sleep that night with his radiant smile in her mind, aching with sadness that he had to go through so much and showing such courage in trying to comfort them by being optimistic. Then a few more times, Trinh was in and out of the ICU visiting him. Just seeing him helpless and pale and weak on the hospital bed made her tears start falling silently. Trinh kept telling herself not to let him see her sadness in such contrast with his recent happiness, at least not in front of him. Against her will, her tears continued to roll. Looking at her sad face and before the nurses wheeled him away, Mac had tried to smile and say some reassuring words to her instead of the other way around! That night, Trinh went home with a heavy heart and could not sleep again, tossing and turning with the image of the cheerful smile he gave her in farewell.

The last time, when Trinh held on to his hand, he was so weak. His radiant smile had gone. Mac said a few words, which Trinh would always remember.

It was that last time when Trinh put both her hands over his, urging, "Mac, please try harder, a bit more, just a little bit more then we'll get there, you must try harder. Okay? Okay?"

He opened his eyes then made an effort to nod his head slightly and reassured her, saying, "It's all right, don't worry. Okay. Okay."

Even in the very last minutes of his life, on the brink of death, he was still thinking of easing their sorrow with his reassurance. With his last phrase, Trinh now realised that he was ready then, happy to depart from this world, and that it was okay with him. He had nothing else to be bothered with. That was the last time he responded before falling into semiconsciousness.

Deep in her reminiscence, her walk came to an end. She reached inside her coat pocket for the keys ready to open the gate of her unit. Trinh was surprised to find nothing! The key ring with every key for the house, the pharmacy, and car was nowhere to be found.

"Oh no, oh no!" Trinh muttered to herself disbelievingly, quivering with fear and anxiety as the night was already dark and cold. It would be impossible for her to look for it in the darkness and at this hour as she had walked not only on the concrete path but on the grass as well. Trinh silently cursed her carelessness as the set must have fallen out of the coat pocket without her noticing when she took the phone out to answer Kim. In utter hopelessness, Trinh started retracing her steps down the path from the beginning, using the slim faint light of her mobile phone pointing it to the ground. It was almost eight now; an hour's walk had ended in huge distress. Shaking her head in despair, Trinh was certain it was gone for good, and thinking of the trouble of changing all the locks of the pharmacy, the house, and the car made it worse!

It was after fifteen minutes in her quest before she thought of asking her brothers, Dien and Mac, for their help in searching for the keys. In despair, the Vietnamese Buddhists almost always ask their deceased relatives or Buddha to assist them with courage, luck, and peace of mind. Trinh was agnostic in nature, but she prayed and chanted silently the names of the two most recently deceased in her family.

"Please help me."

With Cadbury as her only companion on the path, the rustling of leaves, the cawing of the crows, and the noises of the dark, empty field in the reserve made her quicken her steps. But Trinh was determined to follow her path till the very end before giving up completely. Coming toward the turn, Trinh kept praying and chanting for Mac's and Dien's help, knowing that this was the end of her walk; and if she could not find it tonight, then there was no hope of peace. Turning around and heading home to the walkway with scattered bushes and tall eucalyptus trees about ten metres on her left, Trinh almost gave up her search.

"Please help me find it. Please," Trinh kept chanting in her head. She wanted to cry and felt so lonely.

Then at the beginning of the thin stretch of bushes and trees on her left, her heart skipped a beat, and Trinh almost jumped for joy as the faintest gleam of metal in the dark night was visible on the concrete path.

"There it is! My set of keys!"

Kneeling down and picking it up, she felt Cadbury suddenly start to strain on her leash, pulling Trinh forward and striding quicker as if wanting to hurry home, away from this part of the wood. The hair on her dog's back was raised, and her tail was high and fluffy.

"Grrr," Cadbury was growling through her teeth with her head pointing toward the left for the entire length of ten-metre shadow, fur spiked and tail high in aggressive state or as if in fear. In those few minutes walking alongside Cadbury in her strange, eerie behaviour and in the unusual quietness of the open field devoid of any sound, Trinh realised without fear that Mac was somewhere around here with her tonight; he had helped her find the set of keys. Trinh knew it was impossible for her to notice that faintest glimpse of metal in the dark without his help. His limbo state was lingering for the last few days on earth, and it happened to be here tonight. Her heart was thumping loudly and fast, but it was not the fear of danger she had experienced in that moment.

Full of apprehension about the rare chance encounter she had never thought possible in her entire life, Trinh thought she could see his lanky silhouette in the empty space. It was the very first time Trinh spontaneously believed that there was a spiritual world rather than just human existence on this planet. Goose bumps formed on her skin when Cadbury resumed her normal pace and stopped turning her head toward the left, facing front again when she was past the length of the bush.

Trinh whispered the words, "Thank you. Thank you!" Then she hurriedly went home while holding on tightly to her set of keys. Trinh had the strong intuition that he was standing in the thin bushes, bidding farewell to her for the very last time before being gone forever as his time was truly up from this world.

"Farewell and so long!"

Trinh prayed again with Mac and Dien on her way back and sincerely hoped that both her brothers were free to go in peacefulness and contentment. Trinh could assure them now that their presence in spirit was always here with the ones who had shared in their happiness, their tragedies, their sadness, and their life. Though they had gone from this earth, their memories were always close by, and Trinh also knew that they would no doubt provide the rest of the family with strength and courage to go on the long road ahead without them till the day they would meet again.

Tet:
The Year of the Dragon and a Virtual Lover

TIME MOVED ON, and here came Tet again.

Smoke from the fireworks welcoming the year of the Dragon was still billowing from the roof of Phu Hau Temple. Its thundering explosions were still ringing in her ears and the sound of drums from the dragon dance was still lingering in the air when Trinh first stepped into her house. The first step of the first person to enter the house on the first day of the lunar New Year is called *xong dat*. This traditional custom quite amused Trinh.

She had put a lot of effort into creating a festive atmosphere for Eddie and herself. She wanted them to feel bright and happy for the special occasion and went about the traditional ceremonies of Tet more diligently than ever before. They had moved into this two-bedroom flat half a year ago from a spacious five-bedroom house. The house, along with the rest of her family and everything else inside it had been left behind as part of her past. It was now replaced by this little unit. It was on the first floor of a business zone, cosy and functional. However, it was different from the house they had left. Both had to fight for space sometimes even though there were only two of them now instead of six. Eddie, her youngest son, had been very attached to Trinh ever since he was born. They had cried and laughed together through many occasions and now he was together with her in their new abode. The rest were scattered about, as broken families happen to be.

Just a week before Tet, she had practised another custom called the farewell ceremony for the spirit of the housekeeper, *dua ong tao*. After the ritual incense burning with traditional sweets, assorted peanut candies, and tea offerings, Eddie and Trinh had fun burning the make-believe paper currency, miniature paper hats, clothes, and car. Those were his means to use to travel all the way from earth to heaven. The housekeeper spirit was to report to the King of heaven the household's internal affairs of the past year and to return to earth on New Year's Eve, in time for New Year celebrations.

"Bring the make-believe money and those other things here, darling," Trinh told Eddie.

She pointed to the pile on the dining table where treats, candles, and incense containers were still on display. The incense had just burned to ashes, marking the completion of the spiritual ceremony, and she could clear everything away now. Stepping outside to the balcony, a bucket in one hand, a gas lighter in the other, Trinh was going to burn the paper money and the other paper objects, as was customary, following the Farewell ritual.

The wind was strong and cool. There was a sudden change in the weather after the hot dry desert air the day before, like the flip of a coin. The sky was dark with a few twinkling stars far away. Only the streetlights from the main road were illuminating the balcony, but it was bright enough. She put the bucket down on the concrete floor, and Eddie excitedly threw in all the stuff in his hands.

"Can I light it? Can I? Please, please, Mammy?" he pleaded, pulling the lighter out of her hand without waiting for Trinh's response.

"Okay, but be careful. Don't burn your fingers," she cautioned the boy. "Wait, it's fun to burn it a little at a time. Let me get some out then you can start, darling."

She took out half the chunk in the bucket and left it beside her. Then Eddie picked up a piece of paper currency and lit it. The paper burned fast in his hands but did not stay long enough to start the flame. The smoke was acrid from the dyes. He had to do it a second time before the flame caught easily with the wind. Its crimson blaze was bright, and it moved in a kind of languid dance, rising and bending this way and that way, as if in silent rhythm with the breeze. They squatted around watching it in pleasant stillness, feeling the raw excitement of real fires. Then the flame grew stronger, the heat increased and the smoke became more dense. The plastic bucket started to fall sideways then part of it melted along with the make-believe paper objects. The blaze was as high as half a metre now and despite the imminent danger, both burst out laughing, even in fright. Trinh had been foolish to use the plastic bucket; she did not think that it would melt with the burning of paper, but apparently, the temperature was high enough to reach its melting point. The smoke and fire rose further, fuelled by the plastic bucket. Mother and son ran in circles looking for ways to snuff it out, bumping into each other, laughing at the same time.

"Eddie, get that rag! Quickly, boy!" Trinh shouted, pointing to the corner.

"Where? Where?" Eddie jumped up from his sitting position, shouting equally with excitement.

"There, there! Oh, never mind!" Trinh ran inside the house, abandoning the idea of using the rag to throw over the small fire that was the cause of so much excitement. She rushed to the dining table and carried out the vase then poured the whole thing into it, flowers, and all, still laughing. Meanwhile, instead of subduing the fire, Eddie was feeding more paper into it, seeing from her cheerful manner that Trinh wasn't very worried about the danger.

"There you are! Our housekeeper's got a bucket to have a bath in as well as some flowers for a romantic dinner on his way to heaven!" Trinh exclaimed triumphantly, taking charge of the situation.

That had been last week. Tonight, she was by herself at home, spending her New Year's Eve alone. The flat was next to the temple, and she had the opportunity to watch the fireworks and dragon dance from her balcony after the customary New Year's Eve incense burning ceremony. This ceremony is to welcome home the spirits of ancestors and the deceased in the family in the Tet celebration. Eddie was with his dad and the older brothers. Her New Year's Eve was being celebrated with her dog. Poor Cadbury! The chocolate Border Collie was frightened out of her wits with the noise of the fireworks and all the commotion around her.

After the firecrackers that marked the new beginning of a new year, they walked hurriedly toward the house. The dog was fighting desperately with Trinh to get to the door first. She leapt forward trying to squeeze her large body through the grills of the security door, albeit unsuccessfully.

"No, Cadbury! No! Out of my way, silly girl!" Trinh shouted.

She had to control Cadbury. She must not let her dog get in front of her. That was definitely a no-no! Trinh shoved the strong dog aside in case she entered the house before her; then the rest of her year would be the same as Cadbury's fate. She laughed aloud, thinking there could not be anything worse. As the first being to enter the house will bring their aura and personality to that household for the whole year, she would not want Cadbury canine's aura or personality at all, obviously! She would not want to go yap yap all day long, waiting to be fed or petted at the whim of the owner. She would rather be independent in her own environment at any cost.

A Virtual Lover

Trinh won the battle. She went in and turned on her iMac. She was going to write. Lately Trinh had formed the habit of writing to her imaginary lover. She had created a fictional character, a listener in her mind without any physical image or resemblance to anyone in real life, to write to and to talk to every day. Her desire to be in love, truly in love, urged her on. Many times, she wondered if she could ever love again—a pure, unblemished love that originated from the heart without any prejudice. Would it be possible after all?

Then one day, she thought of a solution. She started to pour her feeling and emotions into her words. A series of love letters materialised. A void was now filled by her creation, and it satisfied her femininity miraculously. She could pretend that she was in love, deeply and profoundly in love with that fictional character and wrote him long, romantic, and loving letters at almost every opportunity when she found the need. She ceased to feel lonely from then on. The days were brighter, and the nights were warmer. Her heart was bubbling with air, and the oxygen coursing through her blood brought vitality to her entire being. There was somebody out there for her to love and be loved by after all, even in her imagination! How wonderful that could be!

The loneliness she felt as a busy single woman was not because she was alone. Trinh was rarely alone. There were her sons, her mother, her friends, relatives, colleagues, customers, and her dog during the days. But many times at night, the loneliness of a woman yearning to find her other half crept over her and pricked at her mind dully, like tiny ants picking away a pile of sugar grains. It was draining her of her courage and spirit to go forward. The pile of sugar grains was being depleted as time moved on. Trinh could not let that happen. She had vowed never to succumb to desperation and loneliness ever again.

So here she was, writing on her first day of the year of The Dragon to her fictional lover. It was the first day that she was alone on an occasion as important as Tet when everyone was supposed to be together. She had known that it was only a start as she would have to face it many more days in the future. But she was ready. She had her confidant, a distant figure somewhere in the universe whose presence continued to help her regain her equilibrium in all those lonely and dispirited days and nights, wherever she was and whenever she needed it.

Second Day of Tet

The footpaths were full of firecracker shells, their empty remains strewn about thickly on the ground like a red carpet. It was business as usual: Trinh opened the pharmacy with more firecracker explosions and the drumming of the dragon dance pounding along the street. This was the way to shoo away bad omens and to bring prosperity for the New Year. In Oriental belief, the dragon is a symbol of power, dignity, fertility, and auspiciousness. The longer the dragon dance, the more power it has to exert upon tenanted property. With that belief, many merchants usually hire the dance group with the most skill to move in a flexible, sinuous, undulating manner mimicking the dragon's movements. The dance usually ends with a reward for the dragon tied on a high pole. The deafening noise from firecrackers is believed to scare off demons and evil spirits.

The pharmacy was quiet. Traditionally, Vietnamese or Asians avoid shopping for medications during Tet.

Trinh had mixed feelings standing in the pharmacy looking out. Happiness and melancholy were all blurry, undefined, as if she was having a hallucination. The festive atmosphere and the gaiety of every passerby brought cheerfulness and merriment for an instant then left her empty as quickly as it had arrived. Somehow, she missed her father. His joie de vivre always brought laughter and glitter to occasions like Tet. The family would gather around him listening to his singing and his jokes.

He used to give them a riddle, asking, "Tell me, children, do you know how far it is from earth to heaven?"

"A million stars away," Trinh shouted, trying to be heard over the chattering of others.

"Two million kilometres!" her brother seconded.

"There is no heaven!" Kim protested.

"Two years to travel there," Hoan cautiously answered.

Her father would laugh uproariously and declared victoriously, "Nah, it's not far at all, in fact, it's very close. Don't you all see? It's only taken a week to travel from earth to heaven and back. The story of the housekeeper and the ritual of bidding farewell to him then welcoming him back to earth within seven days proves it!"

Everyone laughed and acknowledged the ingenuity of the riddle.

Trinh missed her childhood, albeit a troublesome childhood full of images of war and despicable living conditions. Returning home after school, her father would pick her up, gave her a cuddle with many kisses on her cheeks, then put her on his lap, and ask, "My darling, do you love me? Did you miss me, my sweetie? How much do you love me, my little sunshine?"

She remembered fidgeting on his lap, longing to jump off and run away with her toys as she always wondered why he had to ask those silly questions. The questions were always the same, and she was being asked many many times over and over again, like a ritual. In her childish mind, Trinh found it a waste of her time, so she replied like an automaton.

"Yes, I do. Love you very much. Miss you too. A lot!"

Then her father continued, "How much is a lot, my doll?" still holding on tightly to Trinh, deliberately not letting her slip off his lap, enjoying his game. "And when will you stop, my little girl?"

At this point, Trinh had run out of patience, and become annoyed with his "childish" game, as she saw it. She wriggled forcefully out of his hold but still tried her best to please him by shouting and extending her short hands to maximum arm length. "As much as this! And forever and ever! Never, never stop!" Then triumphantly, she darted away laughing, free of him.

Those questions from her father about love were very real. However, the answers to them would be as surrealistic as love itself. How would one measure one's love? Trinh wondered. Now, in her reminiscence as a mature adult, Trinh understood her father's poetic passion better. He was such an affectionate, romantic, and sentimental soul. If she had known that it was her father's way of reassuring himself that there were forever in this universe a someone whose love toward him was unconditional and lasting, "As much as this much and forever and ever, never never stop!" then Trinh would have put more emotion into her replies, with more sincerity for the sake of her father's confidence. To declare the love of a daughter toward her father was unique and ongoing even when his presence had already gone from this earth many years ago.

She had asked her imaginary love in her letter last night similar questions as if seeking the same reassurance her father had sought. *"Do you love me? Do you miss me? How much is your love for me and would you ever stop?"*

The unmeasurable or immeasurable state of love: the consequences were so vast in having it or not having it, that Trinh thought no one would be able to explain. The contrasting effect of one state to the other, from a positive yes and a feeling of joie de vivre to the negative one of no, with an indifference to life, was truly remarkable.

But Trinh was feeling very positive now. She was happy and content with the love she created, a warm feeling of sensuality spreading through her entire being and she wondered if she was really missing that imaginary darling by being so rooted in her melancholy all this time.

The Creation

"You know, baby. It's been a while since I've had a chance to say the word to anyone?" Trinh heard herself talking to her confidant. She was day dreaming now.

"The L-O-V-E word." She enunciated each letter of the alphabet. *"And it's been a while since I've been anyone's sweetheart. These terms of endearment seem as strange to me as a different language, lost for so many years. But I've got you now. You are now 'my darling'! I'm so glad, my love. My yearning to say those terms of endearment has been satisfied now by whispering to you!"*

Trinh laughed. The benefits of having an imaginary character were enormous. Her confidant had to be agreeable. He had no choice.

So she continued. *"I'm writing to express my feelings to a love which I've found. That's you! Yes, baby! You're going to receive it all, darling. Every emotion from deep in my heart, every sense, every perception, every consciousness from my hours of living is now devoted to you. My sensuality and my passion are now yours. Without you, they might fade away in time. Don't you see? So here I am, transcribing my femininity into words to you to preserve them for me. As I'm afraid of living a life without romance, you are now my romance, my choice. There was not much choice out there, regretfully. Don't you see, darling? To have someone of similar interests and intellect on the same wavelength, so to speak, is extremely difficult. The problem lies in the evolution of humankind; changes are taking place faster than any other time in the past. The roles of the two sexes in the universe, male and female, need to be preserved in this century, the twenty-first century. The roles are switching and mixing together so much that sometimes I find myself wondering which one is mine!"*

Trinh smiled at herself. She felt warm and glorious. She was in love.

Didn't someone just stop in his tracks and tell her this morning, "You've got a beautiful smile! I'm sorry, but I must tell you that!" when she was having a morning walk with Cadbury.

Her face must have lit up even more as the stranger continued on his bike, repeating, "Your smile is so beautiful!"

Time

THE CLOCK KEEPS ticking, the sun keeps rising and setting, the moon keeps shining and disappearing, and lines and wrinkles keep forming on the once smooth, translucent skin.

"You know, not so long ago, I was terrified of old age, especially looking at your grandmother and at how frail she is now," Trinh said to her children.

"Ha, curiously, nothing has changed. Now the prospect is even more frightening." She laughed at her ambiguity.

"However, I've learnt to think of that process as a matter of course and seem to accept it on better terms, a natural aging process that all living things approach from birth to death."

People in her profession, pharmacists, are in daily contact with ailments, afflictions, substance abuse, the elderly, and disease. It is an unromantic or unglamorous way to earn a living but a fundamental one, nevertheless. Working in a local pharmacy in the southwestern Sydney area, she faced a constant reminder that the human body and mind change with time. One only had to consider the frequent visits of her regular customers whose aging process could be seen in a sudden drop of their independence. Optimal physical well-being and a sound state of mind are threatened as we get older, and it is always heartbreaking for her to witness all these changes. To observe a feeble mind that goes even further astray with the help of medications; to watch a patient once living independently on her own, briskly getting around with her daily chores, then suddenly a few weeks later, on crutches, moving about with little shaking steps aided by a relative, a daughter or son, and to be in almost daily contact with patients on Methadone, the registered addicts' narcotic drug that is used as a replacement for heroin users and dispensed in a pharmacy under a supervised dosing system. To be in shock after hearing sad news from a relative or the neighbour of a regular patient informing of her or his death, this regretfully was only discovered weeks later due to her infrequent visits and her absence from the pharmacy. Added to all these professional duties as a pharmacist was the emotional side of the profession. Being local means a friendliness and attachment that get deeper and deeper with interaction over the years.

"You're all fortunate in a way, being close by my side most of the time from birth to kindergarten," Trinh reminded her children.

Trinh became the proprietor of her own pharmacy after she became pregnant with her first son and with the fantastic help of her mother, who made it possible for her children to follow her to her shop every day until the age of kindergarten. The shop was divided into living quarters at the back for her children. She felt that was the most rewarding and happy achievement for them and for her as a full time working mother.

"I was able to watch each of you growing up from babyhood to kindergarten and then becoming a teenager. That was the most fantastic time of my life, even though I was busy as a bee!" Trinh said.

When all four were little, Trinh told them on the way home by car one evening, "Oh, would you all be quiet? I'm so tired and stressed out. If you keep going on like this I'll end up in a mental hospital soon!"

She was about to accelerate straight ahead after the green light at an intersection when Adam said in surprise, "Mammy, you didn't turn right. The hospital is that way!" He pointed toward the indicated direction, very please with himself for being able to help his mother.

How sweet children are! Trinh knew that for most working mothers, juggling between her career and motherhood was the most difficult mission a woman had to undertake in her life, especially in this modern digital age, and especially for a professional like her. They often have to sacrifice either one or choose to lean toward one or the other. However, Trinh was able to manage them both, a mother and a pharmacist on the same road at the same time.

"Where's your mother, Karl?" her mother would ask, looking for Trinh one morning.

"She's gone to play her computer games," her two-year-old second last son would answer. In his innocence, looking at her working in front of the computer in the pharmacy was just like playing games!

Thinking back over all those years, she was very glad that she had done what she had. Her sons had rarely been out of her sight since birth and were under her care until the age of teens. She had brought four beautiful human beings into this world, and they had grown into beautiful young adults.

She had learnt from them very much as they had learnt from her. They are now in such a friendly relationship that a friend has commented admiringly, "You are just like a sister to them, and I mean that as a compliment!"

She and her customers cheerfully reminisced about the childish act of her second eldest, Adam, who was twenty-two years old now, but a toddler at that time, playing with lipsticks and make-up in the pharmacy.

She said, "How peculiar that I could remember like yesterday his tiptoeing on the shelf with a lipstick on one hand and mascara on the other hand. It's a vivid image lasting in my memory down to the last detail regardless of years gone by. But don't you dare ask me what I had for dinner last night! Whatever there was on the table might not even register in my brain!"

They laughed together at the fond memory. Some commented on how pregnant she was not so long ago with Eddie, the last of the four sons, or how young, healthy, and active her mother used to be, bustling around at the back of the shop with her grandchildren.

They were her close friends as much as her customers. Her kind of pharmacy was now facing extinction by brutal competition with the arrival of huge chain store pharmacies, from which a personal touch might not be essential anymore. Trinh had cried heartily the day one of her neighbours informed her of Mrs. Smith's death in April this year. Every Christmas ever since her first year in this pharmacy, Mrs. Smith had crocheted tea towels personally and gave one to each of them, her assistant and her, a Christmas parcel wrapped up nicely and accompanied by a handwritten card, without fail, for nineteen years continuously. At Easter, they had coat hangers or soaps covered with frilly romantic ribbon and silk or lace, her skilful craft, which seemed to belong to yesteryear now! Her psychotic bachelor son looked lost and aged quickly in the last few months after her death. He was a lonely soul who had been seen to keep carrying his mother's wicker chair to the front garden for their regular afternoon sittings, everyday, as if he did not know that his only companion for the last fifty years or so had gone from his life for good! Trinh wished she could have gone to her funeral, and that wish made Trinh even more mournful as her death had occurred at the beginning of the year without her knowledge. This simple gesture from a thoughtful and caring customer had made a strong impact on her mind! It had helped Trinh draw the conclusion that after death, the everlasting memory of a person comes from their heartfelt caring acts, which have more value than the vastness of gold itself. Her customer's personal touch on those simple cotton tea towels and her sincere loving manner had meant more than any other expensive or extravagant gifts Trinh had received. How rich a person was in life, unadorned and inconspicuous in reminiscence, compared to how kind, and loving he was in death. The act of kindness is always notable and lasts a long time in their absence, Trinh believed.

Some of her Methadone patients had been dosing in the pharmacy for more than a decade. They saw her more often than their parents or children, who either had deserted them or been deserted by them or taken away from them by social security service. Drug addiction is a curse nevertheless, as even with much time and effort many can never get out of this vicious habit. At best, they could lead a relatively normal life with affordable legal Methadone as the substitute rather than the exorbitantly priced, outlawed heroin from which nasty crimes were being committed in order to possess and use. Trinh was very reluctant to enter the program providing Methadone dosing at first and was very scared and naive in the beginning. They were an entirely different category from the regular customers in the pharmacy. Some were plain drug addicts by choice, but the majority were driven to it by circumstances, Trinh believed. Many had served jail terms and had lived the kind of disturbed life that was often reflected in creative television dramas. They were actually true-to-life stories.

Some told lies like truths. The nasty things about their lies were that they probably believed in them wholeheartedly, as their mind was somehow an obscure zone where imagination and reality were mixed up here, there and everywhere. In between alertness and delirium, they got totally confused.

A pharmacist has to outsmart them by being calm and authoritative all the time. Trinh was very confused in her first few years handling them, as she was a believer in human goodness. But as time moved on, she learnt to act accordingly. Sometimes they just needed a strong, authoritative voice to stop them from sliding further into the abyss and prevent them from falling deeper into their drug use habits in certain days and time.

There was Deanna, whose first word was always a "sorry," a customary utterance which Trinh suspected resulted from childhood abuse. At first Trinh tried to convince her not to say "sorry" from the start of each sentence, but she gave up eventually as she kept saying frantically "sorry" over and over again the more she told her not to! Poor soul!

She often commented on Trinh's appearance, "You look fresh and glowing! I wish I could look and feel like that!"

Trinh thought at least she had given someone inspiration!

There was Thomas, another one. Travelling to the city by train at one time, Trinh was greeted warmly and personally, like an old friend, by a man with full-body-tattoos, lizard hair, toothless, grimy, dishevelled, and carrying in one hand a bottle wrapped in a brown paper bag.

"Hi Trinh, how are you! It's good to see you! You're looking sensational as usual!" He almost gave her a hug at the station.

She laughed and gave him a salute, avoiding the potential hug coming her way. Indifferent to the astonished look of passersby directed toward the spectacular scene, Trinh replied, "Good to see you too, Thomas! Still downing the bourbon at ten o'clock in the morning?"

"Back to the other habit yet?" she asked jokingly as he had left the pharmacy over a year already.

It was sad to see them struggling with their habits, both drinking and using drugs for their whole lifetime! Some could move on with their living as best they could, but some stayed with the habits.

Trinh often reminded her children, "Stay away from heroin or anything that causes addiction, but most of all, heroin. It's lethal, once you're hooked on it. It's your life sentence, kids."

They would all chorus, "Yeah, yeah, yeah, Mammy."

Then Trinh told them that her book was almost finished.

Eddie said, "I'll buy one, Mammy. And I'll ask my friends to buy some too."

"Ah, that's great to know, darling! Very comforting to know that." Trinh smiled.

The others would look as if she was joking, "That's very good, Mammy!"

"Very proud of you, Mammy!"

At the time while writing her book, she was confident that she would be able to explain to the rest of the world what she was trying to say, the conflicts of the Vietnam War, the exodus of Vietnamese boat people, the difficulties of resettlement and life in general, being a woman and a mother. Then she was afraid that although the story was still unfinished her words had all dried up. Finally, she hoped that her dilemma and her experience would help people of similar circumstances regain their equilibrium by reading her book.

However, at the time, Trinh kept wondering if it was a futile attempt, with her crude efforts to write in a language still foreign to her even after almost forty years. Would anyone be interested enough to read it? She often had to light three incense sticks with the offerings of tea, fruit, and cakes in front of her Buddha shrine, asking for courage and determination and begging the spirits of perished soldiers, deceased refugees, boat people, her ancestors, her father Nguyen, her sister Betty, and her brothers Dien and Mac, the lot, to give her strength and enough vocabulary to write page after page as promised.

"You know, I disciplined myself to write at least five hundred words a day five days a week, and I was counting them every day! Hey, but I did read them back some time as I was afraid of falling into the same nightmare as Jack the writer in the movie, *The Shining*. Do you remember that movie? Was it Jack the writer or Jack Nicholson who played him?" Trinh told Helen, a close friend of Kim and hers since they first arrived in East Hills Hostel.

"Yeah, that's a scary one. 'All work but no play makes Jack a dull boy.' Or something like that. Wasn't it that he kept clicking away at his typewriter on the same phrase for hundreds and hundreds of pages?"

"Yep, you're not wrong there, Helen. However, believe me, some of my pages are different. And I'm not going insane or trying to kill anyone with an axe." Both would laugh at this joke.

"At the same time, my assistant would ponder for a while about my dilemma of writing five hundred words a day, then say, "But some of the words are the same, aren't they? They're not at all five hundred different words, are they?" She was clearly puzzled about it.

"Yeah, by luck, some of the words were repetitive to the point that my editor had to scream, 'Stop, stop! Cut, cut!' telling me to chop out many paragraphs in the book, as in my writing fever about Communist and Communism, I kept returning to that as an obsession! I almost became Jill the writer with the phrase 'the Communists and Communism are the main enemies of my people and we detest them' over and over again." They laughed again with that discomforting statement.

"But you know, ask any refugee who escaped during the exodus of boat people in the eighties. Those two words raised hell in their mind, and I'm the same. I'm one of them!"

"If it was not that horrible, we would not have left," Trinh explained to her children.

Trinh often wondered what her life would have become if she had stayed back in Vietnam. But she knew that she had given her children the best start in life in Australia. She would not think of herself as anything else but Australian now and was so proud of it.

Following ODP, Ms. Mien and Dr. Quang migrated to the US in 1989.

Thanh remained in Vietnam, a childless widow, and became a successful merchant after the normalisation of trade in her country.

Anh and Sue continued their open-street bar trade for a while then disappeared without a trace, perhaps suffering a fate similar to many others who perished at sea in the exodus.

Mai migrated to the US a few weeks after her recuperation period in a hospital in Terengganu. However, she suffered a mental breakdown when she stepped down onto Californian soil and has stayed in an institution from the age of eighteen in 1978 until now. Her parents were so distraught without news from their only daughter that they tried to escape several times but unsuccessfully. In the end, their final trip, with a hundred others, was lost in the Pacific Ocean.

Truyen drowned with most of her family, her mother and her two sisters, when her boat was scuttled too far out, leaving her father, Lam, the only survivor in their escape in 1979.

Uncle Tam was arrested in his attempt to escape shortly after Truyen left, and no one knew of his fate after that.

Mike was forever searching for his identity. He managed to assimilate into his new home in California, doing odd jobs in Little Saigon but remained a lost soul wondering whether he belonged anywhere. He never found his parents.

Little Lien, who was so excited to leave Saigon during the chaos, grew up to become a successful restaurant owner specialising in Pho in Paris, France.

Giang, a retired Australian tax officer with a master degree in Asian study, moved on after a few years grieving for her husband and then migrated to Washington, DC, USA.

Kate, Giang's daughter, is married with a son and a daughter. She is working for the Australian Department of Finance with a law degree and living in the capital city, Canberra. Anthony, Giang's son, works for the Australian government with an IT degree.

Vy remains a single woman. After more than thirty years working as an electronic technician for a telecom company, she has recently retired as well.

Dien passed away with liver cancer within six months from his diagnosis. His wife and two sons remain in Vietnam.

Hoan, a computer programmer, divorced after more than a quarter of a century marriage with his first love. He is living in Texas and is searching for a new beginning. He has two grown-up daughters.

Kim works for Australian Department of Defence as an assistant director with an IT degree. She is married with two daughters.

Luc, a social worker helping street kids and delinquents, has a son and a daughter. He has recently reversed to being a bachelor again!

Trinh's macular degeneration is under control. She believes in the advancement of technology and hopes for the perfection of "bionic eyes" invention in the future. A friend of her commented recently, "I don't know how macular degeneration might have affected you in any way, but I can see that your eyes are still as bright and shine as a barn owl which can spot a spider one hundred kilometres away at night!"

Chi is so proud of her children and remains a soft spoken, timid person despite her years of dealing with the world out there.

President Tran Van Huong was placed under house arrest by the Vietnamese communist regime after the Fall of Saigon. In 1977, his civil rights were restored, but he declined. Instead, he asked for all officials of the ARVN to be released from prison before he would take his place among the freed. His request was ignored. The former president died quietly in his own home in Vietnam in 1982.

President General Duong Van Minh was never seen again in public from that historical day, April 30, 1975. It seemed Hanoi compensated him for his inert warfare tactics during the last few weeks of the war and allowed him to live quietly. By surrendering readily, the president had managed to avoid for both sides—the bloodshed and carnage of the fighting during the chaos. He was kept in seclusion in his own home for several years before being allowed to migrate to France in 1983. He remained silent and stayed out of politics until his death in California in 2001.

After forty years, the communist Vietnam has introduced nothing to the outside world, both in terms of productivity and acclaimed intellectuals or academics, but prospered on falsified wealth from which a majority of party members and their family have gained through bribery and inside trading on the expenses of the Vietnamese citizens. Rural developments are minimal, and the peasants are still living in the similar environment without running water and basic sewage system as of half a century ago.

Epilogue:
A Summer in England

2015

THE WATER WAS green and slimy, but Trinh could see that the wild drakes and the family of six ducklings were enjoying it contentedly. The handsome male pack had returned after a half-hour's absence. They flew off all at once, leaving the mother duck with her brood behind, when Trinh joyously ran into their flock while picking wild daisies on the lawn. Trinh was so delighted with the wildflowers. They were in several places, here and there, haphazardly breaking the green patch into colourful sections. Amid the little white daisies, there were yellow dandelions and pinkish dog-roses, which added variety to the lot.

The handsome drakes, with distinctive shiny jade-green smooth heads, a ring on the neck, and bright lemon beaks, swam around leisurely in groups of two or three. Not too far away was the modest mother duck with her brood, the six little plain greyish ducklings, clumped together protectively. They were all happily dipping their beaks in and out of the green water searching for titbits. Some even dived head down underneath the surface, leaving half of their body and tail pointed vertically in the air. The partial bodies with the wiggling tail and missing head made Trinh chuckle with amusement at the peculiar forms.

The sound of a small splashing fountain in the middle of the pond was soothing to her ears. The chirping of birds added to the serenade of the morning.

It was so tranquil here, she almost said aloud. On the edge of the irregular oval shaped pond, there were purple irises on one side and healthy white lily-in-the-valley bush on the other side. Scattered on the right side of the water surface, the miniature water lilies were in bloom. The clusters were moving slightly in the water, bending sideways as if trying to duck out of reach of the mischievous carp underneath. They were tickled by the feathered snipping touch of the carps. Trinh was sure. The fish thoroughly enjoyed disturbing those arrogant water lilies from time to time. See, the flowers had the chance to show off their pure white colour blooms in the air; even the timid, subtle pinkish ones were proud of their beauty and stood high under the bright yellow sun. Nevertheless, the carp could not have that privilege. They were hidden below the surface. Trinh had tried very hard to look for them, peering through the thick slimy greenish water, but they seemed to be introverts. Their wide bright orange lips peeped up on the surface as if gasping for air for a very brief moment or two then disappeared quickly. Cowards! She was curious to see how big and how colourful the carp could be! She even walked along the bank by the perimeter of the pond following their movements. Pity, the water was so murky that Trinh could not see anything underneath; not even a glimpse, and they were so adept at quickly swimming into hiding once her shadow fell upon the surface.

The black crow was strolling alone at the far side of the park after swirling around the air a few times at the tops of tall, ancient trees. The trunks were as wide as a big wheel, some at least half a metre in radius.

Her first time in England, and the beautiful town of Walton-on-Thames had given Trinh a sense of peace the moment she arrived. The weather had been so kind, the sun was bright, and there was not even a cloud in the sky. It was blue, blue like the ocean. The town had had a few days of rain before she came, and the luxuriant lush green vegetation in the area somehow enhanced its romantic, enchanting atmosphere.

"Oh!" Trinh exclaimed. A squirrel had ventured out of the wood. She jumped up and pointed it out to Charles, sitting on the park bench, immersed in the glorious summer day.

She walked toward him, in her hand a bouquet of wildflowers and dried pinecones she had collected in a short while.

"Mwah!" She kissed him playfully on the cheek then sat down beside him. He put his left arm around her shoulder, bent down, and kissed her lips in return. Then they both fell into a comfortable silence, observing the natural activities around the pond. The bouquet of wildflowers was arranged in front of Trinh's feet, surrounded by pinecones on the green lawn.

From a distance, the squirrel's tiny body was brown and its fluffy tail was high in the air. It was busy scurrying in and out of the bush nearby for a few minutes looking very industrious, and then it took all the courage it could muster to hop tentatively toward the pond. It went closer to the edge, putting its head down to drink a bit of the murky greenish water and then shook its body as if the water was somewhat strange to the taste. *It must be that, of course!* Trinh thought amusedly.

"It's thirsty!" she told Charles, as if he did not know.

"How could one live and thrive happily in that slimy water?" Charles wondered aloud.

"I've thought the same, Charles!" Trinh had had a similar reflection a moment ago.

"But look! All the creatures, the ducks, the fish, the birds, the water lilies, the irises, and even the squirrel seem to love it and bathe in it quite happily," she added triumphantly.

She had seen the fauna of the park, and the drakes and the ducks, enjoying it tremendously; and all the vegetation and flowers were blooming exuberantly. They seemed to love their environment, unlike human beings who had judgments about all kinds of appearances, especially slimy green water! Trinh smiled inwardly at her thoughts.

"Would you fancy a stroll?" Charles stood up when the squirrel retreated inside the wood.

"Okay, where to?"

"The River Thames."

"Great! Okay, let's go."

It was only a short drive to the Thames Path through Walton-on-Thames, an approximately three-hundred-kilometre route which opened in 1996 to give the walkers a pleasant, unspoiled view of the English villages along the path. The river and its habitat reminded Trinh very much of her father's hometown in Vietnam in an unusual way. The two towns might not have had anything in common except the stream of muddy water slowly drifting by and the dirt path alongside the bank. Yet, it had somehow jogged her memory of the similar dirt path along the river southwest of Saigon, thousands and thousands kilometres away from here. She had taken that path many times when she was a little girl visiting her grandmother with the family in summer vacations. Her river was more alive with dense clumps of floating water plants, lilies, and hyacinth on the surface, living-in sampans with elongated shapes crowded with families and children splashing and swimming noisily in the water. Trinh remembered that there was one time she sat on the riverbank with her feet dangling, holding to a branch of water lily. Then it slipped from her tiny hand and fell down to the river below. Without thinking, Trinh reached out after it and fell in with a splash. The little girl would have drowned if not rescued swiftly by her much older cousin. The incident was still clear in her memory now, even though she was only four or five at the time. What a fright that had been, but she rescued the lily at least. Wet and scared as a little mouse the girl had held tight to it as if it was her most precious possession!

The Thames was cleaner and quieter with a few speedboats moored placidly and a large houseboat at anchor, showing no sign of anyone living there. But there was a group of young women rowing steadily along with harmonious movements. The usual distinctive shiny green drakes of England and the plainer female ducks were swimming leisurely. A lone, sophisticated white swan swam among the ducks, showing off her beauty. Her flock might be somewhere upstream.

There were native bushes and trees on the riverbank, the extraordinary variety of wildflowers showing themselves exquisitely in different colours: white daisy, violet bluebell, yellow agrimonies and spearwort, purple opium poppy, and many more. A few pedestrian bridges joining the two banks were also present but it seemed they were hardly used these days.

"Wait, wait!" Trinh stopped abruptly and walked over to the big tree with hanging leaves and dangling fruits. She reached up and picked a fruit off the branch.

"Look! This is unusual. What tree is it? Do you know, Charles?"

"Ah, this is a helicopter flower tree, and when the fruits are dry we used to pluck off the upper leaves and throw the lower part up in the air. Then it falls down with a movement like a helicopter rotor blade. Let me show you."

He threw up a few fruits before Trinh could see the rotor blade action. She squealed in delight.

"It could be that the fruits aren't dry enough. They're still too green, too fresh. It might not be in season yet," Charles explained the few failed attempts.

"Back home in Vietnam, we have the *Dipterocarpus zeylanicus* tree, we call it 'cay dau' in our language, and its fruit has double wings, much bigger and heavier than your helicopter one. We also used to collect them on windy days then throw them up in the air for them to swirl around like a yo-yo. It's quite fun. My brothers, sister, and I used to love playing the childish, simple game."

"Yeah, funny. Sometimes those playful acts seem insignificant at the time, but when years and years go by, they become the most remarkable memories a person can recall from their childhood."

"I also used to ride along this path many times in summer," he added. "I remember, I bought a bicycle when I was at boarding school, about thirty kilometres away from here. I did not know how to get it home. It's quite a dilemma, you know! In the end, when summer vacation came, my parents drove there to pick up my belongings and I rode the bike home by myself." He laughed at the memory, a faraway look on his face.

"It must be fun, Charles!"

"Sure, back in those days, riding a bike somewhere was almost an occasion. The boys and I did the tour of the Seven Hill Road, the most spectacular one, counting the hills one by one until we reached the last of the seven, yelling and making a noise all the way!"

"Ah, those carefree younger days! Too long gone now for you, darling!" she teased him, smiling. She knew that he hated to be reminded of his age.

They walked on further, holding hands. It was a beautiful, picturesque trail, and the walk was pleasant for both of them.

"You know, this trail must have been in existence for thousands of years, and I am sure there are many charming love stories as well as ghastly horrific stories for every bush and trees, or for every spot, every corner," she said again after a while.

"Gruesome murders and eerie ghost stories," Trinh added.

"Eeee!" She hunched her shoulders, making a scary gesture with her hands folded across her chest.

"For example, don't walk too close to that underbridge over there, there might be hands with long black claws poking out through the bars of that window beneath and pulling your legs over!" She laughed aloud at her gobbledygook.

"Yeah, you're right! That comes with history, I think. For a town this old, I am sure we have plenty of stories," Charles agreed.

The day ended wonderfully. That night, lying in the crook of Charles' arm, Trinh thought of the day before.

"You've come to England at the right time, very good choice of season!" a friend of Charles had said to her at an old pub, the 1505 Duke of Cumberland in Haslemere.

Trinh answered. "Indeed, it could not be any other time!"

Yes, the time could not be any better for Trinh to be acquainted with Charles's hometown, and it was an enchanting trip for her.

Destiny and circumstances, either or both, had influenced her sentiments in the past. Moreover, right now, in the setting of a gorgeous historical town so far from home, she had begun to feel closer to Charles. She had seen in him a person with charisma and warmth. She had fallen in love with him or his hometown. Trinh was not sure, but she felt so at peace, lighthearted, and happy in his presence here. Her heart mellowed with the childhood memories he recounted to her and with the magical river Thames and its surroundings.

Trinh suddenly came to realise that she had to say goodbye to something old but very dear to her heart before she could embrace something new in return. Her mind had to be exorcised of the past loves and images before it was ready to accept a new one. Perhaps it was time.

CieCie Tuyet Nguyen

**Former Statue of an ARVN soldier
at Bien Hoa Military Cemetary**

Photo courtesy of Dr. T. D. Dang

Appendix

- "Alpha History: Because the past Matters." Alpha History. http://alphahistory.com/.

- "American Experience: TV's Most-watched History Series." PBS. , http://www.pbs.org/wgbh/americanexperience/films/lastdays/

- An Loc Battle, https://en.wikipedia.org/wiki/Battle_of_An_Lộc

- Archibald Fountain–The City of Sydney : Water, water every... http://history.cityofsydney.nsw.gov.au/waterexhibition/OrnamentalFountains/ArchibaldFountain.html

- ARVN: Army of the Republic of Vietnam—the South Vietnamese Army

- "Boat Arrivals in Australia since 1976."—Parliament of Australia. Boat Arrivals, http://www.aph.gov.au/About_Parliament/Parliamentary_Departments/Parliamentary_Library/pubs/BN/2012-2013/BoatArrivals

- 'Cambodia Facts and History' by By Kallie Szczepanski Asian History Expert

- "Cambodia and Vietnam War." Cambodia and Vietnam War, http://olive-drab.com/od_history_vietnam_cambodia.php.

- Cu Chi Tunnels, http://vietnam-war.commemoration.gov.au/combat/viet-cong-tunnels.php

- Hyde Park, Sydney–Wikipedia, the free encyclopedia, https://en.wikipedia.org/wiki/Hyde_Park,_Sydney
- "Life Has No Endings, Only Beginnings…": Vietnamese Boat People, http://pinkycactus.blogspot.com/2012/03/vietnamese-boat-people-death-tolls-and.html.
- List of animal sounds–Wikipedia, the free encyclopedia https://en.wikipedia.org/wiki/List_of_animal_sounds
- "Military Factory."–Military Weapons, http://www.militaryfactory.com/.
- "New American Nation." Refugees and "boat People", http://www.americanforeignrelations.com/O-W/The-Vietnam-War-and-Its-Impact-Refugees-and-boat-people.html.
- "Operation Babylift." Operation Babylift, http://www.thebabylift.com/. http://en.wikipedia.org/wiki/Operation_Babylift.
- "Paris Peace Accords Signed." History.com, http://www.history.com/this-day-in-history/paris-peace-accords-signed.
- "The Cold War Museum." Cold War Museum, http://coldwar.org/.
- "UNHCR and Malaysia Close Camp for Vietnamese Boat-people." UNHCR News, http://www.unhcr.org/3ae6b81838.html.
- "Vietnamese Re-Education Camps: A Brief History." Vietnamese Re-Education Camps: A Brief History. http://www.choices.edu/resources/supplemental_vietnam_camps.php., http://en.wikipedia.org/wiki/Reeducation_camp.
- "Vietnam's Forgotten Cambodian War–BBC News."BBC News, http://www.bbc.com/news/world-asia-29106034.

- 18th Infantry Division—of the South Vietnamese Army, was led by Major General Le Minh Dao

- Battle of Xuan Loc, https://en.wikipedia.org/wiki/Battle_of_Xu%C3%A2n_L%E1%BB%99c , http://vnafmamn.com/xuanloc_battle.html, http://www.history.com/this-day-in.../thieu-flees-saigon-as-xuan-loc-falls

- Beri-beri, vitamin B1 Deficiency, http://www.fitday.com/fitness-articles/nutrition/vitamins-minerals/5-signs-of-vitamin-b1-deficiency.html#b

- https://en.wikipedia.org/wiki/Beriberi

- Bien Hoa is thirty kilometres East of Saigon

- Brigadier General Tran Quang Khoi was in the III Corps Armored Task Force of ARVN

- Buon Me Thuot is the largest city in the central highlands region of Vietnam

- Can Tho, a provincial city, 100km to the South West of Saigon

- Da Nang is the largest city in central Vietnam, 759km (472miles) south of Hanoi, 960km (600miles) north of Saigon

- Dipterocarpus zeylanicus trees–It is a large tree that grows up to 40–45 m tall and 4–6 m in circumference. The bark is light pinkish brown or light yellowish brown. Leaves are big and oval, 5 to 8 inches long. The sharp-edged leaves are covered with silver hairy. Flowers bloom in April and seeds have two wings to spread from wind. (Wikipedia)

- Dong is the currency of Vietnam, like the dollar in Australia.

- General Nguyen Khoa Nam and General Le Van Hung were in the Air Force of the Republic of South Vietnam Armed Forces

- Gia Long High School—a renowned public high school in Saigon

- Hanoi is the capital city of The People Republic of Vietnam in the North.

- Ho Chi Minh, Uncle Ho—political leader of the Democratic Republic of Vietnam until 1969

- Hue is an imperial city, central Vietnam, 700km (430miles) south of Hanoi and about 1,100km (680miles) north of Saigon.

- Irving Berlin's 'White Christmas'—the song signalling the total evacuation of the US

- Long Khanh—a highland country 100km from Saigon

- Major General Le Minh Dao, 18th Division of the Army of Republic of Vietnam

- Newport Bridge—Cau Tan Cang

- Ninh Kieu Market Place in Can-Tho

- Ngo Dinh Diem, https://en.wikipedia.org/wiki/Ngo_Dinh_Diem

- Operation Frequent Wind, http://en.wikipedia.org/wiki/Operation_Frequent_Wind.

- Orderly Departure Program, ODP, http://en.wikipedia.org/wiki/Orderly_Departure_Program.

- Palace of Independence—Dinh Doc Lap—the Republic of Vietnam President's residence and office

- President Duong Van Minh was in charge from 28th April till 30th April 1975

- President Nguyen Van Thieu—Former President of the Republic of Vietnam until 21st April 1975

- President Tran Van Huong was in charge from 21st April till 28th April 1975

- Rambutan—a prickly red tropical fruit that Long-Khanh is renowned for.

- Saigon—capital city in the South of the Republic of Vietnam before 30th April 1975, renamed Ho Chi Minh City after the Fall of Saigon

- Tan Son Nhat airport—the international airport in Saigon

- Tet Offensive—The 1968 Grand Offensive

- Tet—What Really Happened at Hue, James H. Willbanks

- The Amerasians from Vietnam:A California Study by Chung Hoang Chuong, San Francisco State University, Department of Asian American Studies and Le Van Bilingual Education Office, California Department of Education   (125 East Bidwell, Folsom CA 95630, 916 355-1100) ©1994 Southeast Asia Community Resource Center

- The Fall of Saigon, The Fall—the total surrender and defeat of the Republic of Vietnam on 30th April 1975, Black April

- The National Liberation Front Viet Cong, the organisation that led the army in Vietnam war and the political organisation and army in South Vietnam that fought the South Vietnamese government and the US during the Vietnam War (1959-1975)

- The Paris Peace Accords of 1973, on 27th January 1973—the Agreement on ending the war and restoring peace in Vietnam

- The People Republic of Vietnam—The Socialist Republic of Vietnam—The Democratic Republic of Vietnam

- The Thames Path, http://www.nationaltrail.co.uk/thames-path, https://en.wikipedia.org/wiki/Thames_Path

- The Vietnam War, http://thevietnamwar.info/vietnamese-re-education-camps/
- UNHCR—United Nations High Commissioner for Refugees, The Office of the United Nations High Commissioner for Refugees (UNHCR) was established by the UN General Assembly on December 14, 1950, and began work in Geneva, Switzerland, a fortnight later on January 1, 1951.
- Vice President Nguyen Cao Ky of the Republic of Vietnam till April 1975
- Vietnam People's Army, http://en.wikipedia.org/wiki/Vietnam_People's_Army.
- Vietnamese Communist Party—the founding and ruling political party of the Socialist Republic of Vietnam
- Vietnamese/Amerasians, http://www.smithsonianmag.com/people-places/children-of-the-vietnam-war
- Vitamin B12 Deficiency, https://en.wikipedia.org/wiki/Vitamin_B12_deficiency
- Xu: The cent in *dong*, currency of Vietnam
- Xuan Loc—a provincial city, 85km North East of Saigon

List of Characters

Anh – Sue's childhood friend

Chi or Mother – Trinh's mother

Dan – the Communist interrogator in the reeducation camp

Dien – Trinh's oldest brother – the twenty-year-old soldier from 18th Battalion

Giang – Trinh's oldest sister

Hoan – Trinh's second oldest brother – the Communist soldier in 1978

Khai – Dien's best friend

Kim – Trinh's immediate older sister

Lam – Truyen's father, a farmer

Lan – Trinh's best friend

Liem – the kid with red boxer shorts on the Fall of Saigon

Luc – Trinh's younger brother

Mac – Giang's husband

Mike – the Amerasian

Nguyen or Father - Trinh's father

Quang – the caretaker in reeducation camp

Sinh – the Northern Communist soldier who stationed inside Trinh's house after the Fall

Sue – the bia om owner

Thanh – the Lieutenant's widow

Trinh – the narrator

Truyen – the cafe vendor in front of Trinh's house

Tuan – the Lieutenant in reeducation camp

Uncle Tam – the disabled South Vietnamese veteran, a secondhand dealer in front of Trinh's house

Vy – Trinh's second oldest sister

Woody Ben – the vanquished soldier in the training camp for the Cambodian war.

An Act of Respectful Altruism

by CieCie Tuyet Nguyen

SHE DIED THIS morning. No, her death was discovered at approximately nine o'clock, but the time of her last intake of oxygen had not been determined yet. Her body was wrapped in a plastic bag, ready to be transported to the morgue. It was an unpleasant surprise; however, we all knew the reason of her sacrifice. It is called Respectful Altruism, a terminology to describe a selfless concern for the well-being of others.

It is sad because it is a wasted sacrifice, in my opinion.

What I mean is her selfless act might not bring about the effects she wanted to establish. She was a poor single woman, or more precisely, a widow. Her partner died a few months ago. Perhaps her loneliness had urged her to make the sacrifice, as there was no reason for her to linger longer on this earth.

Yes, after giving births to thousands of roes resting on the bottom of the tank, my fish died the following day! She had died from exhaustion to make sure her babies or her line of fish remained in existence. That is an act of Respectful Altruism, which describes a behavior normally of an animal benefiting others at its own expense.

Nevertheless, the roes might be empty as she was not with a partner for so long already! She was a loner since I picked up her partner's carcass floating on the tank's water surface a while ago one morning. Furthermore, her partner might be a female as far as I know. What a waste!

CPSIA information can be obtained
at www.ICGtesting.com
Printed in the USA
LVOW04s0911150816

500060LV00034B/289/P